K

Ethnographies and Archaeologies

CULTURAL HERITAGE STUDIES

UNIVERSITY PRESS OF FLORIDA

Florida A&M University, Tallahassee
Florida Atlantic University, Boca Raton
Florida Gulf Coast University, Ft. Myers
Florida International University, Miami
Florida State University, Tallahassee
New College of Florida, Sarasota
University of Central Florida, Orlando
University of Florida, Gainesville
University of North Florida, Jacksonville
University of South Florida, Tampa
University of West Florida, Pensacola

CULTURAL HERITAGE STUDIES

Edited by Paul A. Shackel, University of Maryland

The University Press of Florida is proud to announce the creation of a new series devoted to the study of cultural heritage. This thematic series brings together research devoted to understanding the material and behavioral characteristics of heritage. The series explores the uses of heritage and the meaning of its cultural forms as a way to interpret the present and the past. The series highlights important scholarship related to America's diverse heritage.

Books include important theoretical contributions and descriptions of significant cultural resources. Scholarship addresses questions related to culture and describes how local and national communities develop and value the past. The series includes works in public archaeology, heritage tourism, museum studies, vernacular architecture, history, American studies, and material cultural studies.

Heritage of Value, Archaeology of Renown:
Reshaping Archaeological Assessment and Significance
Edited by Clay Mathers, Timothy Darvill, and Barbara J. Little (2005)

Archaeology, Cultural Heritage, and the Antiquities Trade
Edited by Neil Brodie, Morag M. Kersel, Christina Luke,
and Kathryn Walker Tubb (2006)

Archaeological Site Museums in Latin America
Edited by Helaine Silverman (2006)

Crossroads and Cosmologies: Diasporas and Ethnogenesis in the New World
By Christopher C. Fennell (2007)

Ethnographies and Archaeologies: Iterations of the Past
Edited by Lena Mortensen and Julie Hollowell (2009)

Ethnographies and Archaeologies
Iterations of the Past

Edited by Lena Mortensen and Julie Hollowell

FOREWORD BY PAUL A. SHACKEL

UNIVERSITY PRESS OF FLORIDA

Gainesville Tallahassee Tampa Boca Raton
Pensacola Orlando Miami Jacksonville Ft. Myers Sarasota

14 13 12 11 10 09   6 5 4 3 2 1

Library of Congress Cataloging-in-Publication Data
Ethnographies and archaeologies : iterations of the past / edited by Lena Mortensen
and Julie Hollowell ; foreword by Paul A. Shackel.
p. cm.—(Cultural heritage studies)
Includes bibliographical references and index.
ISBN 978-0-8130-3366-2 (alk. paper)
1. Archaeology—Social aspects. 2. Ethnology—Social aspects. 3. Ethnoarchaeology—
Social aspects. 4. Cultural property—Protection. 5. Intercultural communication.
6. Community life. 7. Archaeology—Philosophy. 8. Archaeology—Methodology.
I. Mortensen, Lena. II. Hollowell, Julia J., 1952-
CC175.E85 2009
930.1—dc22   2009004170

The University Press of Florida is the scholarly publishing agency for the State University
System of Florida, comprising Florida A&M University, Florida Atlantic University, Florida
Gulf Coast University, Florida International University, Florida State University, New College
of Florida, University of Central Florida, University of Florida, University of North Florida,
University of South Florida, and University of West Florida.

University Press of Florida
15 Northwest 15th Street
Gainesville, FL 32611-2079
http://www.upf.com

Contents

Illustrations

Foreword

Understanding the ways that heritage is created in local and international communities has become a significant avenue of inquiry for many disciplines. The authors in this volume demonstrate how different groups of stakeholders create meanings of the past and also how these meanings are used in the present. Their work indicates that our scholarship is not value free and that the practice of archaeology can be tied to issues such as class, economic justice, social justice, and identity politics. By using the lens of an ethnographer, the authors demonstrate that the past is more than history, and archaeology is more than providing heritage to a community. They explain that the practice of archaeology and the interpretation of places and objects can have many ramifications that can impact host communities.

Why the past matters and how we remember the past are two main themes in this volume, and the ethnography of archaeologies is one way to understand these issues. In many places throughout the world, there is a growing demand for knowing the past, because it can also be manipulated for social, political, and economic purposes. These iterations of the past create a usable heritage that serves present needs. In some cases, heritage authorities clarify and even simplify the past to make it usable in the present. However, as social, political, and ideological conditions change, the meanings of the past can also change. Understanding how and why we remember a particular past, while forgetting or ignoring another past, is an important issue to address as we critically evaluate how we understand the development of heritage.

The archaeologist has a long tradition of playing an important, and sometimes an authoritative, role in creating heritage and is often seen as the heritage authority. Engaging communities is now an important part of many research programs, although struggles between authority (the academic) and authenticity (the community) sometimes develop, each with different ideas about which values need to be made public for a wider audience. Those in control of the resources may also insist on reinforcing a consensus history, while subordinated groups may try to claim a more inclusive past. This book is about how the meaning and work of archaeology have lives beyond those given by archaeologists. In some cases, the authority has been challenged, such that diverse stakeholders are now involved in many archaeology projects. The archaeologist, who may be seen as the authority but is often an outsider, must now work in a collaborative manner. Although the archaeologist has traditionally controlled the production of knowledge at a site and developed a perceived truth, the meaning of archaeology often has other values and meanings in communities, beyond those sanctioned by archaeologists.

The authors explicitly de-center archaeologists so that an archaeologist may be seen as merely one among many who are concerned with the past. Ethnography is one way to search for how a variety of stakeholders make sense of their lives and the past. The articles in this volume critically address the social lives of sites and objects and show how the past is created and used in the present. The authors use ethnography to study archaeology and examine issues related to tourism, identity, authenticity, power, and ownership of the past and the role of the archaeologist in this discourse. Future generations of scholars need to think about how archaeology will be used within broader social and political contexts. *Ethnographies and Archaeologies: Iterations of the Past* introduces valuable case studies related to the production of archaeological heritage and understanding the dialogue of how the past is created.

Paul A. Shackel
Series Editor

Preface

It seems that almost daily, news outlets bring us headlines about clashes between land developers and native groups; negotiations between art collectors, museums, and indigenous communities; the repatriation of art, sacred objects, and human remains; tourism development of archaeological ruins; or contemporary protest at World Heritage sites. Whether the controversy is over the Bamiyan Buddhas, the Elgin Marbles, or WalMart at Teotihuacan, the meanings and uses of the so-called past are very much matters for present-day concerns. As these concerns take over more and more ground in public arenas, they call out for nuanced, detailed assessments of the contexts and histories that give them potency.

This volume, like so many others, began as a conversation—a conversation that took note of the burgeoning academic attention to present-day contexts and concerns about archaeological heritage. As our conversation continued, we, the editors of this volume, became aware that the growing accumulation of case studies emerging in academic meetings, edited volumes, and new research programs addressing this broad topic seemed to be reaching a critical mass. Seeking to take advantage of this moment, we organized a session for the 2002 American Anthropological Association meetings in New Orleans, entitled "Beyond Description: Theorizing Heritage and the Archaeological Past," for which many of the chapters and commentaries in the present volume originated. Our goal in this initial effort was to move the discussion beyond a mere critique of contemporary uses and configurations of the past to a more complex, multilayered analysis of the interplay between imagery, power, and interest in the political economy of archaeology and heritage.

However, the collection of papers that resulted seemed to converge on something slightly different and more intellectually provocative to us—a move to de-center the practice of archaeology and instead examine how present-day communities in diverse contexts mediate identity and cultural capital through varied embodiments and interpretations of the past: iterations, if you will. As the project developed through various incarnations, additional chapters were solicited from authors (ethnographers and archaeologists) whose work represented a distinct ethnographic approach to archaeological—or archaeologized—subjects and objects. The result is an endeavor that occupies the disciplinary borderlands between archaeology and cultural anthropology, calling on ethnography to make sense of this undefined terrain.

Much like any iteration of the past, the conversation that began this volume is part of a specific moment but also is grounded in a longer history that draws on many more interlocutors and wider contexts. We, the editors, met during graduate training at Indiana University, in an anthropology department that was uniquely open to inter-subfield exploration. Part of a small group of students who found neither the subfield of cultural anthropology nor archaeology complete enough to address our interests in emerging topics, we were encouraged by a dedicated group of faculty—K. D. Vitelli, Anne Pyburn, and Rick Wilk—to draw on our training in both subfields and attempt to come up with something new. What emerged through the combined efforts of faculty and students was the formal Ph.D. track in archaeology and social context, designed to "bridge the subfields of Sociocultural Anthropology and Archaeology to address archaeological issues as they apply to contemporary peoples" (as noted on the Web site). Solid training in anthropological methods and theory, combined with freedom to explore and experiment, laid the necessary groundwork for our research projects in Alaska and Honduras. Our ongoing and evolving conversations with mentors and colleagues provided inspiration that sustains us to this day. It is in this spirit that we offer the volume to readers—and look forward to the next iteration.

We would like to extend our thanks to Paul Shackel, whose continuing interest in and commitment to this project allowed it to be realized in print. Thanks also to John Byram, Michele Fiyak-Burkley, and Eli Bortz, who have been encouraging and attentive editors, and to Matthew Hoffmann and our anonymous reviewers, who provided valuable feedback along the way. We wish especially to thank our teachers—K. D., Rick, and Anne—who guided us along these explorations and helped shape our insights and our ethics.

Additionally, Lena Mortensen thanks the Center for Heritage Resource Studies at the University of Maryland and the University of Toronto–Scarborough for critical support at various stages. Julie Hollowell wishes to thank the Killam Foundation and the Departments of Anthropology at both the University of British Columbia and Indiana University, and the Prindle Institute for Ethics at DePauw University for their generous support.

Introduction

Ethnographies and Archaeologies

JULIE HOLLOWELL AND LENA MORTENSEN

Ethnography is known for casting light on people, relationships, and situations that otherwise remain dim, out of sight, or at the margins. While predominantly used in anthropological approaches to the present, ethnography also plays—and has long played—a variety of roles in archaeological attempts to interpret the past. Yet, for the most part, these two trajectories have remained separate epistemological endeavors. In recent years, however, this situation has begun to change, resulting in an array of research approaches and findings that beg closer attention, showcased in the pages that follow. This volume charts dynamic new ground emerging in the interstices of ethnographic and archaeological practice. Here we develop a broad argument for an ethnographic approach to dialogues and debates on what is often considered "archaeological heritage," which we might refer to instead as "iterations of the past." This perspective recognizes that the terrain and fragments of the past often claimed by archaeologists have other lives—other iterations—that resurface or rematerialize in transformed, contingent, and unintended ways. Each of the contributors addresses a particular relationship between ethnography and those subjects and objects that are typically deemed archaeological—however, this volume focuses not on what ethnography can do for archaeology but rather on ethnography's ability to illuminate the complexity, potency, and possibility of the past in the present. While these ethnographies may well have implications for archaeological practice, their concerns lie more with the implications of archaeological practice for others.

From Alaska to Australia, Ecuador to Lebanon, archaeological practices have created certain structures for and modes of speaking about the past, ways of handling the material remnants of human activities, and engagements with landscapes that bear markers of past human presence. In many cases, these modes and structures are shifting, intensifying, and in some cases exploding. While archaeologists may claim material culture and sites as their "data," the cultural and intellectual products of archaeology have all along been lived, altered, claimed, and commodified by others in innumerable ways. As William Roseberry (1989: 45) reminds us, "Cultural production is not limited to those who control the means of cultural production."

Indeed, whenever archaeologists come to a place, they walk into ongoing conversations and perceptions of "archaeology" and "the past," encountering people and places that already have a history of engagement with sites, artifacts, and stories about the past, as with explorers, exploiters, and other archaeologists (Roseberry 1989: 91; see also Lane and Herrera 2005; Mortensen 2005; Nicholas 2005). While some contest the pasts that archaeological interventions have created, others embrace these pasts as their own, strategically deploy essentialized versions, or find such pasts irrelevant; these responses result in infinite "iterations," such as the ones explored here.

Inherent in the concept of "iteration" is the element of generative connections—that various products and perceptions of the past reflect back on histories of entanglements. Though these iterations may be distinct, they are never fully separate but instead are linked by ongoing historical encounters, practices, and discourses. This volume explores a sampling of these iterations of the past using ethnographic perspectives to foreground the social lives of sites and objects and the political and economic repercussions of archaeology's work in the world. Archaeology is but one way of knowing the past or of inscribing a cosmopolitan set of meanings; here we look to both engagements with and divergences from this discipline. Each author presents a broader frame for thinking about things, landscapes, and sites of memory that have in some way been claimed by archaeology but have never remained bounded by it. Together, the chapters illustrate how various interests—the state, commercial entities, environmentalists, subsistence diggers, or local farmers—claim or rework material and intellectual aspects of archaeology, whether incorporating these aspects as part of their own identities or as sites of alterity, challenging social cleavages or contributing to greater social inequality. The willingness and propensity to selectively remember, forget, or silence contributes to the interplay of identity and politics of place and highlights the volatility of the past as a resource for the present (Meskell 2002; Shackel 2001; Trouillot 1995). These iterations are often tied to global phenomena, such as tourism or commodification, or they may reflect local practices and predicaments or be implicated in nationalist strategies and policies—sometimes all of these at once. In these ways, the authors probe the edges of archaeology—looking not for its boundaries but instead for ways that relationships with the past render our disciplinary categories porous.

Below, we map out some of the ground in this terrain from two vantage points that call attention to the permeability and potency of these fields of inquiry: the emergence of archaeological subjects within ethnography on one hand, and the development of a distinctly critical, reflexive standpoint within the history of archaeology's articulation with ethnographic subjects on the other. By focusing on these edges and interstices, this volume tackles what Lisa Breglia has called "the challenging task of comprehending a continuously deterritorializing object of study" (2006: 182) and, in doing so, locates some provocative and productive spaces of inquiry.

Ethnography and Archaeology

Ethnography, broadly defined as descriptions of people and their ways of life (Angrosino 2005), refers at once to a research process that involves fieldwork with specific methods, and to a form of descriptive writing that results from that process.[1] Ethnographies come in many styles and forms,[2] but all use this approach as an epistemological tool to get at deeper understandings of how people make meaning in their lives and to uncover what shapes, constrains, or inspires thoughts and actions. As with archaeology and anthropology, ethnography has been roundly criticized for its early entanglements with colonialist practices. Ethnography's "crisis of representation" in the early 1970s occurred when those who were the subjects of ethnographic writing also became part of the audience and hence part of the critique (Clifford and Marcus 1986; Marcus and Fischer 1986). Ethnographers, as a result, began to take seriously the inherent power differentials and potential effects of their voices and actions.[3] Today's ethnographies no longer describe people and places in a timeless "ethnographic present" but take account of the contexts of power and history that reflexively shape cultural memory, the choices people have, and the ethnographic process (Lassiter 2005). By starting with particular lives and locales, ethnography is able to give voice to marginalized and colonialist tendencies.

The appearance of archaeology as an ethnographic subject is driven by several broad trends. One is the increasing public appetite for experiencing, manufacturing, and manipulating the past—or facsimiles of the past—in the present, desires that have continued to proliferate and transform (see Holtorf 2001; Lowenthal 1985; Schnapp et al. 2004: 3). This trend has engendered a related one, the constant reworking of signs and meanings of the past that confront us in our daily lives, deployed by and for varied interests, leading to a kind of cacophony—or, in some places, silence (see Colwell-Chanthaphonh, this volume). Third, attention to ethnographic approaches comes with a growing recognition of the political and ethical implications of the production of knowledge within archaeology and anthropology. Finally, the trend toward archaeology as a subject of ethnography is also inspired by a desire to document and communicate the creativity and resilience of people in various corners of the world who forge new relations with the past under conditions of colonialism, global economic pressures, war, and other circumstances.

Archaeology is commonly defined as "the scientific or systematic study of past peoples and lifeways based on material remains as evidence."[4] Indeed, the term *archaeology* has come to delimit a profession, naturalized to stand for "what trained archaeologists do," although it need not be relegated to such a narrow epistemic footing. The realization that archaeology is "one among many" ways to interpret the past (Foucault 1972: 186) defines archaeology's "crisis of representation," which is still in evolution. Conceptions of archaeology have gradually begun to move beyond these narrow parameters, in a process that mirrors the questioning of "official" or disciplinary definitions of "history" in recent decades (see Roseberry 1989, and below). At the same time, the term *heritage,* although likewise problematic, has come to stand for both personal and popularized knowledge about the past, placed in living contexts and understood through the frames of performance, practice, and, increasingly, "intangibility" (for example, Kirshenblatt-Gimblett 2006; L. Smith 2006). In this slippery code switching, archaeological heritage becomes a territory where certain voices count. A deeper understanding of how concepts such as "heritage" or "the past" acquire meaning and of how people experience, interpret, and benefit from them may well require the kind of contextualized and particularistic ethnographic approaches illustrated here.

Ethnography *in* Archaeology: Current Iterations

Today ethnography plays numerous important and increasingly diverse roles within the field of archaeology (see Hollowell and Nicholas 2008). Some archaeologists, for instance, use ethnographic information to help them understand local attitudes about archaeology, beliefs associated with ancestral sites, or the social situations they encounter (Dowdall and Parrish 2003; Lane and Herrera 2005; McDavid 2004; Pyburn 2003). Ethnographic methods also bring other voices and alternative histories to interpretations of the past. As participatory and collaborative approaches become more prominent (Colwell-Chanthaphonh and Ferguson 2008; Silliman 2008), ethnography is used to identify questions and concerns that community members have, so that these can be incorporated into a project's research agenda (for example, Green et al. 2003; Reeves 2004; Swidler et al. 2000) or applied in developing hybrid, culturally appropriate theories and practices (Dowdall and Parrish 2003; Ferguson and Colwell-Chanthaphonh 2006). Finally, there are a growing number of examples of ethnography and archaeology being used in tandem in projects that aim to deepen indigenous or other local histories, revitalize neighborhoods, solidify land claims, repatriate cultural objects, or legitimate customary authority (Derry and Malloy 2003; Ferguson 2003; Shackel and Chambers 2004).

Obviously, ethnography has an integral role to play in an archaeology that sees itself as accountable to living peoples. Much of this has taken place in concert with the growth of "public archaeology," which relies heavily on the use of ethnography and ethnohistory by archaeologists working in the public sector (museums, heritage sites, parks, government agencies) to build bridges between and among various publics and the past (Jameson 1997; Little 2002; Merriman 2004). Applied archaeology also turns to ethnographic methods to inform policy and practice and to solve problems relevant to community needs (Downum and Price 1999; Pyburn and Wilk 2000; Shackel and Chambers 2004). As archaeology's role in community development and other public realms continues to expand, ethnography is likely to become ever more important, particularly in conveying understandings of community attitudes about place, heritage, and identity that are more nuanced.

Another focus for ethnography in archaeology is as a reflexive method for documenting and critiquing the research process: from excavation practices and discourse, to the phenomenological nature of sensory and bodily experience, to understanding the influences a project has on the surrounding community. These and similar postprocessual approaches began to demarcate the terrain for an "ethnography *of* archaeology" by turning the ethnographic gaze onto the processes and experiential aspects of archaeology. *Ethnographies of Archaeological Practice,* a landmark volume on this topic edited by Matt Edgeworth (2006), focuses particularly on situations in which the ethnographer is embedded "in situ" within the archaeology project (see Breglia 2006: 181–82). Edgeworth (2006: 1–2) traces the origins of this ethnographic genre back a half century (Dupree 1955) but locates its real emergence in ethnographies of excavation from the early 1990s (Edgeworth 1991; Gero 1996; Goodwin 1994; Roveland 2000) and in the explicit incorporation of ethnographic approaches by the Çatalhöyük research project (see Bartu 2000, 2006; Hamilton 2000; Hodder 2000; Shankland 1997, 1999).[5] The case studies in the volume edited by Edgeworth embrace archaeology as sociocultural practice, envisioning archaeological projects as sites of cultural production punctuated by the voices and critiques of local people, who always have their own interpretations of what archaeologists do (Edgeworth 2006: 13).

Ethnography *of* Archaeology

In many ways, the present volume begins where Edgeworth's leaves off, by shifting the focus from ethnographies of archaeological practice, which center primarily on what archaeologists do, toward investigating the various ways in which nonarchaeol-

ogists—such as site workers, art dealers, and homeowners—perceive their relationships to places, ideas, and things elsewhere defined by archaeologists. This move
leads us away from hermeneutic discussions of archaeology's disciplinary authority
and toward investigating how things typically defined as archaeological have other
lives, meanings, and consequences, often well beyond a disciplinary scope. These
iterations of the past are Escher-like, not linear but reinterpreted and used in diverse
ways, showing that what archaeologists long claimed as their own is not theirs alone
(see also Hamilakis 1999).

The primary inspiration for this approach to an ethnography of archaeology
comes from works that typically lie beyond the margins of archaeology, within a trajectory that originates in the emergence of interest in archaeological subjects and objects from thoroughly ethnographic standpoints. This interest is rooted in studies of
domains including material culture, alternative histories, and heritage and identity.
Foundations such as Pierre Bourdieu's (1977, 1984) emphasis on cultural capital and
fields of practice, David Lowenthal's (1985) critique of the past as a foreign country,
and Arjun Appadurai's (1986) attention to the social lives of things demonstrated the
(per)mutability that sites and objects from the past have as a resource for meaning
and agency in the present. Michael Herzfeld has talked about this form of ethnography as a lens that brings "the disputed ownership of history" into sharper focus or
"high relief," thus making particular sites of contention available for closer analysis and comparison (Herzfeld 1991: xi–xiii). Many of the issues raised in Herzfeld's
work appear in the chapters here: competing rhetorics of heritage and ownership
on the part of the state, the community, and the individual (Lisa Breglia, O. Hugo
Benavides, Gastón Gordillo, Christopher N. Matthews and Matthew Palus); divergent notions of management and preservation (Jon Daehnke, Laurajane Smith, Julie
Hollowell); the visibility of heritage in everyday practices and land- or cityscapes
(Jennifer Jacobs and Benjamin Porter, Lena Mortensen); and the layers of history,
imagination, or other aspects of the past that may go undisputed or unspoken (Chip
Colwell-Chanthaphonh, Helaine Silverman).

Several full-length studies have taken up this ethnographic lens to explore archaeology's entanglements with the present, thus laying groundwork for the array
of research included here. Quetzil E. Castañeda's *In the Museum of Maya Culture:
Touring Chichén Itzá* (1996) offers a genealogical analysis of the historical complici-
ties among political officials, national and foreign archaeologists, and commercial
interests in the service of specific agendas of meaning at this world-renowned archaeological site in Mexico. Castañeda argues that local, national, and transnational
interests and agendas have transformed Chichén Itzá into a "factory of knowledge"
that participates in the very invention of "Maya" culture. Richard Handler and Eric
Gable's 1997 study, *The New History in an Old Museum: Creating the Past at Colonial*

Williamsburg, goes behind the scenes at one of the most celebrated sites of public memory in the United States to portray how a veneer of authenticity is created for public consumption. Their research details the contingency of choices made in historical interpretation and the connection of these choices to the important corporate machinery of a national tourism attraction. Finally, Nadia Abu el-Haj tackles the subject matter of archaeology and nationalism in ethnographic detail in *Facts on the Ground: Archaeological Practice and Territorial Self-Fashioning in Israeli Society* (2001). In this volume, she examines the nature and specificity of archaeological practices and their historical entanglements with colonial and state projects in Israel, illuminating the role of archaeology in creating an explicitly politicized nationalist discourse. One important common thread among these accounts is that they were produced not "in the service of" archaeology but altogether outside of it. Only recently have archaeologists paid attention to such studies, and many examples still lie beyond the archaeological gaze.[6]

Within archaeology, this form of ethnography, with its explicit concern for the social and political nature of the archaeologized past, had surfaced occasionally in case studies that foreground the politics of the past or the contested ownership or representation of the past (Gathercole and Lowenthal 1990; Kohl and Fawcett 1995; Lavine and Karp 1991; Layton 1989a, 1989b). But in just the past decade, the shape of this field has changed. "Archaeological ethnography," as described by Lynn Meskell (2005) and practiced by a growing number of both archaeologists and ethnographers, has come into its own. An even broader vision for this particular genre of ethnography of archaeology, with a clear grounding in anthropology, characterizes the studies assembled here, wherein the primary concern is not what this approach can do for archaeology—though there are obvious applications. Instead, it is about the implications of archaeologized places, pasts, and ideas for others, and how people make these things their own.

Part of the intention of this volume is to de-center or reposition the role of archaeologists and archaeological practice in the discussion of constructing the past. Nevertheless, this is not meant as a critique of other applications of ethnography within archaeology, which generate rich understandings on many levels. Nor do we want to reinforce a disjunction between archaeologists and others who hold an interest in the past (compare Roseberry 1989: 53). On the contrary, we see the emergence of creative and productive intersections gathering critical momentum. As the boundaries between interests and discourses on archaeology and ethnography are coming into focus, they are simultaneously becoming subject to dissolution. Engaging with these intersections means that more and more people are combining experience and training in ethnography and archaeology, planning to use ethnography to examine, for instance, the role of archaeology in society, elucidating "multiple sites of constitution and contestation" in an attempt to "understand how the value of the past is calibrated across a wide social spectrum" (Meskell 2005: 82).

To some extent, all the authors in this volume, whether primarily cultural anthropologists or archaeologists, work at these margins, employing conceptual analyses and training derived from both trajectories as well as their crossings. This leads to diverse visions of what constitutes an ethnographer of archaeology. For instance, Lynn Meskell (2005: 85) feels that her insider status and expertise as an archaeologist lends a particular groundedness and deep reflexivity to archaeological ethnography, while others contend that ethnography is best left to trained ethnographers. In either case, both positions agree that archaeological ethnography is about fracturing the boundaries between these two disciplines and illuminating previously hidden terrain that has implications for both. If the experience of many of the authors here is any indication, an individual may very well move over time or place between the position of ethnographer and archaeologist. This does not mean, however, that one person should try to fill both roles simultaneously, which may be inadvisable not only for reasons of time and energy but also because of the very different vantage points and positioning each role requires. Nevertheless, we foresee a time when ethnographies of archaeology such as these (which describe the social context, local reverberations, or political economy of archaeological ideas or objects) are considered just as significant to the field of archaeology as is excavation or artifact analysis.

"Archaeologies"

This volume expands upon the concept of "ethnography of archaeology" in another important sense, transposing it to "ethnography of archaeolo*gies*" to signal a shift toward recognition of the validity of multiple ways of knowing the past. The term *archaeologies* has surfaced in only the past decade, first in reference to the diversity of intellectual approaches within various subfields of archaeology (see Ashmore and Knapp 1999; Pollock and Bernbeck 2005) and also to recognize the slippery nature of the archaeological "object" in modernity (Schnapp et al. 2004: 9). More recently, the term has been used to acknowledge the diversity of theoretical and methodological approaches to the past, constructed from different standpoints—feminist archaeologies, phenomenology, indigenous archaeologies, contemporary archaeologies (Conkey 2005; Holtorf and Piccini 2007; Smith and Wobst 2005).[7] This marks a shift in archaeology from research that seeks "truths" to epistemologies that consider how different people make sense of, or use, the past. Along with Nick Shepherd (2005), we recognize Sigmund Freud, Michel Foucault, Walter Benjamin, and others who have used "archaeologies" as a metaphor for deep explorations into the genealogies and foundational concepts of histories, ideas, and texts.

Expanding from these vantage points, here we use the term *archaeologies* in two broadly applicable ways. First, the term refers to the complex range of ways that people construct relationships to the past, many of which defy the centricities of a "discipline" or a specialist science (see also Pagán-Jiménez 2004). Second, we also employ *archaeologies* to reference the genealogies, trajectories (social lives), and predicaments of things deemed archaeological.

Ethnographies and Archaeologies

The volume's title, *Ethnographies and Archaeologies,* receives its inspiration from William Roseberry's classic *Anthropologies and Histories.* Both volumes attest to the insights that come with bringing together perspectives from what have been perceived as separate-yet-related disciplines engaged in understanding people over place and time. But there are other substantive points of convergence as well. For example, Roseberry (1989: 4) advocated that to understand controversy or contradictions of power and meaning anthropologically, we need to know something more about the larger context and structure of any particular situation and how individuals have acted within these structures or contexts. History, then, becomes much less a theoretical study of patterns of human activity than an exploration of what differently positioned actors actually did in the context of contradictory social situations. Respectively, we, along with others (for example, Castañeda and Matthews 2008; Hamilakis and Duke 2007; Meskell and Pels 2005; Schmidt and Patterson 1995), contend that understanding the dilemmas and interplays of power and meaning infused in archaeological sites, objects, and interpretations requires a deeper and more nuanced investigation of these "archaeologies" within broader social contexts, and we advocate a turn to ethnography to help accomplish this.

Roseberry also called for anthropology to attend to alternative histories that challenge dominant hegemonies, wherever and in whatever form they may take. He insisted that we recognize that the ability or desire of people to construct these alternatives depends on many factors—class, geographic or political positioning, access to information, and other indexes of relative social power. Here again, we see ethnographies as an integral way to discern these nuances and inequalities in alternative readings of the past. In this volume, they illuminate ways that people in particular corners of the world remember, reconstruct, or otherwise find themselves entangled with the past. For instance, the middle-class residents of Eastport have little trouble constructing their own views of archaeology and what it can do for them (see Matthews and Palus, chapter 6), and economic need can serve to rationalize the mining of "gifts from the ancestors" as commodities for a global market (Hollowell, chapter 10). Or, as Breglia (chapter 2) and Porter and Jacobs (chapter 3) demonstrate, residents of Chunchucmil, Yucatán, or local communities in Jordan seem to find much more salience in recent registers of history than in state-sponsored, archaeologically defined pasts. We also see that it is the living histories of relations of inequality, rather than discourses of preservation and veneration of "ruins," that define places in the everyday lives of local farmers and wage-earners in northern Argentina (Gordillo, chapter 1) or site workers at Copán (Mortensen, chapter 8).

Furthermore, Roseberry (1989: 13) finds fault with accounts that portray the anthropological "Other" as cultures or people "without history," uninfluenced by global happenings (see also Wolf 1982). To this we would add that just as there are no people without history, so too are there no people without some (real or imagined) connection to a more distant past, few people "without archaeology," and fewer yet who have not been "archaeologized."

Finally, one of Roseberry's primary aims in *Anthropologies and Histories* was to insist on the importance of a political economy approach to anthropology, one that took account of the embedded nature of all human lifeways in political, economic, and social contexts across place and time. Indeed, throughout the following chapters we see how the imbrication of archaeology with global capitalism plays out in the crosscurrents of social class and economic fortunes or instability. The development of a political economy of archaeology is long overdue and sorely needed for investigating the implications and trajectories of archaeology in the world (compare Appadurai 2001). We anticipate that ethnographies such as those in this volume will be fundamental to giving form and substance to this endeavor.

Organization of the Volume

We have chosen to organize the volume into three related themes, each introduced by a commentary (by Lynn Meskell, Quetzil E. Castañeda, and Richard Handler) that touches upon chapters in the section and broader issues they raise. The first section (chapters by Gastón Gordillo, Lisa Breglia, Jennifer Jacobs and Benjamin Porter, and Helaine Silverman) looks at how official renderings of heritage and archaeology articulate with local discourses that inscribe alternative meanings of landscapes, sites, and ruins. As Meskell notes, these chapters underscore how the interests of national and international agencies charged with managing the past as heritage are typically fueled by the proliferation of globally defined agendas of development and tourism rather than locally based concerns, conceptions, or needs. The chapters also demonstrate the variability and contradictions that arise in identifying temporal and spatial registers for what counts as heritage. The second section (chapters by Laurajane Smith, Christopher N. Matthews and Matthew Palus, and O. Hugo Benavides) centers on the foundations of control over archaeology and the basis of authority in archaeological practices or claims. Rather than re-creating the tensions inherent in questions of "who owns the past," instead we find instances of archaeological control being relinquished by or wrested from the hands of practitioners, challenging the notion that it was ever firmly within their grasp. Chapters in this section also highlight the tensions between groups with unequal access to or ability to control or manage their "heritage" or "past," showing how archaeological authority can be appropriated to turn these traditional power relations on their heads. The final section (chapters by Lena Mortensen, Jon Daehnke, Julie Hollowell, and Chip Colwell-Chanthaphonh) maps a variety of standpoints for valuing the past (or not) and the manifold practices and discourses that inform such standpoints. Taking frames as divergent as the antiquities market, regulation of human remains, the industry of archaeological tourism, and a "landscape of history," these chapters explore historically situated claims made to places and things that (also) have archaeological value, questioning how such value is derived and promoted. Across this spectrum of cases, Handler challenges us to consider how the development of a particular past, or way of valuing one past over others, is in most cases entirely arbitrary. He calls our attention to the known and knowable past as the product of historical contingencies that call for continuing scrutiny but are, at the same time, bound by universalistic notions of time that often go unquestioned.

Although this organizational schema offers a measure of conceptual convenience, the chapters within clearly speak to many overlapping currents that crosscut the entire volume. They could fit within frameworks other than the one we have described, such as studies of archaeological tourism, of commodification of the past, of archaeological practice itself, landscape studies, or histories of place-making. Yet none of these frameworks would capture the scope of the work addressed in the case studies and commentaries presented here. Individually, the chapters reveal the entanglements of archaeological pasts with nationalisms, identity politics, privilege, and domination and highlight the importance of historical and political context to understanding the conflicts, contradictions, and standpoints of various interpretations and claims on the past. Taken together, they remind us that the subjects and objects traditionally claimed by the discipline of archaeology do not remain "disciplined" by it but have other, nonarchaeological lives. They tell us about the complexities of cultural heritage and the layers of morality and politics that undergird various discourses and silencings, and they show us places where local iterations of the past take on creative, hybrid, and meaningful forms. Finally, each author deals in some way with concepts of authority and knowledge construction, because fixing the meaning of objects, sites, heritage, and identity is about codification and control, which in turn requires us to understand, case by case, how power relations are situated.

One of the main contributions ethnography can make is to reveal the diverse and innovative responses that humans have to different local and global circumstances in various places and times. The contributors to this volume illustrate the challenging and productive work that is occurring at the dissembling margins of ethnography and archaeology, marking an expansion of what constitutes "ethnography of archaeology" and exploring the rhetoric of heritage and archaeology alongside actual lived experiences. This, we hope, moves beyond common descriptions of various "stakeholders" in an amorphous "past" and toward a more textured approach that highlights the meanings that particular remnants of particular pasts have acquired (or lost) for particular people(s). As Michael Herzfeld (1991: 257) remarks, "The choice of pasts is negotiated in a shifting present." Ethnographies can help us to better understand these choices as historically, politically, economically, and culturally situated, and they remind us that real livelihoods are often at stake. The ethnographic cases presented here bring the broad category of "the past" into sharper focus and expand our perspectives on the salience, agency, mutability, and uneven valence of the archaeological and archaeologized past.

Notes

1. Some see ethnography primarily as a textual and interpretive device or genre (for example, Clifford 1988; Geertz 1988); others traditionally put more weight on it as a distinctive practice or method (Marcus 1998; Marcus and Fischer 1986: 18). Others define ethnography as a discipline in its own right, not simply a method in anthropology but as a craft with its own specialist goals, methods, theory, and data (Lassiter 2005; Spradley 1979: 10–11).

2. Some of these forms include critical ethnography, with its emancipatory aims (Thomas 1993); multisited ethnography, which transcends boundaries of place by tracing the local in the global and vice versa (Marcus 1995); institutional ethnography, whose results inform institutional policies and practices (D. Smith 2006); collaborative ethnography, within which the process of producing the account is dialogic and shared (Lassiter 2005); and reciprocal ethnography, which juxtaposes different accounts and evaluates their differences (Lawless 2000).

3. Referring to what has been called anthropology's "crisis of representation," Nancy Mithlo (2004: 241–42) reminds us, "What is a crisis for some is the inheritance of centuries of genocide for others."

4. See http://archaeology.about.com/od/archaeology101/a/archaeologyis.htm.

5. See Dural 2007 for the next iteration in ethnographic reflexivity at Çatalhöyük—a book-length example of a local view of an archaeological project.

6. One of the first to receive notice from archaeologists was Thomas Heffernan's (1988) *Wood Quay: The Clash over Dublin's Viking Past*.

7. At precisely the same time that we developed the volume's title, the World Archaeological Congress independently christened their new journal *Archaeologies* and changed their motto from "One World Archaeology" to "One World, Many Archaeologies" in explicit recognition of the multivocality of concerns and interests in archaeology today and the challenges that this

situation presents for an organization dedicated to inclusivity and equitable, ethical practice (Shepherd 2005).

References Cited

Abu el-Haj, Nadia. *Facts on the Ground: Archaeological Practice and Territorial Self-Fashioning in Israeli Society.* Chicago: University of Chicago Press, 2001.

Angrosino, Michael. *Projects in Ethnographic Research.* Long Grove, Ill.: Waveland Press, 2005.

Appadurai, Arjun. *The Social Life of Things: Commodities in Cultural Perspective.* Cambridge: Cambridge University Press, 1986.

———. "The Globalization of Archaeology and Heritage: A Discussion with Arjun Appadurai." *Journal of Social Archaeology* 1, no. 1 (2001): 35–49.

Ashmore, Wendy, and A. Bernard Knapp, eds. *Archaeologies of Landscape: Contemporary Perspectives.* Oxford, U.K.: Blackwell, 1999.

Bartu, Ayfer. "Where Is Çatalhöyük? Multiple Sites in the Construction of an Archaeological Site." In *Towards Reflexive Methodology in Archaeology: The Example at Çatalhöyük,* edited by I. Hodder, 101–9. Cambridge, U.K.: McDonald Institute for Archaeological Research, 2000.

———. "Entanglements/Encounters/Engagements with Prehistory: Çatalhöyük and Its Publics." In *Çatalhöyük Perspectives: Themes from the 1995–99 Seasons,* edited by I. Hodder, 27–38. McDonald Institute Monographs. Cambridge, U.K.: McDonald Institute for Archaeological Research, 2006.

Bourdieu, Pierre. *Outline of a Theory of Practice.* Translated by R. Nice. Cambridge: Cambridge University Press, 1977.

———. *Distinction: A Social Critique of the Judgement of Taste.* Cambridge, Mass.: Harvard University Press, 1984.

Breglia, Lisa. "Complicit Agendas: Ethnography of Archaeology as Ethical Research Practice." In *Ethnographies of Archaeological Practice: Cultural Encounters, Material Transformations,* edited by M. Edgeworth, 173–84. Lanham, Md.: AltaMira Press, 2006.

Castañeda, Quetzil E. *In the Museum of Maya Culture: Touring Chichén Itzá.* Minneapolis: University of Minnesota Press, 1996.

Castañeda, Quetzil E., and Christopher N. Matthews, eds. *Ethnographic Archaeologies: Reflections on Stakeholders and Archaeological Practices.* Lanham, Md.: AltaMira Press, 2008.

Clifford, James. *The Predicament of Culture: Twentieth-Century Ethnography, Literature, and Art.* Cambridge, Mass.: Harvard University Press, 1988.

Clifford, James, and George Marcus, eds. *Writing Culture: The Poetics and Politics of Ethnography.* Berkeley: University of California, 1986.

Colwell-Chanthaphonh, Chip, and T. J. Ferguson, eds. *Collaboration in Archaeological Practice: Engaging Descendant Communities.* Lanham, Md.: AltaMira Press, 2008.

Conkey, Margaret W. "Dwelling at the Margins, Action at the Intersection? Feminist and Indigenous Archaeologies." *Archaeologies* 1, no. 1 (2005): 9–59.

Derry, Linda, and Maureen Malloy, eds. *Archaeologists and Local Communities: Partners in Exploring the Past.* Washington, D.C.: Society for American Archaeology, 2003.

Dowdall, Katherine M., and Otis O. Parrish. "A Meaningful Disturbance of the Earth." *Journal of Social Archaeology* 3, no. 1 (2003): 99–133.

Downum, Christian E., and Laurie J. Price. "Applied Archaeology." *Human Organization* 58, no. 3 (1999): 226–39.

Dupree, Louis. "The Artificial Small Group and Archaeological Excavation." *American Antiquity* 20, no. 3 (1955): 271.

Dural, Sadrettin. *Protecting Çatalhöyük: Memoir of an Archaeological Site Guard.* Walnut Creek, Calif.: Left Coast Press, 2007.

Edgeworth, Matt. 1991. "The Act of Discovery: An Ethnography of the Subject-Object Relation in Archaeological Practice." Ph.D. diss., University of Durham, U.K.

———, ed. *Ethnographies of Archaeological Practice: Cultural Encounters, Material Transformations.* Lanham, Md.: AltaMira Press, 2006.

Ferguson, T. J. "Archaeological Anthropology Conducted by Indian Tribes: Traditional Cultural Properties and Cultural Affiliation." In *Archaeology Is Anthropology,* edited by S. D. Gillespie and D. Nichols, 137–44. Archaeological Papers of the American Anthropological Association 13. Washington, D.C.: American Anthropological Association, 2003.

Ferguson, T. J., and Chip Colwell-Chanthaphonh. *History Is in the Land: Multivocal Tribal Traditions in Arizona's San Pedro Valley.* Tucson: University of Arizona Press, 2006.

Foucault, Michel. *The Archaeology of Knowledge and the Discourse on Language.* Translated by A. M. Sheridan. New York: Pantheon, 1972.

Gathercole, Peter, and David Lowenthal, eds. *Politics of the Past.* London: Unwin Hyman, 1990.

Geertz, Clifford. *Works and Lives: The Anthropologist as Author.* Stanford: Stanford University Press, 1988.

Gero, Joan. "Archaeological Practice and Gendered Encounters with Field Data." In *Gender and Archaeology,* edited by R. Wright, 251–80. Philadelphia: University of Pennsylvania Press, 1996.

Goodwin, Charles. "Professional Vision." *American Anthropologist* 96, no. 3 (1994): 606–33.

Green, Lesley Fordred, David R. Green, and Eduardo Góes Neves. "Indigenous Knowledge and Archaeological Science: The Challenges of Public Archaeology in the Reserva Uaçá." *Journal of Social Archaeology* 3, no. 3 (2003): 366–98.

Hamilakis, Yannis. "La trahison des archéologues? Archaeological Practice as Intellectual Activity in Postmodernity." *Journal of Mediterranean Archaeology* 12, no. 1 (1999): 60–79.

Hamilakis, Yannis, and Philip Duke, eds. *Archaeology and Capitalism: From Ethics to Politics.* Walnut Creek, Calif.: Left Coast Press, 2007.

Hamilton, Carolyn. "Faultlines: The Construction of Archaeological Knowledge at Çatalhöyük." In *Towards Reflexive Method in Archaeology: The Example at Çatalhöyük,* edited by I. Hodder, 119–37. Cambridge, U.K.: McDonald Institute for Archaeological Research, 2000.

Handler, Richard, and Eric Gable. *The New History in an Old Museum: Creating the Past at Colonial Williamsburg.* Durham, N.C.: Duke University Press, 1997.

Heffernan, Thomas. *Wood Quay: The Clash over Dublin's Viking Past.* Austin: University of Texas Press, 1988.

Herzfeld, Michael. *A Place in History: Social and Monumental Time in a Cretan Village.* Princeton, N.J.: Princeton University Press, 1991.

Hodder, Ian, ed. *Towards Reflexive Methodology in Archaeology: The Example at Çatalhöyük*. Cambridge, U.K.: McDonald Institute for Archaeological Research, 2000.

Hollowell, Julie, and George Nicholas. "A Critical Assessment of Ethnography in Archaeology." In *Archaeological Ethnographies: Reflections on Stakeholders and Archaeological Practices,* edited by Q. E. Castañeda and C. N. Matthews, 63–94. Lanham, Md.: AltaMira Press, 2008.

Holtorf, Cornelius. "Is the Past a Nonrenewable Resource?" In *Destruction and Conservation of Cultural Property,* edited by R. Layton, P. Stone, and J. Thomas, 286–97. London: Routledge, 2001.

Holtorf, Cornelius, and Angela Piccini, eds. *Contemporary Archaeologies: Excavating Now.* Oxford, U.K.: Berg, 2007.

Jameson, John H., ed. *Presenting Archaeology to the Public: Digging for Truths.* Walnut Creek, Calif.: AltaMira, 1997.

Kirshenblatt-Gimblett, Barbara. "World Heritage and Cultural Economics." In *Museum Frictions: Public Cultures/Global Transformations,* edited by I. Karp, C. A. Kratz, L. Szwaja, and T. Ybarra-Frausto, 161–202. Durham, N.C.: Duke University Press, 2006.

Kohl, Philip L., and Clare Fawcett, eds. *Nationalism, Politics, and the Practice of Archaeology.* Cambridge: Cambridge University Press, 1995.

Lane, Kevin, and Alexander Herrera. "Archaeology, Landscapes and Dreams: Science, Sacred Offerings, and the Practice of Archaeology." *Archaeological Review of Cambridge* 20, no. 1 (2005): 111–29.

Lassiter, Luke. *The Chicago Guide to Collaborative Ethnography.* Chicago: University of Chicago Press, 2005.

Lavine, Steven D., and Ivan Karp, eds. *Exhibiting Cultures: The Poetics and Politics of Museum Display.* Washington, D.C.: Smithsonian Institution Press, 1991.

Lawless, Elaine J. "Reciprocal Ethnography: No One Said It Was Easy." *Journal of Folklore Research* 37, no. 2–3 (2000): 197–205.

Layton, Robert, ed. *Conflict in the Archaeology of Living Traditions.* London: Routledge, 1989. [1989a]

———. *Who Needs the Past? Indigenous Values and Archaeology.* London: Routledge, 1989. [1989b]

Little, Barbara, ed. *Public Benefits of Archaeology.* Gainesville: University Press of Florida, 2002.

Lowenthal, David. *The Past Is a Foreign Country.* Cambridge: Cambridge University Press, 1985.

Marcus, George. "Ethnography in/of the World System: The Emergence of Multi-sited Ethnography." *Annual Review of Anthropology* 24 (1995): 95–117.

———. *Ethnography through Thick and Thin.* Princeton, N.J.: Princeton University Press, 1998.

Marcus, George, and Michael Fischer. *Anthropology as Cultural Critique: An Experimental Moment in the Human Sciences.* Chicago: University of Chicago Press, 1986.

McDavid, Carol. "From Traditional Archaeology to Public Archaeology to Community Action: The Levi Jordan Plantation Project." In *Places in Mind: Public Archaeology as Applied Anthropology,* edited by P. A. Shackel and E. Chambers, 35–56. New York: Routledge, 2004.

Merriman, Nick, ed. *Public Archaeology.* London: Routledge, 2004.

Meskell, Lynn. "The Intersections of Identity and Politics in Archaeology." *Annual Review of Anthropology* 31 (2002): 270–301.

———. "Archaeological Ethnography: Conversations around Kruger National Park." *Archaeologies* 1, no. 1 (2005): 81–100.

Meskell, Lynn, and Peter Pels, eds. *Embedding Ethics.* Oxford, U.K.: Berg, 2005.

Mithlo, Nancy. "'We Have All Been Colonized': Subordination and Resistance on a Global Arts Stage." *Visual Anthropology* 17 (2004): 229–45.

Mortensen, Lena. "Constructing Heritage at Copán, Honduras: An Ethnography of the Archaeology Industry." Ph.D. diss., Indiana University, 2005.

Nicholas, George P. "The Persistence of Memory, the Politics of Desire: Archaeological Impacts on Aboriginal Peoples and Their Response." In *Indigenous Archaeologies: Decolonizing Theory and Practice,* edited by C. Smith and H. M. Wobst, 81–103. London: Routledge, 2005.

Pagán-Jiménez, Jaime R. "Is All Archaeology at Present a Postcolonial One? Constructive Answers from an Eccentric Viewpoint." *Journal of Social Archaeology* 4, no. 2 (2004): 200–213.

Pollock, Susan, and Reinhard Bernbeck, eds. *Archaeologies of the Middle East: Critical Perspectives.* Malden, Mass.: Blackwell, 2005.

Pyburn, K. Anne. "Archaeology for a New Millennium: The Rules of Engagement." In *Archaeologists and Local Communities: Partners in Exploring the Past,* edited by L. Derry and M. Malloy, 167–84. Washington, D.C.: Society for American Archaeology, 2003.

Pyburn, K. Anne, and Richard R. Wilk. "Responsible Archaeology Is Applied Anthropology." In *Ethics in American Archaeology,* edited by M. J. Lynott and A. Wylie, 2nd ed., 78–83. Washington, D.C.: Society for American Archaeology, 2000.

Reeves, Matthew B. "Asking the 'Right' Questions: Archaeologists and Descendant Communities." In *Places in Mind: Public Archaeology as Applied Anthropology,* edited by P. Shackel and E. Chambers, 71–84. New York: Routledge, 2004.

Roseberry, William. *Anthropologies and Histories: Essays in Culture, History, and Political Economy.* New Brunswick, N.J.: Rutgers University Press, 1989.

Roveland, Blythe. "Contextualizing the History and Practice of Paleolithic Archaeology: Hamburgian Research in Northern Germany." Ph.D. diss., University of Massachusetts, 2000.

Schmidt, Peter R., and Thomas C. Patterson, eds. *Making Alternative Histories: The Practice of Archaeology and History in Non-Western Settings.* Santa Fe, N.Mex.: School of American Research Press, 1995.

Schnapp, Jeffrey T., Michael Shanks, and Matthew Tiews. "Archaeology, Modernism, Modernity: Editors' Introduction to 'Archaeologies of the Modern,' a Special Issue of 'Modernism/Modernity.'" *Archaeologies of the Modern* 11, no. 1 (2004): 1–16.

Shackel, Paul A. "Public Memory and the Search for Power in American Historical Archaeology." *American Anthropologist* 103, no. 3 (2001): 655–70.

Shackel, Paul A., and Erve Chambers, eds. *Places in Mind: Public Archaeology as Applied Anthropology.* New York: Routledge, 2004.

Shankland, David. 1997. "The Anthropology of an Archaeological Presence." In *On the*

Surface: The Re-opening of Çatalhöyük, edited by I. Hodder, 186–202. Cambridge, U.K.: MacDonald Institute for Archaeological Research, 1997.

———. "Integrating the Past: Folklore, Mounds and People at Çatalhöyük." In *Folklore and Archaeology,* edited by A. Gazin-Schwartz and C. J. Holtorf, 139–57. London: Routledge, 1999.

Shepherd, Nick. "From 'One World Archaeology' to 'One World, Many Archaeologies.'" *Archaeologies* 1, no. 1 (2005): 1–6.

Silliman, Stephen W., ed. *Collaborative Indigenous Archaeology at the Trowel's Edge: Exploring Methodology and Education in North American Archaeology.* Tucson: University of Arizona Press, 2008.

Smith, Claire, and H. Martin Wobst, eds. *Indigenous Archaeologies: Decolonizing Theory and Practice.* London: Routledge, 2005.

Smith, Dorothy E., ed. *Institutional Ethnography as Practice.* Lanham, Md.: Rowman and Littlefield, 2006.

Smith, Laurajane. *Uses of Heritage.* London: Routledge, 2006.

Spradley, James P. *The Ethnographic Interview.* New York: Holt, Rinehart and Winston, 1979.

Swidler, Nina, David Eck, T. J. Ferguson, Leigh Kuwanwisiwma, Roger Anyon, Loren Panteah, Klara Kelley, and Harris Francis. "Multiple Views of the Past: Integrating Archeology and Ethnography in the Jeddito Valley." *CRM: The Journal of Heritage Stewardship* 23, no. 9 (2000): 49–53.

Thomas, James. *Doing Critical Ethnography.* Newbury Park, Calif.: Sage Publications, 1993.

Trouillot, Michel-Rolph. *Silencing the Past: Power and the Production of History.* Boston: Beacon Press, 1995.

Wolf, Eric. *Europe and the People without History.* Berkeley: University of California Press, 1982.

Part 1

Official Narratives, Local Visions

Commentary

Cosmopolitan Heritages and the Politics of Protection

LYNN MESKELL

As the editors of this volume suggest, simply addressing "archaeological heritage" per se may fall short of the scale and complexity of the situations encountered by practitioners on the ground today. Broadening our scope somewhat, we might consider that these more encompassing "iterations of the past" make us more attentive to the shifting and sometimes conflictual global terrain within which we are currently enmeshed. This newly acknowledged set of iterations might be framed within a larger discourse of cosmopolitanism, permitting us to consider the politics of heritage protection as a universal trope and to uncover how such modalities unfold in the particular contexts discussed by the contributors to this volume.

Cosmopolitanism has become a nodal issue in regard to internationalism and postnationalism, development and sustainability, cultural preservation and protectionism, and the shortfalls of multiculturalist discourse (Appiah 2006; Breckenridge et al. 2002; Cheah and Robbins 1998; Habermas 2000, 2005; Ivison 2006; Ivison, Patton, and Sanders 2000). Reasons for this upsurge are manifold: from crises in humanitarian intervention, the upsurge in genocide, and recent military adventures in the Middle East to the global concerns and connections of indigenous groups, the desire to exercise mastery of World Heritage sites, and the circulation and subsequent calls for return of cultural properties. Cosmopolitanism dates back to the fourth-century BC Cynics, who talked about the rights and responsibilities of being a "citizen of the cosmos" (Appiah 2006: xiv). One strand of cosmopolitanism recognizes our obligations to others beyond our immediate kin or even a shared citizenship, while the other is the acknowledgment of human diversity and the inherent value of cultural difference. "Cosmopolitanism is infinite ways of being. To understand that we are already cosmopolitan" (Pollock et al. 2002: 12).

Impacting fields such as geography, anthropology, political and social theory, law, and international relations (Beck and Sznaider 2006: 1), cosmopolitanism is not tantamount to the global, to the world system, world polity, and so on, as each of these rests on the basic dualisms of national/international and domestic/foreign, which have become increasingly polymorphous and ambiguous. These clear-cut categories no longer serve us, nor do they describe the situations we find ourselves in as international researchers. One need only consider the international character of the settings within which we work: transnational field projects, multinational cooperations, conservation agencies, funding bodies, and so on. Certainly, the construction of "national" as an analytical category is severely inhibited in archaeology, whether we confront ethnic diversity, indigenous activism, local and regional difference, minority enclaves, or international interventions at the large scale such as the European Union; United Nations Educational, Scientific, and Cultural Organization (UNESCO); U.S. Agency for International Development (USAID); or the World Bank. Nor can we conversely consider the local, situated contexts in which we work as archaeologists or ethnographers as isolated, traditional, disengaged, or disconnected from larger processes, institutions, organizations, consumer networks, and knowledges. The subject of our research, the archaeological past and present, is situated firmly within a suite of cosmopolitan dispositions and practices (Szerszynski and Urry 2006: 114–15): extensive mobility and travel; consuming places and environments; curiosity about people, places, and cultures; experiencing risks in encountering others; mapping various cultures and societies; semiotic skills in interpreting others; and openness to different languages and cultures.

Additionally, within the cosmopolitan heritage sphere, it is ethically incumbent upon practitioners to recognize that the "politics of protection" does not represent a neutral practice, nor is it free from political machinations on a variety of spatial scales. The politics of heritage protectionism and philanthropy have been traditionally mobilized from a Euro-American platform based on the presumed universalism of something called "world heritage"—the logics of which have widespread effects in international and localized settings. Indeed, some of the case studies here illuminate the fallouts from such networks. I am critical of unthinking forms of heritage humanitarianism; although many examples of these seemingly positive practices might be perceived as nationally or even locally constructive and desirable, most could be seen as direct outcomes of the now-familiar global processes of sustainable development, neoliberalism, and governmentality, with their attendant arrays of concerns.

Beyond the transnational nature of archaeological practice, the new focus on multisited fieldwork has led archaeologists to adopt a suite of hybrid practices such as ethnographic archaeologies, using anthropological methodologies in conjunction with their archaeological sensibilities (Meskell 2005a, 2007). Employing a diverse and rich set of techniques, archaeologists and ethnographers are coming to terms with dimensions of heritage that have been previously elided, often because of complicated political, ethical, and economical implications. These disciplinary developments firmly situate practitioners and their practices at the core of interventions that have unequal repercussions for various stakeholders. From the outset, "heritage" has been associated with value judgments premised on indices of identity, locality, territory, ethnicity, religion, and economics. The dominant Western concept of heritage crystallized in Europe in synchrony with the origins of the nation-state, with its own set of politically motivated entanglements. Then as now, the idea of the past as a resource for the present was a vital component (Ashworth 1995). Intimately connected to the Enlightenment project, the formation of national identity relied on a coherent national heritage that could be deployed to fend off the counterclaims of other groups and nations. Even today, the name of the United Nations reveals that world society is composed politically of nation-states and that the type of state that emerged from the French and American revolutions has achieved global dominance (Habermas 2000: 105). The deployment of heritage today, as several of the chapters in this section show, is inextricably tied to the same nexus of issues. Other chapters in the volume identify troubling new global phenomena such as extensive international tourism and commodification and the newly crafted roles of nongovernmental organizations (NGOs) and international agencies.

The case of Chunchucmil, in the Yucatán, is a salient example (chapter 2), through which Lisa Breglia presents an ethnographic study based on the variant perceptions of the archaeological landscape, its occupants, and the consequences for numerous stakeholders in the multilayered ethnoscapes, culturescapes, and finanscapes of the Yucatán. She documents tensions over complex understandings of ownership and foreign intervention; archaeologists are also centrally implicated in these negotiations. She underscores the problems with both archaeological and global interventions, troubling the notion of the "common good" of world heritage. Those of us working in the Middle East or Africa see that the implications of UNESCO and world heritage listing are often detrimental to local communities (Breglia 2003; Joyce 2005; Meskell 2005c). World heritage is simply one facet of the move toward globalization; while a shared world heritage may be desired by certain constituencies, this is by no means a universal presumption. The notion of a common heritage has recently been amplified by the burgeoning global museum, heritage park, and tourist industries. Visiting civilization(s) has become paramount. World heritage and world tourism recursively reinforce and enhance each other in an ever-growing and influential lobby (Ashworth 1995). Within that movement is almost a century's worth of conflation between natural and cultural landscapes, especially if one thinks back to President Theodore Roosevelt's 1906 Antiquities Act in the United States and similar European statutes. Natural resources and places provide the model for this paradigm of nonrenewability and similarly mark sites that deserve both protection and visitation. When the same language and criteria for inclusion on the World Heritage list (that is, outstanding aesthetic and scientific value, universal value, and historical import) are applied to archaeological remains, these remains become literally naturalized under a weight of moral authority (perhaps even perceived as "god given"). However, that the two—sites described as "natural" or "cultural"—are ideologically or conceptually comparable (although living communities are similarly marginal to each) is unlikely, and the conflation eschews the social construction and value systems inherent to each (Meskell 2002).

The very nature of archaeological practice asks us all to question how ideas about the "local" (that is, about difference, new legal framings, and, say, historical restitution for indigenous and descendent communities worldwide) are interpolated into recommendations and policy. Heritage may be our arena of investigation, but beyond heuristics, archaeologists have largely accepted now that decisions about the past have real-time implications for living communities. Identifying competing conceptions of the "common good" and the practices by which new and emergent social realities come into being is very much at issue within this set of chapters. In chapter 1, Gastón Gordillo's fieldwork grapples with the spatial debris of sites in northern Argentina, reflexively interrogating the familiar hegemonic notions of stewardship, patrimony, and universal protection. The politics of protection here depend very much on the construction of history: the ruin, decay, and even the constitution of sites. Universal notions of preservation and protection often fall short of cultural understandings of use and continuity: what inevitably gets cast as looting, vandalism, and reuse of historic materials is thus used to demonize local constituencies by national and transnational authorities. Archaeological sites are purified through the march of time and the cultural amnesia that accompanies temporal passing. How can we define or apprehend an arbitrary moment in time that transforms the product of the past into an object of heritage? Preservation privileges the construct of historical respect rather than the needs of the present. Only the arbitrary passing of culturally determined time sanctifies the past as truly past.

As many of the contributions in this volume make clear, heritage agencies often have little concern with local communities; their efforts are geared more toward global directives and developmental politics that harness tourism and other economic forces. Perhaps this is why ethnographers, rather than archaeologists, have taken up the challenge of heritage practice and representation so effectively in the past decade (for example, Abu el-Haj 2001; Bartu 2000; Benavides 2005; Breglia 2006; Castañeda 1996) and why archaeologists have been slow to seize on the topic as crucial to our self-description. We archaeologists, after all, provide the some of the raw materials for the related spheres of heritage, tourism, and nationalism.

Jennifer Jacobs and Benjamin Porter, writing on the situation in Jordan (chapter 3), underline the narratives of development and sustainability that cohere around specific heritage sites, successfully bolstered by international agencies such as the European Union and USAID. In chapter 4, Helaine Silverman underscores the atomization and localization that archaeological materials can promote and instantiate, namely, a sense of identity outside the metropoles. By her account, the conscription of an archaeological past allows for new notions of Mochica to be forged in contemporary Peru. Undoubtedly, this has always been the case historically; however, in modern times, we have better access to the mechanisms and can effectively track the machinations, which is perhaps why we are witnessing a burgeoning of studies that bridge ethnography and archaeology. The domestication of the past has happened at all times and in all places, and this leads us to question the very notion of authenticity. Over vast expanses of time, the texture of memory cannot cohere in its original form; it is constantly reworked, fabricated, and cast as politically desirable. Selectively, the past is remembered and forgotten in the present, and thus, certain pasts are sanctioned as heritage. This particularly interests me at present in my ethnographic work in South Africa, a newly crafted nation built on only a decade of democratic process that has espoused a tacit policy of reconciled forgetting and Rainbow Nation social doctrine. This necessary forgetting helped to forge a new nation out of the violence and repression of the apartheid past, yet in the process, the specificities of the colonial past (and even more recent times) have often been elided—and with this elision, a glossing over of archaeological heritage and its attachments for particular stakeholders (Meskell 2005b). Tacking between archaeological and ethnographic researches has offered a productive strategy to monitor the progress of the past in the crafting of the new nation.

Breglia (in chapter 2) likewise alludes to the recent convergences between archaeology and sociocultural anthropology. She is correct in stating that we require more than ethnographies of archaeological field practices per se—that such studies are contextually impossible—because of the nature of the wide-ranging cosmopolitan engagements in which we are enmeshed. What is appealing about the cosmopolitan turn, however, is that while the processes of globalization lay claim to an overarching homogeneity of the planet in economic, political, and cultural spheres, the term *cosmopolitanism* can be employed as a counter to globalization from below. As anthropologists, we are primed to be attentive to specific local contexts and histories that plan and project global designs and understandings in particular modalities (Mignolo 2002: 157). Studies of the archaeological present have lately evinced this local dimension, placing local communities and understandings at the forefront of our research agendas. At the same time, many practitioners want to demonstrate global relevance, the impact of global networks and forces and the implications of international efforts: aid, development, protectionism, conservation, humanitarianism, and so on. Both ends of the spectrum, local and global, have their limitations if considered in isolation and do not fully consider the "processes of self-transformation in which new cultural forms take place and where new spaces of discourse open up leading to a transformation in the social world" (Delanty 2006: 44). How the world is imagined in particular places is greatly at variance.

On a more dystopian note, it has become obvious that over the past decade, heritage, conservation, and culture have increasingly entered both political and military arenas. The following provides a brief example of the kind of cultural contextualism that I believe is necessary, as it considers transnational forces but also reflects back upon a specific historical and political moment. UNESCO's recent intervention in Afghanistan provides a high-profile example, underpinned by the organization's explicit desire to create disciplined heritage subjects by developing didactic programs of governance. Interventionist adventures of this kind (whether military, economic, or cultural) are often conducted against the interests of people in the poorer and less-developed regions of the earth; however, that fact does not register, because their experience is not accepted as part of our world's portrait of itself as a world (Gilroy 2005: 59). Iraq would provide another salient contemporary example. UNESCO's stated strategy for Afghanistan is to "help re-establish the links between the populations concerned and their cultural history, helping them to develop a sense of common ownership of monuments that represent the cultural identity of different segments of society."[1] Archaeological materials are thus seen as recuperative objects directly serving the "nation-building process within the framework of the UN and international concerted efforts for rehabilitating Afghanistan." For Paul Gilroy, "the discourse of human rights supplies the principal way in which this shared human nature can be made accessible to political debate and legal rationality," yet under the rubric of "humanitarianism, these particular moral sensibilities can promote and justify intervention in other people's sovereign territory on the grounds that their ailing or incompetent national state has failed to measure up to the levels of good practice that merit recognition as civilized" (Gilroy 2005: 59). United Nations–mandated policies and activities for the safeguarding of Afghanistan's cultural heritage focus on training and capacity-building activities premised on the preservation of the cultural history of the Afghan people. In this case, culture is being instrumentalized through internationally sanctioned modes of salvation, betterment, and development. In large part, non-Western cultures cannot escape the secularization and a pluralism of worldviews stemming from modernization, yet their cultural individuality against a capitalist world culture is severely curtailed (Habermas 2005: 28).

We have to ask whether the safeguarding in Afghanistan specifically serves the nation or, more probably, benefits the world as understood by Euro-American constituencies. UNESCO recommendations stress preservation first and foremost within the new Afghan constitution. Training in the management of heritage/archaeology is another priority, as is the inventorying of cultural property, itself reminiscent of colonial scientific ventures of mapping, surveying, taxonomizing, and collecting (Dirks 1992; Hayden 2003). The reification and control of heritage landscapes is paramount, harnessed by a strong didactic element: disciplined modern subjects foreground monumental preservation and privilege international imperatives over local concerns. From a governmental perspective, UNESCO endorses projects that raise awareness of and foster values around cultural heritage via educational curricula and public information. If the didactic route fails, there are stated disciplinary or military options. One recommendation argues for a "special security force to protect Afghan sites with the support of the international community." National elites must be similarly co-opted through the creation of an "Inter-ministerial Committee on Cultural and Natural Heritage and Development to be established in Kabul in order to enhance the awareness of cabinet members and those policy makers whose decisions would have an impact on the cultural heritage of Afghanistan." The role of local communities is to be brought into the fold and educated about the value of preservation efforts to ensure the sustainability of projects. Paralleling the language of global biodiversity and conservation, the taxonomic call to arms for heritage registers, the threats of endangerment and loss, and the push for community involvement are all markers of pragmatic concerns about the most effective ways to ensure conservation on the one hand and socioeconomic management and intervention on the other (Hayden 2003: 59–60). This briefly sketched example illuminates what different parties have to win or lose within the framings of heritage humanitarianism that tacitly foreground a global heritage for a common humanity (Meskell 2009). It also underlines the complexities of global engagement at a postnational level and problematizes the dangerous borderlines of salvage, aid, development, intervention, and hegemony.

As researchers, we must be ethically mindful when the "politics of protection" is mobilized in efforts to demonize or subjugate peoples with whom we disagree on issues of heritage management or other cultural values, especially under the false rubric of neutrality. This does not represent cosmopolitan engagement; instead, it reinforces hegemonic practices of heritage salvage under the sign of philanthropy. We are obligated to interrogate our motives in the constructs of helping and heritage humanitarianism and to ask whether we are invited participants or are imposing our views and values on others. While a cosmopolitan ethos stresses that we have *obligations* to others, it takes "seriously the value not just of human life but of particular human lives, which means taking an interest in the practices and beliefs that lend them significance. People are different, the cosmopolitan knows, and there is much to learn from our differences. Because there are so many human possibilities worth exploring, we neither expect nor desire that every person or every society should converge on a single model of life" (Appiah 2006: xv). Cosmopolitanism is the challenge, not the universal solution to our cultural diversity, and the past remains the central foundation on which we constitute others and ourselves on the world stage.

Notes

1. http://portal.unesco.org/culture/en/ev.php-URL_ID=24246&URL_DO=DO_TOPIC &URL_SECTION=201.html.

References Cited

Abu el-Haj, Nadia. *Facts on the Ground: Archaeological Practice and Territorial Self-Fashioning in Israeli Society.* Chicago: University of Chicago Press, 2001.

Appiah, Kwame Anthony. *Cosmopolitanism.* New York: Norton and Company, 2006.

Ashworth, Gregory. "Heritage, Tourism and Europe: A European Future for a European Past?" In *Heritage, Tourism and Society,* edited by D. Herbert, 69–84. New York: Mansell Publishing, 1995.

Bartu, Ayfer. "Where Is Çatalhöyük: Multiple Sites in the Construction of an Archaeological Site." In *Towards Reflexive Method in Archaeology: The Example at Çatalhöyük,* edited by I. Hodder, 101–9. Cambridge, U.K.: McDonald Institute for Archaeological Research, 2000.

Beck, Ulrich, and Natan Sznaider. "Unpacking Cosmopolitanism for the Social Sciences: A Research Agenda." *British Journal of Sociology* 57 (2006): 1–23.

Benavides, O. Hugo. *Making Ecuadorian Histories.* Austin: University of Texas Press, 2005.

Breckenridge, Carol A., Homi Bhabha, Sheldon Pollock, and Dipesh Chakrabarty, eds. *Cosmopolitanism.* Durham, N.C.: Duke University Press, 2002.

Breglia, Lisa C. "Docile Descendants and Illegitimate Heirs: Privatization of Cultural Patrimony in Mexico." Ph.D. diss., Rice University, 2003.

———. *Monumental Ambivalence.* Austin: University of Texas Press, 2006.

Castañeda, Quetzil E. *In the Museum of Maya Culture: Touring Chichén Itzá.* Minneapolis: University of Minnesota Press, 1996.

Cheah, Pheng, and Bruce Robbins, eds. *Cosmopolitics: Thinking and Feeling beyond Nation.* Minneapolis: University of Minnesota Press, 1998.

Delanty, Gerard. "The Cosmopolitan Imagination: Critical Cosmopolitanism and Social Theory." *British Journal of Sociology* 57 (2006): 25–47.

Dirks, Nicholas. "Introduction." In *Colonialism and Culture,* edited by N. Dirks, 1–26. Ann Arbor: University of Michigan Press, 1992.

Gilroy, Paul. *Postcolonial Melancholia.* New York: Columbia University Press, 2005.

Habermas, Jürgen. *The Inclusion of the Other: Essays in Political Theory.* Cambridge, Mass.: MIT Press, 2000.

———. "Equal Treatment of Cultures and the Limits of Postmodern Liberalism." *Journal of Political Philosophy* 13 (2005): 1–28.

Hayden, Cori. *When Nature Goes Public: The Making and Unmaking of Bioprospecting in Mexico.* Princeton, N.J.: Princeton University Press, 2003.

Ivison, Duncan. "Emergent Cosmopolitanism: Indigenous Peoples and International Law." In *Between Cosmopolitan Ideals and State Sovereignty,* edited by R. Tinnevelt and G. Verschraegen, 120–34. New York: Palgrave, 2006.

Ivison, Duncan, Paul Patton, and Will Sanders, eds. *Political Theory and the Rights of Indigenous Peoples.* Cambridge: Cambridge University Press, 2000.

Joyce, Rosemary A. "Solid Histories for Fragile Nations: Archaeology as Cultural Patrimony." In *Embedding Ethics,* edited by L. Meskell and P. Pels, 253–73. Oxford, U.K.: Berg, 2005.

Meskell, Lynn M. "Negative Heritage and Past Mastering in Archaeology." *Anthropological Quarterly* 75 (2002): 557–74.

———. "Archaeological Ethnography: Conversations around Kruger National Park." *Archaeologies: Journal of the World Archaeology Congress* 1 (2005): 83–102. [2005a]

———. "Recognition, Restitution and the Potentials of Postcolonial Liberalism for South African Heritage." *South African Archaeological Bulletin* 60 (2005): 72–78. [2005b]

———. "Sites of Violence: Terrorism, Tourism and Heritage in the Archaeological Present." In *Embedding Ethics,* edited by L. Meskell and P. Pels, 123–46. Oxford, U.K.: Berg, 2005. [2005c]

———. "Falling Walls and Mending Fences: Archaeological Ethnography in the Limpopo." *Journal of Southern African Studies* 33, no. 2 (2007): 383–400.

———. "Introduction." In *Cosmopolitan Archaeologies,* edited by L. M. Meskell. Durham, N.C.: Duke University Press, 2009.

Mignolo, Walter. "The Many Faces of Cosmo-polis." In *Cosmopolitanism,* edited by C. Breckenridge, H. Bhabha, S. Pollock, and D. Chakrabarty, 157–88. Durham, N.C.: Duke University Press, 2002.

Pollock, Sheldon, Homi Bhabha, Carol A. Breckenridge, and Dipesh Chakrabarty. "Cosmopolitanisms." In *Cosmopolitanism,* edited by C. Breckenridge, H. Bhabha, S. Pollock, and D. Chakrabarty, 1–14. Durham, N.C.: Duke University Press, 2002.

Szerszynski, Bronislaw, and John Urry. "Visuality, Mobility and the Cosmopolitan: Inhabiting the World from Afar." *British Journal of Sociology* 57 (2006): 113–31.

1

The Ruins of Ruins

On the Preservation and Destruction
of Historical Sites in Northern Argentina

GASTÓN GORDILLO

In May 2003, while doing fieldwork at the foot of the Andes in northwestern Argentina, I arrived at the ruins of San Juan Bautista de Balbuena, a mission founded by the Jesuits in the 1700s on the western edge of the Gran Chaco plain. A local man in his fifties named Juan took me to the place, leading me for about an hour down a winding trail carved through the forest. As we walked, he told me several stories about "the church" (as he called the site); he referred to the ghost of a Catholic priest wandering the surrounding hills, the rumors about riches buried nearby, and the *fiestones* (large celebrations) that local people had organized there decades earlier. On finally seeing the overgrown ruins emerge from the vegetation, I was in awe. Those were by far the best-preserved vestiges associated with the conquest of the Chaco that I would encounter in the region. Three of the church walls stood about seven meters high, and the altar was in relatively good condition. A door on the right wall, leading to a small room, formed an arch decorated by a stucco frame. Weeds and vines crawled on some of the walls, and several trees had sprawling roots anchored in broken bricks scattered on the ground.

As we explored the site and I took photos, Juan emphasized how old the place looked. "At least a hundred years," he repeated several times. I told him the place was even older and had been built in the eighteenth century. He nodded and pointed to a large algarrobo tree growing in what had been the church center: "That tree must be a hundred years old. This place is very old." To make his point clearer, he pointed to the stucco frame decorating the side door to our right and punched it with his fist. A piece of stucco fell off. "See?" he said. He punched it again and another section broke off. "Look, this place is really old! At least a hundred years. These chunks come off easy." I was horrified. I was about to stop him for doing what clearly seemed an act of senseless destruction that was damaging an invaluable historical site; instead, I felt paralyzed. I was puzzled by my own reaction, especially by the realization of the gap that existed between my view of those ruins and his. Furthermore, in feeling that such an action had to be stopped, I realized I was claiming authority over that place and over Juan's conduct in it, even though I was a stranger to the area and had found the site only with his help. Juan, after all, lived only a few kilometers away and interacted with that place on a regular basis, for he worked on the cattle ranch on which the ruins are located, looking after the cattle that roamed those forests. This incident made me begin exploring several questions: What values, senses of place, and conceptions of social memory lie behind the seemingly self-evident idea that even the most minute components of the ruins of historical sites *have* to be preserved? How does one account for Juan's apparent disregard for the physical integrity of that place without falling into views that condemn popular "ignorance" from the self-ascribed heights of academic knowledge? What view of the past lies behind Juan's brisk, disarmingly casual attitude toward the spatial debris of history?

In this chapter, I explore these questions by drawing on my fieldwork in this and other nearby sites in the province of Salta, in the region where the Juramento River—called "Salado" farther downstream—flows from the Andean foothills into the Gran Chaco. In particular, I compare the case of the Balbuena mission with the remains of the seventeenth-century town of Esteco, located about sixty kilometers to the southwest,[1] and contrast local people's experiences of these sites with that of officials and academics, especially involving their respective reactions to alterations of these places' physical integrity. These contrasts shed light on conflicting views of the spatiality of social memory, on the historical contingency of the concept of "ruin," and on the paradoxes posed by the ruining of ruins: that is, by the partial destruction of sites that are already in a state of decay.

Ruin-Preservation and the "Will to Remember"

Many authors have argued that the current preoccupation with ruins and their preservation is a relatively recent product of modernity—in particular, of the rise of nation-states and nationalist projects in the nineteenth century (Jusdanis 2004; Lowenthal 1985; Woodward 2001).[2] In Europe, for instance, the spatial traces of Roman and Greek antiquity coexisted for centuries with the everyday, living geographies of local populations, as is illustrated by the prolonged use of the overgrown remains of the Roman forum as pasture fields (Woodward 2001). Breaking with this attitude, modernist narratives gradually produced new sensitivities toward physical markers of decline, and the latter became seen as sites of contemplation, spiritual illumination, collective identity, or knowledge. State agencies, in particular, asserted a new "will to remember," to use Pierre Nora's (1989) expression, which found a particularly strong spatial foundation in the practice of ruin-preservation, supported by the emerging discipline of archaeology. Physical traces from other eras were turned into "ruins" that required special care, spatial rearrangement, and control. As Michael Roth (1997: 1) argues, "When we frame an object as ruin, we reclaim that object *from* its fall into decay and oblivion and often *for* some kind of cultural attention and care that, in a sense, elevates its value. In the European traditions the classical ruin is elevated out of oblivion into a particularly exalted position of contemplation or even worship."

By becoming "historic ruins," in other words, remains from the past are produced as entirely new places: as sites in which the forces of material decay are to be halted in the name of their intrinsic value as carriers of history. This process implies fencing off these places, severing them from the practice of local populations, and deploying on these spaces the authority of state agencies and academics, particularly archaeologists and historians. This authority draws much of its force from the labeling of nonacademic appropriations of those sites—such as the practice, widespread worldwide, of using ruins as sources of construction materials—as "looting" or as "destructive." The academic knowledge set to preserve those sites, in other words, is highlighted by the alleged ignorance or disregard projected onto the people living near them. Certainly, many archaeologists have distanced themselves from the most hierarchical of these positions and now work together with local populations, especially in contexts where the sites in question are politically charged and local groups claim authority over them (such as in many parts of North America). Yet archaeological research remains based on the tenet that the physical integrity of these sites should be protected from damage.

It is important to note, however, that the meaning and scope of the concept of "preservation" have been a source of debate. Many philosophers, poets, and writers have valued ruins not so much for carrying knowledge about the past but for being sources of contemplation or inspiration; thus, they have been drawn to ruins to put the human experience in perspective in relation to the unrelenting forces of nature and history and to reflect, depending on their viewpoint, either on the fragility or on the resilient grandeur of historical products (Woodward 2001). Advocates of this humanist approach have criticized state and academic attempts to "preserve" these sites for tampering with their original layout and have pointed out that archaeologists have substantially modified, and hence undermined, these spaces. Christopher Woodward has argued, for instance, that in fencing off ruins, trimming them of vegetation, and partially restoring them, archaeologists and officials have produced sanitized, cold places devoid of mystery. Thus, whereas in the nineteenth century, the overgrown ruins of the Roman Coliseum inspired English poets and travelers, today, he argues, "it is the most monumental bathos in Europe: a bald, dead and bare circle of stones" (Woodward 2001: 31).

This nostalgia for allegedly untouched ruins can be criticized for being romantic and elitist, for it longs for a time when upper-class, northern European travelers could enjoy the Roman ruins as relatively private, intimate spaces. Yet one should note that this view is still firmly grounded in modernist sensibilities. Max Page (2003) has pointed out that Woodward's "ruinlust"—and, I would add, the humanist fascination with overgrown ruins—owes much to the work of generations of archaeologists and the subsequent creation of a public record of ruins. Humanist and archaeological views, in short, have not run parallel, separate courses but have influenced and interpenetrated each other (see Riegl 1982: 35). More important, despite its particular take on scholarly preservation, the humanist position shares with archaeology a negative view of the obliteration of ruins other than by "natural decay" and would also condemn "every willful destruction of monuments as a desecration of all-consuming nature" (Riegl 1982: 32).

In the following sections, I will try to show how these views on preservation are largely alien to the experience of people living in rural areas in the Juramento-Salado River region, who are for the most part criollos, as poor rural dwellers of mestizo background are called in northern Argentina. Because of this region's cattle-herding tradition, many criollos see themselves as gauchos (cowboys). Some of them own small or midsize farms (of several hundred hectares) and rely on the labor of their families, but most criollos are wage-laborers who in some cases own a few head of cattle but do not own the land on which they live. For the most part, they work on the cattle and agricultural *fincas* (farms) that dominate the regional landscape, which is dotted by debris from one of the oldest colonial frontiers in South America. Overgrown remains of the settlements, forts, and missions once built to subdue the indigenous groups of the Chaco are scattered in hills, open fields, and forests. All of them are on private lands, in relatively out-of-the-way places, and not easily accessible from public roads. And none of them, including Esteco (the most prominent site), have been turned by state agencies into sites of cultural or historical patrimony.

First, I analyze the most prominent of these sites, Esteco, and the recent transformations and conflicts involving its shifting configuration as a "ruin." Next, I examine the case of the Jesuit mission at Balbuena as a counterpoint to the ways in which criollos have historically related to some of the ruins in the area. In the final section, I draw on both cases to reflect on the ruining of ruins and on the contrasting ways in which different actors spatialize their social memory.

Esteco, 2003

When in the 1550s the Spanish began conquering what is today northwestern Argentina, the Salado River became a contested geography separating the Spanish territories in the Andean highlands from the Gran Chaco, which remained under the control of indigenous groups. In 1566, Spanish troops founded on this river the town of Esteco, at a site located relatively deep in the Chaco plains. Initially a stopover on the road to Peru, Esteco became a center for the exploitation of thousands of indigenous laborers through *encomienda* (servitude) relations. Yet this then was a poorly protected frontier, and by the end of the sixteenth century, the main trade routes had shifted closer to the Andes. In 1609, in fact, the regional authorities decided to move Esteco a hundred kilometers to the west, at the foot of the first mountain ranges. There, it became one of the largest towns in what today is northern Argentina. However, indigenous attacks, the recurrent flight of laborers subjected to encomienda, and economic stagnation contributed to its gradual decline, until an earthquake in 1692 destroyed much of the town and marked its subsequent abandonment (Poma 1995; Tomasini and Alonso 2001; Torre Revelo 1943).

Legends, poems, and songs about the fate of Esteco have long been well known all over northwestern Argentina. They tell the story of an immensely rich town where horseshoes were made of gold and people were arrogant and faithless. This is also a story of a cursed wealth. The inhabitants of Esteco were so rich and proud, so the legend goes, that God punished them by causing the earthquake that destroyed the city in 1692. As a result of this cataclysm, Esteco *se perdió* (got lost, disappeared), a term that accentuates the perception that the city vanished, leaving behind no noticeable ruins but an invisible presence.[3] In this regard, the fame of Esteco as a place doomed by its wealth and faithless arrogance was for a long time heightened by the relative mystery of its exact location, which is commemorated only by the name of a small, abandoned train station located a few kilometers northeast of Metán, the largest town in southeastern Salta.

In May 2003, I arrived in Metán searching for the traces of Esteco. This town had been severely hit by the downsizing and privatization schemes begun by the 1976–83 military dictatorship and deepened in the 1990s by the laying off of thousands of workers employed in the formerly state-run railways. As occurred in most of northwestern Argentina, following the near-collapse of the national economy in 2001–2, unemployment and poverty were then rampant. However, I found that in this town, the nostalgia for better times characterized by semifull public-sector employment was particularly strong. On my first day there, a man in his fifties, a former railway worker, summarized this feeling when he told me, "This used to be a land of plenty" (*ésto era un vergel*). This nostalgia for a past prosperity, and the experience of decline nourishing it, seemed particularly fitting for a region that centuries earlier had alleg-edly also fallen from grace from a prior pinnacle of riches.

When I asked in Metán about Esteco, everybody knew details about its curse and subsequent destruction and remembered its wealth not so much as legend but as historical fact. Yet many were unaware of its exact location and pointed (wrongly, it turned out) to the train station of the same name. Eventually, several people told me that the remains of Esteco were hidden in a patch of forest located more than twenty kilometers to the north, on a citrus farm east of the village of Río Piedras, near the Juramento-Salado River.

A few days later, I drove to Río Piedras. After talking to several people and getting directions from them, I headed to the finca following a dirt road. On arriving at a cluster of houses, I stopped to ask for permission to get on the farm and see Esteco. The finca administrator nodded casually. "No problem." He pointed east and said, "In two kilometers, you'll see a forest on the right side of the road. That's Esteco." It was a rainy, gray Sunday. When I arrived at the site and got out of the car, I felt that the foggy landscape looked relatively unremarkable and devoid of historical traces: it was a densely forested area of about fifty hectares, surrounded by fields of citrus trees. This farm was a counterpoint to the poverty that dominated Metán, Río Piedras, and the rest of the region. The free-trade policies of the 1990s had triggered a boom in export-oriented agribusinesses in southeastern Salta, based on capital-intensive cul-tivation of soybeans, citrus, and white beans. The cattle ranches that had dominated the regional landscape since the nineteenth century, usually raising cattle in forested areas, were ceding terrain to open fields such as the one I was walking on.

I met two young men who worked at the farm and were enjoying their day off, wandering in the rain. We began walking along the forest perimeter and talking about *la ciudad de Esteco* (the city of Esteco), which they knew was there. I soon no-ticed that there were broken tiles scattered on the ground around the lines of citrus trees: some small, some up to five inches long, but all with a distinctive red tone that made them stand out against the mud. Drenched by the rain, we began picking and comparing pieces. One of my companions, César, commented that they had been unearthed by the plowing machines that had prepared the fields for citrus planting. The more we looked at those pieces of tiles and talked about them, the more I was drawn to the forest a few meters away, the source of those traces of buildings de-stroyed centuries earlier. Those distant histories that had initially looked elusive to me were emerging in front of my eyes as sediments firmly inscribed in the landscape.

Thrilled at the sight of debris from another era, I suggested to my companions that we explore together the interior of the forest. They seemed wary at first. Even though they were not from the area but from Santiago del Estero, they told me that they had heard stories from local people about the curse haunting Esteco and those who entered the forest. But it did not take them long to change their minds, probably piqued by my own curiosity. We first followed what seemed to be a trail but soon began walking with difficulty through dense entanglements of trees, vines, and shrubs, becoming wetter from the raindrops accumulated on the foliage. There were no more broken tiles on the ground, just a thick layer of plants and weeds. As we slowly made our way through, the terrain became much more irregular, and we found ourselves climbing and descending steep mounds. We could distinguish what seemed to be the layout of old streets: long, straight depressions surrounded by mounds on both sides. The forest suddenly became a different place—not just an expression of nature but a green veneer covering the grid of an ancient city. On a couple of occasions, we stumbled upon deep and wide holes, which, I learned later, had been dug by the treasure hunters who, over the centuries, had entered those forests in search of the riches of Esteco. At one point, Mario, my other companion, felt compelled to jokingly invoke those memories of wealth. He stood on the edge of one of the mounds, pretended to see something in the distance, and shouted, "Gold! Gold!" We all had a good laugh. I felt as though we could not escape the haunting presence of the past hovering over that place.

We wandered that intricate space for over an hour, until, soaking wet and tired, we reached the other edge of the forest and again found ourselves in citrus fields. César and Mario invited me to drink mate tea at their camp, two kilometers away, and half an hour later we were sitting by a fire listening to stories about Esteco from their *capataz* (foreman), a man from the area in his sixties named Pedro. He was excited to hear that we had been in Esteco and listened approvingly to our accounts of the mounds, the streets, the holes. "Many people are afraid of getting in there," he said. He told us about a farmworker who, years earlier, had abandoned a tractor on the edge of the forest and mysteriously disappeared. People thought he had either been swallowed by Esteco or found a treasure and surreptitiously left so that no one noticed. Pedro also told us about the ghosts of schoolchildren that some swear to have seen walking in the morning next to the forest, mimicking the actions of times past, and about the roosters that wander the area and suddenly disappear. I asked Pedro what the new farm owner, who had bought the finca in 2000, thought of the forest and whether he would try clearing it to plant more citrus. "He's going to leave it like this," Pedro said. César agreed: "He says he's going to leave it like this. People around here don't like working there."

I spent several days in the area, mostly in Río Piedras, and returned to Esteco a few more times. Most local people referred to "the city of Esteco" as the embodiment of the past splendor of the whole region and pointed out that prior to its destruction it far surpassed Salta, the provincial capital, in size, wealth, and importance. In drawing that contrast, they were bringing to light that after the earthquake the regional center of power and wealth shifted toward Salta (hence, toward the valleys of the Andes) and that the Juramento-Salado River region then sank into relative oblivion. The demise of Esteco and the subsequent rise of Salta, therefore, loom large over current perceptions about the relative marginality of the region, even if in the twentieth century the employment provided by the railways had temporarily countered it.

On leaving Río Piedras to do fieldwork farther east in the ruins of Balbuena, I was left with the impression that the quasi-invisible remains of Esteco created a remarkable palimpsest with capitalist spaces of agrarian production and with current geographies of poverty, as part of a mosaic in which these spaces shaped each other in manifold ways. In particular, the high levels of unemployment that, back then, marked the experience of most people living in the area seemed to highlight the wealth projected onto Esteco. And that sense of vanished (if cursed) wealth accentuated the feelings of loss that pervaded the memory of Esteco's past glory. Yet on my next visit, that experience of poverty would inform views of that site in further and—at least to me—unexpected ways.

Esteco, 2005

In July 2005, I returned to Argentina to begin a new fieldwork season in the area of Esteco. In the evening of my arrival in Metán, I met an acquaintance from my previous trip while eating at a diner. Since he knew of my research interests, he immediately asked me, "Did you know what happened in Esteco?" I did not. "The finca owner sent bulldozers in. It was on the radio and in the papers. This happened only a few months ago." He had no further details about the extent of the damage, so I did not know what to make of the news. I was planning to visit Esteco the next morning, but after dinner I headed to a local cybercafé to search for news of the incident in the provincial media. "Ruins of Esteco razed," read a headline in El Tribuno, Salta's most important daily. "The damage to the site is absolute and irreparable" (El Tribuno, February 4, 2005). I felt numb and depressed. The memories of my visit to the site two years earlier, the flashes of my hike through a history-drenched forest that was apparently gone, acquired a totally different meaning.

The next morning, I drove straight to the finca. The newspaper articles did not fully prepare me for what I saw. The forest that I had explored, and which had such a strong presence in the middle of the farm, did not exist anymore. The trees, plants, and weeds uprooted and crushed by the bulldozers had been piled up in neatly organized lines parallel to each other, fifty meters apart. I was particularly disturbed by the mathematical order of the destruction that the farm administration had brought upon the site of Esteco. I entered the barren space of what had once been the forest, taking pictures and contrasting my memory of that same place with the landscape I was then witnessing. The uprooting of the veneer of vegetation that covered Esteco had unearthed countless pieces of tiles and bricks. The mounds I had walked through two years earlier, however, were still there. In fact, the destruction of the forest made visible what up until then had been hidden in the misleading naturalness of that green cover: the rough layout of buildings and streets from another era, now exposed to the light of day.

In contemplating the traces of Esteco from the top of the highest mound, I reflected on my initial impression, two years earlier, that the cultural and historical thickness of that site would somehow stop the expansion of capitalist forms of spatiality onto it. The rubble that surrounded me was proof of how wrong I was. It also suggested that, at least from what I had gathered in my previous fieldwork, local people had also been led to believe that Esteco had an aura that would make the finca owner "leave it like that," even though the site was located on private land and was not under the official protection of state agencies.

Yet the owner, I soon learned, had decided to clear those fifty hectares of forest to build a fruit-packaging plant. In late January 2005, several bulldozers began working around the clock, and by the first days of February, the clearing had been almost completed. It was then that the provincial legislator for the Metán district saw the bulldozers at work while driving on the paved road that passes a few hundred meters south of the site. Being from the nearby town of El Galpón, he knew that the forest being cleared was the site of Esteco. He made his lawyer file a class-action suit in the Metán courts, and a judge ordered the *desmonte* (clearing) and any other alteration of the site to stop. But it was too late. The news of "the destruction of the Esteco ruins" immediately hit the media in the province.

A notable consequence of this incident was that it gave Esteco a public, spatially grounded visibility. Despite Esteco's fame throughout Salta, few people in other parts of the province had known where exactly this place was. Now, its coordinates were unambiguously identified for a wider public, paradoxically as a result of its semidestruction. More important, the bulldozing created a generalized uproar in the academic community and among members of the regional cultural and political elites. In previous years, some of them had pushed for timid attempts to protect the place. In 1998, the Salta legislature had declared the site a "provincial historic patrimony," and in 2000 a research team based at the Universidad de La Plata signed an agreement with the provincial government and local municipalities to do archaeological research on this and other historical sites. But even though archaeologists had conducted brief surveillance work at the site, the latter remained within the firm grip of the finca owner, as the clearing had crudely confirmed, and no signposts or fences identified its significance. The scholars behind these attempts at preservation and research were, not surprisingly, dismayed at the news of the clearing. A few days after I visited the ruined ruins, the most prominent historian living in Metán told me, "It was a disaster. It's a great loss for Salta and for the whole country." Likewise, the archaeologist at the Universidad de La Plata who had worked at Esteco declared to the media, "I'm really appalled. . . . It's something horrific, terrible, incomprehensible, awful, brutal" (*El Tribuno,* February 5, 2005).

The finca owner was certainly the main target of criticism. He was accused of following a purely economic, quantitative rationality indifferent to the historical, qualitative value of space. Indeed, one could argue that the act of sending bulldozers into Esteco was informed by the logic of what Henri Lefebvre (1991) has called "abstract space": the commodified space of capitalism, relatively free of the cultural and religious meanings that for Lefebvre defined the "absolute space" of previous epochs. Yet in the elite discourses that were critical of the bulldozing, this conflict revealed not so much a dichotomy between economic and cultural views of space as variations of neoliberal strategies of spatialization ultimately aimed at commodifying the regional geography.

When the legislator from El Galpón visited Esteco to assess the damage, he was joined, among others, by members of the Chamber of Tourism of Southeastern Salta and the secretary of culture and tourism of El Galpón (*El Tribuno,* February 8, 2005). In fact, part of the criticism of the clearing revolved around the potential of sites such as Esteco to become tourist attractions. The province of Salta is one of the most popular travel destinations in Argentina, yet the most important tourist circuits are located in the valleys and highlands of the Andes. The lowlands of Metán and El Galpón attract almost no visitors from other provinces, and over the past few years, the municipalities of the area have begun coordinated efforts to change this situation. This has included the promotion of the several "ruins" scattered in the area in brochures and on maps and murals, even though they are on private lands, there is no infrastructure to make these sites open to the public, most of them are hard to access, and no signposts guide potential travelers to them. Although framed within the language of historic patrimony, and despite these contradictions, these strategies signal the interest by some influential local actors to impose on these ruins forms of commodification and state management that up until now have been beyond their reach.

In addition to the conflict this incident created with the farm owner, some officials and academics blamed what had happened on the "ignorance" and "disinterest" of the local population at large, which had for generations allowed for the actions of *huaqueros* (looters). The archaeologist cited earlier noted that even though the bulldozing of Esteco was in and of itself shocking, "it was not something new" but a new addition to the damage caused by "archaeological pirates" (*El Tribuno,* February 5, 2005). The historian based in Metán declared to *El Tribuno,* "The loss of that historic patrimony of all *salteños* [people from Salta] has to do with the little concern that we have for our past. There's a notable disinformation and lack of culture involving these issues" (*El Tribuno*, February 7, 2005).

Some officials echoed similar concerns involving the preservation of other historical sites in the region. A few kilometers north of El Galpón, in a clearing on a hill, an adobe wall marks what remains of the Franciscan mission of San Miguel de Miraflores (1880–88), a site that people in the area simply call *la misión* (the mission). Despite being only over a century old, in the past few decades these ruins have attracted an annual procession to commemorate the alleged presence in the site, in the early 1590s, of the patron saint of El Galpón, San Francisco Solano. In July 2005, I interviewed the secretary of culture and tourism of El Galpón about the mission and about what had happened in Esteco. We met at his impressively beautiful house, one of the oldest in town and decorated with many valuable antiques. That setting seemed to accentuate the topics of our conversation: history, heritage, preservation. We began talking about the incident in Esteco, and he then referred to the deterioration of the mission because of the careless actions of the procession participants. "Fifteen or twenty years ago," he said, "people went to that mission and came back with a piece of brick, with a tile. . . . That's why people destroyed it. Because people began to take a brick to sit on in order to drink mate tea. And that's how it was totally destroyed. . . . People's ignorance makes them destroy things that have an enormous value." As is apparent, this official saw people's appropriation of the site through casual, everyday practices as eminently destructive. In making reference to these practices in our conversation about the bulldozing of Esteco, he was, like many others, locating the actions of the finca owner within a broader regional culture of disregard for sites with historical value.

As part of this discourse, a recurrent comment I heard was that, as a result of this alleged ignorance, ordinary people in the region had remained largely indifferent to what had happened with Esteco. Indeed, when I visited Metán a few months after the clearing, most people seemed to have forgotten about it. I was not too surprised, for the actual site of Esteco has always been relatively distant to most inhabitants of this town. But I had initially assumed that in Río Piedras, because of its proximity to the ruins, things would be different—that ordinary people would share at least some of the consternation voiced in the media and see the bulldozing as a destructive appropriation of what was a culturally dense marker of local identity. In Río Piedras, however, I encountered a persistent indifference about the effects of the clearing. Unlike the indifference I had encountered in Metán, this one involved a place these people knew well.

Diego, a man in his forties and my closest acquaintance in Río Piedras, was the first person I talked to about the incident involving the clearing. In a casual way, and only when I pressed him with my questions, he suggested that there could be a connection between the curse of Esteco and the decision to stop the bulldozing. He told me, "The government caused problems for the finca owners because they don't want them to occupy that place, because that place is damned. They want them to leave it just like that." For Diego, "the government" stopped the clearing not because of the historical value of the site but because of the curse haunting it. In other words, he projected onto state officials the imaginaries that many criollos associate with the site as a damned place that should be left undisturbed. Yet it was clear to me that his comments expressed neither sympathy for the decision of "the government" nor condemnation of the finca owner. His attitude included a distancing that bordered on indifference. Yet he was indifferent to the impact of the clearing on those mounds, not to Esteco as a place drenched in histories and personal memories. As a boy, he had lived for many years right next to "the lost city," in a camp for people working at the finca, and had seen "the streets" and "the mounds" countless times. As our conversation progressed, he told me once again stories about the place and at one point asked me whether I wanted to hear him sing a *zamba* (a type of folk song) about Esteco. I said yes. He reached for his guitar, cleared his throat, and began singing:

> The zamba that I here sing
> I sing it with a lot of pain
> A disappeared little town
> That never knew what sunk it

> Silver was its love
> Gold its great passion
> . . . .

> The gauchos used to have
> Well-arranged horses
> With gold horseshoes
> And a shining shield

> But the curse arrived
> Heaven punished them
> Ay, poor city of Esteco,
> It didn't know what a prayer was!
> Ay, poor city of Esteco,
> It didn't know what God was!

I could not help associating the lyrics, which evoked the Esteco vanquished in 1692, with the destruction of the ruins of Esteco that had just taken place in 2005. I also felt that there was a telling parallel between those lines about the disappearance of Esteco because of its faithless devotion to wealth and the bulldozing of its remains because of a businessman's attempt to maximize his profits. But I soon realized that this was my own, analytic interpretation. Diego's singing clearly evoked not so much the mounds affected by the clearing but a town that had been destroyed over three hundred years earlier. The sense of loss and, literally, "pain" transmitted by those lyrics implied a melancholy for a prosperity that had vanished together with the town. This melancholy created sympathy for Esteco ("poor city of Esteco!") and its people, remembered as "gauchos" just like the criollos in Río Piedras, while recognizing its un-Christian arrogance. The sense of loss hovering over the ruins of Esteco, made all the more real by current conditions of poverty, was precisely what caused people to be relatively indifferent to the integrity of those overgrown mounds located on private land they do not control.

Among other local people equally familiar with Esteco, their seeming indifference to the bulldozing masked something else: a critique of the decision by "the government" to prevent the citrus farm from building the fruit-packaging plant. On one of the many occasions I drove from Río Piedras to Esteco, I stopped to chat with a part-time municipality employee who was clearing bushes by the road. His name was Horacio, and he seemed happy to talk to me. When I asked him about the bulldozing in Esteco and about local people's reactions, he shrugged: "People here have nothing to do with that. They said nothing. That's a problem between the farm and the government." A few days later, we talked again at the same site by the road. This time he was more outspoken. I asked him to elaborate on his previous claim that local people had "said nothing" about the incident, and he replied: "People here said nothing because the farm owners were going to give them jobs. . . . The *pueblo* [the town], us, we were happy because of the jobs this would bring, because in this area the tobacco harvest [on other farms in the area] passes and there's nothing."

The more I asked around, the more I detected a subtle yet persistent sense of frustration over the loss of a source of badly needed jobs. This view also included the Wichí living in El Galpón, one of the few people who identify as indigenous in a region that had once been a violent frontier raided by "wild Indians." In the *barrio aborigen* (indigenous neighborhood) of El Galpón, I talked with Arturo, an articulate man in his twenties and member of a Pentecostal church, about the clearings in Esteco. He said, in a bitter tone,

All those government officials from around here don't want that people have jobs. A person from Buenos Aires came and bought the farm. . . . That man was surprised to see the poverty in Metán and El Galpón and decided to buy the farm. But when he bought the farm they didn't tell him that it was Esteco, that there had been a city there. Many people from around here work for him. People go over there to harvest mandarins, oranges, lemons. I think that those [politicians] from around here were a little bothered by this, and they came out saying, "This was Esteco." It's been a thousand years since this city disappeared. No one ever said: "We're going to preserve here. We're going to put a wire fence. We have to look after this place." They only say that now because there's work.

Arturo openly criticized the local political elites by accusing them of trying to prevent people living in poverty from getting jobs from businessmen from other regions. These jobs, he elaborated later, would undermine the relations of patronage through which local politicians keep people dependent on them. But he also criticized what he saw as the hypocrisy of those who for too long ("a thousand years") had done nothing to protect Esteco and intervened only when badly needed jobs were at stake.

For the academics and officials quoted earlier, opinions such as this would probably confirm their point: that ordinary people in the region ignore the historical value of ruins and that this is the result of a conceptual, cultural distance from the actors who can appreciate these places' "true" value. Yet such a view would overlook the oppositional tone of statements such as this, which emerge not from a well-bounded, self-enclosed local "culture" but through a critical engagement with hegemonic practices and discourses. Like the preservation narratives cited earlier, defined in negative relation with tropes of subaltern ignorance, these critical statements are produced through conflicts involving different class experiences and perceptions of space. Furthermore, the concern for jobs does not mean that local subaltern actors have a short-sighted, purely utilitarian view of space and are oblivious to its historical and cultural dimensions. These people are well aware of the weight of past collective experiences on local places: not only through the narratives or songs involving Esteco but also through the inscription of relations of inequality on a landscape of private farms. Their subjectivity and social memory, in other words, are informed by an awareness of the power relations that have produced the regional geography.

These spatial sensitivities counter the veneration of ruins that some officials and academics naturalize as the indisputable measure of historical consciousness. This is a habitus that is not grounded in, or dependent on, the view that places that have long been abandoned and are semidestroyed need to be physically preserved. Implicit in this assumption is that places not inhabited or used by living humans are not necessarily worth preserving and that the grounding of memories in spatial traces does not turn the latter into objects that should be located beyond the diluting forces of history. After all, as Diego reminded me in his zamba, Esteco had been destroyed centuries ago. Those bulldozers uprooting trees and bushes could not change that.

Ruins and Distancing

This gap between academic and local views of ruins is certainly not exclusive to this area, and many authors have noticed similar tensions in other parts of the world (see Breglia, this volume; Clifford 1997; Rodriguez 2002; Wilde 2003). Writing about the holocaust memorial at Auschwitz, for instance, James Young reflected on the contrast between the experience of visitors to the former extermination camp and that of the ordinary people who live nearby and see it as part of their everyday landscape:

> Teenagers fish quietly on the bank of the little pond behind the crematoria, its shallows still white with human ash. They mean no harm. Our memory space is, after all, their city park and state preserve. Whether we like it or not, the local citizens become part of our memory here, reinforcing our own prejudices perhaps, feeding our distrusts. But we must recognize that this awful place remains sacred only in the great distance between it and ourselves, between its past and our present. The site retains its symbolic power over us *partly because we do not live here,* because we must make this pilgrimage to memory. For those who call Auschwitz their home, there may be no other choice: every day and its small chores are framed not merely in the remembered image of this place, but in its hard reality. (Young 1993: 280–81; emphasis added)

This contrast between the experience of local people and what Young calls "memory tourists" does not mean that places such as Auschwitz should not be preserved, especially in cases in which the commemoration grounded in them becomes a political statement against genocide and social suffering. But the veneration of memorials or ruins implies a distancing that is usually alien to those who experience those sites as part of their daily lives. For ordinary people living near Esteco, that everyday reality implies a landscape of poverty and unemployment in which jobs are more pressing than the view that mounds and piles of broken bricks and tiles should remain intact. The local politicians and officials who opposed the clearing may also live in the area, but their class experience clearly distances them from the farm as a working space. As Alois Riegl (1982: 42) noted, "Only works for which we have no use can be enjoyed exclusively from the standpoint of age-value, while those which are still useful impede such pure contemplation." This contemplative distancing is behind what Young (1993) has called the "fetishistic veneration" of this type of site, a concept he does not elaborate but that captures much of what is at stake in my discussion. The veneration of ruins is fetishistic, I argue, because it sees them as objects whose value comes *from within* their materiality rather than from the relations of sociality they articulate. And this is a preoccupation grounded in particular class, cultural, and spatial experiences that imply a separation from those ruins.

As we have seen, local people's indifference to the fate of the site of Esteco does not mean that the latter is not important in their collective memory and sense of identity. Yet this is an importance free of the mandate to remember through traces preserved intact in space. For generations, people in Río Piedras and El Galpón related to these ruins through myriad practices, not only through their work on the farm but also through their search for potentially valuable objects such as bricks used as construction materials, pieces of ceramic, old coins, or artifacts that could be sold to visitors: practices, in sum, that many archaeologists and officials would call "looting." But there is another point worth noting. The appropriation and use of ruins by ordinary people do not necessarily lead to their destruction. And this takes me back to the ruins of the former Jesuit mission of Balbuena.

The Church of La Manga

When I first visited "the church" at Balbuena in 2003, I was impressed by how well preserved it was. That construction dated from the mid-eighteenth century, when the Spanish were consolidating their control over the frontier after the setback created by the demise of Esteco. San Juan Bautista de Balbuena was one of the five mission stations that the Jesuits founded on the Salado River (see Furlong 1941). When the Crown expelled the Jesuits from its territories in 1767, these missions entered a period of decline under the management of the Franciscan order, regular priests, and civilian administrators. By the early nineteenth century, following the wars of independence from Spain, most of these missions had been abandoned.

On my first visit to the ruins of Balbuena, I had assumed that "the church" had survived since the early 1800s simply because of its relative isolation in an out-of-the-way, sparsely populated place covered by large tracts of forests. Yet I soon learned that the building had not simply stood on its own. First, I noticed that Juan and everyone else in the area referred to the ruins as *la iglesia de La Manga,* "the church of La Manga" (after the finca on which it is located). The name of the old Jesuit mission (and of the fort built in its vicinity) had been passed onto the nearest hamlet, Balbuena, located a few kilometers to the east on the main paved road. But no one made a connection between the name "Balbuena" and the ruins at La Manga. Second, I also learned that locals called the place "the church" not simply because it resembled one but because it had been used as one in the not-too-distant past. People in the area argued that decades earlier, there was a hamlet next to the church, the clearest traces of which are a small cemetery (with some tombs dated to the mid-1970s) and the overgrown ruins of what used to be a school. One family in particular, the old owners of the finca, was in charge of looking after the church building and its religious images. Once a year, in mid-August, hundreds of criollo men and women converged on the church and its surroundings to venerate San Roque (Saint Roch), its patron saint, and the Virgin of Transit, whose images were then taken out on procession. That night, people played music, danced, ate, and drank around the church. Those were the large celebrations (fiestones) that Juan had told me about on my first visit to the site. People used the church for these and other religious events (often with the presence of a priest who came from nearby towns) at least until the 1940s, when the building seems to have been semiabandoned. The celebrations for San Roque and the Virgin continued for a few more decades, but they were conducted two hundred meters away, in the home of the family looking after the images. These images were still kept most of the year inside the now-semiabandoned church, and as a result, members of this family did occasional repairs to it. According to people living in the area, these social and religious gatherings came to an end in the 1980s when the man who hosted them became increasingly ill and eventually died, an event that led to his family's decision to move elsewhere.

Partly because of these collective practices carried out by local people over many decades, what once was the Jesuit mission of Balbuena is currently the best-preserved Spanish ruin in the Juramento-Salado region. Criollos maintained this place without the intervention of state agencies or archaeologists and following no explicit attempt to preserve it because of its historical significance. The building was kept in relatively good condition despite being semiabandoned for several decades, in other words, because it was a place of sociality incorporated within local practices. Criollo identity in Salta is strongly anchored around religious processions, and each town has a patron saint venerated once a year at a big public celebration. At La Manga, people appropriated for this practice the remains of an eighteenth-century Jesuit mission, most probably informed by the memory of Christian evangelization that this site evoked. People in the area know that the church was originally built by *los jesuitas* (the Jesuits) and in fact make a direct link between the stories of riches that circulate in the region, including those of Esteco, and the treasures that the Jesuits allegedly buried prior to their departure. Now that the processions at La Manga have ended and no one looks after the building anymore, the church has slid into the relative decay in which I encountered it. The ruins of San Juan Bautista de Balbuena became the ruins of the church of La Manga. In other words, they also became the ruins of ruins: debris charged with memories but that local people feel no need to preserve and that is gradually being reclaimed by the surrounding forest.

Some criollos in the area, however, do express bitterness about the fate of objects associated with those annual religious celebrations. This leads me to a further tension between local and state interventions. In our conversations about "the church," people living around Balbuena told me that, probably in the 1980s, the priest from a nearby town arrived on a pickup truck with police officers and took away the two bells that had been hanging from a pole next to the ruins and were probably from the original Jesuit mission. In 2005, partly with the aim of hearing a firsthand account of that event, I visited a man in his forties named Martín, the son of the man who had looked after the church and its images for several decades. He lived approximately ten kilometers from the ruins of Balbuena, in a small house surrounded by corrals. As with most criollos in the area, he was a gaucho who spent much of his time on horseback and working with cattle. Martín was a man of few words but confirmed that he had been at La Manga during the raid and agreed to tell me about it. He recalled that in seeing the priest and the police officers taking the bells away, he reached for his shotgun to stop them. His father, however, prevented him from intervening. The policemen, he remembered, treated them roughly, like "thieves," and claimed that they were taking the bells away because they were too valuable to be kept there, "in the middle of nowhere." Currently, no one I talked to in the area or in the nearest towns knows where the bells are.[4] Up until then, relics such as these had been preserved locally without the intervention of state actors, and those who eventually took the bells away were, one could argue, "looters" associated with the state and the Catholic Church. Certainly, this is not something new, here or elsewhere. As is well known, the history of European colonialism (and of archaeology) has also been the history of the state-sponsored appropriation of objects wrested away from the control of local actors.

The case of the ruins at Balbuena presents some differences from and parallels with those of Esteco. In contrast to Esteco, only people living around the hamlet of Balbuena and in nearby towns know about the vestiges of this Jesuit mission. And whereas the ruins of Esteco are now immersed within a geography of capital-intensive agribusinesses, those of Balbuena are on a cattle farm covered with forests and based on the labor practices that once characterized the region as a whole, dependent on criollos who roam those lands on horseback. As in the case of Esteco, the people who live near "the church of La Manga" do not see its physical remains with reverence and do not regard an action such as a punch on a stucco frame as destructive. Yet some of them do resent that outsiders, whom officials would probably not view as "looters," took away old objects that had been central to their practices and identity.

This takes me back to the debates surrounding archaeological preservation and to the social and conceptual implications of further destroying what is already partially destroyed.

The Ruins of Ruins

Sigmund Freud (1955: 176) once wrote, referring to ruins, that "their burial had been their preservation: the destruction of Pompeii was only beginning now that it had been dug up." Freud, in other words, is reversing here the hegemonic ideology of restoration by moving the concept of "destruction" away from nonacademic spheres and placing it in the very attempts at preservation conducted by scholars. Likewise, John Ruskin (1963: 134–35) argued that the term *restoration* "means the total destruction which buildings can suffer: a destruction out of which no remnants can be gathered: a destruction accompanied with fake description of the thing destroyed. Do not let us deceive ourselves in this important matter; it is impossible, as impossible [as] to raise the dead[,] to restore anything that has ever been great or beautiful in architecture."

Certainly, the modifications produced by restoration work are aimed at mimicking the allegedly original state of the site, and hence it could be argued that this action is not destructive but "productive." Yet one should consider Karl Marx's warning that production and consumption, while not identical, are part of the same movement, in which production implies the consumption, and therefore the destruction, of raw materials and means of production (see Marx 1970). I would add that this destructive production is central to the understanding of any spatial formation. Max Page (1999) has analyzed, drawing on the work of Joseph Schumpeter, the "creative destruction" that has characterized the spatial history of Manhattan, based on the relentless destruction of its prior landscapes and spatial configurations. Yet while it could be argued that in places such as New York City, or Los Angeles (Klein 1997), spatial erasures have been particularly dramatic, this process is at work in any landscape.

Because of the relative marginality of the ruins of the Juramento-Salado River in the archaeological and historical imaginaries of the Argentinean and international academy, restoration work on them (and hence the potential for creative destruction) has been minimal. Yet, as noted, the ideology of preservation is gradually emerging in regional narratives, especially after the incident in Esteco in 2005. In this view, a practice is "destructive" of ruins when it undermines their resemblance with their allegedly original condition, an action that would affect them at different levels. First, the damage could undermine the ability of specialists to understand the spatial and social organization of these sites in the past and thus the capacity to generate knowledge from them. Yet proponents of this view would also agree that something deeper is at stake here and that such destruction devalues the symbolic, historical, and aesthetic aura of ruins as crumbling yet not fully shattered products of human labor. It is precisely their *partial* destruction that makes some ruins particularly grand and evocative. Georg Simmel (1959: 261) argued that in order to speak of a "ruin" and not of "a mere heap of stones," the power of nature must not have sunk "the work of man into the formless of mere matter." In 1928, Riegl (1982: 32–33) wrote, addressing a similar question, "It is probably fair to say that ruins appear more picturesque the more advanced their state of decay. . . . Of course, this process has its limits. When finally nothing remains, then the effect vanishes completely. A shapeless pile of rubble is no longer able to convey age-value; there must be at least a recognizable trace of the original form, that is, a man's handiwork, whereas rubble alone reveals no trace of their original creation."

In short, these authors suggest that when a ruin is destroyed to the point of becoming "a pile of rubble," it somehow ceases to be a ruin or, following Riegl's reasoning, it ceases to convey "age-value" to those who cherish it. This perspective, which places value on the physical form of the objects to be labeled "ruins," is particularly strong in the humanist tradition that reveres the ruins' aesthetic components. Among archaeologists, in contrast, the existence of "formless heaps of rubble" has not prevented many of them from seeing those spaces as "ruins." For them, what makes a site a ruin is not necessarily its shape or aesthetic beauty but its nature as container of past labor sedimented in space. When first excavated, for instance, famous sites such as Troy or Palenque were not more than huge piles of debris (Clifford 1997: 232; Schmidt 2002: 221). But the fact that those piles were eventually destroyed and turned into partially reconstructed "ruins," which would fascinate both academics and visitors, shows that archaeologists are not free of the aura that Simmel and Riegl have associated with not fully collapsed ruins.

In the case of Esteco, when I explored that forest prior to its destruction, the site was nothing more and nothing less than "piles of rubble" hidden by layers of vegetation. This did not stop academics and writers from referring to them as "the ruins of Esteco." Its aura as a place haunted by past histories was apparent, for different reasons, both to the local population and to the scholars who knew the site. For potential tourists, those mounds may not have the aesthetic effect conveyed by the overgrown walls and altar of the church at Balbuena. Yet those scarred mounds are still spatial testimony of the labor and experiences of actors now gone. Today, after the bulldozers, Esteco is still in ruins. But these ruins are different; they are the debris not just of Esteco but of its ruins.

Ruins are physical expressions of negativity: that is, they affirm that the places that are now in ruins exist no longer; they convey a fracture made apparent in space between the decay one sees in the present and the configuration that same space may have had in the past. They evoke tensions, ruptures, and absences: what is no more. In the Hegelian and Marxist traditions, the expression "the negation of the negation" refers to the contradictory, unrelenting unfolding of the dialectic. Marx (1977: 929), for instance, famously drew on this dialectical double negation when he referred to socialism as "the expropriation of the expropriators": that is, the expropriation by workers of the bourgeois class who had expropriated them of their means of production in the first place. In this and other cases, the negation of the negation implies not the cancellation of the initial negation but the creation of something qualitatively new (in Marx's example, socialism; see also Adorno 1973: 159).

The examples examined so far reveal that a ruin, already an expression of negativity, can be negated in altogether different ways. Archaeological restoration is one such negation, as is particularly clear in sites that have been thoroughly transformed. This process of double negation is not dissimilar from the reconstruction of sites destroyed by warfare, violence, or natural catastrophes. The ruins of San Francisco after the 1906 earthquake and fire, the rubble of the European cities bombed during World War II, the debris of the World Trade Center in New York City, all were marks of negativity (reminders of absences and destruction) that were in turn, and very quickly, negated and destroyed (see Sebald 2004; Solnit 2006). In these cases, the negation of the negation erased the traces of destruction from the landscape, even if memorials were simultaneously built next to them to commemorate that destruction. This process created places that are clearly new, qualitatively different from the original buildings they replaced.

Hegemonic discourses see this type of reconstruction not as destructive but as sheer positivity. They would reserve the term *destruction,* as noted above, to refer to only those practices that alter the integrity of ruins without the control of state officials or academics and without the aim of re-creating its alleged original state. The ruins that fall into further decay without disappearing as ruins go through, from this view, a peculiar double negation. And this has implications for the way in which different social actors spatialize their social memory.

In Esteco, the bulldozing evoked among academics and officials not the original state of the town but the previous configuration of the site *as a ruin.* In other words, the uproar created by the incident produced among these actors nostalgia not so much for the place that had existed in the 1600s but for the piles of rubble hidden in that patch of forest until January 2005. I cannot think of a clearer example of a fetishistic veneration of ruins, even if I cannot help but count myself among those who have fallen under its spell. Local people who would have benefited from the jobs provided by the fruit-packaging plant to be built in Esteco clearly did not venerate the integrity of those overgrown mounds. For them, the double negation triggered by the clearing was different from the one analyzed above, because it drew on a different type of nostalgia. That was nostalgia not for the traces of Esteco but for the social conditions (however imaginary they may be) that had once made that place a prosperous town and the imagined geopolitical center of what is today northwestern Argentina. Because of this, the destruction of that which was already destroyed, the negation of the negativity already inscribed in Esteco, offered them the possibility of partially overcoming that loss through the production of a new place (the packaging plant) that could open the possibility of a modestly better future. That new place would have been grounded within overall conditions of domination and would have further reproduced capitalist forms of exploitation over a privately owned space. But for local people living in poverty, that plant was more than what the well-off defenders of the traces of Esteco had to offer them, which was the reproduction of the imaginaries of loss hovering over them.

Conclusions

In 2005, I returned to the ruins of the Balbuena mission for a second time. I first visited Juan at his home, and we were both happy to see each other again. We chatted for a while and he agreed to take me to *la iglesia* (the church) again. In addition to wanting to explore the place in more detail, I wanted to measure its exact location with a GPS device. As we entered the site at the end of our hike, Juan began emphasizing, again, how old the place was. This time, he picked up a small stick and began casually drilling a hole with it in a wall. Small pieces of adobe fell on the ground. "See?" he told me. "This place is really old!" I felt the same cold, disturbing shiver I had experienced two years earlier. My past reflexive rationalization of the cultural specificity of notions of ruin-preservation did not prevent me from feeling, once again, distressed by Juan's careless disregard for the integrity of those walls.

   In concluding with this anecdote, my aim is simply to point out that my overall argument has not been to downplay the importance of protecting sites such as Esteco or San Juan Bautista de Balbuena, especially if these places serve to publicly promote a critical memory of the history of conquest that has constituted the region. But these two cases also shed light, in different ways, on some of the contradictions embedded in hegemonic assumptions about ruins that, first, fail to reflect critically on the hierarchies of knowledge they rely on and, second, do not match the experience of those who know these places best: the people living in and around them.

   The main threat to the physical integrity of these ruins is the expansion of agribusinesses in the region rather than the everyday actions of subaltern local actors. Contrary to what dominant regional discourses claim, many of the people otherwise viewed as ignorant of their history have been keen to maintain sites that they see as relevant to their practices. The absence of concerns for ruin-preservation among them represents, rather than indifference to the past, a social memory that, even though profoundly spatialized, does not participate in the academic and state-sponsored veneration of the material integrity of ruins. This memory does not fall into this fetishism because these sites are not separated from their experiences and are not viewed as places of contemplation. In the case of the old bells at Balbuena, what some local criollos objected to was the loss of control over them, not that they were not included within a neatly preserved place. As much as I could not help that my academic habitus informed my initial reaction toward the minor and major forms of destruction that I witnessed in both sites, in the end I could not but sympathize with the ways in which the people I met around Balbuena and Esteco related to them.

No ruin is everlasting. As is true for any place, ruins are permanently shaped and reshaped by the social relations and practices that local and extralocal actors weave through them. When people around Esteco viewed the bulldozing with indifference or with expressions of support for the jobs it could provide and when Juan left minor marks on the walls of the church at Balbuena, they were simply making this point clear: that these places are inseparable from the productive, everyday geographies in which they are immersed. These views also highlight that relations of inequality have profoundly shaped the layout of these places and local people's relationship with them. In objecting to the halting of the bulldozing or to the appropriation of artifacts by police officers and priests, local people also make commentaries that, directly or indirectly, are critical of the power relations that are often overlooked by discourses on "preservation."

Acknowledgments

I am grateful to Julie Hollowell, Vinay Kamat, Lena Mortensen, Shaylih Muehlmann, and Anand Pandian for their comments on earlier drafts of this chapter. My greatest debt goes to the people in Río Piedras, El Galpón, Metán, Chorroarín, and Balbuena who welcomed me in their homes and shared with me their stories and experiences about Esteco and the church of La Manga. I conducted fieldwork in southeastern Salta in May–July 2003, July 2005, August 2006–February 2007, and July–August 2007. This research was funded by a Hampton Grant from the University of British Columbia and a Standard Grant from the Social Sciences and Humanities Research Council of Canada. All the names of people interviewed in the field are pseudonyms.

Notes

1. This site is also known as Esteco II, to differentiate it from the original site of the town (Esteco I), located about one hundred kilometers farther east.

2. The first efforts at preservation, especially in Italy, go back to the Renaissance in the 1500s. But those early efforts were quite different from those that would emerge centuries later, in the sense that they were guided more by artistic than by historical or commemorative considerations (Riegl 1982: 28).

3. At least until the early nineteenth century, the ruins of Esteco were partially visible and were visited by several travelers. Yet by the 1870s they were overgrown with vegetation (Torre Revelo 1943: 118), a fact that probably accentuated perceptions that Esteco "got lost."

4. Locals argue that years later, probably in or shortly after 2000, the man with legal titling over the finca (a relative of Martín's) arrived from the city of Salta (where he lives) to take away the images of San Roque and the Virgin of Transit, which had been venerated for decades in the church of La Manga. No one in the area has seen or heard of these images since.

References Cited

Adorno, Theodor. *Negative Dialectics.* Translated by E. Ashton. New York: Continuum, 1973. (Orig. pub. 1966.)

Clifford, James. *Routes: Travel and Translation in the Late Twentieth Century.* Cambridge, Mass.: Harvard University Press, 1997.

Freud, Sigmund. "Notes upon a Case of Obsessional Neurosis." In *The Standard Edition of the Complete Psychological Works of Sigmund Freud,* vol. 10, edited by J. Strachey and A. Freud, 153–257. London: Hogarth Press, 1955. (Orig. pub. 1909.)

Furlong, Guillermo. *Entre los Lules del Tucumán.* Buenos Aires: Talleres Gráficos San Pablo, 1941.

Jusdanis, Gregory. "Farewell to the Classical: Excavations in Modernism." *Modernism/ Modernity* 11, no. 1 (2004): 37–53.

Klein, Norman M. *The History of Forgetting: Los Angeles and the Erasure of Memory.* London: Verso, 1997.

Lefebvre, Henri. *The Production of Space.* Translated by D. N. Smith. Oxford: Blackwell, 1991. (Orig. pub. 1974.)

Lowenthal, David. *The Past Is a Foreign Country.* Cambridge: Cambridge University Press, 1985.

Marx, Karl. *A Contribution to the Critique of Political Economy.* New York: International Publishers, 1970. (Orig. pub. 1859.)

———. *Capital: A Critique of Political Economy,* vol. 1. New York: Vintage, 1977. (Orig. pub. 1867.)

Nora, Pierre. "Between Memory and History: Les Lieux de Mémoire." *Representations* 26 (1989): 7–25.

Page, Max. *The Creative Destruction of Manhattan, 1900–1940.* Chicago: University of Chicago Press, 1999.

———. "Succumbing to Ruinlust." *Metropolis* 4 (2003): 45–49.

Poma, Eduardo. *Historia de Metán y de la frontera Salteña.* Salta: Centergraf, 1995.

Riegl, Alois. "The Modern Cult of Monuments: Its Character and Its Origin." *Oppositions* 25 (1982): 21–51. (Orig. pub. 1928.)

Rodriguez, Timoteo. "Maya Perceptions of Ancestral Remains: Multiple Places in a Local Space." *Berkeley McNair Research Journal* (2002): 21–46.

Roth, Michael. "Irresistible Decay: Ruins Reclaimed." In *Irresistible Decay,* edited by M. Roth, with C. Lyons and C. Merewether, 1–23. Los Angeles: Getty Research Institute for the History of Arts and Humanities, 1997.

Ruskin, John. "The Lamp of Memory." In *The Genius of John Ruskin,* edited by J. Rosenberg, 134–50. Boston: Routledge and Kegan Paul, 1963.

Schmidt, Dietmar. "Refuse Archaeology: Virchow, Schliemann, Freud." *Perspectives on Science* 9, no. 2 (2002): 210–32.

Sebald, W. G. *On the Natural History of Destruction.* Translated by A. Bell. Toronto: Vintage Canada, 2004. (Orig. pub. 1999.)

Simmel, Georg. "The Ruin." In *Essays on Sociology, Philosophy and Aesthetics,* edited by K. Wolff, 259–66. New York: Harper Torchbooks, 1959. (Orig. pub. 1911.)

Solnit, Rebecca. "The Ruins of Memory." In *After the Ruins, 1906 and 2006: Rephotographing the San Francisco Earthquake and Fire,* edited by M. Klett and M. Lundgren, 18–31. Berkeley: University of California Press, 2006.

Tomasini, Alfredo, and Ricardo Alonso. *Esteco, El Viejo: Breve historia y localización de Nuestra Señora de Talavera, 1566–1609.* Salta: Gofica Editora, 2001.

Torre Revelo, José. *Esteco y Concepción del Bermejo, dos ciudades desaparecidas.* Buenos Aires: Talleres Casa Peuser, 1943.

Wilde, Guillermo. "Imaginarios oficiales y memorias locales: Los usos del pasado Jesuítico-Guaraní en misiones." *Avá: Revista de Antropología* 4 (2003): 53–72.

Woodward, Christopher. *In Ruins: A Journey through History, Art, and Literature.* New York: Vintage, 2001.

Young, James E. "The Veneration of Ruins." *Yale Journal of Criticism* 6, no. 2 (1993): 275–83.

2

When Patrimonies Collide

The Case of Chunchucmil, Yucatán

LISA BREGLIA

Maya residents of Kochol, Yucatán, cannot seem to escape their reputation as *gente rebelde* (rebellious people), as ascribed by social workers, bureaucrats, and residents of Kochol's neighboring communities. In this former hacienda town of nearly two thousand inhabitants, routine administrative meetings may quickly become shouting matches, and an occasional machete may be drawn. In the words of one resident of a nearby town, "hasta las mujeres pelean en la calle" (even the women fight in the street). A visiting health promoter from the county seat of Maxcanú described her frustration with getting Kochol's families to comply with a state-sponsored nutrition program: the local children were so rebellious that they even refused to drink their free milk. A district representative of Mexico's National Indigenous Institute (INI) found the community as a whole "challenging." Nor is this reputation confined to human behavior; Kochol's animals are cast by passers-through as equally insubordinate. Large pigs spend hot afternoons lolling about in mud holes along the town's main street, determined not to be fenced in. The beginning of an archaeological excavation project at the site of Chunchucmil—whose official borders include a significant portion of Kochol's *ejido*, or federal land grant—reveals yet another aspect of the unshakeable obstinacy of this Maya community: Kochol's residents are so rebellious, they do not even consider themselves to be descendants of the ancient Maya.

In the days and weeks I spent as an ethnographer working alongside hired excavation workers from the rural Yucatec Maya town of Kochol, we shared many a laugh regarding the "rebellious" nature ascribed to this multifaceted, diverse community.[1] In the long, hot hours spent moving dirt from trowel, to buckets, to sifting tables, men aged sixteen to sixty told me the anecdotes I refer to above with more humor than consternation. Yet this otherwise playful discourse has serious implications. The initiation of archaeological excavation of the ruins sitting upon their ejido agricultural land presented an occasion for residents of Kochol to yet again find themselves positioned as rebellious, this time through their construction of a competing notion of heritage that challenged the nascent archaeological discourse on heritage introduced by a U.S.-led excavation project. Among the dozens of Kochol residents who had been employed in the six seasons of excavation at Chunchucmil under the auspices of the Pakbeh Project at the time of my research, few embraced the archaeological significance of the site.

For contemporary Maya communities within and around Chunchucmil, mounds delicately underscore rather than boldly punctuate the contemporary agricultural landscape. These mounds, or *cerros* (hills), were, for local residents, neither new nor discovered upon the initiation of the archaeological excavation project. Outside of the discourse of archaeological science, mounds are both mysteriously and imprecisely "ancient" and are understood by many local residents as a "natural" as opposed to built feature of the terrain; the mounds, hills, or "ruins" of Chunchucmil were not previously significant to the current residents of Kochol as built, tangible, or material heritage or monuments. In addition, community residents counter the locally emergent discourse on archaeological heritage occasioned by the entrance of a U.S.-based excavation project by reasserting their patrimonial claims to the land on which the mounds sit. The constitution of land patrimony has a more recent history, dating back to the dismantling of the hacienda system, the liberal land reforms of the 1930s, and the subsequent establishment of the ejido land-grant system. This patrimony of the natural landscape is not predicated on ancestral ties of living Yucatec Maya people to ancient Maya civilization. Instead, descent is articulated according to an alternative genealogy based not on archaeological ruins but in relationship to the *henequen* industry.

Genealogies of Ruins

One of the nearly two thousand such zones in the Yucatán Peninsula, Chunchucmil (located just three kilometers from Kochol) is part of a landscape that is, in a sense, one big archaeological site. Mounds of crumbling stone, some up to eighteen meters high, sit on either side of the modern roadway that connects Kochol to the archaeological site and beyond, to another, smaller community that shares the archaeological site's name. Though initial exploration and preliminary site mapping occurred decades ago, sustained academic investigation of Chunchucmil's sixteen square kilometers is relatively recent, begun by the U.S.-based Pakbeh Project in the mid-1990s.

While archaeologists' eyes and interpretive skills are trained toward uncovering evidence that might reveal the site's Classic period instantiation as a specialized trading center (Dahlin, Ardren, and Stanton 2000: 1), local residents seem less keen to speculate on what they perceive of as a remote, if not irrelevant, ancient history. "Not even my dead grandmother knew how this place used to be," commented Rodolfo, an excavation laborer from Kochol, as I worked alongside him digging a one-meter-square test pit at the base of a cerro (mound). "We in Kochol are *gente humilde* [humble people], we are campesinos, and not very well educated. We know little about the cerros and what might be inside them." Rather than overtly asserting claims to the cultural patrimony of the mounds of Chunchucmil by means of oral historical narrative, Kochol's current residents exhibit a very strong sense that what has not been seen with one's own eyes should not be recounted. Many feel that this would be disingenuous and particularly misleading—especially to the foreign researcher.[2]

Excavation laborers from Kochol did not, however, shy away from engaging in lively and emotional discussions of the more recent history of the landscape. Detailed accounts of daily life in and around Kochol under the hacienda system of the late nineteenth and early twentieth centuries are readily evoked and willingly relayed with embodied gestures and affected emotion by contemporary Maya men and women not as "history" or fact, per se, but as stories forming an oral tradition passed from generation to generation. Though some of these narratives touch upon the ruins of Chunchucmil, the majority displace the ancient significance of the mounds in favor of the more recent lived experiences of Kochol's older generation, who cultivated the same stretch of land that is now the archaeological zone, working for decades under the enforced servility of the hacienda system until the mid-1930s.[3]

Kochol (like many other contemporary settlements, or pueblos) was, from the 1880s until 1937, a henequen hacienda. The hacienda system orchestrated and intensively utilized resources of the region in terms of both land and labor-power through the cultivation of henequen, or sisal, a spiny plant of the agave family whose stripped, separated, and desiccated leaves were, for a time, a highly profitable export product for an otherwise agriculturally poor region. At the hand of powerful white landowners supported by state policy, tens of thousands of Yucatec Maya were settled on the haciendas as debt-peons. The years of the henequen boom (1880–1918) are referred to by contemporary residents of Kochol as the *tiempo de esclavitud*—the time of slavery. During these decades, a father's patrimony to his son was a terrible legacy: his lifelong accumulated debt to the hacienda's *tienda de raya* (hacienda store). But now, Kochol's farmers have a tangible patrimony in the form of agricultural land: *patrimonio ejidal,* as one Kochol municipal authority expressed to me.

While cultural patrimony is linked with state, national, and international discourses of universal cultural value and "good," calling to mind the examples of great civilizations to be found across the globe, the concept of patrimonio ejidal is a locally constructed and historically embedded concept tied to experiences of "slavery" (or debt peonage) and the socioeconomic transformations of the rural landscape in northwestern Yucatán, and indeed across Mexico, throughout the twentieth century. The discourse on archaeological or cultural heritage today flourishes in a temporal space that directly ties knowledge of the ancient past together with promises for a bright future of tourism development. Within this space, local residents find themselves out of joint, so to speak, in their commitments to another kind of "ruins," those of the old-style liberal Mexican state that initiated and promoted land distributions to indigenous people throughout the nation. Recent land re-reform allowing for the privatization of the ejido together with collaborative development programs involving both archaeologists and the private sector are disturbing the ground, so to speak, upon which the concept of patrimonio ejidal rests. In a patrimonial juxtaposition between "nature" and "culture," or land versus monumental heritage, how will local Maya residents negotiate the newly archaeologized space of Chunchucmil?

Ethnography of Archaeology as Spatial Genealogy

"These days, a tour of the Maya ruins means a visit to our henequen haciendas," commented Yucatec writer Abreu Gomez (quoted in Joseph 1982: 228). Yet for today's visitors to Yucatán—tourists and researchers alike—the archaeological monuments to ancient civilization that cover the peninsula outsignify the "ruins" of more recent attempts at modernization and industrialization in the rural countryside. These "modern ruins" are evidenced in both the visible built space of abandoned hacienda properties, which continue to serve as the spatial and often social centers of many contemporary communities, and local historical memory. At what point do these ruins of the ancient and the modern converge? According to Amy Gazin-Schwartz and Cornelius Holtorf (1999: 5), "Archaeological approaches to sites and monuments most frequently focus on the time of their construction and intensive use. However, visible monuments have life histories as well, extending from their construction up to the present." In this chapter, I attempt to create such a "life-history" of an archaeological site toward the goal of both illustrating and, in a sense, answering the problematic of different kinds of ruins and their distinct manifestations of patrimony in Yucatán. Because strict disciplinary approaches to this research question fail to sustain its depth and complexity, I turn to a specialized transdisciplinary field-based inquiry: ethnography of archaeology (Breglia 2006a).

Although neither archaeological data nor archaeology's scientific methods of investigation figure in any way into my own research, the activities of archaeology, particularly as they relate to the local communities, serve as a springboard for much of my ethnography. Unlike other investigators conducting ethnographic research at archaeological sites (see, for example, Bartu 2000; Shankland 1996, 1999), I did not restrict my investigation only to the local communities' perceptions of the mounds, archaeology, or a combination of the two. Nor did I find it sufficient, in this particular case, to examine purely contemporary practices characterizing the archaeological heritage site of Chunchucmil in different registers of legal, political, and lived space.

Instead, the archaeological project and its traditionally composed site of research (the official archaeological zone of Chunchucmil) became an occasion upon which other local histories were narrated, political ideologies were espoused, and hopes and fears about the past, present, and future were expressed. My experiences in working with an archaeological project prompted the generation of a series of ideas—methodological, theoretical, and practical—that led me to develop my own sense of ethnography of archaeology. At the outset of my research as an invited guest of the Pakbeh Project, I was quite unfamiliar with the literature of just the past few years dedicated to linking, at least nominally, ethnography and archaeology. Only recently have I have come to realize that my understanding is not the predominant one, at least in terms of recent formulations from the discipline of archaeology. For those trained as practicing field archaeologists, ethnography of archaeology is most often an inquiry centered on the discipline's reflection back on itself, particularly in terms of archaeology's methods and interpretive practices (Edgeworth 2003). It is, in effect, a closed hermeneutic referring to the intimate, self-conscious examination of the processes of archaeological fieldwork practice and the identification and interpretation of material culture.

In the past decades, ethnography has played a role in the development of particular kinds of archaeological practice, figuring prominently in ethnoarchaeology and experimental and reflexive archaeologies (Hodder 2000). Recently, some practitioners of archaeology in the field of social archaeology have begun producing "archaeological ethnographies" as they find resonance between the enterprises of ethnography and archaeology through both theoretical frameworks and interpretive schema (Robin and Rothschild 2002). However, most of these movements are situated exclusively within the realm of archaeology, and their primary lines of inquiry center on material culture and its interpretation. The "ethnography of archaeology" approach I use here takes as its point of departure a concern for identifying the social contexts of material cultural embodiments as they exist in assemblage with systems and articulations of meaning. This ethnography of archaeology carries an awareness of the contingencies and complexities of ethnographic as well as archaeological research and knowledge in its exploration of difference at the local and global levels.

To contribute empirically and methodologically to multiple disciplinary fields in which ethnography of archaeology is situated, I attempt here the production of what I call a "spatial genealogy" of the archaeological zone of Chunchucmil and its environs. Defined as "the union of erudite knowledge and local memories which allows us to establish a historical knowledge of struggles and to make use of this knowledge tactically today" (Foucault and Gordon 1980: 83), genealogy as a method runs counter to the linear, regularized production of knowledge of the past. As I formulate it here, a spatial genealogy examines the production and circulation of historical knowledge at the nexus of history/memory and built "monumental" space/ alternative landscapes. Genealogy and ethnography go hand in hand in the examination of local, flexible, and provisional articulations of patrimony as they critically reveal the multiple patrimonial regimes that exist in the territories of archaeological zones. As a method of sociocultural research, genealogy isolates the coincidence of power/knowledge regimes as "problems" to be unraveled. In the specific case of the Chunchucmil site, I focus on the problematic of competing meanings of patrimony articulated by archaeologists and local residents. I thus pose the following question: what is the "site" overlap between land-tenure regimes, local politics, historical knowledge, belief, and archaeological development?

Patrimony Indeed . . . But What Kind?

Archaeological zones, insofar as they constitute cultural patrimony, are, according to the Mexican Constitution, inalienable possessions of the nation. Ancient remains, visible across the national landscape, have historically been drawn into the service of the state in its attempts to develop a coherent Great Tradition that would serve as a rallying point for the country's diverse populations. Since the time of the conquest, legislatively speaking, all archaeological zones and monuments have been considered part of the national cultural patrimony. Under colonialism, archaeological properties, as with all land, were territory of the Spanish Crown, thus forming a part of the Spanish royal patrimony. Under the independent Mexican state, these properties were transformed into national cultural patrimony, the material embodiment of the developing nationalist project. Currently in Mexico, all archaeological excavation and restoration work is carried out through the National Institute of Anthropology and History (INAH) under the constitution and a supporting body of federal and state laws.[4] Because all archaeology in Mexico is state or governmental archaeology, foreign researchers must receive official permission from INAH to work in the archaeological sites within Mexico's national territory.

My comparative research in Yucatán demonstrates that distinct regional and even local (site-specific) understandings of Maya cultural heritage exist both in tandem and in tension with the Mexican nationalist discourse on cultural heritage, as well as with the criteria of universal cultural value defined by UNESCO, the United

Nations Educational, Scientific, and Cultural Organization (Breglia 2003, 2006b). For regional and national institutions charged with preserving and promoting culture, heritage comprises material spaces of intervention, such as archaeological ruins, used to produce symbolic meanings that forge identity, belonging, and community at regional and national levels. In other words, cultural heritage sites are key accoutrements of the Mexican state as an "imagined community" (Anderson 1983). But their material and symbolic significance does not stop at the nation's territorial borders. Cultural heritage sites are sites of international interest for tourism and conservation/preservation interests, as well as for academic researchers. For international agencies, heritage is a set of policies and practices that create, regulate, and celebrate humanly built cultural spaces.

Yet for residents of local Maya communities, heritage is part of an everyday experience and commonsense knowledge, which includes a repertoire of folkloric references to both the mounds and their builders. Over the course of many months of my working, living, and visiting in communities whose borders overlap the Chunchucmil archaeological site, interpretations of the landscape emerged that point to a break in the assumed "cultural continuity" argument put forward by generations of (mostly foreign) anthropologists as the critical hinge that links living populations with ancient civilizations (Breglia 2006b). Local residents offer the following discordant if not rebellious interpretation: the mounds, or hills, were built and used by another race of people that came before the people who are living today. This other race of people looked different, spoke a different language (*hach* Maya, or true Maya language), and lived in stone houses. The conviction that the builders of the archaeological ruins were a distinct race of people is, for some working as laborers for the Pakbeh Project, reinforced through artifactual evidence.

In the several seasons of excavation at the site to date, various burials were unearthed. In one instance, local workers who witnessed the burial excavations interpreted the remains of a young person to confirm beliefs that the ancient Maya people were very small, like dwarves. The small body size refers to two different groups of personages, often labeled as other "races" in Maya legends or folklore: the *ppuzob* and the *alux*. In most accounts, based on narratives recorded in other regions of the peninsula, the personages identified as this other "race" of people corporeally distinct from living Maya people are commonly referred to as "hunchbacks," or the ppuzob (see Burns 1983: 51; M. Redfield 1935: 24; Redfield and Villa Rojas 1934: 330). Ppuzob were mound builders who no longer exist, having died off in the Great Flood.[5] They suffered the misfortune of living in stone houses at the time of the flood and drowned. The ppuzob seemed to have suffered a double misfortune at Chunchucmil: local residents have suggested that the proliferation of carved stone metates found on-site served as the boats of the ancient Maya race: no wonder they did not survive the Great Flood. Aluxes, in contrast, are still present today. These childlike trickster figures are said to run about naked. They find ruins to be a most auspicious environment. During the day, they hide from humans by morphing into the figures decorating the carved stone of ancient ruins.

Maya folklore and legend lend support to the reasoning that the farmland of Kochol that is coterminous with the archaeological zone of Chunchucmil is not spatially (or temporally) distinct from community life. Many residents of Kochol suspect that an ancient serpent guards the largest of the mounds. Others feel strongly that the ruins are an inauspicious or even dangerous place to frequent or live within. Perhaps as a result, the physically uninhabited site carries an ambience of desolation, disuse, or even abandonment. In high contrast, David Shankland (1999: 145) describes the rich diversity of the habitus of the mounds at the site of Çatalhöyük for the residents of nearby Küçüköy: "There is a complex but subtle and tolerant interaction between the villagers and the heritage that fills their landscape. Mounds, for example, may have a number of different roles in the life of the community. They may act variously as field boundaries, modern-day cemeteries, picnic places at festival times, repositories of water-proof earth, sources of buried treasure, the souls of those past or of the devil."

If Shankland characterizes this kind of relationship as subtle, the interaction between Kochol residents and the mounds at Chunchucmil barely registers at all. Though many residents of Kochol hold usufruct rights and even certificates of title over plots in the territory of the archaeological zone, the land is unimproved—meaning that it is suitable for traditional maize cultivation but not for growing papaya, the community's current intensive agricultural enterprise. One key requirement of papaya cultivation in this region is irrigation—which without electricity is nearly impossible. Farmers may use gas-powered water pumps, but such pumps present an insurmountable cost for growers who typically have no capital resources. Thus, agricultural activities are, to date, quite limited. At the same time, recreational activities of the sort that Shankland notes are typically not carried out at Chunchucmil.

In efforts to expand the potential of the site as a new kind of resource for local communities as well as foreign and national researchers and visitors, since 2001 archaeologists have been working toward building a model of community archaeology at Chunchucmil. Thus, the Pakbeh Project "has shifted the research focus from a clearly outlined processual program concerning the ethnic nature of an ancient trading enclave, to a collaborative plan of research and development that uses academic archaeological inquiry as a foundation from which to generate tourism in the local communities" (Ardren 2002: 380). In short, the Pakbeh Project has as its goal a community archaeology that takes into account local needs, perspectives, and priorities for development. The project's relationships with surrounding communities that hold communal farming rights to the land on which the archaeological zone sits have been, particularly in the case of one community, Kochol, strained and tense. The underlying causes for these tensions are multiple, but most have deep historical roots that predate the archaeological project. Most are based in the history of the regional political economy and the prominent role played by land, alongside a marked tension between de jure and de facto ownership on the part of both private interests and the state, on the one hand, and, on the other hand, usufruct rights of local residents.

The ideology of the land reform of the post-Revolution period (1911–34) sought to bring capitalism to the countryside, requiring the dismantling of haciendas and other large estates that retained an almost feudal flavor. The reforms also bolstered the social (and scientistic) project of nation building through the incorporation of Mexico's indigenous population into the progressive, modern state. Land reforms as prescribed under Article 27 of the Mexican Constitution allowed for rural, mostly indigenous, people to have access to farmland. The initial reforms (which did not reach the henequen haciendas of Yucatán until 1937) allowed for protected land tenure but not ownership. Land re-reform under Mexico's nascent neoliberal agenda in 1992 made possible the privatization of the ejido.[6] Recently, collective landholders in Kochol received certificates of title to individual parcels of land, some of which is coterminous with the archaeological zone. The land, including pieces considered to be within the archaeological site center, is used for subsistence corn crops and for papaya cultivation for local and national markets. With permission from an assembly of the entire group, these parcels may be sold, either within the ejido or to outside interests. Residents of Kochol claim that they would never sell their land; if they do not have land, they have nothing. In the words of one *ejidatario:* "If I sell my land, I'll get money which won't last long anyway. If I sell my land, what will I leave for my children?" For this person, land is his patrimony, the particular, material, and symbolic inheritance he will pass on to his children.

When archaeological work began at the Chunchucmil site, a new discourse and practice of heritage and patrimony came into play. This concept of the ruins as national or even world cultural heritage was to a certain degree irreconcilable with the historically embedded, deeply meaningful everyday understanding of "the land" to local residents. For most of the duration of the archaeological project, these differences in the register of interpretation have not been explicitly articulated as points of contention between the two groups. However, with complications brought about through federal zoning, questions of local access and of the material value of the property and its contents, specifically in terms of future tourism development, concern both groups, though their stakes in the outcomes may differ dramatically.

Residents of Kochol have caused consternation for the U.S.-based archaeological team working in the nearby ruins of Chunchucmil. Suspicions about the real motives of the archaeologists, the specter of state intervention on Kochol's agricultural land, and age-old tensions between Kochol and its neighboring communities underlie local apprehension toward the project's community-oriented, public archaeology agenda. Through public presentations, a general program of sensitivity, and flexibility toward local circumstances and attitudes, Pakbeh Project leaders have repeatedly attempted to quell local anxieties regarding land-use practices and future development of the site. For the project, one key vehicle for communication between archaeologists and community residents is the promotion of a new notion of cultural patrimony over the more contentious local assertions of patrimonio ejidal. According to one project director, Traci Ardren, "The archaeological message of cultural inheritance and empowerment at first stood in stark contrast to the messages from local workmen of fear and anxiety that we would take away the site or facilitate the Mexican government taking away the site" (Ardren 2002: 386). Rather than asserting technical legal rights to carry out their excavation work, project leaders deferred to local practices and community authorities. While it is reasonable to say that many of Kochol's residents, particularly those who worked as temporary laborers in excavation and other aspects of the project, were curious, it would be equally reasonable to conclude that a large number of Kochol's inhabitants—even those with a vested interest in the land coterminous with the officially delimited archaeological zone—were ambivalent toward archaeology, its practitioners, and the vague promises it held for the community's future.

For archaeologists excavating the ruined structures of Chunchucmil alongside the hired laborers from Kochol—the presumed descendants of the ancient Maya builders and dwellers—excavation provides an opportunity to espouse a model of cultural continuity through a program both scientific and moral/ethical. Working as an ethnographer at on-site excavations alongside laborers from Kochol, I was privy to more than one pedagogic intervention on the part of archaeologists aimed toward educating the people of Kochol about their history, their heritage, and the great works and civilization of their ancestors, the ancient Maya. Archaeologists made efforts to promote and valorize the cultural descent and affiliation between the contemporary residents of the communities adjacent to the archaeological zone and the people, better known as the ancient Maya (in Spanish, *los antiguos*), who built and used the structures being excavated. I agree with Ardren (2002) when she claims that the archaeological project at Chunchucmil has occasioned a new awareness of cultural patrimony in the archaeological ruins. However, I am not convinced that excavation laborers from local communities have come to appreciate the ruins as their cultural inheritance according to the logics of archaeology and the discourse on monumental cultural heritage.

Heritage, or patrimony, is definitely in play at the archaeological site of Chun-chucmil, with distinct groups of social actors vying to name and claim the patri-mony of the site. If these communities complicate the grounds from which to make claims for cultural descent, what does this imply for conceptions of heritage? As one director of the Pakbeh Project explains, "Descendant groups that are comprised of people with culturally continuous or territorially historical claims to an archaeo-logical resource must be given priority of control over the management of cultural materials" (Ardren 2002: 392). Community archaeology, thus, Ardren continues, attempts to position itself to "become more aware of, and responsive to, the other members of descendant communities with which we work" (2002: 392). Yet in the process of constituting cultural or archaeological heritage, who has to claim the site as part of their cultural ancestry? Can something be heritage if there is no descendant community? We easily assume that we can identify the objects of cultural heritage (buildings, artifacts, material remains of the past), but what (and, better, who) are the subjects of heritage? Can there be heritage without inheritors? If the residents of Kochol do not claim to be the descendant community of the ancient Maya who built the structures whose ruins cover the landscape, whose heritage is it? Can it even be heritage?

"Heritage" at Chunchucmil is thus caught within a double negation of descent—the archaeologists' de facto negation of Kochol's patrimonial claims based on their descent from henequen workers and Kochol's negation of archaeology's insistence on descent from the ancient Maya. Nevertheless, if representations are indeed so-cial facts (Rabinow 1986), then the monumentalized mounds at Chunchucmil are unquestionably the stuff of "heritage." Situated at the nexus of archaeological sci-ence, state policy, and international convention, archaeological mounds are indeed "heritage" in the strong sense: univocally, nonreflexively, and hegemonically proper symbols of both the patrimonial possessions of the Mexican state and examples of universal cultural value promoted by heritage institutions at the international level. Thus, the question of "heritage without inheritors" becomes a relatively unimport-ant, if not moot, ethnographic detail. The universal discourse on heritage territorial-izes landscapes of ruins and promotes specific ideals of preservation, promotion, and appropriate site uses—simultaneously effacing and containing competing claims over its meanings. At Chunchucmil, the locally specific double negations of descent cancel each other out and pave the way for development.

How, then, does archaeology contend with its patrimonial competitor—the pat-rimony of the ejido? From my observations and discussions with both archaeolo-gists and local residents, this contentiousness is neither wholeheartedly expressed nor more tacitly acknowledged. Rather than producing "conflict" (Hodder 1998), the distinctions in the patrimonial claims of different social actors currently playing out at Chunchucmil more closely resemble an array of coexisting "multiplicities" (Bartu 2000), or iterations, if you will. The intersection of claims to *patrimonio cultural* and *patrimonio ejidal* manifests as negotiations over legitimate "sites" of heritage, played out simultaneously on top of, underneath, and through the codified surfaces and borders of the officially defined (whether by science or the state) archaeological zone. These interstices, captured here as *lieux de mémoire,* are fertile spaces for the articulation of "monumental ambivalence" (Breglia 2006b). Quite literally, the ambivalence of the archaeological mounds at Chunchucmil for local communities is, I would argue, of overwhelming or monumental proportions. At the same time, the phrase *monumental ambivalence* refers also to an undecidedness or uneasiness at the recent attempts on the part of the Pakbeh Project to interpolate the Chunchucmil mounds into what I call the "heritage assemblage" (Breglia 2006b). By this, I refer to the fluid set of codes and practices emanating from a series of institutional, legal, and disciplinary sources (that is, archaeology, heritage resource management, tourism and its agents, the Mexican state, and now ethnography), all of which contribute to the fashioning of new subjectivities for local Maya, as ill fitting as they might be.

According to Pierre Nora, "What makes certain prehistoric, geographical, archaeological locations important as sites is often precisely what ought to exclude them from being *lieux de mémoire:* the absolute absence of a will to remember and, by way of compensation, the crushing weight imposed on them by time, science, and the dreams of men" (1989: 21). Displacing the mounds in favor of the land, so to speak, illuminates the *lieux de mémoire* that generate local ideas of history. The archaeological site—as both the built "monumental" space of national cultural heritage and a contested terrain of land, labor, and social relations—produces a heterotopic space situated between (official) history and (local) memory (Owens 2002). If we attempt to comprehend Chunchucmil as a complex social space in itself rather than as a blank slate for the inscriptions of archaeology and the state (Castañeda 1996), the veil of transparency that lends the mounds their mysterious and ancient flavor falls away and the unexplored territory of the contemporary landscape is revealed.

As archaeological development continues at the site of Chunchucmil, the Maya residents of its surrounding communities are increasingly faced with the questions of what is their heritage and how will they negotiate the new semiotics of the landscape. Although heritage sites are constantly constructed as spatial locations, it is through a temporal understanding—of the specific historical constructions of a site that precede archaeology—that we might reframe questions pertinent to the constitution of heritage in the site of Chunchucmil. Ethnography of archaeology intervenes at this juncture of context: not artifactual, if you will, but vibrantly and dynamically contemporary.

The Future of the Past at Chunchucmil

> There can be no greater failure for archaeology than to accept that children will feel no connection to their archaeological heritage or that native peoples will reject the entire discipline as exploitative. (Ardren 2002: 396)

> Two hundred thousand Maya toil for foreign masters today in the henequen fields of Yucatán, all memory of their former significance gone as completely as if it had never been. . . . With such a glorious past, it would seem as though [the Maya's] future might be made of more promise than this. (Morley 1925: 86)

For the many residents of Kochol who are descendants of henequen hacienda workers, the genealogy of their reputation for rebelliousness is only occasionally a laughing matter. "Rebellious . . . ," mused one elderly *milpero* (corn cultivator), who typically plants on the low mounds in the Chunchucmil archaeological site center. "If I was at one time, I certainly am not now." He gestured across the landscape; in the distance, a group of locally hired excavators hauled boulders out of a pit at the top of a mound. The farmer shook his head. "The henequen stole all of my strength." Sylvanus G. Morley suggested, and the tradition of Maya archaeology would concur, that the "glorious past" of the Maya will always be ancient. Yet for many contemporary Maya communities, there is a more recent past and a commitment to a more tangible future that is not wholly archaeological.

Seventy-seven years and two-hundred-odd kilometers away from Morley's mecca of Maya cultural heritage, I was in Kochol, watching images of Chichén Itzá projected on the scarred wall of a corn-grinding shop. Through the courtesy of a representative of Mexico's National Institute of Anthropology and History, the federal agency charged with the custodianship of the nation's heritage, a World Heritage site was being revealed to Kochol's Maya residents. The occasion was the invitation extended by archaeologists of the Pakbeh Archaeological Project to the INAH representative as an effort to increase community knowledge and interaction with Maya cultural patrimony. The slides showed the thousands of visitors, both national and international tourists, who gather at Chichén Itzá each March 21, the day marking the spring equinox.

There we were in the same state of Yucatán, yet a world away. At the site of Chunchucmil, only recently declared an officially delimited archaeological zone, there is no restored architecture, no pyramids that visitors may climb and take their picture. In fact, there are very few visitors to the mounds at Chunchucmil, including these local community residents, even though most of the land that constitutes the site center belongs to community members as an ejido land grant. From my perspective on the history of archaeological site development in Yucatán, especially through my ethnographic research at Chichén Itzá (Breglia 2003, 2005, 2006b), the words of the INAH representative promised a future in heritage tourism that was distant and intangible. "Maybe none of you will live to see the cerros on your ejido look like the Castillo, the Great Ball Court, or the Temple of the Warriors like at Chichén Itzá," he said. "But maybe your children or their children will." That evening, it was perhaps difficult for Maya residents of Kochol to imagine that the tree-covered hills that lay within their ejido property on the outskirts of town might be versions of the grand monuments such as those at Chichén Itzá. The few seasons of archaeological work at the site could not compare with the decades of excavation and reconstruction efforts in the internationally recognized World Heritage site.

In the discourse of archaeological science and world heritage, Abreu Gomez's observation that the real ruins of Yucatán are the henequen haciendas is counterintuitive. Yet for the descendants of henequen laborers—as Morley notes above—the "glorious past" of the ancient Maya civilization may be forgotten but the memory of the hacienda system, as embodied by the ejido, remains.

Acknowledgments

I would like to thank the volume's editors and other contributors. I would also like to thank Lynn Meskell and Quetzil Castañeda for their feedback when this work was originally presented. A special thank you to Traci Ardren, Aline Magnoni, Scott Hutson, and other members of the Pakbeh Project, who generously hosted me in the 2001 field season.

Notes

1. First at the invitation of project directors, then during the project's off-season, I conducted ethnographic research within the archaeological site and in surrounding communities in 2000–2002. For a discussion of this research, see Breglia 2006a and 2006b.

2. It is quite possible that, as Julie Hollowell has suggested to me, also at work here is a reticence to venture into the realm of "expert" archaeological knowledge and discourse.

3. Kochol was a hacienda dedicated to the production of henequen, a fiber used in the highly profitable manufacture of rope and twine from the mid-nineteenth century until well into the twentieth. Although the 1910 Mexican Revolution formally brought an end to the debt peonage of the hacienda system, residents of Kochol continued to work the henequen hacienda untouched by the revolutionary land reform established by the 1917 Constitution, which began in earnest in 1924. Not until 1937 did President Lazaro Cárdenas finally bring about a mass expropriation of the lands comprising the henequen zone of northwestern Yucatán (see Joseph 1982).

4. See Breglia 2006b (34–41) for a discussion of the development of cultural heritage legislation in Mexico.

5. According to Burns (1983: 30), "The appearance of biblical characters and other features of the European world is expected in Yucatec Mayan tradition, since the Yucatán Peninsula has been under Spanish and Mexican control for over four hundred years." In Kochol, Catholics and Protestants alike are familiar with Bible stories, particularly those of Noah and the flood and the tower of Babel, both of which events figure in contemporary "ancient conversations" concerning the mounds.

6. Article 27 of the Mexican Constitution put into effect in 1992 a change in the nature of land tenure. Prior to the reform, land-grant holders enjoyed use of the land while the state retained the land title. In other words, the land was inalienable. The neoliberal administration of President Salinas (1988–94) made possible private titling of ejido land parcels.

References Cited

Anderson, Benedict. *Imagined Communities.* London: Verso, 1983.

Ardren, Traci. "Conversations about the Production of Archaeological Knowledge and Community Museums at Chunchucmil and Kochol, Yucatán." *World Archaeology* 34, no. 2 (2002): 379–400.

Bartu, Ayfer. "Where is Çatalhöyük? Multiple Sites in the Construction of an Archaeological Site." In *Towards a Reflexive Method in Archaeology: The Example at Çatalhöyük,* edited by I. Hodder, 101–9. Cambridge, U.K.: McDonald Institute for Archaeological Research, 2000.

Breglia, Lisa. "Docile Descendants and Illegitimate Heirs: Privatization of Cultural Patrimony in México." Ph.D. diss., Rice University, 2003.

———. "Keeping World Heritage in the Family: A Genealogy of Maya Labor at Chichén Itzá." *International Journal of Heritage Studies* 11, no. 5 (2005): 385–98.

———. "Complicit Agendas: Ethnography of Archaeology as Ethical Research Practice." In *Ethnographies of Archaeological Practice: Cultural Encounters, Material Reflections,* edited by M. Edgeworth, 173–84. Walnut Creek, Calif.: AltaMira Press, 2006. [2006a]

———. *Monumental Ambivalence: The Politics of Heritage.* Austin: University of Texas Press, 2006. [2006b]

Burns, Allan F. *Epoch of Miracles: Oral Literature of the Yucatec Maya.* Austin: University of Texas Press, 1983.

Castañeda, Quetzil E. *In the Museum of Maya Culture: Touring Chichén Itzá.* Minneapolis: University of Minnesota Press, 1996.

Dahlin, Bruce H., Traci Ardren, and Travis Stanton. "Introduction." In *Pakbeh Regional Economy Program Report of the 2000 Field Season,* edited by T. Stanton. Jamestown, N.Y.: Jamestown Community College, 2000.

Edgeworth, Matt. *Acts of Discovery: an Ethnography of Archaeological Practice.* BAR International Series 1131. Oxford: Archaeopress, 2003.

Foucault, Michel, and Colin Gordon. *Power/Knowledge: Selected Interviews and Other Writings, 1972–1977.* New York: Pantheon, 1980.

Gazin-Schwartz, Amy, and Cornelius J. Holtorf, eds. *Archaeology and Folklore.* New York: Routledge, 1999.

Hodder, Ian. "The Past as Passion and Play: Çatalhöyük as a Site of Conflict in the Construction of Multiple Pasts." In *Archaeology Under Fire: Nationalism, Politics and Heritage in the Eastern Mediterranean and Middle East,* edited by L. Meskell, 124–39. London: Routledge, 1998.

———. *Towards Reflexive Method in Archaeology: The Example at Çatalhöyük.* Cambridge, U.K.: McDonald Institute for Archaeological Research, 2000.

Joseph, Gilbert. *Revolution from Without: Yucatán, Mexico, and the United States, 1880–1924.* New York: Cambridge University Press, 1982.

Morley, Sylvanus G. "Chichén Itzá: An Ancient American Mecca." *National Geographic* January (1925): 63–91.

Nora, Pierre. "Between Memory and History: Les Lieux de Mémoire." *Representations* 26 (1989): 7–25.

Owens, Bruce McCoy. "Monumentality, Identity and the State." *Anthropological Quarterly* 75, no. 2 (2002): 269–316.

Rabinow, Paul. "Representations Are Social Facts: Modernity and Post-Modernity in Ethnography." In *Writing Culture: The Politics and Poetics of Ethnography,* edited by J. Clifford and F. Marcus, 234–61. Berkeley: University of California Press, 1986.

Redfield, Margaret Park. *The Folk Literature of a Yucatecan Town.* Publication 456. Washington, D.C.: Carnegie Institution of Washington, 1935.

Redfield, Robert, and Alfonso Villa Rojas. *Chan Kom: A Maya Village.* Publication 448. Washington, D.C.: Carnegie Institution of Washington, 1934.

Robin, Cynthia, and Nan A. Rothschild. "Archaeological Ethnographies: Social Dynamics of an Outdoor Space." *Journal of Social Archaeology* 2, no. 2 (2002): 159–72.

Shankland, David. "Çatalhöyük: The Anthropology of an Archaeological Presence." In *On the Surface: Çatalhöyük 1993–95,* edited by I. Hodder, 186–202. Cambridge, U.K.: McDonald Institute for Archaeological Research, 1996.

———. "Integrating the Past: Folklore, Mounds and People at Çatalhöyük." In *Archaeology and Folklore,* edited by A. Gazin-Schwartz and C. J. Holtorf, 139–57. London: Routledge, 1999.

3

Excavating *Turath*

Documenting Local and National Heritage Discourses in Jordan

JENNIFER JACOBS AND BENJAMIN PORTER

The year was 1999 and I (Benjamin Porter) had just arrived in the city of Madaba, Jordan, to begin excavations with a Canadian team of archaeologists. The assistant director offered me a tour of the excavation site, centered in a thriving mixed Christian and Muslim shopping district. Accompanying us was Mohammed,[1] a Jordanian student of archaeology. His family had lived above the excavated space a century ago in the latest Ottoman structures. After my guide pointed out the vaulted arches of the Ottoman houses, Mohammed exclaimed, "No, you have it all wrong, this house is not 'Ottoman.' It is Abdullah, the house of my grandfather." Mohammed went on to explain that his grandfather had refused to pay his taxes and the Ottoman officials had chased him into the nearby Jordan Valley, subsequently killing him in a gunfight.

Mohammed's claim resonated with me throughout that season. Perhaps the archaeology of Jordan could be interpreted at several different levels, where the individual, the family, the tribe, and the nation understood the past—and their link to that past—differently. Recent discussions in the academy have represented the relationship between archaeology and heritage as adversarial, mired in conflict and "under fire" (for example, Appadurai 2001; Meskell 1999). The location of the discipline's assailants has remained unclear. Is one such foe Mohammed—or any number of people living in communities adjacent to antiquity sites? Or is it the Jordanian government, which (with good reason) regulates archaeological practices in the kingdom? Perhaps it is an internal disjuncture within the archaeological discipline, a division between positivist and reflexive practitioners. In subsequent visits to Jordan, Jennifer Jacobs and I felt a need to uncover the extent of this conflict in the region in which we work. In attempting to do so, we were required to go beyond armchair anecdotal musings and institutional rhetoric and speak directly with those who encountered the physicality of the past in their daily lives.

In this chapter, we argue that the investigation of heritage requires careful ethnographic scrutiny. We examine heritage using a discourse-centered approach that considers how individuals and groups employ language, objects, and practices when expressing their relationship to the past. Jordan serves as an ideal locale in which to take up the investigation of heritage. Despite incongruities in Jordan's social fabric, the past remains a rhetorically powerful concept within Jordanian political, economic, and cultural spheres that targets the public using the Arabic word *turath*,[2] "heritage," a term closely related to ideas of inheritance (*warata*). Previous examinations of heritage in Middle Eastern contexts demonstrate how it is packaged for public consumption at formal, institutionalized levels such as government publications, museums, and tourist sites (see, for example, Kelly 1998). We demonstrate that although turath is defined and practiced in legal, nationalist, and commercial environments, it is also done so in local and socially contingent ways. Our work in Jordan is teaching us that national and local heritage discourses circulate differently and as a result are variable and unevenly distributed across social space.

A Discourse-Centered Approach to Heritage

While it is possible to speak of multiple and nested types of heritage—global, diasporic, and national, for instance (Appadurai 2001; Dominguez 1986; Meskell 1999)—often missing from these discussions are definitions that acknowledge heritage at its basic, generative levels. Many understandings of heritage denote a sense of self in the past, whereby the subjective component of "self" is implicit and the links between such a self and its past are based on perceived genealogical, biological, or community connections. This definition, while broad enough to cover varied cases around the globe, does little to flesh out the details of any particular society's conceptualization, much less communicate how such ideas operate, circulate, and carry political, religious, or intellectual weight in the world.

One way to solve this problem is to depart from understandings of heritage as a phenomenon segmentable from politics, religion, or the economy and instead understand heritage as a part of culture and its meanings as constituted by culture: all ways of behaving, conceptualizing, and valuing the world insofar as they are socially learned and socially transmitted. This seemingly innocuous statement bears empirical implications, for it grows from theories that understand culture as located in concrete, publicly accessible signs (Sherzer 1987; Urban 1991). To be passed among social actors, the abstract patterns and meanings that people share must become lodged in perceptible objects, even if only momentarily. Therefore, if a group conceptually links itself to a past—more specifically, if archaeologists and historians link peoples to particular pasts—then the iterations of such ideas can be investigated empirically in the present.

Where do we discover such iterations of the past circulating in a society? The most abundant instances are those found in the language through which human understandings of the past are expressed. Indeed, the sheer volume of utterances from dialogues and interviews can quickly fill pages of transcripts; thus, a keen ear is required to find systematic regularities in speech across multiple speakers. Practices and objects that come to embody ideas about and alignments with the past are also available for analysis. While no single utterance, practice, or object completely represents a society's "heritage," these instances are bound in various publicly accessible discourses that unfold in the present and circulate throughout society.

Given the increasing rate and exchange of ideas across societies today, the character of *discourse*—continuous, dynamic, reflexive, and responsive—makes it an exciting and appropriate means by which to investigate heritage. A discourse-centered approach brings two important advantages to the investigation of heritage. First, we can subject to empirical investigation the degree to which ideas are shared and continuous over time and social space. Because they are material in nature, discourses circulate, enabling the mapping and comparison of the "substance" of one heritage discourse with another. The more packageable and portable a discursive entity, the more susceptible it is to movement, decontextualization, and transplantation. This is true of certain museum objects and the word *heritage* alike: both are discrete entities. Of course, upon such movement, the meanings of discrete entities shift, are gained and lost, and, in the case of "heritage," become so vague that they come to co-occur with surprising terms: "Heritage Bank," "Heritage Auto," "The Heritage Foundation," "Warplane Heritage." Though these uses may seem meaningless, other instances more clearly convey a message of inalienability from the identities and objects to which they are attached.

A second advantage of a discourse-centered approach is that we can recognize inconsistencies and contradictions in both speech and practice that may exist within societies. That is, rather than assume a homogenous, unchanging understanding of "heritage" that simply requires one interpretation, we employ the phrase *heritage discourse* to describe the type of data we analyze here. Because they are rarely distributed evenly across a society, heritage discourses are most salient when collaborating with and competing against other discourses, such as globalization, development, and democracy. Nowhere is this phenomenon more readily observed than when examining heritage within the confines of nation-states that use the past to foster identities and assert claims of primordial antiquity. To do so, nation-states may seek to eliminate competing narratives that potentially undermine their legitimacy, while promoting a unified heritage that consolidates their constituent population. Museums, textbooks, national festivals, and legal codes are modes through which states inscribe definitions of heritage. State management of an official heritage discourse can extend beyond territorial borders, linking externalized images of the state's antiquity to tourism, diplomacy, and trade. States' abilities to mask the details of their participation in crafting officializing discourse about the past can sometimes create difficulties for researchers who wish to discern how these narratives are placed in motion. A discourse-centered approach to heritage therefore helps point out differences between the official and the vernacular, or the national and the local.

A Jordanian National Turath: "Half as Old as Time"?

Match me such a marvel, save in Eastern clime
A rose-red city, half as old as time.

From "Petra," by John William Burgon, 1845[3]

A Middle Eastern country with almost six million citizens covering an area of approximately ninety thousand square kilometers, the Hashemite Kingdom of Jordan is a relatively young monarchy founded in 1946, following almost thirty years of British colonial rule. Throughout its six-decade rule, the Hashemite monarchy has faced the challenge of ruling a fractious, multiethnic, sectarian population consisting of Muslims, Druze, and Christians, of Jordanians, Palestinians, Armenians, and Circassians. Complicating matters further is the growing divide between urban and rural social classes. In and around Amman, the kingdom's capital, a middle and upper class expands, desiring access to cosmopolitan symbols and global prestige goods. Outside of the capital, however, a rural agrarian society persists where traditional Islamic and tribal practices structure social life. The kingdom's attempts to craft a national heritage discourse that could potentially unite these sometimes opposing groups make Jordan an exciting ethnographic context in which to examine the mechanics of national and local heritage.

Like many other nation-states founded in the twentieth century, Jordan inherited millennia of accumulated archaeological ruins strewn throughout the kingdom. The extent to which the state is concerned with these ancient remains is visible in the kingdom's legal codes. Jordan's most recent statute, Law 21 for the Year 1988 Antiquities Law,[4] legally distinguishes "antiquity" as

Article 2
a. Any object, whether movable or immovable, which has been constructed, shaped, inscribed, erected, excavated, or otherwise produced or modified by humankind earlier than the year 1700 A.D. including caves, sculpture,

coins, pottery, manuscripts and all sorts of artefacts that indicate the rise and development of sciences, arts, manufactures, religions, and traditions relating to previous cultures, or any part added thereto, reconstructed or restored at a later date[.]

A juridical understanding of antiquity is stipulated in this passage, taken from the first pages of the 1988 law; the rest of the statute specifies how state agencies such as the Ministry of Tourism and Antiquities and the Department of Antiquities are to manage the kingdom's antiquity sites and artifacts. This legal code, particularly this brief passage, affords us the opportunity to understand how the state defines antiquity with special reference to itself. Most interesting is the fact that the state claims legal ownership over pre-1700 materials but not a genealogical connection between itself and the societies—Moabite, Nabataean, Roman, Byzantine, and Islamic—that inhabited the region in antiquity. Such claims suggest that Jordan seeks an official and deliberate means of distancing the state from earlier societies. In our discussions with employees of Jordan's Department of Antiquities, we discovered that this juridical definition of antiquity is readily employed in administrative practice. These distinctions are widely known and easily discussed in conversation. Employees say that most objects created post-1700 are assigned not to the Department of Antiquities but to the Ministry of Culture, which manages their preservation and display.

This contradiction between Jordan's concern with ownership and the simultaneous genealogical disavowal of its creators is resolved when we understand just how important these ancient resources are to the kingdom's tourism industry. Lacking the lucrative oil reserves of neighboring Iraq and Saudi Arabia, the kingdom has depended on tourism as an alternative industry that supports both the public and the private sector. Since the country's founding, the combined efforts of the kingdom's Ministry of Tourism and Antiquities, its Department of Antiquities, and foreign-aid granting agencies such as the United States Agency for International Development (USAID) have transformed Jordan's antiquity sites such as Petra and Jerash into revenue-generating tourist destinations. The past decade, in particular, has witnessed improvements including the participation of nongovernmental organizations such as the Royal Society for the Conservation of Nature, an increased interest in hospitality training in Jordanian universities, and a greater participation of small businesses in the tourism sector. And with the help of recent Japanese and European Union investments, the kingdom is building new national and regional museums and restoring undermanaged antiquity sites. The goals of the recently published *Jordan National Tourism Strategy 2004–2010*—increasing revenue to almost two billion dollars and creating an additional fifty-one thousand jobs—suggest that both the public and the private tourism sector will continue to expand into new niche markets (including ecotourism, well-being, and conference travel) and build on their original achievements in cultural heritage and religious tourism.

Jordan's success in creating a sustainable tourism industry is, in part, attributable to its ability to provide opportunities for visitors to explore their own heritage in the kingdom's historical sites. The kingdom wisely recognizes that its antiquities attract visitors with different interests and concerns. North American and European tourists, for instance, are drawn to Jordan not only for the colonial romance of Lawrence of Arabia and familiar Roman theatres but also for Jordan's links to the Bible, early Christianity, and the Medieval Crusades. Pope John Paul II's millennial visit created an opportunity for the kingdom to carve fresh tourist trails to religious sites that Christian travelers would follow in the years after the papal visit. A contrasting and emerging group is Middle Eastern tourists. With the growth of foreign investment from Persian Gulf countries, Jordan has become an attractive destination for Middle Easterners seeking a cooler climate and a more tolerant and less-expensive social scene. Not frightened off by regional conflicts in neighboring Israel/Palestine and Iraq, these guests provide steady annual revenue on which Jordan can depend. These guests' demands are quite distinct as well: large, family-friendly restaurants and long-term rentals of cars and residences. Although Petra and Jerash are attractive destinations for them, Middle Eastern travelers exhibit more interest in Islamic antiquity sites—castles, battlefields, baths, mosques, and saints' tombs.

Yet Jordan's hospitality industry does not cater equally to Middle Eastern and Western visitors. Rather, the ways in which Christian and Muslim tourism is managed are distinct and, as Erin Addison has demonstrated (2004), manifest in tourism infrastructure; while roads to Christian sites are wide, well paved, and marked with conspicuous signs directing travelers to their destinations, Muslim sites are poorly marked with small signs, and access is often limited to small, sometimes unpaved roads that make tourism impossible. Addison rightly explains these differences as a strategic and pragmatic decision to foster a sanitized Christian encounter with the "Holy Land." Islamic sites consequently do not receive the attention given to and resources required for heavily visited antiquity sites. The greater implications of Addison's conclusions are that religious heritage tourism in Jordan is not haphazard but is instead a carefully crafted industry that fosters links between (some) tourists and their religious heritage at the expense of other groups.

The question of why 1700 AD was chosen as the terminal date for "antiquity" in the 1988 Antiquities Law is conspicuous. The date is no accident; it marks the beginning of migrations from Arabia into Jordan of groups with which "native" Jordanians draw a genealogical connection. Buildings and artifacts dating from 1700 to the mid-twentieth century are still found throughout the kingdom, and they are currently undergoing a process of revaluation and incorporation into national and local heritage discourses. The official code hesitates to define these remains as "antiquity," and only under special circumstances may post-1700 materials be redefined:

Article 2

b. Any movable or immovable object as provided for in Clause "a" of this definition which dates back after AD 1700 and which the Minister requests to be considered an antiquity by a decision published in the Official Gazette[.]

Clause b therefore suggests that the state exercises some flexibility in classifying buildings and objects produced after 1700 as antiquities. In reclassifying such objects, the state may assume ownership of these materials and, as with the objects of a much more remote past, manage them as instruments of the tourism industry.

The clause cited above, then, is a fortunate loophole that permits the Jordanian kingdom flexibility in crafting the category of national heritage. The last decade has indeed seen several changes in the way the Jordanian state defines its relationship with the past. Now, the state readily departs from the legal distinctions and instead collapses pre- and post-1700 buildings and objects into a broad national heritage not constrained by time. In a brief example, recent advertising campaigns promote national unity using images of Roman and Byzantine Petra (once considered the product of "other civilizations"), linking them to images of national pride such as the flag and expressions such as "Jordan First" (*al-urdun awalan*). This newly packaged heritage discourse becomes a vehicle through which the state may bolster a unified national identity that has remained fragile over the past six decades.

The private commercial sector has taken up these state-sponsored notions of heritage and packaged them in purchasable commodities, practices, and places. Salient examples of this process are evident in the Arabic and English-language newspapers that avidly promote a consumption-driven attitude toward heritage. Who takes part in this exciting, sophisticated turath, however, is highly restricted and far from inclusive among Jordan's national population. Because participation requires capital, urban middle and upper classes most easily take part in these nationally and commercially defined heritage practices. Rugs, furniture, paintings, and jewelry are advertised as part of a national heritage that is owned and displayed in one's house. Moreover, Roman theaters in Amman, Jerash, and Umm Qais annually host European classical as well as Arabic pop musical performances, where audiences suffer the uncomfortable stone seating to be entertained "like Romans." One can spend the weekend at the Moevenpick Resort on the Dead Sea, where a nineteenth-century Ottoman village comes to life, this time with an abundance of water, flowers, sumptuous ice cream, and Shiatsu massage.

The transformation of dilapidated Ottoman buildings into heritage cafés and restaurants provides the best example of commercially defined heritage spaces. In Amman as well as in smaller communities in the vicinity of the capital city (for example, Madaba, Fuheis, and al-Yadudah), several scholars (see Daher 1999; Nagy and Abu-Dayyeh 2002; Shryock 2004) have investigated the politics behind these establishments, where international tourists dine alongside wealthy Jordanians eating traditional foods and purchasing rugs and coffee pots in nearby gift shops. We concur with these writers' observations that local residents do not visit, and remain largely unaffected by, these heritage restaurants. While these initiatives to restore old buildings and embark on new commercial ventures should be lauded as part of a growing and much-needed Jordanian private sector, these exclusive heritage cafés—as well as hotels and theatres—pose a problem for the national initiative to foster a unified heritage ethos.

Figure 3.1. This house in a wealthy neighborhood of Amman (*left*) finds inspiration in the rock-hewn buildings of Petra, an expansive Nabataean and Classical city that is Jordan's most admired tourist destination. The ancient city has quickly become a popular symbol of Jordanian national heritage. (Photograph by B. Porter.)

"Drink Tea?" Documenting Local Heritage Discourses

Curious to learn the extent to which government-sponsored discourses about Jordanian heritage were shared, as well as how local culture is expressed in language and practice across the kingdom, we engaged in long-term ethnographic fieldwork in 2002 and 2004. Charting such discursive terrain required us to leave the capital, its bureaucrats, and growing middle-class suburbs and venture into the rural countryside, to individuals' homes and to personal and local social events. From investigating talk and practices, we posit that turath, as understood at the most local levels, incorporates some familiar elements already mentioned, such as items for display in the home and "traditions," yet it also emphasizes social propriety, continuing and emergent personal relationships, and the contingencies of life in the present day.

Across central Jordan, locals say that most of the ancient ruins in their vicinity were occupied by civilizations to which they hold no genealogical relationship. For example, many antiquity sites are thought to be from the ʿasur romanī (the Roman period), and locals believe that Romans (not indigenous to the area) were the first to substantially occupy the region, building cities, forts, and villas. Ancient cemeteries, especially, are labeled "Roman," as the ancient graves that locals encounter are much "taller" than themselves, a claim based on their estimation of tomb cairn lengths. Romans, they assert, were tall with fair skin, and the people in the ground possessed "European" rather than "Arab" racial features. Because almost no bioarchaeological analyses of human remains are available in central Jordan, the "racial" descriptions of these ancient societies currently rest in local knowledge alone.

This genealogical distancing of antiquity sites from previous civilizations in local understandings is remarkably reminiscent of the 1988 Antiquity Law, which likewise distances the state from pre-1700 civilizations, and noticeably different from recent attempts to inscribe all of Jordan's culture history within a single national heritage. At first, we were surprised to discover that the Jordanians we encountered placed little symbolic importance on the antiquity sites in their vicinity although without a doubt they had respect for these monuments and the ancient societies that had produced them. Most intriguing is the fact that the kingdom's push for a national heritage inclusive of pre-1700 societies, while resonating around the capital, was having little effect on local rural society. Given our discovery, we were curious to learn what ordinary Jordanians considered heritage.

We discovered a tacit agreement within local communities that a genealogical relationship exists between the eighteenth- and nineteenth-century residents of the area and themselves. The late nineteenth century is celebrated as a time of resistance against foreign Ottoman occupation, followed by a period of self-determination under the Hashemite monarchy. This period weighs heavily in the memory of older Jordanians; not surprisingly, much local talk about heritage is drawn from this time, because of its perceived historical import and relevancy. Jordan's Ottoman period is remembered for independent and noble tribesmen who raided the flocks of their neighbors and eluded Ottoman tax collectors. The celebration of this independent spirit is even seen in the valorization of events from the British Mandate period by those who remember through discussions of T. E. Lawrence (of Arabia) and Glubb Baša, Britishman John Bagot Glubb, who trained and led Transjordan's Arab Legion from 1939 to 1956. Residents commemorate traditions from these periods by displaying heirloom rugs, antique coffeepots, and weapons in their homes. Locals also stress the notion of *karam,* the hospitality that their nineteenth-century ancestors showed to fellow tribesmen and traveling strangers alike. Demonstrating hospitality indeed remains an important virtue today, although it too is undergoing changes. Andrew Shryock (2004) has recently discussed how an invitation into a Jordanian home is a sacrosanct ritual in which both hosts and guests are obligated to enjoy coffee or tea, exchange news, strike bargains, and arrange marriages. Pleased guests reward their host after the visit, proclaiming his (or her) generosity around town, garnering the host much social capital.

Karam is a practice linked with Jordanian turath, and we inadvertently discovered that the notion conveniently facilitated our ethnographic fieldwork. More than once was our car stopped by a concerned sheikh or interested young man. The *ahlan wa sahlan*, "welcome," was quickly followed by invitations to *šrab šāi*, "drink tea"; chairs were quickly assembled, and water boiled. To refuse an invitation is very difficult, not only because hosts are persistent and that "no" might carry long-standing feelings of rejection but also because these visits are very useful loci of gossip and local discourse circulation. During our conversations, hosts would acknowledge our unfamiliarity with local customs and attempt to make explicit that which may be taken for granted in local interactions. Such comments were valuable as we traveled the region, visiting with families, landowners, nomadic herders, and shopkeepers who provided explicit commentary on the region's history, archaeology, cultural practices, and values.

Among the subjects that I (Jennifer Jacobs) discussed over the warmth of coffee, tea, and karam in peoples' homes was *m-ha-ha*, a type of vocal tribute consisting of four parallel lines of poetry and followed by *zaġarīt* (ululation). Although these tributes are most typically performed at wedding parties, I was introduced to them in the living room of my first host, eighty-four-year-old Munira, who performed one for me as a generous welcome:

aaiihaa ahla wa sahla yā līdituna se͓a!
aaiihaa haī lil-baḥse il-amrīkīya wa hīyam ma͓ha
aaiihaa ḥalefit kuba lā manu kabīrkū
aaiihaa kabīrna kabīr la gal ͓an ma šahada
lilililililililililiiii!

aaiihaa Welcome, our pleasure at this moment!
aaiihaa This is for the American researcher and Hiyyam with her.
aaiihaa I swore to vouch for the favor of your greatness.
aaiihaa Our great are big for speaking about what is seen.
lilililililililililiiii!

To my surprise, there were further performances that she assumed would please me: one to George W. Bush, another to baby Jesus. From a discourse-centered perspective, the varied content of these poems intrigued me. Could someone recite m-ha-ha extemporaneously, crafting new words on the spot, or were the words truly "traditional," that is, words that have come before? A younger interviewee offered a tempered clue to understanding this poetic genre: "Sometimes we add new words, but we cannot change the words, because they are turath." The link between tradition and heritage is unmistakable here: heritage is a condition under which traditions are sought to be fixed. From such a standpoint, only elements that are consciously seen as traditional are maintained. In the case of m-ha-ha, these valued elements would include conventional words that have been passed from generation to generation and the rigid elements of the genre, including distinctive pitch intonations, parallelism in the line, and the zaġarīt at the end (Jacobs 2007). New terms, such as the name "George W. Bush" or "*il-baḫse il-amrīkīya*" (the American researcher), are subject to a different scheme of value and might change the next time the poem is uttered.

Women like Munira are remarkable, not only because they know how to perform m-ha-ha but also because they still practice this oral poetry in their daily lives. Like offering a guest coffee or tea, this mode of performance is seen as proper, friendly, and appropriate, at least from her standpoint. The words incorporated into her m-ha-ha are meaningful in terms of earnest expression and the personal relationship created in the immediate moment, not necessarily as items from the past on display.

Like oral poetry, antiquities play an important role in Jordanians' daily lives, our observations suggest. For farmers, townspersons, and herders, it is nearly impossible not to encounter archaeological sites daily. A visual reminder of the long-term human occupation in the region, numerous *tilāl* (mounds), *xirāb* (ruins), and *quṣūr* (palaces) lie adjacent to modern settlements, and they continue to be used for a variety of purposes. Pastoralists, for example, use large, open architectural features such as Roman forts to corral sheep and goats. Stone buildings and pits, even those cordoned off and marked with government signs, are commonly used as restrooms. Families who search for a quaint location and a nice breeze will often picnic at antiquity sites after Friday prayers. Others visit simply to find some privacy, watch the sunset, and escape the watchful eye of their families. On the tallest of antiquity sites, communities have even founded cemeteries in recent centuries. These behaviors suggest that local communities value antiquity sites for their immediate, pragmatic uses—that is, the contingencies of life in the present.

There is, however, a vast blurriness between value stemming from the "here and now" and value from "the past," as one interviewee clearly demonstrated. Abla Hamarneh, the remarkable author of the 2001 *Aġānīna il-Urdunīya Miṯl Nebaʿ il-Maīa (Our Jordanian Songs Are Like a Gush of Water)* (see figure 3.2), came to writing a book late in life. She sat with me in her home that summer explaining the book's contents: the words of songs and oral poetry for different kinds of ceremonies and social events, or what she calls *turathi* songs. These words are not known by all people, she explained: "The old women, like me, less than five years [younger than me] and more than five years [older than me]—they know." Mrs. Hamarneh's lifetime of experiences contributed to the book's contents. She told me, "When we were small, life was very simple. We . . . if there [was] any party in Madaba, we went and heard. And came back to the home and repeat[ed] what we hear[d] in the other party. So when I wrote this book, I didn't need any other people. It was all from my mind." As an effort to document past practices, her book intrigued me. "You must know Arabic to understand every word in this book," the author advised. But as we sat together, it became clear that the stark words on the page could not communicate many important things to an outsider, despite clear section titles to categorize the texts. Precisely when and where to perform the songs; their tunes, rhythms, intonations, emotional meanings; and most important, the social relationship of the performer to the others present at the event—these are presupposed elements that readers must already understand to comprehend the book. And as our conversation unfolded, such social contingencies—relationships, emotions, sensory-laden memories—were

Figure 3.2. Cover of Abla Hamarneh's book (in English, titled *Our Jordanian Songs Are Like a Gush of Water: A Catalog of Jordanian Heritage from Memory*). The woven antique textile displayed on the cover appears again alongside images of embroidery, coffee grinders, and water pipes inside the book.

clearly among the highly valued elements in Mrs. Hamarneh's turath: "All the things in my home." She pointed to photographs on the wall. "My mother, my mother-in-law, my sister, the oldest one, this one." She gestured to a circular stone on the floor. "The stone to cut the corn, wheat, the *za'atar* [thyme]."

The discursive intermingling of present-day blood relations with family heirlooms, such as grinding stones, carpets, and coffeepots, provides some of the tangible links by which we can understand displays in private homes, architectural decoration, and even some practices of "looting." Not only are cut stones easily salvageable from antiquity sites, but so are statues and inscriptions, which can adorn a doorway or a niche. Display of items of turath, as they are embedded in local contexts, can be an expression of deep sentiment and a source of personal pride, so that they are fervently guarded against loss.

Present-day concerns over losing traditions—the words, practices, sensations, and values from the past—motivate a type of local stewardship in which individuals vested with authority or inclination write books and sheet music and collect items. One afternoon in Fuheis, a small, mostly Christian town northwest of Amman, a very warm and musical family indulged me with descriptions of songs and various wedding customs. I was unfamiliar with one genre—*faṭīre*. Faṭīre, they explained, is a type of sweet made from bread sliced with ghee and topped with sugar-water. It is distributed to neighbors following a wedding, when people are returning from the church. During its preparation, male family members cut the bread, and as they slice it, they sing these special songs for the moment. The eldest grown son told me, "In Fuheis they are keeping with their traditions. . . . In their weddings, they still follow the old traditions. This faṭīre, it's not done in many places. In Salt they used to do this, but they don't anymore. So they are trying really hard to keep the traditions."

This is not the first time that I had heard my hosts so neatly distinguish their wedding practices from those of other towns. Indeed, in interviews from Salt, Dhiban, Karak, Husun, Birein, and Deir Alla, people explicitly recognized extant variations in practice across Jordan—from the ways in which single words get pronounced to musical tunes and rhythms. And while the town (or locality) is frequently employed in these conversations as the bounds of such differences, tribal and religious backgrounds are widely recognized as elements that constitute these towns' demographics.

Circulation and Accessibility of Heritage Discourses

Our work is helping us to understand the mechanics of heritage, especially how any particular discourse is distributed unevenly across the social landscape. Although we discovered that some sentiments, objects, and practices were widely shared across

Central Jordan, certain talk about heritage was confined to particular communities and absent from others. Moreover, individuals with expertise in a given field—such as archaeology, vocal performance, or the hotel and hospitality industry—have the ability to situate heritage from such a vantage point in their talk. Identifying and explaining these differences in local heritage discourses according to social relations, expertise, socioeconomic class, personal abilities, and interest was easy. The distribution of state-sponsored discourses of heritage, however, was more difficult to pin down. Despite the kingdom's efforts to foster a unified discourse about national heritage, we found that concepts such as "al-urdun awalan" are not explicitly reiterated by locals speaking amongst themselves; rather, turath is more likely to be discussed in regionalist terms. Yet we identified little critique of or resistance to this nationalist heritage discourse either. That is, internalization of such ideas may come in the form of unarticulated participation, such as increasing attendance at turath festivals. The means and extent to which nationalist discourses ultimately are expressed and shared is still an unanswered question for future investigation. This conclusion contrasts with studies that assume that state-sponsored heritage discourses will become a totalizing discourse that the government formulates and distributes to passive constituents. Currently in Jordan, the state is managing certain notions of heritage with which only a few groups actively engage.

This continuing disjuncture between the local and the national is noteworthy in an age when the state seeks to manage (and often succeeds in managing) individuals' and community members' understandings of themselves as citizens. Such patterning is explained, in part, if we consider how national and local heritage discourses are accessed and come to circulate in different ways. National heritage discourses are theoretically accessible to all citizens, but because they are often disseminated commercially via one-way media, only certain members possess the economic capital and social competency needed to participate. Those who adopt such broad notions thus tend to be educated and cosmopolitan elites. Foreign visitors, archaeologists included, are offered the same totalizing understanding of a "Jordanian" heritage as an easily consumable discourse for explaining the complexities of local society.

Local heritage discourses are also accessible but in ways very different from the national. Economic capital is not as important as is the social competency required to grasp local meanings. Stories, traditions, and subtle differences in language vary greatly over the landscape; Jordanians from one village will not always comprehend local practices of another. And despite being uneven and different for each person, extant networks of family and social relationships provide the means by which local discourses travel. One other important difference between local and national discourses is that local discourses are largely transmitted through face-to-face talk and direct sentiment-laden experiences rather than billboards and television programs. The personal, face-to-face encounter is one that necessitates dialogue and participation, and this participation comes in the form of more talk—a chain reaction, if you will.

Conclusion

Our work suggests that archaeology is not yet under fire in Jordan. Despite differences between local and national heritage discourses, both the kingdom and local communities currently welcome foreign archaeologists and the funding they bring. Once concerned primarily with scientific explorations, foreign archaeologists working in Jordan are beginning to take an equal interest in the country's economic development and tourism infrastructure. Foreign archaeological research institutes such as the American Center of Oriental Research (ACOR) and the Council for British Research in the Levant (CBRL), for example, partake in projects aimed at developing the kingdom's antiquities for tourism. Local communities are not ambivalent toward archaeology and indeed recognize the economic benefits of site development. When antiquity sites are developed for tourism, their public and fluid nature (as described

Figure 3.3. Antiquity sites are commonly used as public spaces in Jordan. Here children are enjoying an early-evening game of football among the ruins of ancient Dhiban. An asphalt road separates the archaeological site from the modern town in the background. (Photograph by B. Porter.)

above) is transformed. Through a combination of fences, guards, parking lots, and ticket booths, sites are segmented from the surrounding landscape, and public access is consequently reduced. The kingdom incorporates the local antiquity site into a discourse aimed at national elites and tourists, crafting formal narratives that disregard local knowledge. Communities do not appear to mind this transference in the use-value of antiquity sites and in fact desire—sometimes even demand—the excavation and development of antiquity sites to stimulate stagnant economies. Communities appear willing to use antiquities as resources to draw greater economic benefit for themselves and their families with little consideration of the drawbacks of tourist development. Similarly and not surprisingly, communities exhibit little fear that development will compromise local understandings of heritage.

Can archaeologists contribute to these local understandings of heritage that are more concerned with the recent rather than the ancient past? The emerging archaeological investigation of the Ottoman period presents a promising opportunity for scholars to make a tangible contribution to local heritage discourses (Baram and Carroll 2000; Walker 1999). Buildings and artifacts such as coins, ceramic vessels, and agricultural tools can complement the meager historical records from the period; restored Ottoman villages and museum displays can be enjoyed by all Jordanians rather than reserved as destination restaurants for the wealthiest. But ethnography, and the practices it employs, is what will seek out and document the most captivating stories of turath.

Acknowledgments

We would like to thank Bruce Routledge (University of Liverpool), Danielle Steen (Knox College), Gordon Witty (Temple University), Greg Urban (University of Pennsylvania), Alexander Bauer (City University of New York–Queens College), Pierre and Patricia Bikai (American Center of Oriental Research), Hilda Ayoub, and the many Jordanians who acted the gracious hosts while tolerating our odd questions. A version of this chapter was read at a University of Pennsylvania symposium, "Ethics and the Practice of Archaeology" (September 2002). The American Center of Oriental Research (ACOR) in Amman provided institutional support while two Council of American Overseas Research Centers (CAORC) dissertation fellowships provided financial assistance.

Notes

1. All ethnographic subjects mentioned in this work are denoted with pseudonyms.
2. Transliteration of Arabic words closely follow Hans Wehr's system (1961). The lone exception is the word *turath,* which has been rendered differently for the sake of simplicity.

3. Today, Burgon's lines are often cited in advertisements to lure tourists to Petra. A complete transcript of the poem is available in Augé and Dentzer 2000: 109.

4. For a full transcript of the law, see http://www.unesco.org/culture/natlaws/media/pdf/jordan/jo_antiquitieslaw21_engtof.pdf.

References Cited

Addison, Erin. "The Roads to Ruins: Accessing Islamic Heritage in Jordan." In *Marketing Heritage: Archaeology and the Consumption of the Past,* edited by Y. Rowan and U. Baram, 229–48. Walnut Creek, Calif.: AltaMira Press, 2004.

Appadurai, Arjun. "The Globalization of Archaeology and Heritage." *Journal of Social Archaeology* 1, no. 1 (2001): 35–49.

Augé, Christian, and Jean-Marie Dentzer. *Petra: Lost City of the Ancient World.* New York: Harry N. Abrams, 2000.

Baram, Uzi, and Lynda Carroll, eds. *A Historical Archaeology of the Ottoman Empire: Breaking New Ground.* New York: Kluwer Academic/Plenum Publishers, 2000.

Daher, Rami Farouk. "Gentrification and the Politics of Power, Capital and Culture in an Emerging Jordanian Heritage Industry." *Traditional Dwellings and Settlements* 10, no. 11 (1999): 33–45.

Dominguez, Virginia R. "Marketing Heritage." *American Ethnologist* 13, no. 3 (1986): 546–55.

Hamarneh, Abla. *Aġānīna il-Urdunīya Miṯl Nebaʿ il-Maīa.* Amman: Azminah, 2001.

Jacobs, Jennifer E. "'Unintelligibles' in Vocal Performances at Middle Eastern Marriage Celebrations." *Text and Talk* 27, no. 4 (2007): 483–507.

Jordan National Tourism Strategy, 2004–2010. Electronic document found at http://www.tourism.jo/PDFs/NTS%20Book.pdf. 2004.

Kelly, Marjorie. "Tourism, Not Terrorism: The Visual Politics of Presenting Jordan as an International Tourist Destination." *Visual Anthropology* 11 (1998): 191–205.

Meskell, Lynn, ed. *Archaeology Under Fire: Nationalism, Politics and Heritage in the Eastern Mediterranean and Middle East.* London: Routledge, 1999.

Nagy, Sharon, and Nabil Abu-Dayyeh. "Village Air for Urban Elites: Heritage Café Complexes in Jordan." *Expedition* 44, no. 2 (2002): 10–18.

Sherzer, Joel. "A Discourse-Centered Approach to Language and Culture." *American Anthropologist* 89 (1987): 295–309.

Shryock, Andrew. "The New Jordanian Hospitality: House, Host, and Guest in the Culture of Public Display." *Comparative Studies in Society and History* 46, no. 1 (2004): 35–62.

Urban, Greg. *A Discourse-Centered Approach to Culture: Native South American Myths and Rituals.* Austin: University of Texas Press, 1991.

Walker, Bethany J. "Militarization to Nomadization: The Middle and Late Islamic Periods." *Near Eastern Archaeology* 62, no. 4 (1999): 202–32.

Wehr, Hans. *A Dictionary of Modern Written Arabic.* Beirut: Librairie du Liban, 1980. (Orig. pub. 1961.)

4

Embodied Heritage, Identity Politics, and Tourism

HELAINE SILVERMAN

The series of spectacular Mochica burials discovered at the site of Sipán in the Lambayeque Valley on the north coast of Peru provides an example through which to interrogate the conjunction of archaeological discovery, narrational packaging of the past for tourism, and discourses of identity.[1] The Sipán burials are interesting as a site of contested and negotiated performances; in particular, the naming of the ancient Sipán rulers by their discoverer and the popular media has embodied and empowered an ideology of regionalism in Lambayeque. This ideology seeks to promote economic development around tourism and social well-being around identity on the basis of a newly valorized archaeological past.

There is currently a widespread Peruvian discourse promoting identity assertion on the basis of ancient glory and the tourism that extraordinary archaeological sites can attract (see, for example, Silverman 2002). The revival and invention of a Mochica identity in Lambayeque and the espousal and conscious construction of *lambayecanidad*—local Lambayeque identity—are embedded in larger national and international contexts. The conjunction of cultural patrimony tourism with Peru's late-twentieth-/twenty-first-century discourse of national identity is the framework within which ancient elite bodies are being manipulated and interpreted.

The Sipán Burials

In 1987, archaeologists began to recover at Sipán the intact tombs and preserved bodies of the rulers of an ancient society known as Moche or Mochica that flourished on the north coast of Peru in the first half of the first millennium AD (see Bawden 1996). These finds have received national and worldwide media attention because they are the richest unlooted burials yet reported for the New World (see, for example, Alva 1988). *National Geographic* has been especially active in keeping the public informed about the ongoing discoveries. The magazine's role in constructing popular attitudes toward the past and foreign ("exotic") societies is well known (Lutz and Collins 1993).

Beyond archaeological interest in Sipán, the most fascinating aspect of the burials, for me, is the naming of the occupants of the excavated tombs. Beginning with the announcement about the first discovery (Alva 1988) and in popular and scholarly accounts about subsequent discoveries, the occupants of the Sipán tombs have been named: the Lord of Sipán (Alva 1988), the Old Lord of Sipán (Alva 1990), and the Priest (Alva 1994). After being named by their excavator, Walter Alva, these individuals, particularly the Lord of Sipán, acquired new lives as the known rulers of an ancient Peruvian realm.[2]

The media immediately seized upon the name "Lord of Sipán." And this mute skeleton became a person (indeed, a celebrity), given life as much by the artistry of *National Geographic* and concomitant media attention as by archaeological interpretation. So important did this named ancient person become that in 1993, Peru's former president, Alberto Fujimori, welcomed back from Germany the conserved skeleton of the Lord of Sipán in a ceremony that treated the skeleton with the same state honors extended by protocol to any visiting head of state.[3] In his speech, President Fujimori said, "Ladies and gentlemen, we greet the return to Peru of the Lord of Sipán, Lord of Lords, with indescribable joy and pride as Peruvians." At the ceremony, the German ambassador to Peru replied, saying, "Mr. President, it is a great honor and pleasure to deliver to you and the Peruvian people the remains of a world-wide famous Peruvian."[4]

For several days after their return to Peru, the Lord of Sipán lay in state at the Presidential Palace in Lima—again signaling the national importance of the body. This event and its discourse of ancestral political genealogy served to legitimate Fujimori as president and the Peruvian people as a deeply historical nation-state. But the appropriation was not uncontested. Critics of Fujimori seized upon the opportunity to mock the president, calling him the "Lord of Sin Pan" (*Caretas,* March 11, 1993) a clever play on the name "Sipán"—the president as the Lord of the Realm of People without Bread (that is, food), a president who glorifies the past and his legitimacy from it but is unable to feed and employ millions of poor Peruvians.

At the local level, the people of Lambayeque basked in the privileging of their region's contribution to the grand civilizational sweep of Peruvian history. When the remains of the Lord of Sipán were returned to their place of origin, they were greeted by massive crowds. At the Chiclayo airport, in a ceremony paralleling that in Lima, Walter Alva reiterated the message of the president, saying, "For us, the Peruvian past is not merely inert objects. It is a vast spiritual presence that nourishes the deep roots of the Peruvian nation." Alva explained the significance of the actual

Lord of Sipán, saying that the remains "are not merely archaeological findings, but the people of Lambayeque are meeting their own Mochica ancestors."[5]

The Mochica Revival and Local Resistance

Although the major archaeological sites and ancient cultures of Lambayeque have been known by local people as a result of the visibility of monumental sites and public education, until the discovery of the Lord of Sipán and his ancient counterparts, *lambayecanos* were more focused on their present and future in terms of the region's productive agro-industrial complex than its pre-Columbian past. Today, many people of Lambayeque also see appropriation of the past as an engine of economic development as well as a motor of local pride. Indeed, identification with Sipán's rulers and ancient Mochica culture is running rampant. A private university, a hospital, shops, and clubs have adopted the name of "Señor de Sipán." There is also a new Sipán brand of a traditional large layered cookie and sweet filling confection called "King Kong." And an extravaganza called the *Sipán Cantata* has been performed since 1990, combining song, music, dance, and drama to present the epic story of the Lord of Sipán and praise Mochica cultural achievements. The *Cantata* explicitly espouses *mestizaje* and cultural continuity between the current population of Lambayeque and the ancient Mochica one. As enunciated by the group's founder, Edgar Dante, the *Cantata* serves to "integrate local culture in the process of continental and universal development" (*La Industria,* June 26, 1999). Walter Alva, the *Cantata's* consultant, says that the performance "exalts the permanent presence of the [Mochica] roots of our nationality" (*La Industria,* June 26, 1999).

This invented link to the past became hyperreal in 2002 when a local politician sought to gain official recognition of the *Cantata* as an authentic element of Peru's intangible cultural heritage. His proposal was categorically denied by a congressional commission's determination that the performance was fully of recent origin, notwithstanding its theme (*La Industria,* March 12 and August 12, 2002). The hyperreal is also evident in the recent establishment of a "Mochica village" of living artisans alongside the Sipán museum (Alva 2004: fig. 480), reminiscent of the ethnic villages at the Chicago Columbian Exposition in 1893 (see, for example, Hinsley 1991). The village is intended to present to the viewer a re-creation of Mochica craft activities, as carried out by "the descendants of this culture" (*La Industria,* October 3, 2002), as if Mochica talents had been genetically transmitted across the centuries.

The local visibility and accessibility of the excavated remains from Sipán and revival of ancient and traditional crafts surely contribute to popular interest in and identification with the Mochica in Lambayeque. Editorials in the local newspaper, *La Industria,* published in the regional capital of Chiclayo, repeatedly emphasize that Lambayeque's tourism potential rests principally in the discovery of the Lord of Sipán. All of this should be viewed with caution in drawing conclusions, however; in Lambayeque, references were being made to the local ancient past even before the Sipán tombs were discovered. A housing development called Los Mochicas already existed, as did a local musical group called Naymlap, after the first king of the Lambayeque dynasty (see Donnan 1990). Indeed, throughout Peru, the names of ancient cultures and ancient kings are frequently used iconically in the names of schools, housing developments, sports arenas, restaurants, manufacturing industries, and stores. Moreover, these names are translocal (not location specific). The use of the name Sipán is therefore hardly the first time that an archaeological name has been appropriated for a civic or commercial venture in Lambayeque or elsewhere in Peru.

What is noteworthy and different in the case of Sipán is the intensity and rapidity with which this nomenclatural borrowing occurred. Sipán fervor is overtly linked to a local movement to establish a regional identity and promote tourism as a competitive response to what is perceived, in Lambayeque, as a lack of a cultural politics in contrast to the inculcation of identity in other Peruvian regions, especially Cusco. This discourse mushroomed in 2000 when, to rectify the perceived disadvantageous situation, the first Lambayeque Cultural Identity Week was organized. The two professors in charge of this project stated that from ancient times a festival spirit has characterized the people of Lambayeque and that agriculture, crafts, fishing, and shamanism still link the past and present. The president of the organizing committee said that the event sought to create "a space in the calendar of Lambayeque festivals for the affirmation of our identity" (*La Industria*, August 20, 2000). Lambayeque's Cultural Identity Week continues to be celebrated yearly.

This hyper-Lambayeque ideology is being orchestrated and disseminated through a frequent exhortation in *La Industria* and by schoolteachers and local civic institutions. *La Industria* has published news of great archaeological finds in the region and guest editorials about them, and it has informed readers about the nature and locations of identity-affirming activities sponsored by civic and private entities. Also, in 2002 the newspaper decided to take direct action by convening a colloquium for its avocational high school journalists to "create awareness about tourism and strengthen the Lambayeque identity and national identity" (*La Industria*, August 11, 2002). Professional journalists, professors, and educated laypeople write frequent editorials in *La Industria* arguing that there should be academies of lambayecanidad (Lambayequeness), professoriates of lambayecanidad, and agoras of lambayecanidad so that "we are catalyzed into knowing who we are and how we should elevate lambayecanidad to the highest category of our identity in concert with all the people of

Peru and the world" (editorial by Estuardo Deza Saldaña in *La Industria,* August 6, 2000).

Sipán has been conscripted into this effort of local identity creation. A professor of pedagogy and history at the national university in Lambayeque, for instance, argued repeatedly that the region's tourist potential lay principally in the discovery of the Lord of Sipán and also that "around this find should be generated a good part of the Lambayeque identity" (editorial by Pedro Delgado Rosado in *La Industria,* May 15, 2000). President Alejandro Toledo said, at the inauguration of the new Sipán museum, "A people without history is a people without culture, a people without culture is a people without soul, and for this reason this museum must be visited first by the lambayecanos" (*La Industria,* November 9, 2002). And an article in *La Industria* (November 10, 2002) contained the comment that "the Lord of Sipán in his new home re-encountered his people, represented by the different communities [of the Lambayeque region] that came to the museum the second day it was open." Walter Alva said, "The rulers of Sipán have awoken to bring us a message of their great cultural quality, of their impressive knowledge about the world and, above all, to show us that the roots of their society are also ours and are the essence of our identity" (quoted in *El Comercio,* November 9, 2002).

Attention to Sipán and the Mochica has facilitated the valorization of regional identity in Lambayeque, already premised upon Lambayeque's distinctive cuisine, traditional handicrafts, particular saints, and vernacular villages. Links to an ancient Mochica identity are being added to these features and foregrounded. The current revival of Mochica identity in Lambayeque is particularly interesting because the Muchik language died out at the beginning of the twentieth century, and Mochica culture has all but disappeared save in the faces of some people, local surnames and toponyms, shamanic practices, and the traditional reed fishing boat. The reinvention of Mochica identity is being conducted as a contemporary project of modernist discourse and practice.

But we would be severely mistaken if we regarded this affection for the past as locally unanimous. Quite the contrary; in the town of Sipán, where the burial mound is located, memory is still fresh of the armed struggle between looters and the police that led to archaeological intervention in the site and the exclusion of town residents from the mound, thereby cutting off a much-needed source of income (see full details in Kirkpatrick 1992).

Moreover, the new state-of-the-art Royal Tombs of Sipán Museum was not constructed at Sipán but was instead built in the town of Lambayeque, more than thirty-five kilometers from Sipán but just a few minutes from the provincial capital of Chiclayo.[6] It was inaugurated in November 2002. The Sipán townsfolk vigorously protested the new museum's location from the time it was announced, but to no

a.

Figure 4.1. The modest site museum at Sipán where the great Mochica burials were found: *a,* exterior; *b* and *c,* interior display. (Photographs by Helaine Silverman, June 2004.)

b.

c.

Figure 4.2. The magnificent Royal Tombs of Sipán Museum in the town of Lambayeque, near Chiclayo. Photography is not permitted inside the museum. For interior views, see Alva 2004: figs. 469–78. (Photograph by Helaine Silverman, June 2004.)

avail. The modest site museum at Sipán (see figure 4.1) is unable to compete with the magnificent new facility (see figure 4.2), which both displays the fabulous original artifacts from the tombs and reproduces the burials, thereby obviating the need to see the original locale among all but the most authenticity-seeking tourists. Place of discovery is superseded by place of representation.

For all the national and international attention that ancient Sipán has received, modern Sipán still lacks basic infrastructure. Townsfolk have been insistent in their demands for electricity, running water, sewers, and roads. Indeed, on September 22, 2001, to draw attention to their demands, residents put up roadblocks to prevent tourists from gaining access to the site. But Walter Alva said, the day after, that although the residents were right in their demands, their social concerns must not be mixed with scientific work. Herein lies the source of conflict and ethical debate. Archaeology should not be removed from its social context. As archaeologists appropriate the lives of the dead, the lives of living people must be considered.

Living alongside an ancient site that yielded incalculable wealth beyond their reach, the contemporary residents of Sipán tried to get a legal piece of the tourist action by setting up vernacular service stands alongside the ruin (see figure 4.3).

Figure 4.3. Kiosks of local townsfolk alongside the Sipán archaeological mound. *a.* This vendor sells souvenir trinkets.

b. The vendors of these kiosks sell food. (Photographs by Helaine Silverman, June 2004.)

Over the past couple of years, infrastructural improvements have begun to be made in and around Sipán by the regional and national government. These improvements are necessary because of the poor impression that modern Sipán is making on tourists, in comparison to its ancient glory. But given the years of antagonism between the townsfolk of Sipán and the archaeological and political establishment, and the relocation of the actual remains from the site of origin to the new museum in the town of Lambayeque, it is difficult to conceive of the residents of Sipán becoming full stakeholders.

The Legitimating Body

As I consider the zeal with which a multidomain and multimedia discourse about lambayecanidad is being locally disseminated, I keep returning to the animating significance of the actual bodies at Sipán. Would the reception of these tombs have been the same without the bodies? I think not. Indeed, it is not coincidental that the new museum is referred to as "the new house of the Lord of Sipán" (for example, *El Comercio,* October 26, 2002) and a "palace of the Mochica dynasty" (for example, *La Industria,* November 8, 2002). In Walter Alva's words, the new museum is "an appropriate space for a ruler, a kind of museum and at the same time a mausoleum, where not only are jewels, emblems, and ornaments exhibited that served to forge cultural identity and establish the rank and power of a ruler of ancient Peru, but also where we are going to conserve for posterity the remains of this person" (*La República,* November 9, 2002).

Furthermore, in Lambayeque, interest in Sipán and the Mochica has led to a resurgence of local interest in other local ancient cultures. Thus, in 1999, the group that performs the *Cantata al Señor de Sipán* presented a theatrical work entitled *Ode to the God Naymlap,* stating that this work reflects the origins of the local Lambayeque culture (see Donnan 1990). The case of Naymlap is especially interesting because here we have a historically preserved pre-Hispanic name but no body. With Sipán, we have no idea what the leaders were actually called, but we do have their bodies in their tombs.

The discoveries at Sipán have been locally managed as a brilliant public relations triumph with major exhibitions of the funerary materials in Lima, the United States, and Japan. That the town of Lambayeque was able to gain possession of the spectacular artifacts and acquire a five-million-dollar state-of-the-art museum for them is remarkable given the strong centralization of archaeology in Lima. Justifiably, Walter Alva has become a local hero—except at Sipán itself—because of the world-class excavation he has conducted, his dedication to Lambayeque, and his support for its rights to its own cultural patrimony, including the contribution that his discoveries make to the economic development of Lambayeque and Peru through attracting tourism. He even appears in illustrated children's books about the Lambayeque past.

Tourism is being managed and promoted locally in Lambayeque, with the agro-industrial and commercial resources of the region significantly liberating it from Lima's control. The presence at the new museum's inauguration of the then current president of the republic, Alejandro Toledo, and the first lady, as well as cabinet ministers, national dignitaries, numerous foreign ambassadors, and international businessmen, indicates how important this ancient assemblage is to the future of Lambayeque and the nation-state.

Comparisons

A couple of valleys to the south of Lambayeque, in Jequetepeque, the intact tomb of a female officiant of the local Mochica court was discovered in 1991 (Donnan and Castillo 1992). She was named the Priestess by her excavators and is referred to as such by local people. Indeed, the Mochica Priestess has been seized upon by the neighboring small city of Chepen as the vehicle for their own claim to attention on the national and international tourist stage. A statue has been erected at the entrance

Figure 4.4. Statue of the Mochica Priestess excavated at San José de Moro, located at the entrance to Chepén. (Photograph by Helaine Silverman, June 2004.)

to town (see figure 4.4), depicting this archaeological skeleton in fully fleshed form, and local people are now talking about themselves as descendants of the Mochica. The Priestess is said to be the *novia* (bride) of the Lord of Sipán.

But in the eponymous Moche Valley, a strong discourse about the past is absent even though the greatest panregional Mochica capital city (Huaca del Sol–Huaca de la Luna) is located here and extraordinary Mochica discoveries are being made on a regular basis, from exquisite murals (Uceda et al. 1994) to ancient massacres (Bourget 2001). And on the other side of the river, on the outskirts of the contemporary city of Trujillo, lie the spectacular ruins of the vast city of Chan Chan, former capital of the Chimu Empire, historical successors to the Mochica (Moseley and Day 1982). Why are Mochica and Chimu not an evident part of daily discourse and public ideology in Trujillo, as Mochica is in Lambayeque? This question is all the more perplexing because Trujillo has long been a tourist city, owing to the grandeur and easy accessibility of Chan Chan, and Trujillo needs tourism far more for its economic well-being than do the richer city of Chiclayo and the larger and more fertile Lambayeque Valley. But Trujillo's fabulous Mochica and Chimu architecture is trumped by the human remains removed from the small mound at Sipán and housed in the town of Lambayeque.

These comparisons can be extended. For instance, at Paracas, on the south coast, in the late 1920s, the discovery of dozens of elite men, perfectly preserved in their exquisite ritual garments, provoked interest not in them as persons but only in their fabulous paraphernalia (see Tello 1959; Tello and Mejía Xesspe 1979). There was no sudden clamor on the south coast or nationally that at Paracas were buried the earliest known rulers of ancient Peru. Indeed, after Peruvian archaeologists had opened the two-thousand-year-old mummy bundles, the skeletons were quickly separated from their glorious textile wrappings and the human remains received no further attention.

And in 1946, in the Virú Valley on the north coast, William Duncan Strong (1947) discovered a rich Mochica tomb containing the remains of an individual he named the Warrior-God, replete with an exceptionally fine array of funerary goods. The body, however, disintegrated immediately upon exposure. But I suspect that even had the skeleton survived, it would have received no further attention, because Julio C. Tello, then Peru's leading archaeologist, was more upset with the fact that a North American project had made a find of great objects than that they had recovered actual evidence of an ancient Mochica lord, known only iconographically until that time.[7]

Izumi Shimada's (2000) discovery of extraordinarily wealthy Sicán culture (post-Mochica) tombs at Batan Grande in the Lambayeque region led to the creation of the superb National Sicán Museum in Ferreñafe to house the excavated archaeological material. Shimada wrote the museum's outstanding exhibition script covering the whole prehistory of the region, much of it revealed by his long-term research.[8] Residents of Ferreñafe created their own *Cantata del Señor de Sicán* and take pride in their own local culture, both archaeological and lived, but the great Sicán archaeological culture and museum have not attracted the same degree of attention as those of Sipán. The Peruvian and international public appear unable to concentrate on more than one great ancient lord at a time, in this case the Lord of Sipán discovered by Walter Alva. And, possibly, they confuse and conflate Sipán and Sicán.[9]

As many nation-states do, Peru has operationalized its magnificent archaeological past at particular moments and for specific political purposes (see, for example,

Silverman 1999). But the social and political realities of Peru prior to recent years were such that a true genealogical connection with indigenous civilizations and indigenous people was eschewed. Indeed, only some fifteen years ago was the wall between the adjacent National Museum of Anthropology and Archaeology and the National Museum of History broken through so that a continuous developmental narrative could be told about Peru. The widely perceived and structurally propagated disjunction between Peru's past and present may account for the object-focused interest in the great mummy bundles at Paracas and the Tomb of the Warrior-God in Virú at the time of their discoveries.

Also, in part, we may understand the current appreciation of Sipán's burials in terms of advances in Mochica iconographic analysis (see, for example, Donnan 1978; Donnan and McClelland 1979; Makowski 2003) and the contemporary engagement of archaeology with particular theoretical paradigms of personhood, legitimation, and materiality. Thus, although William Duncan Strong explicitly stated that the old man buried in the Virú Valley tomb was a priest, a warrior, and the impersonator of a Mochica god, Strong did not theorize his conclusion, and his idea received no further discussion. But today's archaeological discourse emphasizes that Sipán and other newly discovered related burials demonstrate that Mochica iconography was depicting individuals who fulfilled in life the ritual roles portrayed on pottery. Indeed, Sipán seems to be claimed as the first evidence of such a link, disregarding Strong's earlier work.

Perhaps the most salient explanation of why Sipán is having such great regional and national impact is that the occupants of the tombs have been named: Lord of Sipán, Old Lord of Sipán, the Priest, and at San José de Moro, the Priestess. Through massive public attention, these inert skeletons have morphed into today's celebrities and cultural icons.

Conclusions

Case studies from around the world demonstrate that a discourse about the past and the practice of archaeology may intersect to play important roles in nation building (see, for example, Kohl and Fawcett 1995). Certainly in Peru, archaeology, understood broadly, contributes significantly to various contemporary projects, from the construction of national and local identities to economic development (see, for example, Silverman 2002).

Throughout time and around the world, particular dead bodies have enjoyed a political life (see, especially, Verdery 1999), whether Evita Perón, Lenin, Rameses II,[10] or the mummies of Inca kings. But why have the Sipán burials become such potent symbols now? Why have the ancient Sipán dead been named, personalized, and paraded? Why have they been enthusiastically adopted by so many lambayecanos? Why were they important to two successive Peruvian presidents?

On the *local* level, the visibility and accessibility of the excavated remains from Sipán, and other archaeological sites in the Lambayeque region, contribute to interest in and identification with the ancient Mochica. The naming of the Sipán burials and their popularization have literally embodied and empowered an ideology of regionalism in Lambayeque. This ideology seeks to promote local economic development through tourism and social well-being around identification with a newly valorized archaeological past. The ideology is animated by popular discourse and a range of civic activities. At the same time, the agro-industrial and commercial wealth of Chiclayo and its surrounding region is significantly underwriting this effort.

Moreover, the burials are localized; they were found alongside a contemporary village. This contrasts significantly with the recent discovery of another, now worldfamous, ancient Peruvian: Juanita, the young woman sacrificed by the Incas atop one of the highest mountains in the Andean range (Reinhard 1996). Here, too, a name was conferred on the anonymous deceased, leading to the humanization of the victim in this formerly sacrosanct burial. However, there is no local community to claim and appropriate Juanita for the purpose of a neo-Inca identity formation, nor can adventure tourism to sacred peaks promote the kind of mass tourism that Lambayeque is encouraging and beginning to enjoy.

Beyond this local framework, there is the *national* position of Lambayeque as it asserts itself among commensurate regions elsewhere in Peru and with regard to the highly centralized government in Lima. Ancient Sipán underwrites calls to strengthen local identity and promote tourism as a competitive response to what is perceived as a lack of cultural politics in Lambayeque, in contrast to the inculcation of identity in other Peruvian departments, especially Cusco, seat of the ancient Inca Empire. Interestingly, former president Fujimori's attention to the returning Lord of Sipán was an attempt to assert national control over the region while seeking to bolster his own position within the country and internationally.

On the *international* playing field, attention to Sipán bolsters the standing of Peru among the community of world nations. The serendipitous discovery of the Sipán burials and Lambayeque's appropriation of ancient Mochica people coincides with the growing insertion of the north coast and the entire country of Peru into the globalized tourist industry. Thus, a strong recursive relationship between the local and the transnational is created and reiterated. Moreover, although subordinated to the International Monetary Fund, World Bank, and other similar institutions of the developed world, Peru nevertheless is able to flaunt itself on the global stage through the display of its spectacular archaeological treasures, particularly mobile ones such as the Lord of Sipán, who has toured the world. Indeed, the Lord of Sipán has been described as "the ambassador of our prehispanic culture" (*El Comercio*, November 8, 2002). Thus, at the inauguration of the new Sipán museum, President Toledo stated, "I assume the obligation . . . of showing the world the greatness of our history and selling—in the best sense of the word—the image of the Royal Tombs of Sipán Museum so that three million tourists arrive by 2006" (*La Industria*, November 9, 2002).

These observations coincide with Barbara Kirshenblatt-Gimblett's (2006) discussion of the cultural economics of heritage worldwide. She argues that intense interest in tangible and intangible heritage (specifically, UNESCO's category of "world heritage") has arisen "from the very processes of globalization" and that heritage "is actually made possible by globalization, in both political and economic terms, the most important form of which is cultural tourism" (Kirshenblatt-Gimblett 2006: 163). The heritage economy is a modern economy (Kirshenblatt-Gimblett 2006: 183), requiring investment based on economic calculation (Kirshenblatt-Gimblett 2006: 192). Both Lambayeque at the local level and Peru at the national level are operating on the basis of this pragmatic reality. And with possession of the stunning funerary wealth of the ancient rulers of Sipán and the personalization and display of those leaders, Lambayeque's Royal Tombs of Sipán Museum has become a new site of cultural production, political engagement, economic incentive, and global intersection: in short, a strategic deployment of the past for contemporary and future goals that range from the deeply personal to the anonymous domains of international and transnational power.

The dead political bodies of Sipán are active social actors in local affairs, national relationships, and foreign dealings at a time of significant change and ongoing economic crisis in Peru. Attention to these dead bodies recognizes and interrogates their importance in contemporary society.

Notes

1. This chapter originally appeared in *Anthropology and Humanism* 30, no. 2 (December 2005): 141–55. It has been edited and updated for the present volume. I thank the editors of this volume for giving me the opportunity to disseminate the paper in this venue.

2. At least ten tombs have been discovered on the platforms of the Sipán mound. In addition to the three named personages, the other tombs correspond to warriors and other elite individuals.

3. The return of the remains of the Lord of Sipán was widely reported in Peru in the print and televised news, and a television documentary was made.

4. The remarks by President Fujimori and the German ambassador quoted here were transcribed from the television documentary, then translated by me. I have translated all other Spanish-language quotations in this chapter.

5. Statements transcribed from the same television documentary, then translated by me.

6. The Lambayeque region has been a center of cultural and political development for more than three thousand years. The contiguity of rivers here creates an exceptionally rich agricultural complex. Indeed, in the late twentieth century, this region accounted for almost one-third of the cultivated land on the entire Peruvian coast. Lambayeque is a Colonial period town built over an indigenous settlement. It was the power center in the region because it had the port. But with the opening up of the Pan American Highway in the 1940s, Chiclayo began to become an important commercial city, growing from about 100,000 inhabitants at that time to at least half a million today. The town of Lambayeque (population, approximately 51,000 in 1995) is separated from the progressive, bustling city of Chiclayo by agricultural fields, although urbanization is fast moving to join them.

7. Letter from Julio C. Tello to Toribio Mejía Xesspe, November 9, 1946, photocopy in possession of the author.

8. http://www.bienvenidaperu.com/English/Ediciones/Edicion42/sican/Body.htm.

9. Sicán culture was originally known as Lambayeque in the archaeological literature.

10. A *Forbes* article on-line (http://www.forbes.com/2002/08/13/0813hot_print.html) states that in 1974, "Egyptologists at the Cairo Museum noticed that the mummy's condition was getting worse rapidly. They decided to fly Rameses II to Paris so that a team of experts could give the mummy a medical examination. . . . Rameses II was issued an Egyptian passport that listed his occupation as 'King (deceased).'"

References Cited

Alva, Walter. "Discovering the New World's Richest Unlooted Tomb." *National Geographic* 174, no. 4 (1988): 510–49.

———. "The Moche of Ancient Peru: New Tomb of Royal Splendor." *National Geographic* 177, no. 6 (1990): 2–15.

———. *Sipán.* Lima: Cervecería Backus and Johnston, 1994.

———. *Sipán: Descubrimiento e investigación.* Privately published, 2004.

Bawden, Garth. *The Moche.* Cambridge, Mass.: Blackwell, 1996.

Bourget, Steve. "Rituals of Sacrifice: Its Practice at Huaca de la Luna and Its Representation in Moche Iconography." In *Moche Art and Archaeology in Ancient Peru,* edited by J. Pillsbury, 89–109. Washington, D.C.: National Gallery of Art, 2001.

Donnan, Christopher B. "The Thematic Approach to Moche Art: The Presentation Theme." In *Moche Art of Peru,* by C. Donnan, 158–73. Los Angeles: Museum of Cultural History, University of California, 1978.

———. "An Assessment of the Validity of the Naymlap Dynasty." In *The Northern Dynasties: Kingship and Statecraft in Chimor,* edited by M. E. Moseley and A. Cordy-Collins, 243–74. Washington, D.C.: Dumbarton Oaks Research Library and Collection, 1990.

Donnan, Christopher B., and Luis Jaime Castillo. "Finding the Tomb of a Moche Priestess." *Archaeology* 45, no. 6 (1992): 38–42.

Donnan, Christopher B., and Donna McClelland. *The Burial Theme in Moche Iconography.* Washington, D.C.: Dumbarton Oaks, 1979.

Hinsley, Curtis. "The World as Marketplace: Commodification of the Exotic at the World's Columbian Exposition, Chicago, 1893." In *Exhibiting Cultures. The Poetics and Politics* of *Museum Display*, edited by I. Karp and S. D. Lavine, 344–65. Washington, D.C.: Smithsonian Institution Press, 1991.

Kirkpatrick, Sidney D. *Lords of Sipán: A True Story of Pre-Inca Tombs, Archaeology, and Crime.* New York: William Morrow, 1992.

Kirshenblatt-Gimblett, Barbara. "World Heritage and Cultural Economics." In *Museum Frictions: Public Cultures/Global Transformations,* edited by I. Karp, C. A. Kratz, L. Szwaja, and T. Ybarra-Fausto, 161–202. Durham, N.C.: Duke University Press, 2006.

Kohl, Philip L., and Clare Fawcett, eds. *Nationalism, Politics, and the Practice of Archaeology.* Cambridge: Cambridge University Press, 1995.

Lutz, Catherine A., and Jane L. Collins. *Reading National Geographic.* Chicago: University of Chicago Press, 1993.

Makowski, Krzysztof. "La deidad suprema en la iconografía Mochica: ¿Como definirla?" In *Moche: Hacia el final del milenio,* edited by S. Uceda and E. Mujica, 343–81. Lima: Fondo Editorial, Pontificia Universidad Católica del Perú; Trujillo: Universidad Nacional de Trujillo, 2003.

Moseley, Michael E., and Kent C. Day, eds. *Chan Chan: Andean Desert City.* Albuquerque: University of New Mexico Press, 1982.

Reinhard, Johan. "Peru's Ice Maidens." *National Geographic* 189 no. 6 (1996): 62–81.

Shimada, Izumi. *Sicán: Lost Tombs of Peru.* Television documentary produced by the Discovery Channel, aired October 4, 2000.

Silverman, Helaine. "Archaeology and the 1997 Peruvian Hostage Crisis." *Anthropology Today* 15, no. 1 (1999): 9–13.

———. "Touring Ancient Times: The Present and Presented Past in Contemporary Peru." *American Anthropologist* 104, no. 3 (2002): 881–902.

Strong, William Duncan. "Finding the Tomb of a Warrior-God." *National Geographic* 91, no. 4 (1947): 453–82.

Tello, Julio C. *Paracas: Primera parte.* Lima: Empresa Gráfica T. Scheuch, 1959.

Tello, Julio C., and Toribio Mejía Xesspe. *Paracas: Segunda parte, cavernas y necrópolis.* Lima: Universidad Nacional Mayor de San Marcos, 1979.

Uceda, Santiago, Ricardo Morales Gamarra, José Canziani Amico, and María Montoya Vera. "Investigaciones sobre la arquitectura y relieves polícromos en la Huaca de la Luna, Valle de Moche." In *Moche: Propuestas y perspectivas,* edited by S. Uceda and E. Mujica, 251–303. Lima: Instituto Francés de Estudios Andinos; Trujillo: Universidad Nacional de la Libertad, 1994.

Verdery, Katherine. *The Political Lives of Dead Bodies: Reburial and Postsocialist Change.* New York: Columbia University Press, 1999.

Part 2

Controlling Archaeology

Commentary

Notes on the Work of Heritage in the Age of Archaeological Reproduction

QUETZIL E. CASTAÑEDA

This is how one pictures the angel of history. His face is turned toward the past. Where we perceive a chain of events, he sees one single catastrophe which keeps piling wreckage and hurls it in front of his feet. The angel would like to stay, awaken the dead, and make whole what has been smashed. But a storm is blowing in from Paradise; it has got caught in his wings with such a violence that the angel can no longer close them. The storm irresistibly propels him into the future to which his back is turned, while the pile of debris before him grows skyward.

Benjamin 1968a: 257–58

From where and when did the proliferation of discourses, policies, investigations, protocols, practices, programs, degree plans, and foundations of and for heritage begin? Twenty years ago, few thought about heritage but instead were hotly debating identity politics, multiculturalism, and the survival of cultures in advanced late capitalism and in nationalist modernities. The decade from the mid-1980s to mid-1990s was the final battle in the great (and global) culture wars over cultural diversity and rights. Ironically, even though culture won—that is, "culture" and "cultures" were finally accepted as really real reality that could not be uprooted by modernization schemes and political solutions to the problem of the Other—Culture itself, that is, culture as a concept and theory, died (valiantly, no doubt). On this battlefield, Heritage itself was erected—pardon my poiesis—as the monument to this war and the ongoing wreckage of culture. An Angel of Heritage must have witnessed this catastrophe and, wishing to restore a lost holism, only managed to convert all the fragments and debris of culture into the detritus of heritage, which continues to pile on high. This, in short, is the origin story of the current proliferation of kinds, types, forms, modes, concepts, conflicts, politics, strategies, and analyses of "heritage" in the globalized world today, as well as in this book that you, dear reader, have in your hands.

In light of this image, consider the differences between Laurajane Smith, Christopher Matthews and Matthew Palus, and O. Hugo Benavides in the following chapters. Smith argues that heritage is a mode of governmentality, that is, a strategy of control and management of "heritage."[1] This implies, even presupposes, that archaeology is deeply interconnected with heritage, even though the force of Smith's argument is to analyze the conflicted tensions between the past constructed as an archaeologically managed heritage and the past pre-given as a heritage whose authentic meaning is constituted by indigenous values. Benavides is not at all concerned with the management of material heritage; instead, he focuses on discourses, symbolic value, knowledge, and meanings of heritage, which archaeology, archaeologists, the state, and indigenous groups struggle to shape and control. Although these two chapters present overtly different conceptualizations of heritage to analyze quite distinct socio-ethnographic situations, their shared perspective and commonality in approach are revealed when contrasted to the chapter by Matthews and Palus. The latter assert that archaeology and heritage are antagonistically opposed and disjunctive. Underlying this proposition is the idea that heritage is like culture and is a manifestation or expression of a "culture" of a social group.

Heritage, for Matthews and Palus, is, therefore, not at all a strategy but a real, material, and meaningful bundle of things that constitute at least part of "the past" of a cultural community. This is not to say that there is not a theory embedded within this latter mode of heritage; in this view, heritage is not a strategy but the goals, objects, objectives, and means of strategies that have a rightful relation of use and ownership over their past. Furthermore, any and all social groups must have, do have, and have a right to have *their* heritage so as to maintain the integrity of *their* culture and identity. Heritage references discernible cultures (cultural communities in the plural). In short, these authors present three visions of heritage: heritage as a management toolkit of social sciences (Smith), heritage as a field of contested interpretations (Benavides), and heritage as a practical materiality lived and experienced on the ground (Matthews and Palus). By clarifying the points of difference and overlap between these three views, I chart my own conceptualization of heritage.

If we position ourselves alongside Walter Benjamin, who envisions history through the figure of the Angel of History (see chapter epigraph), we can begin to deepen our understanding of why *heritage* has so often replaced *culture* as the term of reference in archaeological discourse, public debate, policy formation, and international intergovernmental discussions. Benjamin construes history as a continuous catastrophe that keeps on accumulating wreckage, which the Angel of History looks upon as he relentlessly moves into the future while facing backwards toward the ever-growing pile of debris, that is, the "past." In this analogy, Benjamin's catastrophe points to the continuous critique of the holism of culture, the irrefutable demise of essentialism, the endless hybridization of identity, the proliferation of split and divided subjectivities, and the defrocking of multiculturalism as strategies of control and consumer diversification that began in the late 1970s. What remains are fragments and shards of cultural wholes that have no unassailable transcendent or even immanent logic of reintegration. To return to my question posed above, why the erasure of holism in this turn from culture to heritage? The answer is identified in the language of the last sentence of UNESCO's definition of "intangible cultural heritage" (UNESCO 2003: Article 2 "definitions" [#1–2]; see also UNESCO 1972: Article 1, "definitions"): heritage, via the "compatible existing international human rights instruments," functions to manage and govern (that is, "legislates") identity, especially in the context of "the requirements of mutual respect . . . and sustainable development."[2]

The application of Benjamin's allegory of history to archaeology provides additional insights. If we substitute the holism, unity, essentialism, and so on of culture for the historical "chain of events," then a curious understanding is revealed: we might very well recognize that we ourselves seek to be "the angel [of Heritage who] would like to stay, awaken the dead, and make whole what has been smashed" (Benjamin 1968a: 258). When I say "we," I refer to all of us who participate in the activity of heritage management, dispute, litigation, claims, interpretation, protection—that is, all of us archaeologists, aborigines, UNESCO heritage administrators, cultural resource managers, anthropologists, indigenous groups, citizens of Eastport, international lawyers, and heritage NGOs—who would like to recuperate the "past" as heritage for an identifiable cultural community as a means that might reestablish the integrity, propriety, and proper ownership (if not also the integrative unity) of culture, community, identity, and belonging via the concept and diverse practices of heritage. Certainly, the archaeological impulse to investigate, know, and restore the historical pasts of humanity in general and of specific societies in particular is evidence enough of this nostalgic desire to make the present moment "whole" by reunifying it with a resuscitated past.[3] In turn, all the various disaggregating techniques that seek to document, classify, quantify, and otherwise isolate artifacts and data (that is, the archaeological record) are, ultimately, always subordinated to the larger project of constituting and constructing wholes out of diverse fragments and by mobilizing these into coherent series, such as styles, horizons, sites, and typologies, and these into encompassing hierarchies of series, such as regions, city-states, societies, civilizations, human civilization, and humanity.

Matthews and Palus (chapter 6) explicitly acknowledge this motivation and ideal in their vision and use of heritage as the material expressions of identity that properly belong to each unique cultural group versus to a universalized humanity. Thus, as already noted, they oppose heritage and archaeology, the latter of which, they are correct to point out, emerges as a Western discipline that tends to transform the particular pasts of distinct groups into the legacy of a generalized human civilization. When archaeology is so able to universalize heritage—that is, reconstitute it as part and parcel of a unitary modernity belonging to everyone—then its "authentic" nature as the property of particular cultures and social groups is radically diminished, if not entirely denied. This oppositional logic, which makes "heritage" and "archaeology" antinomies, is also evident in Smith's theorization of heritage as governmentality, á la Michel Foucault (chapter 5). Although archaeology and heritage are conceptualized as interlinked processes via governmentality, Smith's application of governmentality presupposes the existence of a heritage-past that lies outside of the hegemony of strategic resource management and is in some sense authentic, aboriginal, and untainted by Western science (Smith, this volume; see also Smith 2004).

To point out this contradiction is not to critique Smith's premise so much as to identify this duplicity in heritage as irreducible. Heritage in a loose, nontheoretical, nonanalytical sense is indeed the property of a cultural community as its (rightfully or wrongfully) inherited past. Yet heritage is a strategy of power in the hands of archaeology as a tool of state control and technology of governance of cultural minorities through the shaping of identity-belonging. Thus, along the lines of Smith's argument, which is also based on Foucault's theory of governmentality, I suggest the need to conceptualize a theory of heritage in relation to power. By coining the term *heritage-power*, along the lines of the French philosopher's well-known notion of bio-power (Foucault 1980), we can begin to think about and investigate heritage in new ways such that we make use of it instead of its simply using us. Despite the Foucaultian basis of Smith's theorizing heritage, there is a lingering leftist-Marxian or Weberian assumption of domination whereby power (more precisely, heritage as a strategy of power, that is, governmentality) is wielded exclusively by the dominant; in this and other intellectual traditions, subordinate groups are categorically and theoretically excluded from having, possessing, and even using power, since it is the very absence of power that subordinates the dominated group and gives them their identity as subordinate! Foucault's notion of power, and thus also his theory of governmentality, however, eschews the conceptualization of power as, first, something that can be possessed and, second, something that works only (by definition) in a top-down fashion (Foucault 1980, 1991a, 1991b, 1991c; Gordon 1991; Hindess 1996; Rose 1996).

It is this significant caveat to the analysis of heritage as a mode of governmentality that Benavides offers. In his chapter, Benavides implicitly argues that the management of heritage discourses of identity is not simply a weapon of "the strong" that is only and always possessed and wielded by the state, science, or other hegemonic institutions. Heritage, as a strategy of power by which to manage the past and to generate narratives of identity, is available for diverse social agents to exercise. Thus, in the Ecuadorian case that Benavides analyzes in chapter 7, archaeological heritage is a resource and strategy for producing discourses of identity by agents invested in the national project and by those involved in the indigenous movement. Certainly, there is differential access to the use and effectiveness of the exercise of this heritage-power. But just as indubitably, heritage is available as a strategy for those who accede—willingly or with friction and resistance—to the conditions and dynamics of its deployment.

Here, and in line with Foucault's notions of strategy and power, specifically bio-power (Foucault 1980), I refer to the necessary transformations in the subject positioning and mode of subjectivity of those who enter the field of contestation in which heritage is generated, managed, and disputed. This effectiveness in shifting aspects of subjectivity is what Smith points to as a significant dimension of heritage as governmentality. This logic also underlies the brief, negative reference that Matthews and Palus make regarding how archaeology, via certain kinds of outreach and engagement with publics, implicitly seeks to convert stakeholders into archaeologists or archaeological subjects—that is, subjects with the proper responsibilities, obligations, viewpoints, attitudes, identities, and habits for the assumption of ownership and management of archaeological heritage. Several recent studies (including Castañeda 2005; Castañeda and Castillo Cocom 2002; Castillo Cocom 2002; Breglia 2006) discuss this dimension of the work of heritage in producing the proper subjects of archaeology to inherit the stewardship of archaeologically produced heritage. Similarly, Benavides in his chapter details a case in which members of the indigenous movement of Ecuador have already entered into the field of power to assert themselves as proper managers and interpreters of the meaning and messages of heritage. In that case, however, the indigenous groups enter the field of contestation as "undomesticated," improper subjects (from the view of science) because the meanings they assert do not comply with the Ecuadorian establishment archaeology.

In focusing on these conflicts of interpretation of heritage, Benavides' chapter stands in contrast to the chapters by Smith and by Matthews and Palus. Whereas Smith attends to the issues of the management of heritage materials or "resources" (as cultural resource management, or CRM), Matthews and Palus focus on the fieldwork negotiation with stakeholders by archaeologists. These authors not only conceive of heritage differently but also, as one might suspect, problematize heritage as an object of study in three distinct ways. These points of difference return us to multiple expressions, forms, and modes of heritage and to the question of how to make sense of this diversity.

To my mind, it is necessary to situate (archaeological, cultural, tangible) heritage in history as a phenomenon that is not at all independent of archaeology but instead exists in strict and intimate relationship to it. Indeed, the work of heritage only begins to become what we now understand it to be in what I would call the "age of archaeological reproduction." This phrase borrows from Benjamin's (1968b) famous analysis of the work of art: he argues that the modern era's technological capacity to create identical or mimetic copies has a transformative effect on the aura of art, or what can be glossed as its attribute of uniqueness and authenticity. In adapting Benjamin's notion to heritage, I first point out that the technologies of archaeological reproduction are not restricted to the discipline and science of archaeology; rather, archaeological reproduction consists of an inclusive panoply of methods and techniques of preservation, conservation, protection, and restoration that are applied within a variety of practical fields—ecology, history, environmentalism, architecture, even tourism—to re-create an origin/original (that is, an *archæ*) or its image. Many have cited Benjamin's quotable phrase that "aura withers away" as a result of technological capacity for mimetic reproduction. However, many studies have demonstrated that this is not actually or empirically the case; aura, authenticity, and the value of uniqueness thrive in modernity. Furthermore, in a less quoted section of his analysis, Benjamin argues not that aura "disappears" but rather that the basis of aura shifts from the holism of "tradition" and ritual to what he calls "politics."[4] Similarly, I suggest that the basis and nature of heritage in the age of archaeological reproduction have been undergoing a profound transformation in the conditions of possibility underlying heritage, that is, from relatively unproblematized "inheritance" based in relations of identity to tradition, to politicized construction of identity and cultural ownership in contexts of advanced, globalized capitalism.

As an ethnographer of archaeology—that is, as one who investigates archaeology ethnographically, using ethnography—I am fascinated by the way archaeology creates reality. Of particular significance is the key difference between the archaeological reproduction of the past and what Benjamin analyzed as the mimetic copying of modern technologies such as photography. Put simply, archaeology invents (that is, literally constructs) complex representations of the past that are not mimetic but simply appear—and not always to everyone, of course—as if they were faithfully identical copies and transparent mimetic representations of a past that, however, actually never did exist as such in the manner constructed for tourists today. As I have argued elsewhere (Castañeda 1996), all archaeological constructions are forms of hyper-reality (Eco 1990) and simulacra (Baudrillard 1995).[5]

Consider one of the primary truisms taught in introductory archaeology classes: archaeology destroys the past in its process of investigation; that is, the possibility of retrieving information and even the materiality of the past is destroyed through specific methodologies of knowledge production. We may note, therefore, that this is one among several reasons why, even in cases where there is restoration, the resulting ruins—which often take form as life-size, scale-model "replicas" of cities or settlements—are never identical to any actual past. That archaeology destroys the past, even as it salvages specific elements of that totality to create a material and partial representation of that past, requires an unquestioned epistemological trick on which to ground the scientific agenda of archaeology. The concept of the "archaeological record" is precisely this epistemological anchorage that allows for the production and accumulation of knowledge based on the destruction of the knowable material of the past. The archaeological record comprises not just the raw, material, disjunctive, and fragmentary remains of the past but also the full gamut of field notes, drawings, photographs, measurements, descriptions, analyses, and recordings created by archaeologists as the documentation of data (also see Patrick 1985).

Without in any way suggesting a philosophical opposition between mind and matter, I do assert that it would be analytically useful to recognize, investigate, and engage the following three forms or registers "of heritage": the material fragments of the past, the archaeological inscription of this materiality as data, and the interpretation of the archaeological past. Even in cases where there is overlap among and intersection of these three forms, each presents distinct fields of power, contestation, knowledge, and practice. Differences among the three chapters of this section illustrate this point. Each of these chapters, I suggest, can be viewed as having analyzed the field of political contestation that is defined and organized by the problems posed by one of these forms of heritage. Smith's analysis of the management of cultural resources as governmentality is situated in the problem of the control of the materiality of the archaeological record—that is, that part of the record that consists of the disjunctive series of object-fragments of the past. Her analysis of how CRM as governmentality impinges on indigenous rights and ownership of heritage in this first register definitely points toward, but is not about, the conflicts of interpretation and meaning of archaeological heritage. Matthews and Palus's discussion of the fieldwork negotiation between archaeologists and stakeholders is centrally focused on the struggle to define the status and constitution of archaeological data out of the fragmentary materiality of the past (or what are called "resources" by Smith). Similarly, this focus on the constitution of archaeological data (the second form of heritage) implicates but really does not address the conflicts in the other two registers of heritage. In turn, Benavides's attention to the competing narratives and discourses by which the past is interpreted as meaningful directly targets the problem of heritage as the politics of knowledge (production). At stake for Benavides are the politics and problem of the interpretation and meaning of archaeological heritage, not the conflicts over the archaeological record—that is, heritage in either form or register of material resources or data production.

Each of these focal points and their attendant analyses emerge from the empirical situation. In other words, the analyses are not imposed from above by the dictates of some (high) theory. Instead, the analyses focus on what the authors view as the significant issues and debates within the context in which they are working. Each gives priority to one of the three specific forms or registers of heritage (material resources, scientific data, interpretation of the past) that I have identified. From these three registers of heritage, we have three different logics of or strategies for analysis. To put it simply, the conflicts over any one of these three registers may not have any connection to conflicts in either of the other two domains. The logic and agenda of analyses must attend to this contextual particularity. The value and insights of these three chapters, including their differences, are due in fact to this kind of close inspection of the ethnographic materials.

Each of these key concepts (heritage in the form, or register, of materiality, data, and interpretation) can include types of objects but also spaces and fields of contention, practices of control and use, and politics and juridical legislation. These three forms can be further differentiated from two distinct strategies of heritage—that is, two strategies by which heritage forms are shaped into objects, means, and targets of struggle. In the first, heritage is a strategy of identity. In the second, it is a strategy of governmentality.

On the one hand, what I mean by heritage as a strategy of identity builds on what Clifford Geertz long ago called "primordial origins." Geertz used this term to designate six types of resources for imagining nation, building national community, and forging shared belonging. In this framework, the symbols and images of the nation are constructed out of a strategic selection of the materials given by history, religion, geography, tradition, and so on. Archaeological patrimony is not one of Geertz's types of primordial origins, yet it is interesting because it crosscuts his categories in a unique way. It is a resource and a strategy to construct and imagine "nation" (and therefore, "national modernity") that is concretely generated, materialized, shaped, and disseminated—via the sciences of archaeology and anthropology (with ancillary help from associated sciences). In other words, whereas Geertz's primordial origins are in some sense inherent to community as lived practices, customs, traditions, and values, the significance of (archaeological) patrimony for national identity formation is that it is constructed outside of the quotidian, experiential life of a community by expert-knowledge producers. The interpretive content of this knowledge is reformulated into narratives of and master debates about the nation as a unified, modern community of identity and belonging. I would call this strategic use of "heritage" patrimony or primordial heritage to contrast it from contemporary lay concepts of "heritage"; equally, these formulations point to distinct conflicts over how community is imagined.

On the other hand, heritage as a strategy of governmentality entails a radically different politics of heritage. In heritage governmentality, identity is not the product of primordial heritage but instead a crucial mechanism and tool crafted to control, regulate, manage, and, especially, claim rights of use and ownership over heritage as data and resource. As a rationality for managing and regulating heritage, identity is displaced as an issue of conflict. As a rationality for claiming rights and ownership of heritage, identity is a powerful weapon that is increasingly supported by a wide array of customary, national, and international legalities.

To conclude these notes, I want to point out that heritage can be used in an untheorized and generic way to reference anything that comes "from the past" and that is claimed as part of one or another group's culture and identity. Heritage in this sense is not an analytical category, much less a concept. It is simply the dictionary definition of the word. But heritage can be theorized and conceptualized as a methodological tool that facilitates analyses of and active engagement with "heritage" issues, conflicts, debates, stakeholders, and publics. The question then becomes, what would be the parameters and elements of such an analytical and methodological tool? In forging an analytical concept of heritage, we must pay attention to the fact that not everything that appears on the surface as "heritage," or is asserted to be such, is indeed heritage in an analytical or methodological sense. Furthermore, not all "heritage" is heritage in the same way, with the same stakes, with the same value, and with the same politics. To create a notion of heritage that is useful to social science, including archaeological research, the concept must not be used as a reified umbrella term that lumps variations and differences together indiscriminately. To be methodologically useful, a concept of heritage must distinguish types, forms, modes, and variations of heritage. Toward this end, I have sketched three forms or registers of heritage—material resource, archaeological data, and discursive knowledge—that comprise distinct, yet at times overlapping and intersecting, fields of power and contestation. It is in and through these fields of power that "heritage" is identified, defined, claimed, legislated, regulated, controlled, managed, owned, used, sold, consumed, and re-created. As well, I have suggested two strategic modes of heritage, which may or may not overlap or intersect in any given or empirical situation. On the one hand, primordial heritage, or "patrimony," is a strategy and resource for narrating and imagining the nation. On the other hand, heritage is a mode of governmentality, that is, a strategic rationality devised to manage, regulate, and control "the past" as it is manifested as data and resource.

Heritage is many things, that is, it can refer to a wide variety of phenomena at any one time. Yet the structure outlined above may help us investigate heritage by facilitating our thinking, formulation of problems, descriptions, and analyses. Instead of working like an Angel of Heritage to reconstruct a grand theoretical whole or singular master concept out of the debris and fragments of heritage, we should perhaps operate more like rescue workers in the ongoing wreckage of "the past" with analytical strategies that attend to the specificity of situations and issues.

Notes

1. See Smith 2004. My thinking of heritage as governmentality was independently formulated based on my work at Chichén Itzá (Castañeda 2005, 2009).

2. The 1972 Convention on World Heritage defines cultural and natural heritage, both of which are defined as manifestations of a "universal" value. Despite this expression of universal significance, there is nonetheless no innate logical coherence, integration, or holism that constitutes world heritage. Heritage in popular discourse (as well as in UNESCO discourse) is or can be both universal/universalized and culturally particular, or only one or the other. Sometimes these two senses are in contradiction with each other and sometimes not, as in, for example, UNESCO's universalizing conception of world heritage and its culturally particularist notion of intangible heritage found in the 2003 Convention on Intangible Cultural Heritage.

3. See Benavides 2005 on the work of nostalgia in archaeology.

4. See Castañeda 2000. Note that Benjamin's use of the term *politics* seems to obliquely refer to political economy, generally, and the politics of capitalism, specifically.

5. There are significant conceptual differences between Umberto Eco's (1990) concept of hyperreal, Jean Baudrillard's (1995) concept of simulacra, and Benjamin's notion of ruin (see Castañeda 2000). On the face of it, Eco's and Baudrillard's ideas of hyperreal and simulacra are the "copies" to Benjamin's idea of ruin, which is posed as the "original." The idea of the ruin is the idea of a unique, sui generis time-space materiality that constitutes the origin-anchors around which are produced, endlessly, copies. "Hyperreal" is the idea of such impeccable, better-than-perfect copies not simply of a work of art but of built environments in which persons experience a reality that corresponds to the time-place that was replicated. "Simulacra" is the idea that such copies "overwhelm" and displace the original with their fabricated materiality; the copy and the experience of the copy precede any encounter with the "original"—if it ever even existed. However, the hyperreal and simulacra come to displace any original of which they are copies and thus become sui generis, unique ruins in themselves. This is what archaeological constructs of the past are: simulacra that have completely displaced the "real" original and substituted themselves as the ruin. The Knossos that one can visit today is perhaps the quintessential example and not unique at all to archaeology.

References Cited

Baudrillard, Jean. *Simulacra and Simulation.* Ann Arbor: University of Michigan Press, 1995.
Benavides, Hugo. "Disciplining the Past, Policing the Present." Paper presented in Wenner-Gren Workshop, Sociological Archaeology, Open School of Ethnography and Anthropology, Chichén Itzá, Mexico, June 1–5, 2005.
Benjamin, Walter. "Theses on the Philosophy of History." In *Illuminations,* 253–63. New York: Schocken Books, 1968. [1968a]

————. "The Work of Art in the Age of Mechanical Reproduction." In *Illuminations,* 217–51. New York: Schocken Books, 1968. [1968b]

Breglia, Lisa C. *Monumental Ambivalence: The Politics of Heritage.* Austin: University of Texas Press, 2006.

Castañeda, Quetzil E. *In the Museum of Maya Culture: Touring Chichén Itzá.* Minneapolis: University of Minnesota Press, 1996.

————. "Approaching Ruins." *Visual Anthropology Review* 16, no. 2 (Fall–Winter 2000): 43–70.

————. "Tourism 'Wars' in the Yucatán." *Anthropology News* 46, no. 5 (May 2005): 8–9.

————. "Heritage and Indigeneity: Transformations in the Politics of Tourism." In *Cultural Tourism in Latin America: The Politics of Space and Imagery,* edited by M. Baud and A. Ypeji, 263–96. Leiden and Boston: Brill, 2009.

Castañeda, Quetzil E., and Juan A. Castillo Cocom. "Deciphering the Archaeology Glyph." Paper presented at the Meetings of the American Anthropology Association, New Orleans, November 22, 2002.

Castillo Cocom, Juan A. "Privilege and Ethics in Archaeology: The Experience as Fiction." Paper presented at "International Symposium: Towards a More Ethical Mayanist Archaeology," University of British Columbia, Vancouver, November 12–14, 2002.

Eco, Umberto. *Travels in Hyperreality.* Reprint, Fort Washington, Penn.: Harvest Books, 1990.

Foucault, Michel. *The History of Sexuality,* vol. 1. New York: Vintage, 1980.

————. "Governmentality." In *The Foucault Effect,* edited by G. Burchell, C. Gordon, and P. Miller, 87–104. Chicago: University of Chicago Press, 1991. [1991a]

————. "Politics and the Study of Discourse." In *The Foucault Effect,* edited by G. Burchell, C. Gordon, and P. Miller, 53–72. Chicago: University of Chicago Press, 1991. [1991b]

————. "Questions of Method." In *The Foucault Effect,* edited by G. Burchell, C. Gordon, and P. Miller, 73–86. Chicago: University of Chicago Press, 1991. [1991c]

Gordon, Collin. "Governmentality and Rationality." In *The Foucault Effect,* edited by G. Burchell, C. Gordon, and P. Miller, 1–52. Chicago: University of Chicago Press, 1991.

Hindess, Barry. "Liberalism, Socialism and Democracy: Variations on a Governmental Theme." In *Foucault and Political Reason,* edited by A. Barry, T. Osborne, and N. Rose, 65–97. London: University of Chicago Press, 1996.

Patrick, Linda. "Is There an Archaeological Record?" In *Archeological Method and Theory,* vol. 3, edited by M. Schiffer, 27–62. London: Academic Press, 1985.

Rose, Nikolas. "Governing 'Advanced' Liberal Democracies." In *Foucault and Political Reason,* edited by A. Barry, T. Osborne, and N. Rose, 37–64. London: University of Chicago Press, 1996.

Smith, Laurajane. *Archaeological Theory and the Politics of Cultural Heritage.* London: Routledge, 2004.

UNESCO. "Convention Concerning the Protection of the World Cultural and Natural Heritage." Paris, November 16, 1972.

————. "Convention for the Safeguarding of the Intangible Cultural Heritage." Paris, October 17, 2003.

5

Theorizing Heritage

Legislators, Interpreters, and Facilitators

LAURAJANE SMITH

In many Western countries, such as the United States and Australia, cultural resource management (CRM) is often defined as simply a technical process concerned with the preservation of sites, places, and landscapes considered to have "heritage value." The objects of management—"cultural resources" or "cultural heritage"—are often defined through the legal and public policy systems that underpin CRM, or by resource managers themselves, as possessing some innate value to science, education, or society as a whole. CRM is often characterized in the archaeological literature and discourse as the job you get when you cannot get a "real" archaeological job. It is often defined as a process devoid of any theoretical interest, as it is simply a technical process that, while it may employ the latest methodological and research developments in archaeology, has no other significant interaction with research and theoretical developments in the discipline.

However, I argue that CRM is a significant area of archaeological practice that plays an important role in legitimizing certain archaeological discourses and, consequently, theoretical positions both within and outside of the academy. The practice and discourse of CRM can also delegitimize or displace other discourses or knowledge systems that focus on the past and its material culture. In effect, archaeological knowledge and practices are given legitimacy and authority within the state via CRM. This has significant consequences for archaeological theory, because the role that archaeological knowledge assumes within the state works to govern or regulate the expression of archaeological discourse. This does not mean that diverse stakeholder groups do nothing to successfully challenge archaeological knowledge and practice; these challenges, however, are often a consequence of the role played by archaeology as a technology of government. Moreover, through these challenges, archaeologists may subvert dominant disciplinary discourses. In developing these arguments, I draw heavily on my previous attempts to theorize heritage (Smith 2000,

2001, 2004, 2006). In developing the idea of archaeology as a technology of govern-ment in previous work, I have tended to concentrate on elucidating and exploring the way in which CRM has regulated and "governed" archaeological theory and practice. However, in this chapter, I explore the consequences that challenges to archaeological expertise have not only for archaeological practice but also, by impli-cation, for the communities with which archaeologists work. In addition, archaeolo-gists working within the constraints of CRM may collaborate with communities and in doing so not only challenge the regulation and governance of archaeological theory and practice but also facilitate the renegotiation of power/knowledge rela-tions between communities and the state.

Legislators and Interpreters

An understanding of how archaeology becomes a "technology of government," and the significance of this for both archaeological practice and the relationship that the discipline as a whole tends to have with communities, rest on several arguments that I have made in detail elsewhere (Smith 2004). The first point consists of the roles played by intellectuals in Western society; the work of Zygmunt Bauman (1987, 1992) is important here. He identifies two roles: that of legislator and interpreter. The legislator role is, as the name implies, an authoritative position, drawing on tradi-tional Enlightenment concepts of the rationality of knowledge and the assumption that intellectuals possess superior knowledge and are committed to the search for "truth." The role of the legislator is to make authoritative and binding statements. The role of the interpreter, in contrast, is to "translate" discourses constructed in one knowledge system so that they become intelligible to other knowledge systems. This is potentially a more socially and politically progressive, though less authoritative, role for intellectuals. However, as Bauman argues, the two forms of intellectual prac-tice coexist, and neither abandons the authority and privilege given to assumptions about the professional and superior rational knowledge of the intellectual.

Bauman's discussion of intellectuals provides a useful critique, which can be drawn on to show how expert knowledge is taken up and used within state institu-tions. This is important for understanding what archaeological knowledge does in the realm of public policy, as it extends our understanding of intellectual expertise beyond the academy and allows us to consider CRM in the context of state negotia-tions over the legitimacy of cultural, class, and social identity. To understand the consequences that archaeological knowledge and practice have for other interests, stakeholders, or community groups, one must recognize that disciplinary knowledge and practice does cultural and political work that extends well beyond what indi-vidual archaeologists may intend. Knowledge, whether conveyed in a legislative or an interpretive mode, is utilized by the state, and its use not only draws on the privi-

lege and authority given to intellectuals within state institutions but also continually legitimizes and re-creates its authority. This has consequences for community
groups and other stakeholders whose knowledge about the past and heritage may be
constructed outside of the knowledge frameworks privileged by Western intellectual
practice. To understand the use that archaeological knowledge is put to in the form
of CRM, one may turn to a consideration of governmentality.

Governmentality and Technologies of Government

The governmentality thesis derives from Michel Foucault's (1991) later work, which
considers how knowledge is taken up within social institutions and identifies the
mechanics of the legislative and interpretative roles assigned to intellectuals. The
literature on governmentality argues that intellectual knowledge is incorporated
into the act of governing populations and social problems by "rendering the world
thinkable, taming its intractable reality by subjecting it to the disciplined analyses
of thought" (Rose and Miller 1992: 182; see also Rose 1991, 1993). Archaeological
rationality, emphasized by the logical positivism of processualism, became useful
in defining populations through both their archaeological pasts and the heritage
objects and places that were defined as representing a specific past (Smith 2004).
The discourse of archaeological science and professionalism that developed during
the 1960s and 1970s found synergy with the stress that liberal modernity placed
on rationality and the search for universal truths. Archaeological knowledge began
to be publicly promoted as based on rigorous scientific "objective" methodologies.
Notwithstanding these internal critiques within the discipline that questioned (and
continue to question) the legitimacy of disciplinary claims to neutrality and objectivity, a *public* archaeological discourse arose in the 1970s that laid claims to traditional
Western intellectual authority and privilege. These claims were disseminated publicly through a growing number of outreach programs by academic archaeological
departments, museums, and professional organizations, as well as through lobbying
by individual archaeologists and archaeological organizations in the 1960s and 1970s
in the form of legislation to protect archaeological sites.

Claims to know the meaning and value of the past or to have special access to
a unique view of the past are often important to diverse groups for defining their
identity, a sense of community and belonging, and a sense of place (Smith 2006).
Communities—whether defined geographically or through shared cultural, social,
or political experiences and values—often come into conflict with each other and
with national projects and perceptions of a wider collective identity. Conflict often
centers on how the past is understood and how it may (de-)legitimize the construction of certain social and cultural identities. Archaeological knowledge is one of the

areas of expertise that is called upon to interpret or legislate over these claims—to in effect arbitrate or govern the legitimacy of these claims—so that they may be rendered tractable by the state.

Expert knowledge thus becomes enmeshed in the political arena—in the exercise of power and the interplay of discourse and ideology. Yet at the same time, expertise is depoliticized, as it is seen to rest on technical rational calculation, which must operate above competing interests. Within archaeology, the epistemological reliance on logical positivism stresses objectivity and the pursuit of technical rigor. This depoliticizes archaeological knowledge and allows it to be utilized in the governance of social problems, which can, if done successfully, then reinforce its usefulness. Moreover, by rendering social problems as subject to the intervention of "rational" knowledge, the problems that are governed in this process are rendered nonpolitical and more technical in nature. Nikolas Rose and Peter Miller (1992: 175) define the process whereby the knowledge, techniques, procedures, and so on of a particular discipline become taken up in the regulation of populations as "technologies of government." Archaeology has been mobilized as a technology of government in the regulation or governance of social problems that intersect with claims about the meaning of the past and its heritage. Archaeological knowledge is particularly useful in this context, because these claims will inevitably be tied to physical objects or places. Material culture, or heritage, renders archaeological knowledge tangible, evidential, and thus "real," and this physicality further renders the social problems that intersect heritage open to technical intervention and regulation.

The heritage management process is the avenue through which archaeological knowledge becomes mobilized within the state as a technology of government. Archaeological knowledge, discourse, and values became largely constitutive of the heritage management process during the 1970s, a time characterized not only by the advent of the discourse of "processual science" in the discipline but also by an increase in competing public demands about the meaning and nature of heritage. As I have documented previously (Smith 2004), the late 1960s and 1970s saw an increase in archaeological concerns about protecting the past, alongside increasing public interest in heritage issues generally, and preservation issues in particular. Also at this time, Indigenous peoples became increasingly politically active in postcolonial nations and, significantly, public awareness of Indigenous land rights issues increased. This consequently presented postcolonial states with a social problem that needed both defining and regulating. This was a coincidental development that facilitated the uptake of archaeological knowledge, through CRM, as a technology of government. The whole process of CRM, which emphasizes the technical application of knowledge and expertise, works effectively to render wider political debates about the legitimacy of cultural and social claims on the past nonpolitical. It does this in two ways: first, by redefining these issues as issues of access to, or even ownership of, certain discrete heritage sites, so that wider social problems become narrowed down and redefined as conflicts over individual heritage sites; and second, by redefining these issues as technical issues of site management.

As John Tunbridge and Gregory Ashworth (1996) point out, all heritage is "dissonant." The cultural resources that are identified as important in defining someone's identity will inevitably exclude someone else. The comforting sense of belonging that some individuals or collectives derive from a sense of shared heritage will inevitably be discomforting for others. The dissonance and conflicts that occur at and around heritage sites and debates over ownership or control of sites, places, and landscapes are well documented in the heritage literature, and within CRM archaeological managers are often tasked with mitigating these conflicts where and when they occur. Although within CRM these conflicts are often seen or characterized as technical issues that may be site or place specific, one should understand that these conflicts actually exist within the context of wider conflicts and negotiations over the resolution of certain social problems. Heritage sites or cultural resources have symbolic authority within Western societies. The tangibility of material culture and its ability to represent, if not stand in for, collective identities makes those items identified as heritage, or as significant cultural resources, important *political* resources. The ability to have a collective's knowledge about the past taken seriously, for it to be given authority and legitimacy, has a consequence for the social, cultural, or political legitimacy with which that collective is regarded by the state. This has important political and cultural consequences for those subaltern communities whose knowledge and perceptions of the past (and the way in which these may underwrite their values and identities in the present) are granted—or not—authority and legitimacy. This is principally the case when demands for economic or political resources or claims for increased political or civil rights, equity, compensation and so forth are based on or legitimized through claims to collective identity. This can be particularly significant for Indigenous populations and communities whose claims for land, equity, and justice often rest on the assertion of their shared identity and the legitimacy of their cultural knowledge and experiences.

Nevertheless, the privileging and authorization of knowledge will also have significant consequences. Archaeology has made noteworthy gains through its position as a technology of government, and the position that the discipline's expert knowledge has attained with CRM ensures the discipline's access to material culture—its database. However, to maintain this access, archaeologists must continually rehearse the discourse of processual rationality and objectivity or risk compromising their usefulness as a technology of government, and thus their authority and privilege. This is not necessarily a conscious process, as collectively and individually archaeologists become implicated within the process of CRM and the role that it plays as a technology of government, and they are governed as much by this process as by the competing and marginalized claims and discourses of other interests and stakeholders. This does not mean to say that individual archaeologists do not attempt to subvert and challenge the authority and nature of archaeological knowledge and its privileged position as a technology of government. For instance, there are many archaeologists in postcolonial contexts who wish to, in various ways, support the aspirations of Indigenous or other communities or may seek to accept the legitimacy of Indigenous and other knowledge claims made outside of the frameworks of "rationality" (see, for instance, authors in Davidson, Lovell-Jones, and Bancroft 1995; Nicholas and Andrews 1997; Swidler et al. 1997; Smith and Wobst 2005). However, these archaeologists must continually confront the paradox of needing the authority of their positions as intellectuals and experts to be listened to by policy makers and other representatives of the state in supporting Indigenous issues, while simultaneously convincing state bureaucracies of the legitimacy of Indigenous knowledge. Archaeologists in this scenario inevitably confront the tension between legislative and interpretive roles—and the impasse caused by this paradox constrains substantive change.

The literature on governmentality tends to privilege the authority of knowledge; however, this point must not be overstated, for in fairness one ought to acknowledge that such authority is continually challenged. As noted above, this has been done not only by archaeologists but also by a range of wider stakeholders and interest groups. The point to be made here is that although archaeological knowledge gains power and authority in its mobilization as a technology of government, this does not mean that it cannot be successfully challenged from time to time. Because of such challenges, the balance of power between archaeologists and specific communities may be reshuffled and the authority of the intellectual, at least temporarily, renegotiated. What emerges from the identification of the role played by archaeology as a technology of government is the recognition that archaeological knowledge, theory construction, and practice sit within wider networks of social, cultural, and political conflict—and that they have, in some measure, consequences for those conflicts. This in turn reveals why the members of many interest groups (particularly Indigenous and community-based) can be so passionate and sustained in their critique of archaeological practice and knowledge (for examples of this criticism, see Deloria 1969, 1992; Langford 1983; Mihesuah 2000; Organ 1994; Riding In 2000; Watkins 2001, 2004). Debates over possession of heritage items, be they religious or secular artifacts or the ancestral remains of Indigenous peoples, are part of wider political negotiations over the legitimacy of a range of claims made on the interpretations of the past.

Case Study—Indigenous Australia

In Australia, Indigenous communities have a long history of contesting archaeological knowledge claims (for recent debates, see McNiven and Russell 2005; C. Smith and Wobst 2005; L. Smith 2004). This should not be viewed simply as a clash of cultural values, although it is that too. Rather, these clashes are part of wider struggles over the cultural and political legitimacy of modern Indigenous cultural claims to land, self-determination, and equitable access to education, housing, health, and other resources. Aboriginal people have argued for the right to control the management and use of their heritage sites, and this is more than a claim to access rights. Rather, the issue here is the right to control the way in which their identity as Indigenous Australians is presented and how the legitimacy of their claims to resources, justice, and equity are viewed in Australian society. By controlling public perception of their legitimacy, Indigenous people gain a modicum of power in wider negotiations with the state about the legitimacy of demands to land and other resources based on cultural identity and links to the past.

In the mid-1970s, when archaeological research at Lake Mungo had pushed the dating of Aboriginal occupation of Australia back to 40,000 years (see Lourandos 1997; Mulvaney and Kamminga 1999), public policy makers under the progressive Whitlam Labor government were able to utilize this knowledge to facilitate positive public debate to help develop controversial land rights legislation—what eventually became the 1976 Aboriginal Land Rights (Northern Territory) Act (Cth) under the conservative Frazer Liberal government. Although this example worked to the benefit of some Aboriginal communities at that time, there are many instances in which archaeological knowledge has been used to depoliticize Aboriginal cultural demands. The point here, however, is that archaeological knowledge works, whether for good or ill, to translate or legislate Indigenous demands, and archaeological knowledge effectively distances Indigenous communities from the nexus of political negotiation with the state and public policy makers.

In response, Indigenous communities have been lobbying archaeologists for decades to ensure that both archaeological research and management are undertaken with informed community consent and participation. The Waanyi Women's History Project, a case in point, was initiated by Waanyi women to record sites of cultural significance to Indigenous women within the confines of Boodjamulla National Park, in far northwestern Queensland. Although this case has been discussed in detail elsewhere (Smith, Morgan, and van der Meer 2003), the project illustrates the tensions that archaeologists and cultural resource managers find themselves navigating, between their roles formed by technologies of government and desires to support Indigenous aspirations. In 2000, when the project began, much of the cultural material within the national park had been effectively alienated from its traditional female custodians. This was in part because the colonial history of the region meant that many Waanyi people had been relocated to regions outside of their cultural territory and in part because women were often simply not consulted in a region of Australia known for its masculine approach to many issues, including land and cultural site management. The machismo culture associated with the Australian bush or out-back often makes the political and social terrain of rural Australia a difficult one for women to navigate (see McGrath 1997; Schaffer 1988; Smith 2006). Furthermore, many of the national park personnel were men, and they tended to assume that the appropriate people to talk to about cultural issues were Waanyi men, while Waanyi women also had difficulty in talking to male land managers about women's cultural business (see Smith, Morgan, and van der Meer 2003).

Much of the knowledge about the sites is sacred knowledge and cannot be im-parted to men, and the women were concerned that their sites were not known by the park managers and could inadvertently be in danger from day-to-day park management activities. The project had many pragmatic, cultural, and political aims. One of the pragmatic aims was to identify site locations and provide map coordinates for the park managers, so they would at least know where sensitive sites were located. A further aim was to establish protocols to facilitate communication between park managers and Waanyi women over site management. However, for the Waanyi women involved in the project, a significant cultural aim was to get back in touch with their heritage and to use the time in the field to pass on information to younger women. The political aim of the project was to assert the legitimacy of the role of women in the management of their cultural sites.

I was one of three female archaeologists who were invited by Waanyi women to participate in the project (Smith, Morgan, and van der Meer 2003). The role of the archaeologists in this project was to record the oral histories about the sites for the women, map them, and help write up the protocols for negotiating with the park managers. We agreed not to keep or publish information about the sites or any other data (Smith, Morgan, and van der Meer 2003). The success of this project may be measured by the fact that park managers now know where sites are and what they need to be careful about, whom to talk to about certain sites, and so on. However, Waanyi women have argued that the project has reaffirmed their connec-tions with their heritage and given them some control over its management (O'Keefe et al. 2001). The political aim of the project was achieved to the extent that Waanyi women have become more visible in the management landscape of Boodjamulla, and one member of the project had been employed to continue recording women's sites (Smith, Morgan, and van der Meer 2003). What is important about this ex-ample is that the political aims were achieved in part because the archaeologists involved surrendered the need to control the data generated; we surrendered our roles as both legislators and interpreters and thus had no role in the regulation of the knowledge obtained. The project succeeded precisely because as archaeologists we had no ability to comment on or interpret the knowledge generated by the project, and we surrendered established CRM practice and values. We did not entirely abandon our authority as experts, of course, as our presence on the project affirmed its legitimacy in the eyes of the park managers. However, we modified our role as experts enough to ensure that the project's nonarchaeological and community values were met. We did not adopt the role of legislators, as we made no pronouncements or judgments about either Waanyi knowledge or archaeological knowledge of the sites or region. Nor did we fulfill a role as interpreters, as we did not comment on or translate Waanyi knowledge for the park managers. Although we helped draft the protocols, these were simply guidelines about whom managers should talk to and when. Our presence *facilitated* the achievement of its aims. The role that we in part remade for ourselves as archaeologists, and which was in part remade for us by the Waanyi women in the project, was that of facilitator. The community values and aspirations of this project could not have been met if, as archaeological heritage managers, we had applied standard archaeological values and aspirations—that is, if we had insisted on controlling, interpreting, and legislating the project's aims and outcomes.

In effect, by reining in archaeology's role as a technology of government in this instance, Waanyi women were able to assert their own sense of cultural identity as reflected in the sites within Boodjamulla National Park. Subsequently, the women involved have been able to assert a positive role for themselves in the wider management of the park. They have been identified as in control of their knowledge and thus of their identity as Waanyi women.

Conclusions

Currently, the management of cultural heritage, or cultural resources, is set within parameters defined by government policy makers, who in turn have drawn upon archaeological knowledge and values to underpin their policies and practices. In particular, archaeological claims to liberal modernity and rationality, via processual theory and scientific values, have become embedded in the public policy process. If practice is theory, and theory practice, then CRM works to govern and regulate the expression and use of archaeological knowledge and values. The Waanyi Women's History Project, although a small project with specific and limited aims, is nonetheless an example of how archaeological privilege, access, and control of material culture and knowledge can be subverted. This is not to suggest that this project challenged the power/knowledge relations anywhere except in a specific place or at a specific time. However, it does establish within the realm of CRM, and thus archaeological practice, a theoretical position that acknowledges not only the political nature of archaeological knowledge but also the role of archaeological knowledge within state negotiations about political and cultural legitimacy. In effect, by incorporating this understanding of power and knowledge into CRM practices, the Waanyi project offers a concrete challenge to the hegemony of processual science. It illustrates one way in which the mobilization of archaeology as a technology of government can be modified or subverted. The issue, then, is to broaden this challenge and facilitate change in archaeological practice in such a way that this change feeds into archaeological theory and discourse. Only through challenges to both theory and practice can the intellectual authority and privilege of archaeological knowledge be renegotiated, so that room is made for Indigenous and other knowledges—or iterations—about the past to be recognized.

References Cited

Bauman, Zygmunt. *Legislators and Interpreters.* Cambridge, U.K.: Polity Press, 1987.
———. *Intimations of Postmodernity.* London: Routledge, 1992.
Curtis, Bruce. "Taking the State Back Out: Rose and Miller on Political Power." *British Journal of Sociology* 46, no. 4 (1995): 575–89.
Davidson, Iain, Christine Lovell-Jones, and Robyne Bancroft, eds. *Archaeologists and Aborigines Working Together.* Armidale, New South Wales, Aus.: University of New England Press, 1995.
Deloria, Vine, Jr. *Custer Died for Your Sins: An Indian Manifesto.* London: Macmillan, 1969.
———. "Indians, Archaeologists, and the Future." *American Antiquity* 57, no. 4 (1992): 595–98.
Foucault, Michel. "Governmentality." In *The Foucault Effect,* edited by G. Burchell, C. Gordon, and P. Miller, 87–104. Chicago: University of Chicago Press, 1991.
Langford, Ros. "Our Heritage—Your Playground." *Australian Archaeology* 16 (1983): 1–6.
Lourandos, Harry. *Continent of Hunter-Gatherers: New Perspectives in Australian Prehistory.* Cambridge: Cambridge University Press, 1997.
McGrath, Ann. "Sexuality and Australian Identities." In *Creating Australia: Changing Australian History,* edited by W. Hudson and G. Bolton, 39–51. St. Leonards, New South Wales, Aus.: Allen and Unwin, 1997.
McNiven, Ian, and Lynette Russell. *Appropriated Pasts: Indigenous Peoples and the Colonial Culture of Archaeology.* Walnut Creek, Calif.: AltaMira Press, 2005.
Mihesuah, Devon A., ed. *Repatriation Reader: Who Owns American Indian Remains?* Lincoln: University of Nebraska Press, 2000.
Mulvaney, Derek John, and Johan Kamminga. *Prehistory of Australia.* St. Leonards, New South Wales, Aus.: Allen and Unwin, 1999.
Nicholas, George P., and Thomas D. Andrews, eds. *At a Crossroads: Archaeology and First Peoples in Canada.* Burnaby, B.C.: Archaeology Press, Simon Fraser University, 1997.

O'Keefe, Eunice, Del Burgan, Anna Morgan, Laurajane Smith, and Anita van der Meer. "Waanyi Women's History Project and Re-engendering the Riversleigh and Lawn Hill Landscapes." Paper presented at Sixth Women in Archaeology Conference, Queensland, Australia, 2001.

Organ, Michael. "A Conspiracy of Silence: The NSW National Parks and Wildlife Service and Aboriginal Cultural Heritage Sites." *Aboriginal Law Bulletin* 3, no. 67 (1994): 4–7.

Riding In, James. "Repatriation: A Pawnee's Perspective." In *Repatriation Reader: Who Owns American Indian Remains?* edited by D. A. Mihesuah, 106–20. Lincoln: University of Nebraska Press, 2000.

Rose, Nikolas. *Governing the Soul.* London: Routledge, 1991.

———. "Government, Authority and Expertise in Advanced Liberalism." *Economy and Society* 22, no. 3 (1993): 283–99.

Rose, Nikolas, and Peter Miller. "Political Power beyond the State: Problematics of Government." *British Journal of Sociology* 43 (1992): 173–205.

Schaffer, Kay. *Women and the Bush: Forces of Desire in the Australian Cultural Tradition.* Cambridge: Cambridge University Press, 1988.

Smith, Claire, and H. Martin Wobst, eds. *Indigenous Archaeologies: Decolonizing Theory and Practice.* London: Routledge, 2005.

Smith, Laurajane. "A History of Aboriginal Heritage Legislation in South-Eastern Australia." *Australian Archaeology* 50 (2000): 109–18.

———. "Archaeology and the Governance of Material Culture: A Case Study from South-Eastern Australia." *Norwegian Archaeological Review* 34, no. 2 (2001): 97–105.

———. *Archaeological Theory and the Politics of Cultural Heritage.* London: Routledge, 2004.

———. *Uses of Heritage.* London: Routledge, 2006.

Smith, Laurajane, Anna Morgan, and Anita van der Meer. "The Waanyi Women's History Project: A Community Partnership Project, Queensland, Australia." In *Archaeologists and Local Communities: Partners in Exploring the Past,* edited by L. Derry and M. Malloy, 147–66. Washington, D.C.: Society for American Archaeology, 2003.

Swidler, Nina, Kurt E. Dongoske, Roger Anyon, and Alan S. Downer, eds. *Native Americans and Archaeologists: Stepping Stones to Common Ground.* Walnut Creek, Calif.: AltaMira Press, 1997.

Tunbridge, John, and Gregory Ashworth. *Dissonant Heritage: The Management of the Past as a Resource in Conflict.* Chichester, U.K.: J. Wiley, 1996.

Watkins, Joe. "Yours, Mine, or Ours? Conflicts between Archaeologists and Ethnic Groups." In *The Future of the Past: Archaeologists, Native Americans, and Repatriation,* edited by T. Bray, 57–68. New York: Garland Publishing, 2001.

———. "Becoming American or Becoming Indian? NAGPRA, Kennewick and Cultural Affiliation." *Journal of Social Archaeology* 4, no. 1 (2004): 60–80.

6

About Face

On Archaeology, Heritage, and Social Power in Public

CHRISTOPHER N. MATTHEWS AND MATTHEW PALUS

The relationship between archaeology and heritage—or the obligations and relations that living people construct with particular pasts to establish a way of life in the present—remains fluid and undefined. Does archaeology produce a material heritage? Does the desire for heritage drive interest in archaeology? Do they somehow produce each other, in an iterative sense? Though we are archaeologists and are writing to this problem in archaeology, we examine this issue by considering neither archaeology nor heritage directly. Instead, we argue that archaeology and heritage together position the past for the purpose of being modern. As we see it, the relationship between archaeology and heritage constructs a divide between neutral scientific and politically interested approaches that legitimizes each as different ways of knowing the past. In particular, by positioning themselves as arbitrators who debate the legitimacy of heritage pasts, in some sense authorizing such pasts, archaeologists sustain concepts of heritage (even if solely in a negative light) as somehow lesser than the scientific discourses that archaeologists produce. We do not think this is an accident. Rather, we argue that archaeology maintains a dialogue with narratives of heritage to pose for its publics what archaeology could be but is not. Manipulating or explicitly offering a counterpoint to heritage, as a mode of publicly engaging with the past, allows archaeology (and thus the association with archaeologists) to become a distinctive credential. That distinction, we argue, is important to the positioning of modern subjects and of archaeology as a technique for being modern.

Our approach follows the structure of Edward Said's argument in *Orientalism.* Said shows that in order to identify itself, the modern West constructs a stereotyped "Orient" as an external reality that embodies all that the West opposes, especially the East's (presumably inherent) tendency for primitive, religious, despotic political societies (see also Asad 2003; Bhabha 1994; Chakrabarty 2000; Spivak 1999). Anthropologist Talal Asad (2003) shows that this negative Western construction of the self (as not-the-Oriental-Other) serves a special purpose in modernity. It supports a powerful Eurocentrism in which the Western self is defined as one who is not guided by enchantments such as ancestral spirits, gods, mystics, or, we add, heritage. Instead, a Westerner rationally lives in the secular or disenchanted "real" world and knows that spirits and enchantment merely cloud our experience of it. For Asad, this claim is vacant. He asks us to explore whether enchantments can ever be fully absolved in our experience of social life. He focuses in particular on the construction of society and self in secular modernity. "Modern" societies are based on the idea of a commonly shared reality that is disenchanted and therefore "real," despite the fact that it is in most other ways undefined. What makes this contradictory, undetermined reality particularly feasible is that it posits an accessible and interchangeable universal subject position that allows societies to form in the absence of interpersonal subjective relations. Modern persons assume that others see the world as they do, because they assume that the world is the object before us all and therefore equally within reach of all persons.

We suggest that the universal subject is epistemologically indispensable to archaeology, especially when it is framed as the abstract individual who may be exchanged between different cultures, places, and, especially for archaeology, times. For instance, to the extent that archaeology relies on analogy as a mode of inference, only through an acceptance of the universal subject can we suppose that the original meanings of the mute material remains of past people are available. If we could not generalize the meaning of material culture in a way that collapsed the distance between archaeological subjects and persons now living or documented, then regardless of the discipline's attempt to establish viable bridging arguments or middle-range theory, the basis for much of what we know as American archaeology would be undermined.

"Heritage" functions similarly as it seamlessly spans the gulf between past and present. Yet although local heritage constructions may be packaged for global consumption, they tend not to employ the universal subject position as their rationale. Following Richard Handler's work on patrimony (1985), we see heritage as a politicized identity project, whose premise is the existence of distinct and particular pasts unique to different persons and groups. Many "moderns," therefore, regard heritage as fictional or imaginary (Lowenthal 1998). However, we think this assessment is off the mark. Our position is that *every* attempt to connect past with present is effectively both systematic and fictional. This position in no way denies the events of the past, nor does it make them available to unlimited possibilities of interpretation (see Trouillot 1995). Rather, our point is that the modernist claim to a universal subject position stands not apart from (as when it claims to be disenchanted) but alongside global, national, cultural, ethnic, or personal heritage claims, as one among many ways of relating modern subjects to the past and, more important, to each other. The seemingly obvious contrast between these approaches to the past—the notion that the now-archaeological universal subject is qualitatively different from the particular heritage subject—reveals an important dimension of modernist ideology, which we are interested in describing here.

Why Faces Matter: An Outline

It is one thing to claim that archaeology and heritage produce modernity through their contrast and cement modern ideologies irrespective of the pasts they produce, and another thing to show it. This chapter illustrates the persistence of the ideology of the universal subject in archaeology by exploring archaeology's metaphorical relationship with the human face. In the following investigations, we approach the human face as a device used by our research subjects—archaeologists and community members—as well as ourselves as authors to project an insistent subjectivity. As a sign of personhood, the face allows us an avenue to assess the public meanings of archaeology. The face symbolizes more than an intersubjective encounter; it also embodies a confrontation, just as it demands recognition. The face brings to the surface the presence of real persons involved with the negotiations that make archaeology possible, as well as attendant personal relationships and expectations, such as trust, fellowship, solidarity, or suspicion. Faces thus matter a great deal in the life and practice of archaeology. Yet in practice, archaeology more typically hides its face in favor of a different basis for subjectivity.

Our investigation explores two examples in the history of archaeology and its relationship with heritage that touch upon the discipline's trend of defacement (following Taussig 1999: prologue). We then describe how the negotiations inherent to invocation, recognition, or absencing of the face also have an impact on the use of archaeology and the way in which archaeologists are viewed by the larger community. That archaeologists can be mobilized by those outside of professional ranks provides an indication of who archaeologists are thought to be and what they are believed to accomplish. Looking at how and why the Eastport neighborhood of Annapolis, Maryland, engaged with our archaeological project shows the value of archaeology's specific credentials in the context of building local heritage. "Archaeology" was sought out and appreciated not so much because of what was found but simply because the investigation could be carried out at all. The actual archaeologists were ambiguously relevant to the project from the public's perspective except in the way in which their presence brought the community a new form of historical significance.

Creating the Faceless Archaeology

The history of archaeology typically locates the discipline's origins in ancient and modern quests for heritage (for example, Fagan 2004; Kehoe 1998; Patterson 1994; Silverberg 1968; Thomas 2000; Trigger 1989; Willey and Sabloff 1974). In particular, archaeology was established as a relevant pursuit by excavating the ancient world and transporting remains, in both physical and symbolic terms, from their original position to a new position of prominence within a living descendant society. This sort of activity is evident in many historical examples, from the postmedieval Italian merchant elite's support for investigations of Roman antiquity (Trigger 1989: 35–36) to the Nazi effort to advance the Aryan cause by rewriting European prehistory (Arnold 1990). The discovery and display of archaeological remains served to legitimize popular and political claims of cultural descent or national heritage. Most disciplinary histories, such as those mentioned above, however, quickly move forward to show how, with modern professionalization, archaeology overcame a reliance on establishing political heritage. Framing the historical intimacy between archaeology and heritage as "irrational" serves as a frequent backdrop for the story of professional archaeology's independence from subjective concerns. Modern archaeology is framed instead as self-directed (at least in the sense that it was directed by academic interests) in its pursuit of objectively understanding the human experience through the study of material remains. To establish disciplinary autonomy, modern archaeology generalized its subjects so that they could be approached by everyone. These shifts have typically been identified in the United States with the New Archaeology, which boldly explained that human behaviors rather than specific cultures produced the archaeological record (for example, Binford 1962, 1965, 2001; Flannery 1972; Schiffer 1972, 1976).

The approach of the New Archaeology was problematized with the rise of postprocessualism, or the expression in archaeology of the radical critique of generalizing approaches in humanistic scholarship (Hodder 1985, 1991; Leone 1982; Shanks and Tilley 1987, 1991). This cultural turn in archaeology called for greater sensitivity to both the diversity of human experience and the particular sociocultural and historical circumstances that create unique cultural constructs. However, to some, following through with postprocessual concerns would severely limit cross-cultural understanding. If all knowledge is generated from within certain cultural frames, to know another way of life would require translation, a process fraught with difficulty and bias. This is the issue that archaeologists Ruth Tringham (1991) and Bruce Trigger (1990) were struggling with as they worked out important applications of the postprocessual critique in reference to meanings of the human face.

Tringham and Trigger found with the human face an important aspect of archaeology that was missing from processualism: an appreciation for the familiar subjective experiences of people. The New Archaeology's subjects were overly determined by "objective" conditions such as environment, economic systems, and rigid social and cultural structures. People were seen in calculable terms such that both archaeologists and their subjects rationally assessed the limitations imposed on human life by external forces. The argument was made that internal motivations and limitations resident in the mind were archaeologically unverifiable and beyond the limits of archaeological inference. Finding a verifiable face is in part the premise of these works by Tringham and Trigger.

Tringham's approach is twofold. First, she employs storytelling to describe how she was challenged to imagine her subjects with faces, and also how multiple approaches toward her European Neolithic site might lead to varied interpretations of the data. These tales bring to the surface insightful evidence of her authorship, and she argues that her project has adopted the goal of "reconceptualizing what writing prehistory is all about" (Tringham 1991: 98). Focusing on writing, she challenges archaeologists to consider their subjects as substantive characters who need to have something more than their mere corporeal existence explained. They need their "gender, age, hopes, fears, [and] aspirations" (Tringham 1991: 125) reconstructed, and this relies on the archaeologist's capacity to envision the faces that mediate these social and personal characteristics.

Second, Tringham cautions that archaeologists need to not only confront a faceless prehistory but also challenge how they produce archaeological subjects. She advocates a focus on the microscale household level, at which everyday lives are played out and where the human face is most relevant. Although archaeologists have long excavated and analyzed households, Tringham points out that for the most part this work "reflect[s] a willingness to accept the generalized assumptions concerning what goes on in and around the house . . . and a corresponding *lack* of interest in challenging the givens of social action at a microscale . . . [as in] linking architectural units with specific social units such as . . . the 'family' or 'household'" (Tringham 1991: 100). An uncritical extension of the heterosexual matrix—a core element of modern subjecthood—obscures the richness and variability evident in the ethnographic record and, worse, overly determines the social context and significance of (domestic) action. Tringham urges an engendering of archaeology by examining variability rather than typological conformity in reference to relational categories such as gender, age, family, and neighbors that are used to define a household. She predicts that we will find more-useful models of social action by tying archaeological data into relationships (for example, male/female or elder/younger) versus seeing households defined by stable social units such as the family set in relation to larger units such as the village or state. Ultimately, Tringham argues that we can build the foundations for "alternative historical trajectories" (Tringham 1991: 99) by starting off with a new system for imagining how archaeological subjects constructed active face-to-face relations with those who supported or challenged their way of life.

Trigger's consideration of the face takes a different approach. While sharing Tringham's interest in the subjective experience of past peoples, he focuses on the relationship between archaeology and the publics it serves—specifically, indigenous peoples. Trigger cites a growing interest in archaeology during the 1980s in two new projects. First, he cites the postprocessual interest in "religious beliefs, art, myths, and other features of specific cultural traditions" (Trigger 1990: 778). He thinks that the investigation of these topics renewed Native American interest in archaeology because the archaeological exploration of symbolic and cultural experience was more compelling than the generalizing cultural ecology of processual archaeology. Native people could connect their interests in revitalization and heritage with archaeological studies that were interested in "culturally specific meanings of art and ritual" (Trigger 1990: 781). Trigger also cites, if not personifies, the importance of the "systematic study of the history of archaeology" (Trigger 1990: 778), meaning work defining the heritage of archaeologists, including both the positive and the negative aspects of the discipline's history that color its practice today. For Trigger, historically informed reflexivity is essential if practitioners of archaeology are to understand its social situation and identify appropriate ethical standards. Yet he believes that reflexivity alone cannot keep archaeologists from alienating native people and similar interested and necessary publics.

Trigger highlights the fact that in 1990, professional Native American archaeologists were almost nonexistent, and he warns that relations between archaeology and native people will decline as long as indigenous people remain objects of study rather than collaborators or, ultimately, peers. Humanizing the face of archaeology, therefore, would require that archaeology broaden its ranks to include people with varied perspectives on how to live in the present and the future, as much as on how to understand the past. Yet for Trigger, what purpose would renewing the professional face of archaeology serve? It seems that a new face for American archaeology comes from a revived interest in studying Native American culture—via archaeology—in ways that would have immediate interest for Native Americans because it would recognize what native people already know *without* archaeology: "[Archaeologists] are again interested in prehistoric religions, art, mythology and other culturally-specific beliefs and values. These themes have more interest to native people than did processual archaeology's preoccupation with ecological adaptation—even though native people who maintain traditional subsistence strategies, especially in the arctic and subarctic, know far more about adaptive behavior than does any archaeologist" (Trigger 1990: 781).

Trigger thus paints an image of archaeology compelled to find its human face to draw out culturally specific meanings of prehistoric practices through an "increasingly holistic engagement with native cultures" (Trigger 1990: 781). The archaeologist's face is thus a mechanism for extracting and representing indigenous knowledge and ways of life for the sake of producing archaeological interpretations that are more convincing and cultural knowledge that is more globally useful. Trigger forecast the contemporary climate in which archaeologists now enter into exactly these kinds of partnerships and collaborations. Even as we critically appropriate ideas from this particular publication, we applaud Trigger's vision and the beginning of its fulfillment, as seen in the edited volume by Swidler and colleagues (1997) and comparable works published since (for example, Castañeda and Matthews 2008; Colwell-Chanthaphonh and Ferguson 2007; Echo-Hawk 2000; Ferguson, Anyon, and Ladd 2000; Little and Shackel 2007; Nicholas and Andrews 1997; Shackel and Chambers 2004; Smith and Wobst 2005; Watkins 2001). Given recent developments that have supported the training and authority of professional Native American archaeologists as well as the rise of varied sorts of collaboration between archaeologists and native elders, scholars, and activists, indigenous contributions are becoming more readily accessible to wider audiences.

By discussing these statements by Tringham and Trigger, we do not mean to suggest that the discipline has not progressed in the two decades since they were written. Certainly, the discipline has grown increasingly diverse, and storytelling and alternative narrative techniques have been examined and adopted by many archaeologists (see, for example, Franklin 1997; Jackman and Whitmore 2002; Praetzellis and Praetzellis 1998; Shanks 1991; Watkins 2001). Rather, we explicitly situate Tringham and Trigger as part of the effort to realize the potential of the postprocessual critique in archaeological practice. For Tringham, this involves making space for the explicit presence of archaeologists within archaeological texts, accomplished through storytelling and the interpersonal relationship between authors and their subjects. For Trigger, it involves re-forming native people into archaeological collaborators and professionals, a focus on the intersubjective professional relations among varied experts. In both cases, the aim is to work *with* subjectivities inherent to archaeology. Yet, surprisingly, in neither case is the subjectivity of the archaeologist examined: for Tringham, an impersonal archaeologist is replaced by a personal author; for Trigger, an impersonal science is replaced by cross-cultural collaboration. Missing is a critical evaluation of the capacity for archaeologists to produce and play these different roles and, moreover, any rationale for why readers would want to engage with archaeologists and their subjects or why native people would want to work with or be archaeologists. Our concern here is that the idea of archaeology as a benefit to modern global life remains an assumption. In contrast, we think that its value must be demonstrated, but not as a matter of fact. We propose that it will emerge only through an ethnographically informed understanding of the more subtle evaluations that are part of the everyday face-to-face encounters archaeologists have with collaborators. More specifically, we explore here how engagements with archaeology serve to support a modern way of life, or a "being-in-the-modern-world," and the political implications that this "being" has for archaeologists working in public.

So instead of asking whether and how archaeology can be relevant to the general public or specific interested publics such as indigenous descendent communities, we ask why and how archaeology already *is* relevant from their perspectives. We might turn Trigger's thought on its head: if native people already know what archaeologists hope to learn, why would they care about archaeology? A more problematic question is why would any indigenous person want to be an archaeologist? Given this interest alone, archaeology is relevant at some level to people living now. That archaeologists are currently struggling to determine their relevance suggests that they have yet to sort out how this relevance relates to the particular modern contexts that sustain it. In this situation, an examination of what archaeologists really do for modern publics is called for: the relevance of archaeology is approachable, but it requires examining not the potential of archaeological results—how they may be used to challenge and change the world—but the potential of archaeology's existence as a distinct practice whose investigations of the past support the agenda of being modern. Given that the human face allows Tringham and Trigger to access a position from which the humanity of archaeological subjects can be seen in the past and the present alike, so too must the face that archaeologists see first be their own.

How and where do we find the archaeologist's face so that we can observe it in action? The archaeologist's face is most evident where the discipline encounters its publics. These spaces of engagement and confrontation help define archaeology by situating it in particular ways within *non*-archaeological spaces. These sites of interaction demand that archaeologists be aware of themselves and those who sustain them through funding, interest, and the use of their results: in these activities, the archaeological face is most vital, for it signifies a subjective and interested presence. However, the archaeologist's actual face is largely absent from these spaces, a feature that reveals archaeology's publicly stated commitment to the universalism within modernity and its primary commitment to actively dissociate from heritage as a way to construct legitimate pasts.

A striking illustration of this absence of face can be seen in a project that Matthew Palus directed in the Eastport neighborhood of Annapolis, Maryland. This project is an example of community archaeology in which the interface between archaeology and the public embodies a conscious though contradictory program defined by concurrent (albeit not necessarily shared) interests in the development of local archaeological heritage as a public resource. Furthermore, archaeology's universalism is expressed here in the facile transplantation of the Archaeology in Annapolis project to a new community of the city and a new, though not unfamiliar, constellation of social powers.

Eastport, Maryland

The space between archaeology and heritage may be framed as the meeting ground upon which archaeologists and their constituents see one another face to face. Archaeologists share this space with constituencies who are themselves producers and users of heritage. This is the space in which the iterations of archaeology and heritage are called out, and they often exist concurrently. Yet this meeting ground too often goes undefined and needs to be examined more closely if archaeology is to be positioned in the modern worldview. With whom, precisely, do we, as archaeologists, share this ground? What do "they" think when "they" meet "us" and view our works? What happens when statements made by archaeologists mingle with those made by others in the crowded territory that is the place for the past in modernity? Answers to these questions can be seen in a public archaeology project undertaken in the community of Eastport, a neighborhood of Annapolis, Maryland, that was developed by land speculators during the late nineteenth and early twentieth centuries.

Archaeology had never been undertaken in the yards of homes in the Eastport neighborhood prior to 2001. Some residents had had their own experiences with archaeology, some professional archaeologists resided there, and many residents had been exposed to publicity about archaeology in Annapolis over the years, but the role that archaeology might play in Eastport had not yet been established. Thus, the value that such research might bring to Eastport was uncertain. We were invited by Eastport residents and homeowners to begin an investigation without a specific mandate. The following discussion is our attempt to frame this question: Who were we, the archaeologists, to Eastport residents?

Eastport is an early suburb of Annapolis that developed on a one-hundred-acre peninsula immediately south of the city. Platted by land speculators in 1868, it represented an important opportunity to own land, albeit outside of the city of Annapolis proper. Eastport homes were owned or rented by professionals, craftspeople, domestics, and laborers, and many of these found employment at the United States Naval Academy on the north side of the city. The community was annexed into Annapolis in 1951 and now constitutes the city's eighth ward. Eastport is within the orbit of gentrification that took hold in the historic district of Annapolis, and since the 1970s, its small wood-frame homes on lots one-quarter acre and smaller have gone from affordable to prohibitively expensive; the millennial boom in real estate projected homes from one or two hundred thousand dollars in value to half a million dollars or more. As such, the most recent wave of homebuyers threatens to completely displace families with longer associations to the neighborhood, and what economic and racial diversity remains is endangered. Still, some diversity persists, and several communities relevant to the project can be distinguished.

In addition to the families with long historical ties in the neighborhood, which count several generations in the community or even extend back to Eastport's founding, there are two distinct recent waves of gentrifiers.[1] The first arrived during the 1970s and purchased homes in Eastport when they were quite affordable, and many have raised families there. Today they constitute Eastport's front porch society, sometimes called "Eastporchers" (Hoffman 2003), and they are among the most politically active and civically engaged members of the community. They are studied experts on what Eastport is all about, maintaining and expressing strong opinions on local issues. A more recent wave of homebuyers began to arrive during the 1990s, after the real estate boom was under way. These recent settlers are sometimes highly visible in their newness and their lifestyles, and they variously appreciate Eastport's character or express indifference toward it. Some see their move as buying a historic home in an interesting neighborhood. Others see Eastport as quantitatively less historic than the neighboring historic district of Annapolis. African-American residents in Eastport are frequently not associated with the later waves of homebuyers. African-Americans founded a community in Eastport during the later nineteenth century, and while this community and much of the property that gives it definition are intact, African-Americans have been moving out of Eastport rather than into it, suggesting the ongoing cost of gentrification over the past thirty years.

Land within the neighborhood is more valuable today than are the small, narrow houses that survive from the original development. At any one time during archaeological fieldwork from 2001 through 2004, several structures were undergoing costly renovations, with their cellars and foundations being re-excavated and new additions—even entire homes—being built, usually according to zoning guidelines designed to protect the character and livability of the neighborhood.[2] Eastport's zoning is called "neighborhood conservation" rather than historic preservation. The local architects of Eastport's zoning never intended to create another historic district within their neighborhood, though even recent settlers have a strong sense of the place and its heritage; that is to say, a quality of "place" is conveyed by the Eastport neighborhood without the extensive legal, infrastructural, and planning work that was undertaken to cultivate a sense of place in the historic district of Annapolis during the second half of the twentieth century.

Field school students from the University of Maryland excavated at eight home sites in Eastport between 2001 and 2004, all of which were owner-occupied at the time the work took place. These excavations, initiated as a component of Palus's doctoral research, were designed to explore the historical relationship between the Eastport neighborhood and Annapolis during the twentieth century. These investigations were undertaken at the invitation of a prominent and respected Eastport resident who had enjoyed a long career in real estate and directed a local historical museum that laid the foundation for the Annapolis Maritime Museum, located in a former oyster-shucking and packing house in Eastport. Her local knowledge and perspective on land use allowed her to obtain permission for the University of Maryland to excavate at two addresses in 2001.

With the exception of street-end parks, all of the land within the peninsular neighborhood is privately owned, and most of the ground surface available for excavation lies within the front and back yards of Eastport homes. As a result, students and staff met with area residents within a variety of personal contexts centering on annual field school excavations. Homeowners and their families saw archaeologists working almost daily, as did those responsible for providing child care, maintenance, and other daytime services in the community. We invited the public to take site tours guided by students, during which there was generally an exchange of ideas and stories between current and former neighborhood residents and members of our project; in part, we use data collected from these encounters to support our discussion here.

Students hosted Eastport residents while making clear to visitors that the residents of Eastport were hosting our project; in many instances, visitors from the immediate neighborhood were more "at home" at excavation sites than were archaeologists, owing to the familiarity bred by local habitation. The result of this style of interaction was substantial visitation, support, and encouragement from some segments of the community, combined with a fluidly structured authority at the actual site of work, where we enjoyed the opportunity to present the findings of our excavations even as Eastport residents with inside knowledge interpreted these findings to us. Support for these undertakings was expressed as permission to conduct additional excavations at more Eastport homes from 2002 through 2004, with a generous welcome. Several other characteristics of Eastport have a bearing on understanding our experience there thus far and also on the reasons why some residents enjoyed our attentions more than others did.

First, as indicated above, Eastport today remains a biracial neighborhood. A distinct African-American community developed during the later nineteenth and early twentieth centuries, organized compactly around a United Methodist church founded in the 1880s. One dimension of the gentrification of this neighborhood has been the dispersal of Eastport's African-American families throughout the surrounding county. The principal mechanism of dispersal is the sale of inherited homes; while Eastport is desirable to commuters from Washington and Baltimore, many African-Americans—but not all—see advantages to selling off family property, which is a principle form of wealth in this land-rich community. Numerous homes in Eastport are still black-owned, but there are far fewer black-owned homes today than there were a generation ago. Mt. Zion, the United Methodist church founded by Eastport's African-American community, still provides an anchor and serves to unify a community that has dispersed through the region.

The experience of project members was that home sites associated historically with African-Americans were made available to our field school by their contemporary white owners, while the relatively limited area still occupied by African-Americans was closed to us, in that African-American property owners, including the trustees of Mt. Zion (which was renovating a multiunit rental property within the neighborhood in 2002) would not give permission for the University of Maryland field school to initiate excavations. The response to our research would best be described as disinterest among all but a very few black Eastporters, and this disinterest almost certainly signaled a more profound disconnect between our project, which included several African-American students each summer (although none among its leadership), and people of color in Eastport.

Moreover, the profile of those who did cooperate with our research was fairly consistent, comprising middle-class families who had very recently come to reside within the community and who owned their homes. As such, most of our hosts had yet to establish their "residency" in the sense that they might become "Eastporters." Many communities have the sort of social criteria for residency that we witnessed in Eastport, where working-class roots and ties to the water extended residency to those who had family of four or even five generations on the peninsula, and to a few who had in the course of their lifetimes become "honorary" residents. Without these extensive qualifications, a person is not from Eastport but from somewhere else, despite owning a house and starting a family there.

We intended to undertake an archaeology that was supported within the community and that addressed salient issues deriving from community concerns. In practice, the base of support for our project was partial and could be seen as quite narrow. Here we question not how we might have garnered wider support and acceptance—a challenge faced by every archaeologist working in community contexts—but why we received any support at all, considering the inevitable disruption and expense that our excavations entailed and the lack of precedents or a genealogy for archaeology in Eastport. We wondered, as would many archaeologists, about each failure to cultivate partnerships with Eastport homeowners, but we also wondered (perhaps counterintuitively) about the several solid successes. What exactly were we expected to bring to this neighborhood? What lay behind the invitation that was initially extended to us, and how can the benefits of having archaeologists at work in a given context be described? What was the reason for the apparent indifference among African-Americans in the community (which we attribute to the agency of that community, its positioning vis-à-vis its heritage, and its historical cohesion as a congregation)?

We raise this issue in large part because the Eastport neighborhood satisfied the usual objectives of historical archaeology in ambiguous ways. Dramatic and surprising finds often provide immediate payoffs and appeal on a different level from conclusions resulting from extended analysis. While a rich site for research, the ground in Eastport produced only a few finds that were visually impressive or conveyed their importance to a nonspecialist. One might even say that there was little to be found using the traditional tools of historical archaeology. On the one hand, this prompted us to consider kinds of archaeological evidence different from that found in abundance within Annapolis's historic district. On the other hand, the familiarity of those materials that we recovered in Eastport indicated the very recent historical contexts available to excavation methods. Much of what we found related to the later occupations of these homes, during the years following World War II. A substantial proportion of this material came from activities carried out on the properties by their current owners, such as landscaping, renovation and construction, raising families, and shade-tree car repair. This research went on in front of our hosts and not infrequently in front of newspaper and television journalists. Why was the value of our work never called into question? The task of students hosting neighbors and residents on site tours was to discover answers to these questions; the answer we found derives from the local sense of who archaeologists are and what they do.

In Eastport we learned that, in fact, there is not much of an extant record of archaeological deposits and features that is not already known. So to understand why we were there, we ask a new set of questions: What is archaeology good for in Eastport? How does it exist in this community? These questions were posed for archaeologically rich historic Annapolis by Mark Leone and Parker Potter (Potter 1994; Potter and Leone 1992), but in the context of a different community we see a new way to answer them.

Our supposition is that "archaeology" is one of an array of modern practices that allow people to dwell in Eastport, a technique for being Eastporters, and for that reason alone they value archaeology even though it has little new to tell them in the short run. As a field of knowledge production (with or without immediate significant discoveries), archaeology relates to one aspect of residing in a community that has a sense of its heritage, which Eastporters inarguably have. We regard becoming knowledgeable about a place to be a way of residing in that place, and we interpret the indifference of African-Americans in Eastport toward our archaeology along these lines.

One example demonstrates the relationship between knowledge of place and residency especially well. There was an uncanny correspondence between the stories told by one lifelong resident of Eastport with many generations of family in the neighborhood, who has over the years received attention from local historians and journalists, and those related by Peg Wallace, a supporter of the project who lived in the area for more than half her life and helped us to make contact with homeowners who would offer access to their properties for excavation. Both of these persons described the sound of caulking hammers used to pack hemp cordage soaked with tar into crevices in a wooden boat's hull in order to evoke a time before Annapolis boatyards—not to mention harbors—were full of fiberglass pleasure boats. The caulking hammer is hollow, with a weight that shuttles back and forth inside the head of the hammer for a double-strike that produces a very distinctive sound. Both the longtime resident and the "naturalized" Eastporter identified this as the quintessential remembrance of pre–World War II Eastport, and both used exactly the same onomatopoeic phrase to evoke the sound of the caulking hammer: a "clink-clink, clink-clink," or the same rhythm sounded out on a tabletop with one's knuckles. These stories circulate, and the native's story is available from oral history recordings and similar materials as well as from his own mouth. But the retelling is crucial here, in that it betrays the role of such knowledge in residing in this community. At the end of the day, it is all retelling, which is a key form of re-membering (Bhabha 1994), and we suggest that it is the narratives rather than residency that are fixed. Recent settlers can achieve legitimacy by becoming knowledgeable, and archaeology (specifically, association with archaeologists) is one opportunity among several others to expand one's range of stories, that is, to demonstrate appropriate local knowledge, to become "at home" and acquire the aura of habitation that differentiated our hosts from ourselves. The point is that we, by virtue of our metonymic relation with archaeology, were a story for the community to tell about itself, a self-authored iteration of Eastport's heritage with our professional authority perforce attached.

Archaeology can deliver new narratives just as it can offer a forum for existing ones to circulate, as in the story of the caulking hammer that reached our ears. Time will show whether the archaeological narratives of Eastport's heritage survive and serve in the same capacity, that of retelling as a mode of *residing*. What we take from the indifference of African-American Eastporters is that we did not offer anything to them with this kind of efficacy. When inquiring with one trustee of Mt. Zion United Methodist Church, who is African-American and a naturalized Eastporter, about where we should excavate in the portion of Eastport that is still home to African-

Americans, we were consistently directed to speak with living people, as though archaeological discoveries could not contribute to the knowledge that exists in the memories of elder African-American Eastporters. This response reveals the partiality of meaning built into most archaeological finds and interpretations. In this case, at least one difference between those in Eastport who could do without archaeology and those who wanted to be associated with it was marked by lines of race, a difference as plain as their and our faces.

Conclusion

To make a question out of the social position archaeologists adopt in public, as granting specific social powers to act as stewards and to characterize debates over heritage as though archaeologists were a third party, we have attempted to examine the relationship between archaeologists in one context—the field—and the publics who encounter this field or reside there. This has meant looking for more than good reasons to do archaeology. The social powers that archaeologists have been allowed to adopt come through an understanding with the communities and the institutions that view and use the results of our work: universities, colleges, and precollegiate educational institutions and their faculty and students; private and public funding agencies; residents and business communities; real estate markets; news media; museums; community and neighborhood groups; municipal authorities; and so on. We have one notion of who we are, and they have notions as well. Too often, the objective of public archaeology is to turn the public into archaeologists who share our ethics and sensibilities—in effect, to make them wear the public (though hidden) face of archaeology. However, this displacement perhaps conceals the real social power that our discipline has sought for itself as an arbiter and promoter of modernity.

Our approach to the problem reconsiders what archaeologists are in such social settings and suggests that our discipline might be less bounded on-the-ground, less autonomous despite our firm belief that archaeology is our domain alone. We do not propose here that it is necessary for the public to become archaeologists, so that we can deliver control over archaeological resources to them and thus dissolve the social power that we wear in public. Rather, we believe that decisions over who or what is an archaeologist have already been made and that these decisions color archaeological discourses in important ways.

The work behind this chapter echoes a question inspired by Michel Foucault: What is an archaeologist? Undeniably, our discipline shares certain standards of professionalism that define who is and who is not an archaeologist. While the specifics of these standards are susceptible to critique, such a dialogue would be less interesting than the critique that comes from considering the public face of archaeology and the public discourses from which it derives. This answer derives from Foucault's analysis of authorship (1984), such that "an archaeologist" (standing in for an author) is some social fact, a statement that elides questions made directly of archaeology as a site of knowledge production, on its value, its origins, and its purposes. The archaeologist, like Foucault's author, is a substitute for the wider practice of archaeology, the social-discursive life of that notion, and the matrices that extend from it. We are left to question whether there is an archaeologist who exists without standing in for archaeology, an archaeologist who is otherwise produced or potentially not produced at all? If not, why not; if so, what could this person be?

While we consider the archaeological record to be an awkward social fact (in that it is constructed by archaeologists in the present as a discovered, if not "natural," occurrence), we wish to recognize that archaeologists are produced by themselves and their publics along the very same lines, as similarly uncomfortably natural. Inasmuch as there is archaeology, there must be archaeologists. Hence our faces, which are a significant part of us despite their public absence, must be examined carefully, for their presence is a vital resource for redefining archaeologists who can bring about change within and outside modernist archaeology. The archaeologist's face sees what happens in every archaeological act, and it records the answers we propose to the key questions we pose below.

To what end archaeology? Largely, it seems to establish a presence in the world of a heritage for modernity. For whom is this done? Learning from the lack of interest among African-Americans in Eastport, we think it is for those who find standing for themselves by playing the modern universal subject. Why did historical archaeology not appeal to African-Americans in Eastport? Perhaps their interest in the past, one that in this case did not require or desire archaeology, indicates a different sort of heritage than those most often represented and debated within archaeology. Theirs is the heritage of substantial interpersonal relationships that produce not an identity for the purpose of gaining standing in a community but the resources required for living every day, including especially the techniques for subverting the forces that run counter to community and its social and personal basis.

The final question is one of iterations, or the processes by which archaeology may be examined and thus found to exist. We have argued that archaeology and heritage are mutual constructions and that these practices serve as nodes of exchange between forms of knowledge, especially such that modern subjects pose their knowledge as valid and reliable largely in opposition to others. Such iterations in heritage debates are therefore between science and history, between history and heritage, and perhaps most conspicuously, between archaeologists in fact and archaeologists in face. By this, we mean to remind ourselves that histories are made and built today, but they are not constructed by people equally. The resources for relating history are diverse but always subject to forms of control. Only an iterative examination of the knowledge-making processes that substantiate not archaeology but archaeologists within existing communities is capable of alternatively respecting or challenging these controls for the sake of opening up the discourse of archaeology to allow its potentials to be better understood.

Acknowledgments

An earlier version of this chapter was presented at "Ethics and the Practice of Archaeology," a symposium at the University of Pennsylvania organized by Alexander A. Bauer. The authors benefited from feedback both at that symposium and at the session organized by the editors of this volume, at the annual meeting of the American Anthropological Association in 2002. Archaeological research in Eastport was made possible through the effort, generosity, and goodwill of Peg Wallace, who was then chair emeritus of the Annapolis Maritime Museum. The project also benefited from the support of Ward Representative Josh Cohen and the mayor and city council of Annapolis.

Notes

1. This assessment of Eastport residents resulted from research completed by lawyer and graduate student Laura L. Hoffman in 2003 (original notes in possession of the authors). Hoffman conducted informal and structured interviews with Eastport residents, attended community meetings, and administered a survey to persons working, visiting, or living in Eastport. Her conclusions were substantiated during several seasons of excavation fieldwork in the neighborhood.

2. This zoning, which was evaluated and revised by a committee of residents beginning in 2002 and passed by the city council in 2005, is significantly less restrictive than that of the adjacent historic district of Annapolis.

References Cited

Arnold, Bettina. "The Past as Propaganda: Totalitarian Archaeology in Nazi Germany." *Antiquity* 64, no. 244 (1990): 464–78.

Asad, Talal. *Formations of the Secular: Christianity, Islam, Modernity.* Stanford: Stanford University Press, 2003.

Bhabha, Homi K. *The Location of Culture.* New York: Routledge, 1994.

Binford, Lewis R. "Archaeology as Anthropology." *American Antiquity* 28 (1962): 217–25.

———. "Archaeological Systematics and the Study of Cultural Process." *American Antiquity* 31 (1965): 203–10.

―――. *Constructing Frames of Reference: An Analytical Method for Archaeological Theory Building Using Ethnographic and Environmental Data Sets.* Berkeley: University of California Press, 2001.

Butler, Judith. *Bodies that Matter: On the Discursive Limits of "Sex."* London: Routledge, 1993.

Castañeda, Quetzil E., and Christopher N. Matthews, eds. *Ethnographic Archaeologies: Reflections on Stakeholders and Archaeological Practices.* Lanham, Md.: AltaMira Press, 2008.

Chakrabarty, Dipesh. *Provincializing Europe: Postcolonial Thought and Historical Difference.* Princeton, N.J.: Princeton University Press, 2000.

Colwell-Chanthaphonh, Chip, and T. J. Ferguson, eds. *Collaboration in Archaeological Practice: Engaging Descendant Communities.* Lanham, Md.: AltaMira Press, 2007.

Echo-Hawk, Roger C. "Ancient History in the New World: Integrating Oral Traditions and the Archaeological Record in Deep Time." *American Antiquity* 65, no. 2 (2000): 267–90.

Fagan, Brian M. *A Brief History of Archaeology: Classical Times to the Twenty-first Century.* New York: Prentice-Hall, 2004.

Ferguson, T. J., Roger Anyon, and Edmund J. Ladd. "Repatriation at the Pueblo of Zuni: Diverse Solutions to Complex Problems." In *Repatriation Reader: Who Owns American Indian Remains?* edited by D. A. Mihesuah, 239–65. Lincoln: University of Nebraska Press, 2000.

Flannery, Kent. "The Cultural Evolution of Civilizations." *Annual Review of Ecology and Systematics* 3 (1972): 399–426.

Foucault, Michel. "What Is an Author?" In *The Foucault Reader,* edited by P. Rabinow, 101–20. New York: Pantheon Books, 1984.

Franklin, Maria. "Why Are There So Few Black American Archaeologists?" *Antiquity* 71 (1997): 799–801.

Handler, Richard. "On Having a Culture: Nationalism and the Preservation of Quebec's Patrimoine." In *Objects and Others: Essays on Museums and Material Culture,* edited by G. W. Stocking Jr., 192–217. Madison: University of Wisconsin Press, 1985.

Hodder, Ian. "Postprocessual Archaeology." In *Advances in Archaeological Method and Theory,* vol. 8, edited by M. B. Schiffer, 1–26. New York: Academic Publishers, 1985.

―――. *Reading the Past: Current Approaches to Interpretation in Archaeology.* 2nd edition. Cambridge: Cambridge University Press, 1991.

Hoffman, Laura L. "Summary Conclusions of Field Work." Unpublished paper for Department of Anthropology, University of Maryland College Park, 2003.

Jackman, Trinity, and Christopher Whitmore. Editorial, "The Narrative Act and Archaeology." *Stanford Journal of Archaeology* 1 (2002). http://archaeology.stanford.edu/journal/newdraft/editorial.html.

Kehoe, Alice. *The Land of Prehistory: A Critical History of American Archaeology.* New York: Routledge, 1998.

Leone, Mark P. "Some Opinions about Recovering Mind." *American Antiquity* 47, no. 4 (1982): 742–60.

Little, Barbara J., and Paul A. Shackel, eds. *Archaeology as a Tool of Civic Engagement.* Walnut Creek, Calif.: AltaMira Press, 2007.

Lowenthal, David. *The Heritage Crusade and the Spoils of History.* Cambridge: Cambridge University Press, 1998.

Nicholas, George P., and Thomas D. Andrews, eds. *At a Crossroads: Archaeology and First Peoples in Canada.* Burnaby, B.C.: Archaeology Press, Simon Fraser University, 1997.

Patterson, T. C. *Toward a Social History of Archaeology in the United States.* New York: Harcourt Brace, 1995.

Potter, Parker B., Jr. *Public Archaeology in Annapolis: A Critical Approach to History in Maryland's Ancient City.* Washington, D.C.: Smithsonian Institution Press, 1994.

Potter, Parker B., Jr., and Mark P. Leone. 1992. "Establishing the Roots of Historical Consciousness in Modern Annapolis, Maryland." In *Museums and Communities: The Politics of Public Culture,* edited by I. Karp, C. Mullen Kreamer, and S. D. Lavine, 476–505. Washington, D.C.: Smithsonian Institution Press, 1992.

Praetzellis, Adrian, and Mary Praetzellis, eds. "Archaeologists as Storytellers." Special issue, *Historical Archaeology* 32, no. 1 (1998).

Said, Edward W. *Orientalism.* New York: Vintage Books, 1979.

Schiffer, Michael B. "Archaeological Context and Systemic Context." *American Antiquity* 37 (1972): 156–65.

———. *Behavioral Archaeology.* New York: Academic Press, 1976.

Shackel, Paul A., and Erve Chambers, eds. *Places in Mind: Public Archaeology as Applied Anthropology.* New York: Routledge, 2004.

Shanks, Michael. *Experiencing the Past: On the Character of Archaeology.* London: Routledge, 1991.

Shanks, Michael, and Christopher Tilley. *Social Theory and Archaeology.* Cambridge: Polity Press, 1987.

———. *Re-constructing Archaeology: Theory and Practice.* 2nd edition. London: Routledge, 1991.

Silverberg, Robert. *Moundbuilders of Ancient America: The Archaeology of a Myth.* Athens: Ohio University Press, 1968.

Smith, Claire, and H. Martin Wobst, eds. *Indigenous Archaeologies: Decolonizing Theory and Practice.* London: Routledge, 2005.

Spivak, Gayatri C. *A Critique of Postcolonial Reason: Toward a History of the Vanishing Present.* Cambridge, Mass.: Harvard University Press, 1999.

Swidler, Nina, Kurt E. Dongoske, Roger Anyon, and Alan S. Dower. 1997. *Native Americans and Archaeologists: Stepping Stones to a Common Ground.* Walnut Creek, Calif.: AltaMira Press, 1997.

Taussig, Michael. *Defacement: Public Secrecy and the Labor of the Negative.* Stanford: Stanford University Press, 1999.

Thomas, David H. *Skull Wars: Kennewick Man, Archaeology, and the Battle for Native American Identity.* 1st edition. New York: Basic Books, 2000.

Trigger, Bruce G. *A History of Archaeological Thought.* Cambridge: University of Cambridge Press, 1989.

———. "The 1990s: North American Archaeology with a Human Face?" *Antiquity* 64 (1990): 778–87.

Tringham, Ruth. "Households with Faces: The Challenge of Gender in Prehistoric

Architectural Remains." In *Engendering Archaeology: Women and Prehistory,* edited by J. Gero and M. Conkey, 93–131. Oxford, U.K.: Blackwell, 1991.

Trouillot, Michel-Rolph. *Silencing the Past: Power and the Production of History.* Boston: Beacon Press, 1995.

Watkins, Joe. *Indigenous Archaeology: American Indian Values and Scientific Practice.* Walnut Creek, Calif.: AltaMira Press, 2001.

Willey, Gordon R., and Jeremy A. Sabloff. *A History of American Archaeology.* San Francisco: W. H. Freeman, 1974.

7

The Recovery of Archaeological Heritage in the Ecuadorian Andes

Ethnography, Domination, and the Past

O. HUGO BENAVIDES

Heritage has an essential place in the production of one's past and identity, though researching and writing about the subject shows that the contours of archaeological heritage are ambiguous and slippery. An example of the immediate complexity of the subject of archaeological heritage is that, unlike other paradigmatic concepts, it has only recently become the focus of anthropological scrutiny and objective analysis. Unlike nationalism and other ethnographic enterprises, heritage is almost always presented as an obvious cultural good (see Trouillot 1995). The question proposed, therefore, has never been one of bringing to the forefront the dangerous implications of heritage claims but rather of concentrating only on those claims that highlight its operationalization. In this manner, the focus is kept on how to better and more efficiently appropriate heritage, rather than whether such an appropriation should be made at all, or at the least to question what some of the most explicit cultural implications are of its successful implementation (Lowenthal 1985, 1996).

In this regard, it is quite telling that conflict, as an essential part of heritage analysis, is very rarely acknowledged, and when it is, the acknowledgment is generally limited to two scenarios. The first only superficially addresses the question of contesting claims to the past. In these instances, conflict is posed in terms of trying to define the contrasting authenticity of claims and to some degree defining who is actually "more right" in these claims to the past (see Handler and Gable 1997). I argue, through my analysis of Ecuadorian archaeological heritage at the site of Cochasquí and the Indian movement (CONAIE), that this particular limited analytical strategy is a slippery slope because supposedly authentic groups become legitimized in this manner, having their claims to the past recognized, to the exclusion of other historical minority groups. The second limited analytical strategy engages heritage contestation as if it is only and exclusively a domain within an explicit and highly politicized context, such as the contemporary Israeli-Palestinian conflict (Abu el-Haj 2001; Silberman and Small 1997) and the Nazi (Arnold 1992; Trigger 1989) or other colonial pasts (Kuklick 1991).

Contrary to these particular understandings of the conflictive nature of archaeological heritage, the past decade has seen an effective interest in assessing the pervasive politicized nature of archaeological recovery in all settings. Research by Quetzil Castañeda (1996), Barbara Bender (1998), Thomas Patterson (1995), and Neil Asher Silberman (1989, 1995), among others, has been paradigmatic in underscoring the political production of the past as an essential element in the recovery and construction of archaeological heritage. All of these authors strive to assess the recovery of archaeological heritage through the ethnographic enterprise, emphasizing the contemporary underpinning that any production of the past entails (see Hall 1997a).

It is in this vein that I offer my research in the Ecuadorian Andes (Benavides 2004) to further elucidate the contested nature of the construction of the nation's past and the incredibly hegemonic enterprise that the recovery of any archaeological heritage implicates. Notions of cultural authenticity, historical rights, and identity claims are highly charged political projects and belie the contested nature of archaeology's enterprise, in all its varied implications and reconstructions of the past. These recent assessments of archaeological heritage are enabled by the postmodern turn in North American and European archaeology that has allowed for myriad approaches to contribute to the ever-changing archaeological discipline (Hodder 1982, 1986; Shanks and Tilley 1987a, 1987b). Although far from a monolithic theoretical approach, this postmodern turn has allowed a series of neo-Marxist (Schmidt and Patterson 1995), poststructural (Gero, Lacy, and Blakey 1983; Wylie 1992, 1995), and postcolonial approaches (see Vargas Arenas 1995; Lumbreras 1981) to assess the past from a much more nuanced position than traditional or New Archaeology paradigms had previously done or allowed.

However, all these recent approaches share several similarities, including the important recognition of the politics invested in the production of the past and the pervasively contested domain that traditional scientific objectivity serves to disguise. This is not a question of denying the existence of the past or its material remains per se but, rather, the recognition that recovery is always already framed within established notions of what is legally recognized and culturally authentic in social terms. This battlefield or "field of force" (Roseberry 1994) is where objectivity is afforded, even before any actual interaction with the archaeological material being discussed, and involvement with an archaeological project, or research at any archaeological site, actually takes place (see LaRoche and Blakey 1997 for a case discussion of the New York African Burial Ground controversy).

Therefore, it comes as no surprise that Indian (Native American) groups throughout the Americas have been claiming control over their ancestral lands, objects, and bodies for centuries despite facing enormous official and anthropological resistance (Deloria 1970; Zimmerman 1989). Only within the changing dynamic of globalization and the recognition (almost obsessive desire, one could say) for that which is authentic (Appadurai 2000, 2002; Tsing 2000), in the Lacanian sense of "the real" (see Zizek 2002), have native rights been finally recognized. Indian claims to the past are not new; their legal recognition and international support is. This empowering of native rights clearly expresses how scientific objectivity is closely linked to power, making it "history's most seductively attired false witness" (Baldwin 1990: 480). In this context, less attention has to be paid to objectivity per se as method and more attention should be given to understanding objectivity as a product and effect of larger empirical constraints and politically paradigmatic social definitions, including colonialism (see Wylie 1992, 1995).

From this positional standpoint, afforded by new forms of globalizations, an ethnographic enterprise of archaeology has become viable. An ethnography of archaeology has benefited from the critical reworking of ethnographic representation in general (Clifford and Marcus 1986; Fabian 1983; Rabinow 1977) and a critique of archaeology's enterprise of domination assessed over its object of inquiry as the "native Other" (Fahim 1982; Harrison 1991; Jones 1970). Therefore, the lived-in assessment of the daily reality of archaeological production has consistently benefited from archaeologists contributing to the discipline from the vantage point of the ethnographer. In this instance, ethnographic-minded archaeologists have been consistent contributors, although perhaps less acknowledged than their trowel-busy companions, to our knowledge of the past.

This ethnographic tradition has been the most successful when archaeologists have taken up the ethnographic task (see Patterson 1995). The ethnographic enterprise allows archaeologists a much-needed outside perspective, an "objective" view (in the contextual sense), of what is it that they do and of the theoretical and methodological underpinnings involved in the production of the past. Many mainstream archaeological circles have been resistant to this ethnographic wave and have mistakenly presented the conflict in terms of an elusive dichotomy between science and humanities, a dichotomy that does not take into account the ambiguously fictive nature of all reality, scientific or not (see Foucault 1991). Perhaps this is the greatest pitfall of the ethnographic enterprise in archaeology— not that it fails to open up the discipline to the scrutinizing effect it had limited to the "Other's past" but that the light brought to shine upon the hegemonic foundations of archaeology is too disturbing for many to accept. Perhaps ethnographic findings that seem to question archaeology's scientific base are in themselves the most disturbing (and rewarding) contributions that ethnography can make to archaeology (see Bender 1998).

Also in this vein, it may be useful to use the insights elucidated by the ethnographic enterprise of another of anthropology's subfields: physical anthropology. Donna Haraway's (1989) work is paradigmatic here. Her study of the colonizing enterprise caught within the tenets of physical anthropology's scientific discourse might continue to be slighted by most physical anthropologists but has been very influential for a generation of emerging scholars of interdisciplinary cultural and postcolonial studies. Haraway's (1989) work (ranging from a thorough assessment of the role of white women as the surprisingly suitable agent to study the primate world of Africa to the total eclipse of native contributions to anthropology) marks the manners in which an implicit colonial agenda underlines the anthropological enterprise.

This poststructural method can handily inform our ethnographic enterprise and help us refocus our archaeological lenses to better assess, if not the past, then our reconstruction of that past and the political effects that such reconstruction always implies. In her work, Haraway elaborates on the discipline's maintenance of a particular image of patriarchal human evolution and global hierarchical racial order that has continuously gone uncontested in the past two centuries.

Furthermore, she elaborates, the scientific aura has been primal in maintaining this authoritative facade and enabling this hegemonic enterprise to serve its foundational role in a field that presents itself as implicitly committed to the betterment of humanity. I would argue that Haraway's findings in physical anthropology are far from limited to this subfield alone. In many ways, archaeology in general and archaeological heritage in particular are invested in hegemonic enterprises that not only secure their own advantageous position in the global ecumene but also allow a series of hurtful practices of historical domination and colonizing effects to continue. These studies also better contextualize the colonial origin of anthropology and through it anthropology's, including archaeology's, contribution to the knowledge of the world at large—always a problematic endeavor (see Trigger 1984, 1989).

Critical auto-examination of this sort must also take into account conceptual frameworks such as Stuart Hall's (1997a, 1997b) insight into the global dynamics in which we live and produce our scholarly work, particularly his engagement with the role of history and historical heritage. For this British scholar, the past plays a central role in the production and maintenance of our contemporary global dynamics (Hall 1997a, 1997b). Hall accurately recognizes that all reconstructions of the past are exactly that: contemporary approximations to the past in which the present always has a pivotal role. In this manner, according to Hall, far from being superseded or ending, history continuously serves to redefine, over and over again, our global relationships, remaking our social relationships in similarly different ways (Hall 1997b; see also García-Canclini 1992).

This recognition of the dynamic production of the past, as well as the insights into its hidden hegemonic enterprise, contributes to our understanding of the pitfalls of archaeological heritage and frames my discussion of the Ecuadorian cases. Hall's approach (1997a, 1997b) is singularly useful in analytically integrating the apparent contradictory ways in which nationality, race, ethnicity, sexuality, and age are continuously reformulated and how they seem to constrain rather than afford greater human agency. For Hall (1997a), the manner in which domination and agency are inherently reformulated is central to the political play of the past in defining both what is called archaeological heritage and whether and how it is claimed and recovered (see Wright 1985 for a brilliant discussion of the Thatcher case).

My study of Ecuadorian archaeological heritage uses Hall's reformulation of the past as a hegemonic enterprise that both aims to secure national control and allows for subtle forms of agency and counterhegemonic contestation. My ethnographic foray into the Ecuadorian nation's archaeological past shows that it is filled with both subtle and explicit forms of national hegemony, as well as inherent forms of progressive Indian rights politics and agency-filled appropriations. The research I carried out at the archaeological site of Cochasquí and my analysis of the contemporary Indian movement speak to the contested nature of archaeological heritage and the pivotal role that the past has in the nation-state's contemporary production of hegemony. The following is not an exhaustive discussion of these two instances of archaeological appropriation (either at the site of Cochasquí or by the Indian movement); instead, I highlight theoretical elements concerned with archaeological heritage that have been subjected to less explicit analysis or critical auto-examination.

Cochasquí: Appropriations of the Past by Any Means Necessary

The site of Cochasquí is an example of the contestation of all archaeological heritage, even though it seems not to be central to the discourse of the nation or any other contending group. It presents elements very similar to those presented by Richard Handler and Eric Gable (1997) in their study of Colonial Williamsburg and in Handler's (1988) study of French nationalism in Quebec. Cochasquí is located in the northern Ecuadorian Andes, just an hour drive north of Quito, the country's capital. My work is the result of a year-long ethnographic exploration at the site, during which I interviewed tourists, workers, the local population, and members of the Programa Cochasquí, who run the site. My first exploration into the contested nature of archaeological heritage at the site served as the central discourse of my work on Ecuadorian racial histories and national hegemony (see Benavides 2004). In what follows, I offer a further contribution and thinking-through of the major tenets present in the historical debates embodied at the site.

The site of Cochasquí is officially represented as a pre- Inca site, thus embodying a pristine national (Ecuadorian) identity over the centuries, even after waves of invasion by the Incas and Spaniards, as well as U.S. imperialism. This central discourse of Ecuadorianess goes uncontested in the official discourse at the site, among the tour guides, in the site museum, and in the sporadic educational pamphlets published by the Programa Cochasquí, the governing program for the site (hereafter referred to as the "program"). This discourse of pristine nationalism is blatantly presented to Ecuadorian and foreign tourists alike, and many of them (unsurprisingly) leave with a revitalized sense of Ecuadorianess or of having come into contact with a primordial image of the nation's past. Particularly for the foreigners, this primordial identity allows them to better digest the exploitative and corrupt society to which they are initially introduced in the major urban centers of Guayaquil and Ecuador. In contrast, the proud ancient mound-builders of Cochasquí are a welcomed image.

Also, the nationalizing discourse that "Ecuadorianizes" pyramids built almost two millennia (approximately AD 500) before the Ecuadorian Republic came into existence (1830s) is an incredibly successful hegemonic device. The fact that the site's Ecuadorianess is presented so naturally only pushes us to analyze and question the contestation and mystification carried throughout the site, rather than tempting us to delineate any true heritage of the site (as if the truth in any sense actually exists— see Miller 1993). What we observe at Cochasquí (I would argue that Cochasquí is a fairly typical example and not an exception to this appropriation phenomenon) is that the heritage of the site goes to the highest bidder—in this case, the Ecuadorian state. The Ecuadorian state, by financing the governing program, fuels an explicit (and implicit) nationalism that secures its ideological future in all the tourists, particularly students, who are enabled by the site visit to proudly reclaim their national identity. The pyramids afford a claim to a national identity that is otherwise visibly problematic in the daily life of political corruption, exploitative class relationships, and unbearable racial oppression, which are continuously normalized in differing social processes as well.

However, this homogenizing and hegemonic national discourse is not without its points of fracture. Although far from causing the national ideology to collapse, these fractures do present interesting devices in which hegemonizing discourse is able to rearticulate itself in interesting and provocative ways to an audience eager to be seduced. The fact that the different tours and the explanations of the site have changed over time or even change through the course of the day, depending on the tourist groups, does not expose the fragility of the national ideology but instead serves to express and reemphasize the discourse's changing and adaptive nature, its concrete hegemonic possibilities (see Joseph and Nugent 1994). At best, these shifting narratives and scenarios can be equated to the emperor's new clothes, in which everybody sees him naked but only naive children or stupid people, both unaware of the devastating effects, point it out (see Sayer 1994).

I explore these points of fracture because I believe that they are instrumental in understanding what Hall defines as "different similarities," in the sense that they serve to express the adaptive manner of hegemonic domination, and they also reflect the ever-changing nature of historical recovery and the agency-filled possibilities of the archaeological past. One of the most interesting points of fracture is found in the local community (the *comuna* of Cochasquí), which, although in close proximity to the site, does not actively participate in the nationalizing Ecuadorian ideology of the site.

At best, the local *comuneros* either serve as cheap labor for the physical maintenance of the site or maintain a coldly distant relationship that tempers the most outlandish of the site's nationalizing proposals. This does not imply that the inhabitants of the comuna are the pristine inheritors of the site—far from it, because the site's territory and its present inhabitants are a product of complex hacienda and agrarian-reform transformations over the last century (Moscoso and Costa 1989). In that sense, nobody can claim an ancestral ownership to the site in a manner legally recognized by the Ecuadorian state, a situation that further maintains the state's hegemony over the site's ideological production.

The comuna has been the object of an insightful and detailed ethnography carried out by José Salcedo (1985). As I revisited and worked at the site, I found many of Salcedo's initial findings to be completely relevant to the current structure or interaction between the site and the local inhabitants. As the following descriptions exemplify, the complex interaction between state-financed and struggling local workers is a more realistic example of the current Ecuadorian national reality hidden beneath the nationalizing archaeological scripts narrated by tour guides and appropriated by tourists at the site.

For Salcedo (1985: 103–5), the difficulties between the comuna and the program have two specific roots. The first are the social differences between the mestizo urban staff and the rural-mestizo peasant community that express two contrasting mentalities, in sociocultural and economic forms. This is especially true because all the decision-making power is retained by the white-mestizo staff located in Quito. The second is the program's portrayal of social development as an abstraction, while for the comuneros there is a tangible need for better economic and social conditions. Overall the comuneros—usually men—who interact with the program's staff (or even become part of the local staff of site guards and guides) gain an enormous amount of prestige, which in different instances translates into economic gain. It is clear to the comuneros that association with the urban, white-mestizo, middle-class staff and sometimes with foreign visitors is a form of accumulating social capital.

When one understands the comuneros' complex life and interaction with the site as a manifestation of daily survival and socioeconomic dependency, this serves as a context for sobering the ideological discourse presented at a surface level about the supposedly past glories of the nation. In this same context, another point of fracture relating to the legacy of racial definition is analytically useful. The ever-present Indian identity in Ecuador—catapulted now into the political scene as the most important social movement in the country, CONAIE (Confederation of Indian Nationalities of Ecuador)—also has strong ideological ramifications at Cochasquí.

The Indian movement (CONAIE) presents an interesting element in the racial production of Ecuadorianess at the site. Throughout this Andean nation, "Indianness" is deemed positive or pride-worthy only when it is talked about in the past tense (Crain 1990; Muratorio 1994), serving in that manner to boost the nation's image and ecumenically unite the nation's past with the contemporary indigenous population. Of course, through this ideological recourse, the genocide and continuous ethnocide of the Indian population is denied and the ongoing enmity of Indians against the state is seductively dissolved for both national and foreign consumption. In this regard, CONAIE presents a most problematic obstacle because the claims of the Indian movement are based precisely on this historical oppression and mistreatment of the territory's indigenous population and the insistence that the socioeconomic situation has not changed significantly in the past five centuries.

At Cochasquí, the ongoing conflict between the state and the Indian population is played out in interestingly provocative ways. On the one side is the homogenizing ideology that provides tribute to dead Indian leaders but leaves contemporary issues of discrimination and oppression unaddressed. This is the place of fracture that is made visible when Indian groups visit the site as tourists and there is a significant resistance, more than usual, among the tour guides to accompanying them. In many ways, it is provocatively obvious that the tour guides' reticence is a result of centuries of racial discrimination and self-hatred, because most of the tour guides are mestizos from a rural population and of indigenous descent (see Stutzman 1981). But more poignantly, the unwillingness of all tour guides to work with the Indian groups expresses the fallacy of claiming an Indian heritage to support Ecuador's mythical identity of a pleasant Indian past, while being unwilling to share that site with contemporary Indians. If the nationalizing ideology were genuine, Indians logically would be the most direct descendants of that pristine national aura that the site so successfully exploits, and Indians would not continue to be discriminated against throughout the country, including at Cochasquí.

This double standard—an appropriation of a past Indian heritage while clearly discriminating against the contemporary Indian population—exemplifies the fragile nature of the site's national hegemonic ideology. Furthering this ambiguity is the fact that Indian holidays such as Inti-Raymi (the summer solstice celebration, which was raised to a state celebration by the invading Inca population) are important dates celebrated at the site. Indian groups, particularly dancers, carry out ritual activities at the site; different Indian communities are welcomed. Yet, again, the presence of these Indian guests and their celebrations is a means by which they are completely appropriated into the nationalizing discourse. Indians are welcomed at the site, but only if they are dead or if they fit within the colorful scriptures of the program's contemporary nationalizing objective.

The local comuna and the Indian "presence" are but two fractures inherent in the national recovery of the archaeological heritage at Cochasquí. However, neither the local comuna nor the Indian presence is an impediment to the nation's success in making Cochasquí its own. Rather, they provide interesting means by which the archaeological discourse at the site must adapt to the ever-changing face of the nation and its different constitutive populations. This changeability of the nation, and therefore of its past, is perhaps even more readily appropriated by the Indians themselves and has enabled them to operationalize the most powerful political movement in the country today.

The Indian Movement in Ecuador: Appropriation of the Past by Ideological Force

I begin my critical assessment of CONAIE's appropriation of the past with an insight from the postcolonial scholar Jamaica Kincaid. In her 1997 memoir of her brother dying of AIDS in Antigua, Kincaid expresses her belief that not only the present but also the past constantly change: when one looks back at the past, it no longer is what one thought it was. More important is that those new notions of the past, transformed through our current understanding of it, continue to affect the way we look at ourselves now, in the present. This very dynamic understanding of the past— as something still with us, ever changing, and currently being retransformed though our lives—is useful in assessing CONAIE's reworking of its pre-Hispanic past (and that of the Ecuadorian nation-state) and, through this, its Indian identity.

A reworking of the Indian past has been central to CONAIE's ability to gain a central place in the political spotlight and thus effect change not only for oppressed Indian communities of Ecuador but also for the larger disenfranchised national populations. Here, I do not completely elaborate on the complex reworking of the Indian movement's pre-Hispanic past, because I have done that elsewhere (see Benavides 2004). Rather, my focus is on some of the most salient fractures that this

Indian heritage exemplifies, particularly because these fractures provide the context through which the facade of the supposedly smooth Indian archaeological heritage is better exposed.

One of the most interesting elements of CONAIE's retelling of the nation's past is the appropriation of the pre-Hispanic history of the Ecuadorian nation-state. For CONAIE, the Indian communities indigenous to the territory—Incas primary among them—are not foreign or distant relatives but are instead considered direct ancestors. In other words, CONAIE and the current Indian communities in Ecuador become, through this appropriation, the living relatives of this pre-Hispanic past. In this manner, a historical unity is forged between the past and present; rather than serving as a record of a distant past to be learned in books and lectures, both archaeological and historical material remains are living remnants of the lives and political struggles of members of CONAIE and other Indian communities (see CONAIE 1989).

This particular recovery of the pre-Hispanic past carries a series of immediate implications. One of the most positive ones is that it has served to propel the movement into the current political mainstream and in that manner give voice to a community oppressed for five centuries through genocidal and ethnocidal mechanisms—mechanisms of oppression that have been central to the maintenance of the Ecuadorian nation-state as such (see Guerrero 1991). An example of the political power of the movement is that 2003 saw the appointment of two Indians, Luis Macas and Nina Pakari, as minister of agriculture and secretary of state, respectively. However, given the discriminatory practices and policies of the nation, the fact that an Indian woman became the international diplomatic representative of the country made Pakari's the most influential and provocative of the two appointments, as it raised questions about national representation abroad and the role of Indians in the international image of the nation.

These "positive/progressive" results are tempered by a complex historical hermeneutic that in many ways continues to express the fragility of any hegemonic recovery of the past (see Sayer 1994) or agency-filled mechanisms of archaeological heritage (see Hall 1997b). As Frank Salomon (1987) has succinctly elaborated, one of the most problematic results of the current pan-Indianism (both in the present and in the past) is that historical facts and cultural differences are overlooked or oversimplified in its new transformation: the Incas are incorporated as ancestors whose wisdom and courage was lost in their decimation by the Spaniard onslaught. Denied in this appropriation process is the ample evidence that the Incas were far from the benign, wise, and peaceful Indian community that CONAIE is invested in representing.

The Incas were among the world's most successful conquering armies and state enterprises. They built an empire from the tip of Patagonia to today's Colombian highlands in little over a century, not through kindness and gift giving but through indiscriminate warring and at times cruel and unrelenting domination (see D'Altroy 1992, 2002; Murra 1989; Patterson 1991). A more locally relevant example of this occurs in the name of the large highland lake on the outskirts of Otavalo in northern Ecuador, called Yaguarcocha—a Quechua word meaning "lake of blood"—which marks the slaughter of many of the Indian communities in the territory that resisted the Inca onslaught. Also telling is that many of the descendant communities from this area (for instance, Cañaris, Salasacas, Saraguros, and others) have a prominent place in CONAIE's leadership. One imagines how startled many of these groups' past leaders, killed by the Incas, would be by the fact that their descendants are claiming the direct ancestry of a group responsible for their own decimation.

This ambiguous nature of archaeological heritage (not unique to CONAIE or the Ecuadorian nation-state, for that matter, but shared by all recovery attempts) tends to be overlooked when one wishes to create a congruent bridge to the past. The past, like the present, is composed of breaks and discontinuities on which only a haphazard order can be imposed, yet what is attempted in the recovery of archaeological heritage is the exact opposite. These breaks and discontinuities are overlooked by pretending that the past is a silent player in the continuous reworking of our contemporary desires and identities (see Alonso 1988). Foucault is quite insightful in this regard, citing (1) the ever-present discontinuities of all historical narrative, because "it operates in a field of entangled and confused parchment, on documents that have been scratched over and recopied many times" (Foucault 1998b: 369); and (2) the pivotal role of language in the enterprise of recovering history because one cannot be "blind to the personal investment there may be in this obsession with language that exists everywhere and escapes us in its very survival" (Foucault 1998a: 290).

For CONAIE, language also marks a pivotal place (as Foucault [1998b] outlines for us), one that is plagued with discontinuities upon which one erases and recopies new meanings. Quechua, an indigenous language introduced by the Incas as a lingua franca in the Incan process of colonization, occupies that ambiguous position for Indians today (just as Spanish does for all Ecuadorians). At an initial level, the pre-Hispanic colonizing undertones of Quechua must be silenced, because this violent rhetoric (Incas as colonizers) has been used by the nation-state not only to divide the Indian communities but also to legitimize its claims against its neighboring Peruvian enemy (Ecuador and Peru have been at war on and off since the inception of the republic in 1830). Yet the colonizing undertone is there, a linguistic emblem of the Incas' prowess in conquering and decimating local northern Andean populations.

This same instrument, Quechua (or Quichua, as the local northern variant) as a pre-Hispanic language, has served to continuously divide the Indian communities, including those within CONAIE—for CONAIE is not the only representative of Ecuador's Indian communities. Tellingly, the Ecuadorian Indian Evangelical Movement has the second largest support base, but unmistakably CONAIE is still the largest and most politically powerful. The Indian divisions are maintained through not only religious (as the Evangelical Movement expresses) and ethnic (different cultural/tribal affiliations) differences but also linguistic ones. Out of the twenty-one Indian nationalities that constitute CONAIE, all but six of them claim Quichua as their official language. It is not surprising that these six groups, most of them from the Amazon, have the least influence in the movement and have the fewest representatives in the decision making of the movement's governing body.

Once again, I use this example of language to show the ambiguous elements in archaeological heritage: how it is continuously plagued with claims of truth, identity politics, and implicit forms of domination, particularly when elevated to a national sphere. Unlike any other contemporary national Ecuadorian population, Indians today embody, in an existential manner, an ethos of the pre-Hispanic past. The nation's continuous rhetoric of courageous Indian leaders—exemplified by the use of their images on currency (until the sucre was replaced by the U.S. dollar), murals, school textbooks, and elsewhere—is embodied by the presence of Indians today and inscribed, however artificially, in the white/mestizo population's appreciation of Indian languages, clothes, and customs. A brief but relevant example is that an avid interest in traditional healing has been revived by middle-class Ecuadorians in recent decades, with places such as Santo Domingo de los Colorados becoming pilgrimage sites for good luck and health seekers. As a result of this, Indians today personalize the incredibly contested relationships among other national Ecuadorian populations, particularly that of whites and mestizo Ecuadorians, and identify such contestation with their troubled pre-Hispanic and colonial past.

This particular mode of looking at the past through its archaeological remains is clearly a historical recourse of the nation; for the past 170 years, the Indian population has carried this burden of proof afforded by the racially normative national ideology. Through CONAIE and the movement's recent reformulation of Indian identity, this embodiment of the past seems to be affected slightly, producing similarly different power effects (see Hall 1997a, 1997b). As the Indians regain a power lost more than five centuries ago, they also develop a powerful national representation, inducing a fear among the white and mestizo populations not known since colonial times, so that traditional national figures, elite landholders, church representatives, and governing politicians find their status questioned in unbearably problematic and dangerous ways.

Perhaps the clearest manner in which this is effected is the continuous production of an ideology of *regionalismo* (regionalism), which mainly depends on the coastal groups' (*costeños*) hatred of highlanders (*serranos*), to the total exclusion of the Amazon or Galapagos Island populations as rhetorically irrelevant. Through this regionalist discourse, *serrano* (formerly merely a descriptive adjective) has come to be understood more as an insult than anything else, a symbolic resignification that the word *costeño* has not undergone. For costeños, CONAIE and contemporary Indians embody their ambiguous hatred of the Indian past, which they associate with the highlands because the Andean mountain range is where most of today's Indian communities managed to survive.

In this sense, CONAIE represents not only a reversal of historical oppression but also an uneasy memory of the coast's genocidal past, which has been singularly erased. These uneasy memories (along with the costeños' fear of losing political control and power, gained only a hundred years ago through the liberal revolution of 1905) are enough to generate enormous resentment against the leaders of the Indian movement today. In this context, fraught with incredible national implications and very real effects of power, CONAIE has been able to succeed, at least in political terms, and continues to reproduce the nation's pre-Hispanic archaeological heritage.

Ethnographic Contestation: Archaeological Heritage and Domination

The two elements discussed above—the state's appropriation of the site of Cochasquí as one imbued with national significance and the traumatic instance of pre-Hispanic recovery by the Indian movement—exemplify but a small part of the larger historical debate and hegemonic implications embedded within any discussion of archaeological heritage in Ecuador. Other case studies, such as that of the archaeological sites of Culebrilla and Agua Blanca, present scenarios in which the local population fought against the state's willingness to destroy the archaeological sites for development purposes. In both instances, the communities reinterpreted the archaeological heritage embedded at the sites to legitimize their claims of defending the archaeological ruins and through this process provided a dynamic reinterpretation of their past and identities (see McEwan 1990; McEwan, Silva, and Hudson 2006).

All of these cases—either of state control at sites such as Cochasquí and Inga Pirca (the largest Inca ruin in Ecuador today) or where local contestation is immediately effected and mobilized through the population's reinterpretation of the official past, as with CONAIE—are dynamic examples of the complex hegemonic burden of the past and archaeological heritage. Rather than seeing these cases as contrasting examples, I argue that they all express similar processes of interpretation, appropriation, and hegemonic ambiguity: in other words, similar constraints of national historical hermeneutics, embedded within the nature of all types of claims of archaeological heritage.

Even though, as anthropologists, we have a political commitment that is traditionally aligned with locally oppressed communities, such as that of the indigenous population of Ecuador, we cannot deny that these local groups and the state are both playing the archaeological heritage game in related political terms, with similar concerns for socioeconomic and cultural survival. What has become clearer in the past few decades is what we have always known: no individual, group, or institution can survive without an inherent and congruent claim to the past. The greatest difference, perhaps, is that we can now theorize about the appropriation of archaeological heritage, mainly because the archaeological discipline has been forced to adapt its hegemonic domain of science and western legitimacy less stringently. This adaptation of the discipline's hegemonic stronghold is enabled by a postcolonial critique that has given a voice, albeit in an extremely complicated manner, to precisely those natives and locals who used to be only objects of study (Mignolo 2000; Spivak 1999).

In this new context of theoretical analysis and shifting domains of scientific inquiry, archaeological heritage claims are as contested as they have ever been (as in the debate over mound builders in the United States, for example, or the reconfiguration of Aztec symbolism in Mexico) but are more clearly understood for what they are: sociopolitical resignifications of the past (see García-Canclini 1992). In this sense, arguing for greater or lesser values of truth in terms of one claim versus another is not a worthwhile analytical endeavor (other than for explicit political effects), because every contesting version is already invested with and formulated within its own logic of truth and evidential constraints (see Wylie 1992). Rather, it is precisely in a limited analysis that looks to validate one version over another in which domination and hegemonic control insinuates itself in the most problematic fashion, specifically because hegemony is so subtle in maintaining its dominance.

All archaeological heritage claims, particularly ones with nationalizing implications (such as those that are evident at Cochasquí and inherent in CONAIE's reformulation of the past), will always imply a political struggle to redefine and legitimize one's identity and therefore one's right to exist. James Baldwin—not indirectly as a result of his ambiguous position as a black, gay, North American intellectual—captured this ambiguous relationship between the past and our identities perhaps better than any other scholar has yet done: "The disputed passage (of our identities) will remain disputed so long as you do not have the authority of the right-of-way—so long, that is, as your passage can be disputed: the document promising safe passage can always be revoked. Power clears the passage, swiftly: but the paradox, here, is that power, rooted in history, is also the mockery and repudiation of history. The power to define the other seals one's definition of oneself—who, then, in such a fearful mathematics, is trapped?" (1990: 481).

I am not advocating that there should be no claims to archaeological heritage of any kind. Ultimately this would mean little, because Indians and the Ecuadorian state will continue this historical process no matter what anthropologists say. Rather, I argue that the process of domination inherent in all claims to the past invites a different form of analysis, one that will not blindly offer itself to hegemonic control, even though it cannot totally escape the dominance of hegemony (for believing in such an escape is yet another form of academic delusion). This is the context within which ethnographic analysis can be useful in helping us to question official and alternative histories.

The ethnographic enterprise, when redirected toward one of anthropology's subfields (such as archaeology), can help us liberate ourselves from complicit games of cultural authenticity (Clifford and Marcus 1986; Rabinow 1977), historical truth (Foucault 1991), and static identities (McClintock, Mufti, and Shohat 1997; Minh-ha 1997). By directing the gaze away from the Other's past to ourselves as legitimizers of historical truth, we may obtain new knowledge central to the ethnographic endeavor; this same process of knowledge production has allowed anthropology to historically distance itself from its colonialist origins. No less ironic is the premise that the postcolonial turn—of the "native anthropologist" making the Western subject the Other—resignifies ethnography's potential as a counterhegemonic tool.

Yet the ambiguous elements of domination and resistance are inherent to ethnographic contestation, just as they are to the recovery of archaeological heritage. The trap is most precisely set when we look only to one—either resistance or domination—instead of seeing how both are inherent to all ethnographic enterprise, reconstructions of the past, and reformulations of our historical identities. Precisely because of the dynamic nature of these social processes, something always eludes signification and thrusts us into new/old reformulations. It is also in that escape that our hopes are most secure and least betrayed, because "true" archaeological heritages will only lead us into greater webs of domination and historical misrepresentations.

Acknowledgments

I want to extend my gratitude to Lena Mortensen and Julie Hollowell for their dedication and hard work; without their support, this enterprise would not be. Much thanks to Bernice Kurchin for her wonderful editorial suggestions and comments. Thanks also to Greg Allen, who in his own way always has an impact on my vision and scholarship.

References Cited

Abu el-Haj, Nadia. *Facts on the Ground: Archaeological Practice and Territorial Self-fashioning in Israeli Society.* Chicago: University of Chicago Press, 2001.

Appadurai, Arjun. "Grassroots Globalization and the Research Imagination." *Public Culture* 12, no. 1 (2000): 1–20.

———. "Disjuncture and Difference in the Global Cultural Economy," In *The Anthropology of Globalization: A Reader,* edited by J. X. Inda and R. Rosaldo, 47–65. Oxford, U.K.: Blackwell, 2002.

Arnold, Bettina. "The Past as Propaganda: Totalitarian Archaeology in Nazi Germany." *Antiquity* 64, no. 244 (1990): 464–78.

———. "Germany's Nazi Past: How Hitler's Archaeologists Distorted European Prehistory to Justify Racist and Territorial Goals." *Archaeology* July/August (1992): 30–37.

Baldwin, James. *Just above My Head.* New York: Laurel Books, 1990.

Benavides, O. Hugo. *Making Ecuadorian Histories: Four Centuries of Defining Power.* Austin: University of Texas Press, 2004.

Bender, Barbara. *Stonehenge: Making Space.* New York: Berg, 1998.

Castañeda, Quetzil E. *In the Museum of Maya Culture: Touring Chichén Itzá.* Minneapolis: University of Minnesota Press, 1996.

Clifford, James, and George E. Marcus, eds. *Writing Culture: The Poetics and Politics of Ethnography.* Berkeley: University of California Press, 1986.

CONAIE (Confederación de Nacionalidades Indígenas del Ecuador). *Las nacionalidades indígenas en el Ecuador: Nuestro proceso organizativo.* Quito: Ed. TINCUI-CONAIE and Abya-Yala, 1989.

Crain, Mary. "The Social Construction of National Identity in Highland Ecuador." *Anthropological Quarterly* 63, no. 1 (1990): 43–59.

D'Altroy, Terence. *Provincial Power in the Inka Empire.* Washington, D.C.: Smithsonian Institution Press, 1992.

———. *The Incas.* Malden, Mass.: Blackwell, 2002.

Deloria, Vine, Jr.. *Custer Died for Your Sins: An Indian Manifesto.* New York: Avon Books, 1970.

Fabian, Johannes. *Time and the Other: How Anthropology Makes Its Object.* New York: Columbia University Press, 1983.

Fahim, Hussein, ed. *Indigenous Anthropology in Non-Western Countries.* Durham, N.C.: Carolina Academic Press, 1982.

Foucault, Michel. *Remarks on Marx.* New York: Semiotext(e), 1991.

———. "On the Ways of Writing History." In *Essential Works of Foucault, 1954–1984,* vol. 2, *Aesthetics, Method and Epistemology,* edited by J. Faubion, 279–96. New York: New Press, 1998. [1998a]

———. "Nietzsche, Genealogy, History." In *Essential Works of Foucault, 1954–1984,* vol. 2, *Aesthetics, Method and Epistemology,* edited by J. Faubion, 369–92. New York: New Press, 1998. [1998b]

García-Canclini, Nestor. "Cultural Reconversion." In *On Edge: The Crisis of Contemporary Latin American Culture,* edited by G. Yudice, J. Flores, and J. Franco, 29–44. Minneapolis: University of Minnesota Press, 1992.

Gero, Joan, D. M. Lacy, and M. Blakey, eds. *The Socio-Politics of Archaeology.* Department of Anthropology Research Reports 23. Amherst: University of Massachusetts, 1983.

Guerrero, Andrés. *La semántica de la dominación: El concertaje de Indios.* Quito: Ediciones Libri Mundi and Enrique Grosse-Luemern, 1991.

Hall, Stuart. "The Local and the Global: Globalization and Ethnicity." In *Culture, Globalization and the World-System: Contemporary Conditions for the Representation of Identity,* edited by A. King, 19–39. Minneapolis: University of Minnesota Press, 1997. [1997a]

———. "Old and New Identities, Old and New Ethnicities." In *Culture, Globalization and the World-System: Contemporary Conditions for the Representation of Identity,* edited by A. King, 41–68. Minneapolis: University of Minnesota Press, 1997. [1997b]

Handler, Richard. *Nationalism and the Politics of Culture in Quebec.* Madison: University of Wisconsin Press, 1988.

Handler, Richard, and Eric Gable. *The New History in an Old Museum: Creating the Past at Colonial Williamsburg.* Durham, N.C.: Duke University Press, 1997.

Haraway, Donna. *Primate Visions.* New York: Routledge, Chapman and Hall, 1989.

Harrison, Faye, ed. *Decolonizing Anthropology: Moving Further Toward an Anthropology for Liberation.* Washington, D.C.: Association of Black Anthropologists, American Anthropological Association, 1991.

Hodder, Ian. *Symbols in Action.* Cambridge: Cambridge University Press, 1982.

———. *Reading the Past.* Cambridge: Cambridge University Press, 1986.

Jones, Delmos. "Towards a Native Anthropology." *Human Organization* 29, no. 4 (1970): 251–59.

Joseph, Gilbert, and Daniel Nugent, eds. *Everyday Forms of State Formation: Revolution and the Negotiation of Rule in Modern Mexico.* Durham, N.C.: Duke University Press, 1994.

Kincaid, Jamaica. *My Brother.* New York: Farrar, Straus and Giroux, 1997.

Kuklick, Henrika. "Contested Monuments: The Politics of Archaeology in Southern Africa." In *History of Anthropology,* vol. 7, *Colonial Situations: Essays on the Contextualization of Ethnographic Knowledge,* edited by G. Stocking, 135–69. Wisconsin: University of Wisconsin Press, 1991.

LaRoche, Cheryl J., and Michael L. Blakey. "Seizing Intellectual Power: The Dialogue at the New York African Burial Ground." *Historical Archaeology* 31, no. 3 (1997): 84–106.

Lowenthal, David. *The Past Is a Foreign Country.* New York: Cambridge University Press, 1985.

———. *Possessed by the Past: The Heritage Crusade and the Spoils of History.* New York: Free Press, 1996.

Lumbreras, Luis. *La arqueología como ciencia social.* Lima: Ediciones Histar, 1981.

McClintock, Anne, Aamir Mufti, and Ella Shohat. *Dangerous Liaisons: Gender, Nation and Postcolonial Perspectives.* Minneapolis: University of Minnesota Press, 1997.

McEwan, Colin. "El sitio arqueológico de Agua Blanca, Manabí, Ecuador." Report on file at the Instituto Nacional de Patrimonio Cultural, Guayaquil, 1990.

McEwan, Colin, María-Isabel Silva, and Chris Hudson. "Using the Past to Forge the Future: The Genesis of the Community Site Museum at Agua Blanca, Ecuador." In *Archaeological Site Museums in Latin America,* edited by H. Silverman, 187–216. Gainesville: University Press of Florida, 2006.

Mignolo, Walter. *Local Histories/Global Designs: Coloniality, Subaltern Knowledges, and Border Thinking.* Princeton, N.J.: Princeton University Press, 2000.

Miller, James. *The Passion of Michel Foucault.* New York: Anchor Books, Doubleday, 1993.

Minh-ha, Trinh. "Not You/Like You: Postcolonial Women and the Interlocking Questions of Identity and Difference." In *Dangerous Liaisons: Gender, Nation and Postcolonial Perspectives,* edited by A. McClintock, A. Mufti, and E. Shohat, 415–19. Minneapolis: University of Minnesota Press, 1997.

Moscoso, Lucia, and Gaby Costa. *Historia oral de Cochasquí.* Quito: Programa Cochasquí, H. Consejo Provincial de Pichincha, 1989.

Muratorio, Blanca, ed. *Imágenes e imagineros: Representaciones de los indígenas ecuatorianos, siglos XIX y XX.* Quito: FLACSO, 1994.

Murra, John. *La organización económica del estado Inca.* Mexico City: Siglo XXI, Instituto de Estudios Peruanos, 1989.

Patterson, Thomas. *The Inca Empire: The Formation and Disintegration of a Pre-capitalist State.* New York: Berg, 1991.

———. *Toward a Social History of Archaeology in the United States.* New York: Harcourt Brace College Publishers, 1995.

Rabinow, Paul. *Reflections of Fieldwork in Morocco.* Berkeley: University of California Press, 1977.

Roseberry, William. "Hegemony and the Language of Contention." In *Everyday Forms of State Formation: Revolution and the Negotiation of Rule in Modern Mexico,* edited by G. Joseph and D. Nugent, 355–66. Durham, N.C.: Duke University Press, 1994.

Salcedo, José. "Al rescate de la identidad cultural en Cochasquí." Unpublished manuscript for Programa Cochasquí, Cochasquí, Ecuador, 1985.

Salomon, Frank. "Ancestors, Grave Robbers, and the Possible Antecedents of Canari 'Inca-Ism.'" In *Natives and Neighbors in South America: Anthropological Essays,* edited by H. Skar and F. Salomon, 23–45. Ethnological Studies 38. Goteborg, Sweden: Goteborgs Etnografiska Museum, 1987.

Sayer, Derek. "Everyday Forms of State Formation: Some Dissident Remarks on 'Hegemony.'" In *Everyday Forms of State Formation: Revolution and the Negotiation of Rule in Modern Mexico,* edited by G. Joseph and D. Nugent, 367–78. Durham, N.C.: Duke University Press, 1994.

Schmidt, Peter R., and Thomas C. Patterson. "Introduction: From Constructing to Making Alternative Histories." In *Making Alternative Histories: The Practice of Archaeology and History in Non-Western Settings,* edited by P. Schmidt and T. Patterson, 1–24. Santa Fe, N.Mex.: School of American Research Press, 1995.

Shanks, Michael, and Christopher Tilley. *Social Theory and Archaeology.* Albuquerque: University of New Mexico Press, 1987. [1987a]

———. *Re-constructing Archaeology: Theory and Practice.* Cambridge: Cambridge University Press, 1987. [1987b]

Silberman, Neil Asher. *Between Past and Present: Archaeology, Ideology, and Nationalism in the Modern Middle East.* New York: Henry Holt and Company, 1989.

———. "Promised Lands and Chosen People: The Politics and Poetics of Archaeological Narrative." In *Nationalism, Politics, and the Practice of Archaeology,* edited by P. Kohl and C. Fawcett, 249–62. Cambridge: Cambridge University Press, 1995.

Silberman, Neil Asher, and David Small, eds. *The Archaeology of Israel: Constructing the Past, Interpreting the Present.* Sheffield: Sheffield Academic Press, 1997.

Spivak, Gayatri Chakravorty. *A Critique of Postcolonial Reason: Toward a History of the Vanishing Present.* Cambridge, Mass.: Harvard University Press, 1999.

Stutzman, Ronald. "El Mestizaje: An All-Inclusive Ideology of Exclusion." In *Cultural Transformations and Ethnicity in Modern Ecuador,* edited by N. Whitten, 45–94. Urbana: University of Illinois Press, 1981.

Trigger, Bruce. "Alternative Archaeologies: Nationalist, Colonialist, Imperialist." *Man* 19 (1984): 355–70.

———. *A History of Archaeological Thought.* New York: Cambridge University Press, 1989.

Trouillot, Michel-Rolph. *Silencing the Past: Power and the Production of History.* Boston: Beacon Press, 1995.

Tsing, Anna. "Inside the Economy of Appearances." *Public Culture* 12, no. 1 (2000): 115–44.

Vargas Arenas, Iraida. "The Perception of History and Archaeology in Latin America: A Theoretical Approach." In *Making Alternative Histories: The Practice of Archaeology and History in Non-Western Settings,* edited by P. Schmidt and T. Patterson, 47–68. Santa Fe, N.Mex.: School of American Research Press, 1995.

Wright, Patrick. *On Living in an Old Country: The National Past in Contemporary Britain.* New York: Verso, 1985.

Wylie, Alison. "The Interplay of Evidential Constraints and Political Interests: Recent Archaeological Research on Gender." *American Antiquity* 57, no. 1 (1992): 15–35.

———. "Alternative Histories: Epistemic Disunity and Political Integrity." In *Making Alternative Histories: The Practice of Archaeology and History in Non-Western Settings,* edited by P. Schmidt and T. Patterson, 255–72. Santa Fe, N.Mex.: School of American Research Press, 1995.

Zimmerman, Larry. "Human Bones as Symbols of Power: Aboriginal American Belief System toward Bones and 'Grave-Robbing' Archaeologists." In *Who Needs the Past?* edited by R. Layton, 211–16. London: Unwin Hyman, 1989.

Zizek, Slavoj. *Welcome to the Desert of the Real.* London: Verso, 2002.

Part 3

Valuing the Past

Commentary

Archaeological Follies

RICHARD HANDLER

When a person is crazy or merely pathogenic and functions in a schizoid way we say he is out of contact or disconnected. When a large group of people acts this way toward us we say that they constitute a separate culture.

Henry 1963: 94

As has often been noted, valuing the past is an activity that can occur only in the present. And such activities can occur only at specific places in the present, places chosen by past-oriented actors as relevant to their work. Yet the phrase *the past* (with its definite article) implies a set of universalistic implications that Benjamin Lee Whorf (1956: 134–59) spelled out long ago. This concept is applicable (we think) to all reality, and it implies that all reality exists within a homogenous temporal regime. That regime can be enumerated in terms of a uniform calculus (in plain language, we count time in equal units that we assume to be objectively quantified). We imagine this temporal regime in spatial terms (blocks, lines), while we imagine time itself as a uniform substance (like the sand in an hourglass). Finally, we imagine this substance, time, as inhering in objects, which are said to "have" a certain age, or to be marked by time and history.

From this perspective, the past exists beneath or within all contemporary places. Our planet as a whole and all places on it are equally possessed of a past. Clearly (as evidenced by the vast literature on the politics of the past and on the social construction of historical memory), not all people agree on which version of the past is relevant for the particular place on earth that interests them. Also clear is that there are plenty of places where people have no interest in the past. Yet another point that should be clear, but is less well discussed, is that there are plenty of people who do not share this contemporary temporal regime and, in particular, this universalistic, objectifying concept of the past (which, after all, is a cultural conceit with its own—dare I say it?—history).

This universalistic concept of time is one that archaeologists and scholars in other historical disciplines have little interest in questioning, since it gives them a prima facie claim to study any place that catches their fancy. Once one decides to study the past of a certain place or people, all sorts of negotiations over access may follow. But the starting assumption is that all places are equally past-saturated and that science thus has a legitimate claim not only to study the past but also to preserve the physical configuration or archival record of the past in a given location, at least until it can be studied. From these assumptions follow the well-known arguments concerning the "destruction" of archaeological heritage by a cast of characters that starts with looters and art dealers and can include anyone who wants to farm, dig, build, or bury on a given plot of land.

Now, there is something just a bit crazy (as Jules Henry uses the term in my epigraph) in the idea that the entire surface of the earth is an archaeological site containing precious information that we may need someday to reconstruct the past in its totality. We will never have the resources to mine anything but a tiny fraction of the earth's surface for its archaeological treasures. The daily activities of human beings and the regular workings of natural processes (climatological, geological, and so on) will destroy far, far more of the archaeological heritage than we will ever be able to study. And we are daily creating vast quantities of new "past" to be studied at some subsequent moment.

Beyond these practical matters, one can also argue that no human vision of the past can transcend its own particular cultural location to arrive at an objective or complete understanding of past human societies and cultures. This argument has both an epistemological and a political strand. Most anthropologists and archaeologists who have delved into the epistemological question agree that we can never reconstruct the past completely or objectively. At best, we can use our current knowledge, concepts, and hunches to ask fairly specific questions about specific locales. As to the politics of the past, a guiding assumption of this volume is that different iterations of the past of a particular place will be constructed by differently situated actors. People have more or less power to construct a version of the past, and more or less power to imbue their particular construction with authority. What is true of the politics of particular pasts is also true of the politics of the modern temporal regime and its relationship to history making, although this relationship has received less scrutiny. Scholars now pay a good deal of attention to political struggles over particular versions of history, but they, and perhaps the people they study, seem less likely to contest the hegemony of modern historical time.

What can the chapters in this section of the volume tell us about the evaluation of a past that is conceptualized in the modernist, universalistic terms I have sketched? Taken together, they do more than present case studies of disputes over the value of particular pasts (although we can take Jon Daehnke's chapter on Hawai'i as paradigmatic in this regard). They also give us a set of possibilities ranging from a local situation in which the past has been archaeologically mined to an extraordinary degree (Lena Mortensen's chapter on Copán), to one in which it is being mined but not in a way that archaeologists would like (Julie Hollowell's chapter on St. Lawrence Island), to one in which it has been mined very little, despite the presence of important archaeological sites (Chip Colwell-Chanthaphonh's chapter on the San Pedro Valley).

Lena Mortensen's portrayal of Copán (chapter 8) is refreshingly unusual in its refusal to discuss the historical or archaeological significance of a world-famous archaeological site. Rather, Mortensen describes the site as a present-day industrial complex (or perhaps an especially elaborate archaeological folly, with *folly* here intended in one of its French senses, to mean an architectural extravagance). Copán is presented as a typical site of resource extraction, in which international capital deriving from Western centers of power takes over an "undeveloped" site and there produces a world (call it a museum or a heritage site or a theme park) that meets and expresses the needs of those who (re-)built it. Mortensen focuses on work relations at this industrial site: not only the hiring of locals for various lower-level tasks but also the apprenticeship of incoming, First World students to established senior scientists and the ways in which relationships between senior scholars and locals are renewed or exploited by both apprentice students and local workers.

In the international world of big-time ("world-famous") sites, it is a grave insult to make a comparison to Disneyland. Yet Copán, like Colonial Williamsburg, has a Disneyesque quality, at least when considered as a present-day factory in the leisure industry. Mortensen's focus on the way the site works in the present recalls, for me, what Eric Gable and I tried to study ethnographically at Colonial Williamsburg (Handler and Gable 1997) and what Stephen Fjellman did in his ethnography of Walt Disney World (Fjellman 1992). In making such a claim, I do not mean to be disrespectful; that the museum sites (leaving Disney out of the discussion, for the moment) are places of significant scholarly achievement is not doubted. But Mortensen allows us to see, in addition, how such scholarly work is organized in a way that is consonant with other kinds of industrial production in our world. And there is something outlandish (a bit insane) in the creation of these vast reconstructions, which, after all, always owe their existence to strange sets of contingencies that brought together "natives" from various places, some of whom had visionary ambitions and others of whom had vast capital resources.

Jon Daehnke's and Julie Hollowell's chapters both concern disputes about how to manage a past that all disputants agree is valuable. Daehnke, however, reports a case that is completely within an archaeological frame of reference, in the sense that "the past" is valued in similar ways by all disputants (chapter 9). What remains at issue is the question of who is to control the objects that contain or represent the Hawaiian past. In chapter 10, by contrast, Hollowell discusses one group of actors (St. Lawrence Islanders) who have consciously rejected some of the implications of the archaeological frame of reference, a decision that another group of actors (archaeologists) laments but is powerless to undo. Hollowell argues that archaeologists need to understand their own ethic of stewardship (and, by extension, their definition of the value of the past) as one among several alternatives, all of which deserve respectful attention. Archaeologists may never agree with St. Lawrence Islanders who dig for old ivory artifacts to sell on the market, but from Hollowell's perspective, the archaeological conception of the scientific value of the past does not by itself trump all other claims concerning the disposition of cultural resources.

This brings us, finally, to Chip Colwell-Chanthaphonh's sketch of a place (the San Pedro Valley, Arizona) "littered" with important Paleo-Indian sites, of some fame in the archaeological literature but not of interest, apparently, to those who are currently stewarding and developing the area for tourism and natural conservation (chapter 11). Lack of what Colwell-Chanthaphonh calls monumentality can be but one reason for the public disinterest in the archaeological resources of the region. The salient point for the present discussion is the arbitrary relationship between the past—which, by definition, is everywhere—and the historical contingencies that lead some pasts to be developed, others forgotten.

The San Pedro Valley illuminates by contrast, by the very absence of developed archaeological sites, the degree of folly required to make such sites bloom, as it were, in the desert (or jungle). The scholarly and philanthropic visionaries who built places such as Copán and Colonial Williamsburg must have been possessed by some divine madness that drove them to apparently heroic feats of historical reconstruction. Ethnographic and historical analyses of such reconstructions, such as Quetzil Castañeda's study of Chichén Itzá (1996), will need to question modern presuppositions about "the past" if their aim is to be critical rather than celebratory.

Finally, historians of anthropology must also note the analogous process that has taken place in sociocultural anthropology, in which there is a similarly arbitrary or fantastical quality to the historical creation of canonical ethnographic examples. The Nuer, Trobriand Islanders, and Kwakiutl are not inherently more interesting (or more interestingly "cultured") than any number of other peoples (Segal 1999). Their fame in the anthropological record can be explained only in terms of historical contingencies that brought together anthropological visionaries (such as E. E. Evans-Pritchard, Bronislaw Malinowski, and Franz Boas) in particular colonial situations at a moment when anthropology was working to institutionalize itself as an eminently sane field of study within an apparently rational scientific enterprise: the mapping of all reality.

References Cited

Castañeda, Quetzil E. *In the Museum of Maya Culture: Touring Chichén Itzá.* Minneapolis: University of Minnesota Press, 1996.

Fjellman, Stephen M. *Vinyl Leaves: Walt Disney World and America.* Boulder, Colo.: Westview Press, 1992.

Handler, Richard, and Eric Gable. *The New History in an Old Museum: Creating the Past at Colonial Williamsburg.* Durham, N.C.: Duke University Press, 1997.

Henry, Jules. *Culture against Man.* New York: Random House, 1963.

Segal, Daniel. "Ethnographic Classics, Ethnographic Examples: Some Thoughts on the New Cultural Studies and an Old Queer Science." In *Kulturstudien Heute (The Contemporary Study of Culture),* edited by I. Korneck and G. Illetschko, 245–62. Vienna: Turia and Kant, 1999.

Whorf, Benjamin Lee. *Language, Thought, and Reality.* Cambridge, Mass.: MIT Press, 1956.

8

Producing Copán in the Archaeology Industry

LENA MORTENSEN .

There are many routes into Copán, an internationally celebrated archaeological park in western Honduras. On almost any day, hundreds of international visitors and Honduran schoolchildren pour through the main gates of the Copán complex and head toward the visitor center, where they purchase tickets to one of the bundled "attractions" that make up the present-day park: the reconstructed city center, the on-site sculpture museum, or perhaps the tunnels built by archaeologists that burrow beneath the tallest of the site's ancient structures. For many, these tickets represent personal access to the ancient Maya past, as embodied in the resurrected monuments that make up the site core. But these visitors, for the most part, have already had access to Copán long before they cross the fence line that separates the archaeological zone from neighboring fields.

First encounters with Copán—primary routes of entry, that is—usually take place through various forms of media: a thumbed-through travel guide for the Mundo Maya, an hour-long documentary produced by *Nova,* a government-issue Honduran textbook for first graders, a new display of stone sculpture from the collection of a university museum, the photo album (or, now, photo blog) of a friend who recently returned from her own visit.[1] Such interfaces, reproduced and dispersed throughout the world, provide passages into Copán that foreground its monumentality and re-create a sense of fame that has been acquiring patina since the site was first described by John Stephens and Frank Catherwood in their 1841 best seller, *Incidents of Travel in Central America, Chiapas and Yucatan.* Given the historical proliferation and cumulative weight of media depicting this place, and its placement within the cultural discourse about the ancient Maya, visitors today have difficulty experiencing Copán in anything other than its monumental form or deviating from the imaginings that have become institutionalized in this place.

But there are other points of entry, those that lead to Copán's backstage. Beyond the mode of "visitor," many others enter Copán, also on a daily basis but through a set of secondary gates and passageways, accessible via unmarked turns off the main road that lead to unscripted spaces in the park's infrastructure. These are the passageways for the scores of laborers, students, "experts," *vigilantes,* and others who participate in what I call here Copán's "archaeology industry," the operations of which collectively produce the Copán experience. Those who enter through a side door rather than the front gate are also usually entering into relations of production that have literally built the monument from the ground up. I came to Copán wanting to know more about these other entrances, these nonmonumental experiences, and how they might condition the way one values the past. The pertinent question seemed to be not so much what people make of the past but *how* they make it.

In beginning this ethnographic project, I found disentangling the various entranceways to the site difficult, if not impossible. Copán's many modes and, subsequently, ways of being valued—a center for scientific research on the ancient Maya, a symbol of Honduran national identity, an engine of economic development in the form of heritage tourism, to name a few—result from dialogic processes of coproduction rather than distinct spheres of meaning or practice. These various modes cannot be taken separately but must instead be considered as part of a working, if fractious, whole. The whole to which I refer is a complex set of operations that produce the site in its physical, discursive, and symbolic form—the archaeology industry. Indeed, any encounter with Copán is always an encounter with the archaeology industry that simultaneously shapes the contours of the contemporary site and channels the economies of value that produce meaning out of place or past. In this chapter, I take a more intimate look at the form and functions of this industry, focusing on its participants and their detailed engagements.

Archaeology as Industry

The "archaeology industry" concept as I use it here is inspired by Robert Hewison's iconic condemnation of England's heritage movement, which he dubs the "heritage industry" (1987). Hewison sees the heritage industry as a trend that stifles creativity, relying on nostalgia for a sanitized past rather than on innovation for alternative futures. While perhaps not exactly creative, the archaeology industry at Copán is certainly better characterized as generative—producing artifacts, entertainment, and histories—even as the forms of these products are limited by the needs and desires of the actors and institutions that regulate them. Rather than merely denounce the archaeology industry as an appropriation and alienation of history in the service of capitalism (á la Marx), I am interested in exploring how employing this concept might afford a clearer perspective on the many entanglements that the work of archaeology entails. The conceptual metaphor "industry" describes the ways in which people engage with the site and the basic economic relationships at the heart of those engagements, as well as the relations of power and inequality they inevitably entail.

Merriam-Webster's Collegiate Dictionary offers a definition for the term *industry* that helps focus this discussion: "systematic labor especially for some useful purpose or the creation of something of value." The site of Copán, in its different formulations and manifestations, has value (that is, it is valued, highly, in a variety of registers) and is the result of systematic labor by various actors. The archaeology industry, then, can be thought of as the collective processes of production and consumption that generate and constitute the site in physical, discursive, and ideological form. This includes highly interactive micro- and macro-level practices, such as excavation, interpretation, management, conservation, tour guiding, providing tourism services, publicity, and producing various forms of knowledge.

Before I turn to details of the processes, products, and participants, some broader notes about the structure of the Copán system are necessary. Industry is a familiar concept in a place such as Honduras, where economic growth depends on the ever-expanding maquiladora (export-oriented manufacturing and assembly) sector, which constitutes links in well-developed global commodity chains. Like maquiladoras, the archaeology industry is organized by global commodity chains that link the flows of people, technology, goods, capital, and services between countries and regions (Gereffi and Korzeniewicz 1994). Some aspects of the archaeology industry—especially intensive excavation, analysis, and reconstruction efforts—require considerable financial capital investment. Others—particularly tourism services and some kinds of archaeological fieldwork—rely primarily on inexpensive labor. One must also note that the archaeology industry is decentralized: although industry processes are negotiated through hierarchies of power, no single institution controls the system (compare Handler and Gable 1997); instead, many different sectors rely on one another in complicated networks of authority and different forms of capital to make the collective industry function. In the production of both discursive and material products, the industry is flexible, maintaining multiple products that circulate in diverse venues. And while products of this industry are not exactly mass-produced, they do conform to what we might call "industry standards," in that they fit within norms that define parameters of academic work, archaeological materials, tourist experiences, and "Maya culture."

As many have noted, the past is neither already remembered nor already meaningful (for example, Bodnar 1992; Bond and Gilliam 1994; Handler and Gable 1997; Kirshenblatt-Gimblett 1998; Trouillot 1995). It must be produced in some form, in this case "materialized"—as memory, as tourism, as heritage—and the work of this production is what gives the past shape. Although saying that the past is produced is no longer novel, it bears repeating, if only to remind us to look more closely at the mechanics and consequences of acts of production. As I use the term, *production* does not mean "fiction." By saying that Copán or Maya archaeology or the past itself is produced, I mean to focus not on its invention in the sense of "inauthentic" or "false" but instead on the very real structures and interactions that manipulate the generation and exchange of symbolic and financial capital. In this way, this approach owes more of a debt to Pierre Bourdieu than to Karl Marx. Taking note of the operations of production and the recognition that a site is a collection of not only discourses but also actions and relations allows us to more intimately assess the ways in which an archaeologized space may intrude upon, or indeed prefigure, the experiences of everyday life (see, for example, Herzfeld 1991).[2]

Creating Copán

The ancient city of Copán occupies a central position in the archaeological imagination of Maya studies and the romantic fashioning of the Honduran nation-state (Joyce 2003; Mortensen 2007). It bears a long history as a constructed place: literally, in the sense of construction phases spanning centuries; and figuratively, as a site of public memory, cultural genealogy, and global spectacle. By the time the Spanish conquistadores arrived in the Caribbean, the city of Copán had already ceased operating as an active political center for several hundred years. In the mid-nineteenth century, when the first archaeologist-explorers from Europe and North America visited the area, they encountered the remnants of the city covered in tropical growth, at that point only peripherally relevant to local residents' lives, more a source of convenient building material than a basis for continuing cultural traditions.[3] Since that time, numerous phases of archaeological projects and tourism development, and their reciprocal practices, have once again transformed Copán into a vital regional center, defined by cycles of politics and circuits of commerce not entirely unlike those negotiated by the original inhabitants (see Mortensen 2005).

Since the 1930s, the government of Honduras has partnered with high-profile foreign institutions to invest in transfiguring the ancient structures that make up the Copán ruins, taming the physical landscape and establishing tourism infrastructure. The first major phase in Copán archaeology as an industry—its production, marketing, and consumption—began with a bilateral project between the government of Honduras and the Carnegie Institute of Washington (CIW), which at that time was the key institution not only conducting research on the ancient Maya but also establishing archaeological parks in the region.[4] The ultimate goal of this massive excavation and reconstruction project at Copán, which lasted into the 1950s, was to transform the ruins into a major tourist attraction, satisfying the Carnegie agenda of creating another showcase for the ancient Maya and the Honduran government's agenda of defining a national past based in a recognized "civilization."[5] Over multiple field seasons, the CIW project established the modern template for the Copán park, producing both archaeological research and the attendant infrastructure for archaeological tourism: reconstructing major buildings in the site core, raising fallen stelae, building a local museum, and writing the first guidebook (see Weeks and Hill 2006).

The groundwork for the next significant iteration of Copán was laid in the 1970s, when the Honduran government turned to Harvard University to renew archaeological excavations as part of a new phase of archaeotourism development through the Proyecto Arqueológico Copán: Primera Fase, or PAC I (1977–80), funded in part by the Central American Bank of Economic Integration (BCIE). The success of PAC I led to a second phase, PAC II (1981–84), this time with financing from the World Bank and foreign expertise provided through Pennsylvania State University. Both phases of PAC were conceived explicitly as archaeology-for-tourism projects and yielded significant additions to the budding Copán archaeological industry, including remodeling and expansion of the local museum, several traveling exhibitions, a visitor center, the first training program for guides, and an interpretive trail. The archaeological projects themselves, although broad in overall scope, also concentrated heavily on restoring structures in the site core and adjacent areas, an expected and proven attraction for visitors.

In the early 1990s, when the tobacco industry—the dominant economic force in the Copán Valley since the 1950s—began to decline, tourism surged, generating the impetus for full-scale development of the modern archaeological industry at Copán (Loker 2005). The mid-1990s are commonly considered the archaeological heyday of Copán, a time when at least three full-time research projects and numerous subprojects were under way at the ruins or in the valley at any given time. These projects (funded through aid agencies, foreign universities, scientific foundations, and the Honduran government) employed several hundred local laborers and technicians, in addition to the approximately fifty permanent employees and contract workers paid by the Honduran Institute for Anthropology and History (IHAH—the government body in charge of the nation's cultural patrimony) to manage and maintain the archaeological park, laboratory, visitor center, and museums.[6] In this period, many residents, looking for new opportunities as they watched tobacco fortunes wither, began to invest in the tourism service sector. Changes at the national level during the late 1990s, specifically the creation of a new Ministry of Tourism, facilitated the overall growth of tourism, always promoting Copán as a cornerstone in new development strategies.

Today, the ancient city of Copán is a tourism park, a national monument, and a

UNESCO World Heritage site. As such, it is subject to regulation by several overlapping institutions at the regional, national, transnational, and even global levels. Experts, technicians, managers, students, and laborers from Europe, North America, Asia, greater Honduras, and, of course, the local area come together to carry out the mutually dependent operations that form the archaeology industry here. Permanent residents of the area surrounding the site—primarily Honduran nationals who identify as mestizos but also indigenous Maya Chortí as well as foreign expatriates—are continually adapting their lifestyles to accommodate the ever-growing tourist economy based in the neighboring town of Copán Ruinas. Copán now receives approximately 150,000 visitors yearly, more than twice as many as all other archaeological parks and historical sites in Honduras combined, making it an integral part of not only the local economy but also the national historical imaginary.

Today in Copán virtually everyone is aware of the role that archaeological tourism plays in the development of the town and region, and more and more local and not-so-local entrepreneurs seek to piggyback on this growth by initiating complementary tourism ventures and services. This trend has recently been strengthened by a World Bank loan dedicating 12.3 million dollars toward sustainable tourism development in the Copán Valley, specifically directed at archaeological tourism and its offshoots and designed to remap the entire region into a circuit of attractions. This Regional Development in the Copan Valley Project effectively marks the latest, and most massive, iteration in the history of Copán's archaeology industry.[7]

Work in the Archaeology Industry

The abstract configuration of "the past" rarely enters into ordinary life, yet the presence of the Copán ruins and the operations of its presentation are nothing if not quotidian encounters. At Copán, I looked for a way to talk with people about the connection between daily life and "the past," wondering often about the ways in which specific experiences shape value, in its myriad forms. But when I interviewed Hondurans who lived in and around Copán about their experiences with archaeology and *las ruinas,* the vast majority spoke in terms of work. From laborers who had spent only a few months cutting grass at the park to midlevel project administrators to the most highly trained specialists working in the laboratory and storage facility of the Regional Center for Archaeological Investigations (CRIA), nearly every conversation touched on fluctuations in pay scales, hiring practices, project histories, and the politics that affect these things. Although I never directly asked about these factors, people would typically describe their engagements with archaeology in terms of hours, conditions, benefits, and wages, and they often offered great detail about the history of changes in labor relations. I was, in fact, reluctant to discuss employment terms in much detail: I was concerned about creating additional tension for those whose employment status seemed particularly insecure, and I did not wish to become entangled in any ongoing disputes. But again and again, many whom I interviewed offered up their intimate experiences with the rhythms and structures of archaeological work, which clarified that this was perhaps the most significant frame for understanding local value for archaeological processes. This recurring focus on pay, conditions, and labor during interviews is what first led me to begin to think about archaeology at Copán as an industry.

The nature of archaeological excavation in this region, and in many others, fits well with the metaphor of industry. Excavation, whether tunneling through the remains of buildings or exposing rural house floors, is labor intensive. A single archaeologist may sit alone confronting a table full of ceramic bits and pieces, but those pieces arrive at the table by way of many hands. The processes that take them there and form the chain of transforming an object from the ground into a source of scientific information[8]—clearing, digging, cleaning, recording, washing, labeling, and others—require labor and inevitably some form of economic exchange. Some of this labor is performed by professional archaeologists, who obtain funding from government, university, and private sources to carry out their research projects. Some labor is performed by technicians, who constitute a secondary level of specialized expertise, though typically with less formal training than foreign archaeologists or conservators. Technicians are usually paid for their services, either on a project-by-project basis by directors who control funding sources or through contracts with institutions such as IHAH that retain specialists on a semipermanent basis to handle different kinds of archaeology-related work. Laborers fill in the ranks of operations that facilitate the excavation and analysis processes central to the archaeological enterprise. Individuals are hired, sometimes with experience but often without, to perform a range of tasks, such as clearing debris, excavating, and washing ceramics. Archaeological exploration also requires a host of support services. Specialized tools and materials, construction, housing, transportation, communication, and storage must all be arranged and paid for, entangling still more layers of human and material resources in the process of carrying out archaeological work. In effect, archaeology is accomplished solely through exchanges of goods and labor articulated through many component parts. That the operations of archaeology, which in some quarters appear arcane, are eminently relevant to many peoples' daily lives at Copán is therefore not surprising.

At its peak in the early 1980s, PAC II directly employed 110 residents of the Copán area to assist with survey, excavation, analysis, restoration, and project administration. Nearly all of these individuals had previous experience in archaeological work, gained in the two projects immediately preceding PAC II and in some cases dating back to the Carnegie project, yielding what PAC II project director William Sanders has referred to as a "professional class of excavators."[9] Dozens more individuals provided transportation, meals, and housing; procured materials; and ran errands for PAC II. For these people, archaeology meant seasonal or sometimes year-round employment. Major funding for the PAC activities came from the BCIE and the World Bank, was administered through the government of Honduras, and was handled locally by a project accountant. This allowed for a fairly stable system of archaeological employment, at least for a time. Workers assigned to excavation and other duties during the months when foreign archaeologists came to direct fieldwork shifted to consolidation and related work in the off season. Archaeological research after the PAC investigations, especially since the mid-1990s, has been primarily funded through research grants channeled directly through foreign project directors, which have provided less continuity and much more variance in the terms of contracts with employees. Many individuals who worked on PAC I and II continued to find work on the numerous subsequent projects. But continuity has waned, and nowadays when archaeology projects wrap up, apart from a handful that remain employed by IHAH, these people are effectively out of work.

Honduras has had a national minimum wage since 1974 that sets standards for different categories of labor, including agricultural labor, factory work, and other industries. Pay scales and benefits for different kinds of work in the archaeology industry, however, tend to vary according to the employer and the project, a delicate balancing act that engages the intricate politics of local economic currents, transnational capital, and social position. By both national and local standards, IHAH salaries have been considered low. In IHAH's operating budget for the year 2000, proposed salaries (not including benefits) ranged from approximately US$800 per month for a high-level department director to about US$150 per month for site guards. Foreign project directors who bring research funds from outside sources (which included the majority of those working at the site in 2001) must respect IHAH pay scales and usually do not contract for much beyond the going rate for different kinds of work. However, the details of employment are generally left to the discretion of the project director. Several directors I spoke with made it a habit to pay slightly higher wages than IHAH dictates, as a way to show workers they are valued, but directors must also balance this impulse with the obligation to not overinflate local wages. More than one middle-class resident in Copán confided in me that a job in the ruins is "not a very good job to have." But by and large, Copanecos also acknowledge that the ruins, historically and continuously, have provided employment for many of the local poor, who for many years have had few alternatives.

As project activity has waned in recent years, many of the people formerly employed directly in archaeology projects have found ways to capitalize on their experience and transfer their energies to other sectors of the archaeology industry, specifically those that facilitate commodification for tourism, now in full swing. Masons, once hired to rebuild fallen walls of 1,400-year-old buildings, have found employment in the housing boom in Copán Ruinas, as tourism businesses remodel and expand and new houses multiply to accommodate the swelling local population. Families who rented rooms and cooked for foreign archaeologists and students have turned their domestic spaces into commercial ventures by opening up small eateries and *hotelitos*. Some individuals who spent years as field crew in different areas of archaeological specialization now employ their knowledge as park guides, explaining and expanding on the details of their previous work. Illustrators and artists who learned the intricacies of Maya design by drawing countless objects or building replicas of sculptures have set up workshops where they make and sell souvenirs for tourists. Many are simply on hand, awaiting the next opportunity to offer their skills to new projects or to any of the ongoing itinerant short projects that seem to characterize the current phase of archaeological activity. I met many of these people during my fieldwork in 2000 and 2001, and they regularly inquired as to whether I knew of any upcoming projects, hoping that I would be able to put in a good word.

Products and Values

Much of what takes place in the Copán archaeology industry happens on the ground, in locally framed or even intimate contexts. Maintaining an archaeological park and keeping the attendant tourism infrastructure functioning is day-to-day work, performed by people earning wages, making a living. But the repeated cycles of production processes connect up with and contribute to larger discourses of value that make the industry much more than the simple sum of its parts. As a way into these levels, I turn to a discussion of some industry products and the narratives they engage.

If we think of activity at Copán as an industry, then the most obvious product of this industry is Maya archaeology—specifically, the Maya archaeology of Copán. The popular (highly generalized) concept of "the Maya," and particularly the "ancient Maya,"[10] forms the basis for assigning value to nearly all products of the industry. Without this form of currency, Copán would be more like Yarumuela or Los Naranjos, that is, like other important archaeological sites in Honduras that, in large part because of their lack of connection to "the Maya," have not enjoyed the same level of constant attention, popular recognition, and nationalist interest. This all-important label of "Maya," not unlike a brand name, is what draws tourists, schoolchildren, scientists, and entrepreneurs to Copán year after year.

Like ancient Egypt, the Mediterranean, and the Andes, the Maya world has developed a devoted following among nonspecialists, fueled in large part by the medium of travel writing, beginning with nineteenth-century explorer accounts and proliferated by such cultural phenomena as the National Geographic institution in the twentieth century; more recently, documentary and even popular film-making; and of course, now, the Internet. Over the years, these channels have played a direct and important role in commodifying the archaeological past, fashioning sites into respectable, desirable destinations, even funding research to generate more subject matter for their readers and viewers. In popular educational media such as *Archaeology* magazine and others, articles about places such as Copán, written by archaeologists who work there, are flanked by invitations to visit and advertisements for specialty tours (sometimes led by the same scholars) produced by companies specializing in the archaeology brand of "edutainment." Television specials and documentaries, even dedicated cable outlets including the Discovery Channel and History Channel, command even wider audiences and, together with the Internet, have overtaken print media as the dominant sources of popular information about the archaeological past.

The prolific attention paid to the ancient Maya in both scholarly and popular media has also made them one of the most prosperous subjects of archaeological tourism. Many tour companies, both independent and university based, now specialize in archaeological tours to the "Mundo Maya" (Maya World), which consistently rate among the most popular "products" offered to clients.[11] Part of what makes Maya archaeology seductive today for both professional and nonspecialist audiences is the constant activity—the constant production of new artifacts, new theories, new places, new decipherment, new media products, new things to see, do, and feel. This very productivity in Maya archaeology helps to ensure a renewable market of interest among scholars, tourists, and aficionados alike.

Although some may argue that the touring public prefers highly stylized, Disney-fied theme park experiences when they travel to and consume the products of heritage sites (see, for example, Kirshenblatt-Gimblett 1998; Rowan and Baram 2004; compare Holtorf 2005), a growing audience for Maya archaeology seems to desire something else. Increasingly, nonprofessional Mayanists are participating on academically oriented Listservs, buying scholarly texts, following theoretical debates, learning to decipher glyphs, and even making their own contributions to scholarly discourse. This specialized audience is looking for "authentic" experiences, not just with archaeological sites and artifacts but with archaeologists themselves (see also Ehrentraut 1996: 17). In the past twenty years, a conference circuit catering specifically to this growing audience has developed. Events such as the UCLA Maya Weekend, the Maya Weekend at the University of Pennsylvania Museum, and the grandmother of this trend, the Maya Meetings at Texas, highlight interactions between scholars and nonprofessionals through a series of presentations, seminars, and workshops given by academics at various stages of their careers. These contexts provide ample occasion to showcase both Maya archaeological research and the personalities who bring this research to the public. David Webster (2002: 7–9) writes, "Like our colleagues everywhere, we Mayanists love to bask in the limelight, and for better or worse, the flamboyant archaeological record we deal with gives us plenty of opportunity to do so." The same specialized tour companies both advertise these meetings and advertise at these meetings and in the pages of popular magazines, such as *Archaeology,* thereby helping to energize the cycle for this specialized demographic. This group of consumers may prefer their archaeology packaged rather than raw, but they still want it recognizable as "archaeology," for this is the product they seek to consume.[12]

In these ways, archaeologists and other "experts," media professionals, and tourism operators are linked in the co-production of Maya archaeology (Castañeda 1996; Medina 2003), sometimes confounding attempts to distinguish academic discourse from popular discourse (for example, Wilk 1985). This does not mean that these discourses are identical; instead, they feed into each other and have co-constituted one another for decades. Peter Hervik (1999) identifies the flow of ideas between popular consciousness and academic research in Maya studies as the "double hermeneutic process" articulated by Anthony Giddens (1984). Hervik examines the discursive practices of cultural producers—particularly the functions of imagery and text in magazines and similar contexts—and their relations to the powerful engines of profit motives in tourism and media to make the point that popular ideas about the Maya inevitably inform academic formulations. Maya archaeology is thus not the sole domain of archaeologists, although their research is a principal element in the industry. In other words, archaeologists do not necessarily orchestrate the industry, nor do I mean to suggest that they are merely cogs in a machine; but their work certainly helps fuel this continuous cycle of production and consumption, often with little control over where the products of their research go. This set of relations makes some scholars, perhaps many, uncomfortable, especially those who have no interest in engaging with the larger Maya media machine.

Archaeological knowledge—that is to say, archaeological reconstructions of past human activity in the Copán Valley—has been an extremely productive sector of the Copán archaeology industry over the past twenty-five years. In this time, scholars have generated no less than fifteen monographs and edited volumes; countless articles, book chapters, and conference papers; and scores of Ph.D. dissertations. The data sets of artifacts, architecture, epigraphy, and skeletal remains from Copán are some of the most extensive in the Maya area (Fash and Agurcia F. 2005; Webster 1999). These products form the basis for secondary ones—peer-reviewed journal articles, dissertations, guidebooks, documentaries, tour scripts, promotional materials, newspaper articles, political essays, children's books, and even souvenirs. In this way, archaeological knowledge and its subsidiaries are subject to consumption, in one form or another, and not simply by tourists. Even the most seemingly exclusively academic product of archaeological knowledge about Copán—for instance, a presentation at an academic conference—can hardly escape the logics of consumption. While no actual material transaction usually occurs in such a forum, the medium of conference presentations is still a form of exchange in which value is determined and ascribed, investing symbolic capital in (and divesting it from) particular modes of inquiry, topics, theoretical approaches, and individuals.

By 2001, IHAH had begun to suspend new projects at Copán. Given the institution's mandate to protect the country's cultural patrimony, IHAH was concerned about the overproduction of archaeology at Copán, such that insufficient time and attention were being paid to conservation. Some business owners in Copán Ruinas were unhappy with this decision and expressed concern that fewer active research projects at Copán or, more specifically, less excavation (at least in the site core) would interrupt the cycle of production or worse, end it. Although they appear to be in opposition, IHAH and business owners are actually trying to protect the same resource base. By focusing too much on excavation and literally mining Copán architecture through extensive tunneling projects, archaeological activities can make the larger Copán resource fragile, threatening the overall tourism product. IHAH's restrictions on new excavation also force archaeologists to analyze and write about the work they have conducted, creating more Copán narrative products. Business owners may appear naive in presenting a limited conception of archaeology as excavation alone and for not always appreciating the importance of conservation at the site. But they are correct in associating the physical process of excavation with new Copán products (and with the creation of local employment). For tourists, the presence of archaeologists actively working on site is perhaps as attractive as the new narratives that may result from their projects. Both the activity of archaeology and the objects and narratives it yields function as products for enthusiasts to consume, and these are what the service sector of the tourism industry depends on for attracting repeat clients.

Many local business owners have a sophisticated understanding of the tourism market; to some extent, with respect to their own interests, they may have cause for worry. The constant activity at Copán, the seemingly endless stream of new projects, distinguishes contemporary Copán from some of its rival sites in the Maya tourism circuit. A number of tourists I spoke with, both at Copán and in other venues of interest to Maya aficionados, expressed excitement at returning to Copán "because there is always something happening, something new there." A well-known epigrapher also once explained to me that he saw no reason to return to Copán anytime soon unless they uncovered some new inscriptions. The lack of ongoing excavation creates a popular conception that a site is static and therefore not exciting to visit more than once. Thus, concern over the physical production processes of archaeological knowledge, or the lack thereof, echoes the observation that Maya archaeology itself is the main product of the archaeology industry. This product is more than a book, more than historical details taught through educational fora, more than even the physically reconstructed remains of the Maya buildings. The *action* of archaeology, as much as all the contingent processes, is what sustains the Copán industry; shifts in activity levels reverberate throughout its many sectors.

Relations of Production and Power

A former archaeology project director once described Copán Ruinas to me as something of a "company town"; the description, although not necessarily accurate in the standard definition of this term, underscores the significance and dominance of the archaeology industry there. The town is certainly well attuned to the seasonal and daily cycles of archaeological work, which help make many visiting students and scholars more quickly feel at home. But Copán Ruinas does not follow the classic structure of a company town, because the fortunes of most of the local wealthy families were not built on archaeological work and no member of these families is an archaeologist. Nor do these families control access to working in the archaeology industry, except in terms of running tourism businesses that supplement the traditional family assets of land, cattle, and tobacco. Authority and power in the Copán archaeology industry rest in national and international networks instead of locally based family networks.

Relations of power are implicit in the structure of the archaeology industry and in the relations of production that connect its participants. As in any industry, access and opportunity are regulated by a variety of gatekeeping practices and reinforcing cycles rather than by a so-called free market. Take academics, for example. Becoming a Mayanist archaeologist typically requires following a route of academic patronage that is familiar to many academic disciplines. That is, opportunity to work at specific sites or on specific projects often derives from who you know, which largely depends on where and with whom you study. Well-known professionals sometimes receive invitations from colleagues or even government representatives to direct projects at high-profile sites. They bring the resources of their universities and the symbolic capital of their affiliation and their career to the process. The profile of the site, combined with the prestige and record of the scholar, helps these individuals receive grant funding from sources such as the National Science Foundation, National Geographic Society, and international counterparts, which in turn allows them to accomplish additional research. Faculty provide opportunities for their students and for students of their colleagues to work on projects, thereby allowing students to gain the "proper" experience (or pedigree) to enter the discipline. The association of work at particular sites adds luster to nascent careers, as does the patronage of important scholars and funding agencies. Under the wing of established professionals, new generations of scholars at high-prestige institutions begin to establish records that mirror those of their mentors, which increase their chances of securing their own positions as faculty.

Most students who train to become archaeologists at Copán are not Honduran. For Hondurans, a career in archaeology is next to impossible, even if it were desirable. Copán locals recognize that to be an archaeologist takes *billete*—cash, and lots of it. Even if a student is lucky enough to have both the financial means and the appropriate (sometimes serendipitous) social connections and support required to travel to study archaeology in Guatemala, Mexico, the United States, or Europe (because despite several concerted efforts, there are as of yet no advanced degree programs in Honduras), there are still precious few jobs at home to return to. The archaeology industry may be based on Copán, but it is not really based *in* Copán. The networks of capital and power operate in other registers that run through places such as Tegucigalpa, New York, and Washington, D.C.

Many Copanecos identify archaeology as a prestige occupation. They observe the attention the site receives and the notable visitors it attracts, and they watch as established archaeologists meet with dignitaries and are treated with deference and respect. They also see archaeologists traveling around the world, commanding impressive resources, and being featured in the press. In 2001, I asked several locals working at the CRIA laboratory, some with many years of experience, whether they would ever want to become professionally trained archaeologists if given the means to do so. Most said no, citing the lack of job opportunities, disinterest in the long hours of studying, or a general disinterest in what they believed the lifestyle to entail. One friend, working as an archaeological illustrator, laughed at my question and called archaeology a *carrera de locos*—a career path for (and of) crazy people. But even though he made light of this personal moment, he and many others expressed a fairly well defined sense of injustice over unequal access to such opportunities, as well as a sophisticated recognition of the potential (although diffuse) value of archaeological resources. He told me, "Here you can study history but not archaeology—it's illogical! Imagine having a country like this and no degree program to study it."

Although the routes for becoming a professional archaeologist are few, there are numerous paths to becoming involved at other levels in the archaeology industry. Many Copanecos have gained access to employment opportunities by means of sheer serendipity. For instance, one CRIA employee began her career as a teenager, living next door to a young archaeologist and initially hired to care for his children. As she showed interest and aptitude, project archaeologists offered her the opportunity to earn more, get training in specialized techniques, and eventually work with ceramics and other materials from the site. She considered this good employment and useful work for her level of education, and she soon became a well-respected technical specialist whose skills have been sought by many subsequent project directors. This case is not unusual. Many others have received training and achieved positions of some prominence in the industry from a chance friendship with those in a position to offer such opportunities. But the majority of individuals who find employment in some sector follow routes of access that are more common: kin and political party networks.

Kin networks are especially important in the archaeology industry, over generations as well as across them. This is true in the traditional sense of family, both close and extended—many families in Copán Ruinas have multiple generations that go into the "family business" of guiding, illustrating, excavating, or running tourism services. It is also true in the sense of the "kin" created through particular projects, especially over the past twenty years, as multiple universities have worked at Copán during the same time. Students who work on the project of a particular university tend to return to the same service providers and the same technical specialists year after year. When new students arrive to work on a project, the directors usually recommend that they find housing with the same set of families and draw from the same pool of workers. As these students develop their own projects, they often return to these families or ask them to recommend others, drawing on these connections to fill both personal and project needs. In this way, individuals in town become associated with particular projects (although rarely exclusively), and host families become focal nodes in extensive service and employment networks. This situation of "project kinship" also means that the politics that play out among projects led by foreign universities sometimes extends to and embroils the Copanecos employed by them. To keep current jobs without closing doors to future opportunities, employees must delicately navigate the feuds and competitions that sometimes surface among project directors and students.

Everyone in the Copán region is aware of the links between traditional politics and job opportunities, particularly for positions that are controlled by Hondurans rather than by foreign researchers. For instance, when a space opens up for a new guard at the Copán park, the position typically falls to a family member or someone who has been active in the political party of the person doing the hiring, sometimes regardless of the individual's background or experience. This also means that individuals can lose their jobs when political parties shift power at the local or national levels. I met many who had obtained their footing in the archaeology industry based on their loyalty and contributions to "the party." From 1994 through 2000, the central government in Honduras was controlled by the Liberal Party of Honduras (PLH), one of the country's two primary political parties. IHAH, as a state institution, was also dominated by Liberals during this period; consequently, so was the administration of the Copán park. Family members in Copán Ruinas who were loyal to the opposing party, the National Party (PN), often complained that no one could get a job at the ruins in those days without a recommendation from the PLH, and they pointed out instances of persecution of those with many years of experience but the wrong party affiliation.

The structural relationships among people involved in the industry reveal conditions of power that move well beyond wage earning. Fundamental inequalities that derive from the relative social and national positions of the participants also play significant roles in defining relationships. Specialists, tourists, and students are always coming to Copán from other places. That they are able even to travel to Copán (relatively easily) means that they have far greater access to resources than do many Copanecos or, for that matter, many Hondurans. The positioning of foreign scholars and other visitors in the global political economy allows them to offer much more than they realize to the many Copanecos with whom they come into contact. For example, a new groundskeeper at the archaeological park may be paid very little for hard labor in the sun. But during the course of the day in his job, he may run into foreigners who are curious about him and regard him as a potential, though anonymous, representative of "local culture." If he can begin a conversation with them, he is no longer anonymous, and this exchange may spark a fortuitous relationship, the likes of which have benefited many of his social peers.

Foreigners who are in a position to hire people for various kinds of work bring with them the power not only of offering short-term employment but also of teaching languages, bringing gifts, buying meals at restaurants, and even facilitating travel and supporting further education. Tour guides, especially, stand to benefit from their relationships with foreign specialists and with tourists. Currently, there is little opportunity for formal guide training at Copán, and most individuals who become guides do so by way of connections to archaeologists and other specialists. Many current guides are former assistants to individual archaeologists, who continue to coach them with knowledge, lend them books, and answer their questions. Tourists grateful for a guide's service will often reward him or her with generous tips, recommendations to friends, and meals in town. Visitors often want to maintain connections with guides they meet, and an exchange of letters or e-mails sometimes leads to further opportunities—for guides to specialize their training, improve the quality of life for themselves and their families, and even to travel around the world. These dynamics of access and opportunity mirror the entanglements of global and local—which are at once intimate and structural—that are present in many tourism contexts. This commonality, however, makes them no less significant for the daily lives and relations of local Copanecos.

From a distance, developing archaeology for tourism by tapping into the Maya media machine seems like a safe economic bet. But the reality for most individuals working in the archaeology industry suggests the opposite. Most of those who had jobs directly related to archaeology in 2001, whether employed by a project director or by IHAH, spoke of the overwhelming insecurity with which they lived. When discussing the experience of working in the ruins or on archaeological projects, I often heard tales of labor disputes, broken promises, and compensation never received, revealing a perception that archaeology, as work, is unstable and unreliable (although perhaps no more so than other kinds of seasonal employment, such as working on coffee *fincas*). The itinerant nature of funding, the fickleness of research priorities, and the seesaw of party politics make for an anxious work environment. Those employed in the tourism-related economy, which is increasingly coming to overshadow all other sectors, shared similar worries and frustrations. Guides, hotel and restaurant owners, souvenir suppliers, transportation companies, and others all rely on the whims of the fluctuating tourism market, which typically responds to political and economic forces well beyond local control. Tourism, like much of archaeology, is seasonal business, easily disrupted by economic downturns, uncooperative weather patterns, and political instability.[13] Business owners and operators follow events at the ruins closely, acutely aware that any disturbance in the operations of the main attraction sends immediate ripples throughout their many ventures.

Conclusions

Dissembling the monumental face of Copán reveals human connections and interdependencies, which, in turn, remind us that "producing" the past is ultimately a fragile enterprise. On any given day, as tourists enter through the park gates and wander among the reconstructed stone buildings, resurrected stelae, and cleared forest paths, they encounter the intimacy of Copán's construction largely as a fait accompli. Yet these coveted moments of imagined access to the "past" are always underscored by ongoing labor, for the most part obscured by the very industry it generates. This labor and its many acts of production demarcate other entryways to Copán, still mostly hidden from public view.

Some of the older residents in Copán Ruinas remember times when the land among the ruins, now manicured by paid groundskeepers, was used for cattle grazing and planting local crops. But I spoke with no one living in the vicinity of Copán who remembered a time before the ruins themselves were thought of as "archaeological." This is not to say that Copán residents have treated the crumbling structures as specimens reserved only for scientific study. However, most residents have long been aware that scientific, state, and visitor interests in Copán are based on a conception of the structures and monuments as archaeological remains.[14] The production of Copán through the archaeology industry only strengthens this perspective. Thus, the relative lack of competing local narratives of Copán should come as no surprise (compare Bartu 2000; Breglia 2006, this volume; Castañeda 1996; Gordillo, this volume). But there are certainly competing interests and uses, and therefore modes of value, predicated on divergent daily experiences and the larger politics in which they are grounded.

Arjun Appadurai (2001: 48) argues that we need to recognize that "the past does have an economy" and that "if indeed the past is a scarce resource, because its construction is subject to cultural as well as material constraints, this means that the economy which governs the production of the past has to be examined even more critically." Many who visited or conducted research at Copán more than a decade ago bemoan the numerous changes that globalization, catalyzed by a booming tourism business, has wrought. Those who lament the recent, rapid growth of the tourism economy, including foreign archaeologists who sometimes wonder whether they are uniquely responsible for their impact on the social landscape, fail to recognize that the archaeotourism machine was set in motion more than a century and a half ago. Recent developments are in some ways the logical outgrowth of forces beyond the control of any single group. Today the lives of individuals who keep the park functioning—groundskeepers, guards, administrators, and others—are inextricably bound to the rhythms of political processes that take place in North American, Japanese, Italian, French, Australian, and other universities, international funding agencies, and the offices of national ministries, which shape the transnational flow of trends in archaeological tourism. However, the future course of this trajectory is not predetermined. In this case, tracing the functioning of the archaeology industry can help to signal moments of rupture and therefore, more hopefully, opportunities to influence its next iteration.

Acknowledgments

I wish to thank the Instituto Hondureño de Antropología e Historia, especially Darío Euraque, Carmen Julia Fajardo, and Oscar Cruz M., who provided generous assistance facilitating the research on which this chapter is based. I owe a much larger debt to the many residents of Copán and elsewhere in Honduras, as well as to various foreign researchers and students, who have graciously offered their time and expertise. Thanks also to Julie Hollowell, Chip Colwell-Chanthaphonh, Girish Daswani, Quetzil Castañeda, and Lynn Meskell, who provided helpful comments on earlier versions.

Notes

1. This framing echoes Clifford's (1997) emphasis on "routes" as a dominant metaphor for understanding the movement of peoples and ideas, and "relations of travel" in the constitution of culture.

2. Several recent studies (including Breglia 2005 and Shepherd 2003) have also notably called attention to the lives of people who perform labor in the pursuit of archaeological production. These analyses fall broadly in line with the recent scholarly focus on the intersections of ethnography and archaeological practice—specifically, social production of archaeological knowledge (see introduction to this volume).

3. There is some limited evidence for interest in the site as a culturally significant locale for local Maya Chortí communities. For instance, archaeologists and other explorers from the late nineteenth through the mid-twentieth centuries occasionally made note of areas within the ruins where small amounts of copal and candles were routinely left as offerings.

4. The Carnegie Institution of Washington (CIW) had initiated a massive Maya research program centered in Yucatán, which then expanded throughout Central America. Chichén Itzá is the most famous example of a reconstructed archaeological park under the auspices of the CIW, but the CIW tradition of research and reconstruction in the Maya Research Program established a pattern followed at many other sites in the region, including Quirigua and Uxmal (Weeks and Hill 2006; see also Castañeda 1996; Sullivan 1989).

5. The Honduran nationalist project during this time period, and its grounding in the ancient Maya, is best described by historian Darío Euraque (1996, 2004).

6. See Fash 2001 and Fash and Agurcia F. 2005 for a summary of archaeological project history at Copán; see Veliz 1983 and Joyce 2007 for a broader contextualization of the history of archaeology in Honduras.

7. World Bank Project #P081172, Regional Development in the Copan Valley Project, was approved in May 2003 (consult http://web.worldbank.org for project details).

8. See Castañeda 1996 and Holtorf 2002 for discussions of this creative, perhaps magical, process.

9. William Sanders, personal communication, 2002.

10. The stylized popular concept of "the Maya" tends to homogenize the rich diversity and complexity of both the past and the present of this region (Joyce 2005; Pyburn 1998).

11. Mary Dell Lucas, personal communication, 2003. A small sample of tour companies includes Maya Expeditions, Maya Tropical Tours, Far Horizons, Explorations, Inc., The Mayan Traveler, Archaeological Tours, Mayan World Expeditions, and many others.

12. See Holtorf 2005 for a related, provocative discussion of "archaeo-appeal."

13. Hurricane Mitch, which hit in October 1998 and devastated much of Honduras, is an example of one such event. Visitation to Copán in the following three months dropped by more than half, and many local residents scrambled to compensate for the disappearance of expected income.

14. See Mortensen 2005 for extended discussion of this history.

References Cited

Appadurai, Arjun. "Introduction: Commodities and the Politics of Value." In *The Social Life of Things: Commodities in Cultural Perspective,* edited by A. Appadurai, 3–63. Cambridge: Cambridge University Press, 1988.

———. "The Globalization of Archaeology and Heritage A Discussion with Arjun Appadurai." *Journal of Social Archaeology* 1, no. 1 (2001): 35–49.

Bartu, Ayfer. "Where Is Çatalhöyük? Multiple Sites in the Construction of an Archaeological Site." In *Towards Reflexive Method in Archaeology: The Example at Çatalhöyük,* edited by I. Hodder, 101–10. Cambridge, U.K.: McDonald Institute for Archaeological Research, 2000.

Bodnar, John. *Remaking America: Public Memory, Commemoration, and Patriotism in the Twentieth Century.* Princeton, N.J.: Princeton University Press, 1992.

Bond, George, and Angela Gilliam, eds. *Social Construction of the Past: Representation as Power.* One World Archaeology, no. 4. London: Routledge, 1994.

Breglia, Lisa. "Keeping World Heritage in the Family: A Genealogy of Maya Labour at Chichén Itzá." *International Journal of Heritage Studies* 11, no. 5 (2005): 385–98.

———. *Monumental Ambivalence: The Politics of Heritage.* Austin: University of Texas Press, 2006.

Castañeda, Quetzil E. *In the Museum of Maya Culture: Touring Chichén Itzá.* Minneapolis: University of Minnesota Press, 1996.

Clifford, James. *Routes: Travel and Translation in the Late Twentieth Century.* Cambridge, Mass.: Harvard University Press, 1997.

Ehrentraut, Adolf. "Maya Ruins, Cultural Tourism and the Contested Symbolism of Collective Identities." *Culture* 16, no. 1 (1996): 15–32.

Euraque, Darío. *Estado, poder, nacionalidad y raza en la historia de Honduras: Ensayos.* Choluteca, Honduras: Ediciones Subirana, 1996.

———. *Conversaciones históricas con el mestizaje y su identidad nacional en Honduras.* San Pedro Sula, Honduras: Litografía López, 2004.

Fash, William L. *Scribes, Warriors and Kings: The City of Copán and the Ancient Maya.* Revised edition. London: Thames and Hudson, 2001.

Fash, William L., and Ricardo Agurcia Fasquelle. "Contributions and Controversies in the Archaeology and History of Copán." In *Copán: The History of an Ancient Maya Kingdom,* edited by E. W. Andrews and W. L. Fash, 1–30. Santa Fe, N.Mex.: School of American Research Press, 2005.

Gereffi, Gary, and Miguel Korzeniewicz, eds. *Commodity Chains and Global Capitalism.* Westport, Conn.: Praeger, 1994.

Giddens, Anthony. *The Constitution of Society: Outline of a Theory of Structuration.* Berkeley: University of California Press, 1984.

Handler, Richard, and Eric Gable. *The New History in an Old Museum: Creating the Past at Colonial Williamsburg.* Durham, N.C.: Duke University Press, 1997.

Hervik, Peter. "The Mysterious Maya of National Geographic." *Journal of Latin American Anthropology* 4, no. 1 (1999): 166–97.

Herzfeld, Michael. *A Place in History: Social and Monumental Time in a Cretan Village.* Princeton, N.J.: Princeton University Press, 1991.

Hewison, Robert. *The Heritage Industry: Britain in a Climate of Decline.* London: Methuen, 1987.

Holtorf, Cornelius. "Notes on the Life History of a Pot Sherd." *Journal of Material Culture* 7, no. 1 (2002): 49–71.

———. *From Stonehenge to Las Vegas: Archaeology as Popular Culture.* Walnut Creek, Calif.: AltaMira Press, 2005.

Joyce, Rosemary A. "Archaeology and Nation Building: A View from Central America." In *The Politics of Archaeology and Identity in a Global Context,* edited by S. Kane, 79–100. Boston: Archaeological Institute of America, 2003.

———. "What Kind of Subject of Study Is 'The Ancient Maya?'" *Reviews in Anthropology* 34 (2005): 295–311.

———. "Critical Histories of Archaeological Practice: Latin American and North American Interpretations in a Honduran Context." In *Evaluating Multiple Narratives: Beyond Nationalist, Colonialist, Imperialist Archaeologies,* edited by J. Habu, C. Fawcett, and J. M. Matsunaga, 56–68. New York: Springer, 2007.

Kirshenblatt-Gimblett, Barbara. *Destination Culture: Tourism, Museums, and Heritage.* Berkeley: University of California Press, 1998.

Loker, William M. "The Rise and Fall of Flue-Cured Tobacco in the Copán Valley and Its Environmental and Social Consequences." *Human Ecology* 33, no. 3 (2005): 299–327.

Medina, Laurie K. "Commoditizing Culture: Tourism and Maya Identity." *Annals of Tourism Research* 30, no. 2 (2003): 353–68.

Mortensen, Lena. "Constructing Heritage at Copán, Honduras: An Ethnography of the Archaeology Industry." Ph.D. diss., Indiana University, 2005.

———. "Working Borders: Contextualizing Copán Archaeology." *Archaeologies: Journal of the World Archaeological Congress* 3, no. 2 (2007): 132–52.

Pyburn, K. Anne. "Consuming the Maya." *Dialectical Anthropology* 23, no. 2 (1998): 111–29.

Rowan, Yorke, and Uzi Baram, eds. *Marketing Heritage: Archaeology and the Consumption of the Past.* Walnut Creek, Calif.: AltaMira Press, 2004.

Shepherd, Nick. "'When the Hand that Holds the Trowel Is Black . . .': Disciplinary Practices of Self-Representation and the Issue of 'Native' Labour in Archaeology." *Journal of Social Archaeology* 3, no. 3 (2003): 334–52.

Stephens, John L., and Frederick Catherwood. *Incidents of Travel in Central America, Chiapas and Yucatan,* vol. 1. New York: Dover Publications, 1969. (Orig. pub. 1841.)

Sullivan, Paul. *Unfinished Conversations: Mayas and Foreigners between Two Wars.* New York: Knopf, 1989.

Trouillot, Michel-Rolph. *Silencing the Past: Power and the Production of History.* Boston: Beacon Press, 1995.

Veliz R., Vito. "Síntesis histórica de la arqueología en Honduras." *Yaxkín* 6, no. 1–2 (1983): 1–9.

Webster, David. "The Archaeology of Copan, Honduras." *Journal of Archaeological Research* 7, no. 1 (1999): 1–53.

———. *The Fall of the Ancient Maya: Solving the Mystery of the Maya Collapse.* London: Thames and Hudson, 2002.

Weeks, John M., and Jane A. Hill, eds. *The Carnegie Maya: The Carnegie Institution of Washington Maya Research Program, 1913–1957.* Boulder: University Press of Colorado, 2006.

Wilk, Richard R. "The Ancient Maya and the Political Present." *Journal of Anthropological Research* 41, no. 3 (1985): 307–26.

9

Responsibility to the Ancestors, Responsibility to the Descendants

Artifacts, Stewardship, and NAGPRA in Hawai'i

JON DAEHNKE

However, long before this law, Bishop Museum was conceived and made real by the *ali'i* and other people of the Hawaiian Kingdom. We remember and honor the vision and love of Bernice Pauahi Bishop. We believe that her dream and our responsibility has always been, and will remain, to be a bridge to the past so that the living remember from whence they came.

Bishop Museum 2004a: 1

We are mindful that our ancestors left us with the *kuleana* (responsibility) to care for their well-being. While they also left us cultural items upon which we maintain our cultural identity and through which we continue to be educated and inspired, this does not include their *iwi* and *moepū*, for those belong to them.

Ayau and Tengan 2002: 184

Archaeologists have a tendency to focus on "things." Randy McGuire has pointed out that even our ethical concerns as a discipline have historically been thing-centric: did we use the proper methods to dig things up? Did we appropriately analyze these things to learn about the past? Did we responsibly publish what we learned from analyzing and digging up these things? (McGuire 2003: vii). No doubt, this "thing" myopia stems from the object-centered basis of most archaeological research. The bulk of archaeological data takes the form of material artifacts—pottery, projectile points, bones, and so forth. Typically, for archaeologists the primary value of artifacts is that they are a "record of the cultural past whose significance lay in its informational content (as evidence), not its aesthetic or sentimental or commercial value" (Wylie 2005: 56). And although a conservation and stewardship ethic grew in importance over recent decades (see Lipe 1974; see also Lynott and Wylie 2000), the primary intention of that ethic is to preserve artifacts because of their value as evidence about the past (see Lipe 1996). The crucial cultural resource laws in the United States, such as Section 106 of the National Historic Preservation Act (NHPA) and the Archaeological Resources Protection Act (ARPA), also reflect this view.[1]

Artifacts, however, have lives separate from archaeologists—or, in the terminology of this volume, other *iterations*. While archaeologists might conceive of artifacts as evidentiary data, descendant communities—those present-day groups of people whose heritage is under investigation (Singleton and Orser 2003: 143)—might place more emphasis on the social or ritual value of the artifact (Watkins 2005: 188) or view artifacts as sources of subsistence (Hollowell, this volume) or as objects that must be used (rather than stored on shelves) or allowed to deteriorate (Clavir 2002). The purpose of this chapter, therefore, is not to look at the archaeological process, but rather to look at the value placed on archaeological things (artifacts) by people who have interests separate from the goals of archaeology. My interest is in the nonarchaeological iterations of tangible objects, especially the role that these objects play in the more intangible processes of stewardship, cultural recovery, and cultural revival. To explore these nonarchaeological iterations, I focus on Hawai'i, where diverse views on the value of objects (including human remains), as well as the role these tangible objects play in recovering and reviving culture, have led to contention and legal disputes.

Ownership, Stewardship, and NAGPRA

As material objects, artifacts are items that can be held, moved, transferred, and thereby potentially owned. Artifacts also have value, both cultural and commercial. This inevitably leads to questions about who rightfully owns these objects, whether they can be owned at all, and who gets to make decisions about ownership. Archaeologists, along with museum personnel, have at times eschewed the issue of ownership by claiming instead the role of stewards of the past, with *steward* denoting responsibility or entrustment rather than ownership. The notion of stewardship, however, contains its own sets of perils (Wylie 2005; see also Groarke and Warrick 2006), and what is considered appropriate stewardship depends greatly on your standpoint (Hollowell, this volume). The role of steward is also a position of privilege that allows the steward to dictate with some authority how the histories tied to objects will be disseminated or whether they will be disseminated at all. But given the powerful role that historical narratives play in shaping history (see Arnold 1990; Habu and Fawcett 1999; Kohl and Fawcett 1995; Schmidt 1999; Sommer 1999), this authority is contested by groups or individuals who believe that they, not archaeologists or museum personnel as stewards, should control the dissemination of what they view as their cultural and intellectual property.

The Native American Graves Protection and Repatriation Act (NAGPRA) was signed into U.S. law on November 16, 1990, in part in response to these ownership and stewardship concerns.[2] This law requires federal agencies and museums (with the exception of the Smithsonian Institution, which is covered under separate legislation) to inventory and repatriate human remains, associated funerary items, sacred objects, and items of cultural patrimony to Native American tribes, Alaskan Natives, or Native Hawaiian organizations (NHOs) in which lineal descent or right of ownership can be demonstrated (see McManamon and Nordby 1992). This important piece of human rights legislation was the culmination of decades of struggle by Native Americans, Alaskan Natives, and Native Hawaiians to retrieve illegally acquired cultural items, protect against grave desecration, and regain control over the dissemination of their history (see Trope and Echo-Hawk 1992). It also fundamentally resituates where ownership of the past resides.

As is the case with most pieces of legislation, NAGPRA is a compromise bill, and the wording of the law reflects this. The bill requires the necessary specificity in language to be meaningful but sufficient vagueness to be applicable in and adaptable to a variety of settings. The law is also equally applicable to tribes, organizations, and individuals who may hold widely disparate views of what constitutes ownership, what can be owned, and who has the right to make these decisions. As a result, the implementation of NAGPRA is often complex and occasionally contentious, as each community struggles to negotiate the balance between the letter of the law, cultural values, and differing ideas regarding appropriate stewardship. This complexity and contention can certainly be seen in the implementation of NAGPRA in Hawai'i, especially in the context of policies of the Bishop Museum, the largest museum in Hawai'i and the premier cultural history institution in the Pacific.

The Bishop Museum and NAGPRA

On June 30, 2004, the Bishop Museum issued an interim guidance document to clarify the steps taken by the museum to implement and comply with NAGPRA. The tenets of the Bishop Museum's interim guidance proved to be quite controversial. Certainly, concerns over repatriation and ownership of the past in Hawai'i did not begin with the issuing of the Bishop Museum's proposed guidance or even with the passage of NAGPRA. In fact, concern over desecration of Hawaiian graves and the appropriation of objects of Hawaiian antiquity by non-Hawaiians has been present since the time of first colonial contact (see Thomas 1991, 1997). What the proposed guidance did was foreground these disagreements over the value of Hawaiian antiquities and who serves as the rightful stewards of Hawaiian heritage.

The "Interim and Proposed Final Guidance: Native American Graves Protection and Repatriation Act,"[3] defined by the Bishop Museum as a legal analysis, outlined the museum's position on key provisions of NAGPRA and also addressed the museum's responsibilities under this law. In the document, the Bishop Museum reached four fundamental conclusions. First, the Bishop Museum declared itself qualified to serve as a Native Hawaiian organization (NHO). Under the definitions of NAGPRA, a "Native Hawaiian organization" is any organization that "(A) serves and represents the interests of Native Hawaiians, (B) has as a primary and stated purpose the provision of services to Native Hawaiians, and (C) has expertise in Native Hawaiian Affairs, and shall include the Office of Hawaiian Affairs and Hui Malama I Na Kupuna O Hawai'i Nei" (NAGPRA, sec. 2[11]).[4] The Bishop Museum is neither an organization made up of predominantly Native Hawaiian membership nor a traditional historic body. But in its proposed guidance document, the museum noted that this does not preclude the organization from serving as an NHO, because NAGPRA definitions for NHO status—unlike the definition for Indian tribes—do not require Native Hawaiian membership or traditional history.[5] Furthermore, the document noted that the Bishop Museum was established to preserve and exhibit the original collections of the last three female high-ranking *ali'i* (ruling class) of the Kamehameha dynasty: Princess Ruta Ke'elikolani, Bernice Pauahi Bishop, and Dowager Queen Emma (Rose 1980: 7–10).[6] When the Bishop Museum opened in 1890, the core of its initial collection was formed by donations from these three *ali'i*. Today, the Bishop is the steward of nearly 1,500,000 artifacts important to Hawaiian history. The Bishop's articles of incorporation were also amended in 2003 to specifically state that a primary purpose of the museum is to provide services to Native Hawaiians and, as noted in the "Interim and Proposed Final Guidance," "over the last five years, nearly 500,000 Native Hawaiians were served through exhibits and educational programs. More than 20 Native Hawaiian organizations and 200 Native Hawaiian individuals benefited directly as participants in Museum cultural programs" (par. 11). Therefore, because of its role as a steward of items of historical importance (including the original collections of the Kamehameha line) and servant to the interests of Native Hawaiians, the "Bishop Museum clearly meets NAGPRA's definition of an NHO, and Bishop Museum here recognizes itself to be a Native Hawaiian organization" (par. 11).

The second conclusion reached by the Bishop Museum is that despite the fact that the museum is neither a traditional historic body nor an organization made up of predominantly Native Hawaiian membership, the Bishop does meet the criteria for "cultural affiliation" as defined by NAGPRA. In fact, all organizations qualifying as NHOs are culturally affiliated with Native Hawaiians. While NAGPRA defines "cultural affiliation" as "a relationship of shared group identity which can be reasonably traced historically or prehistorically between a present-day Indian tribe or Native Hawaiian organization and an identifiable earlier group" (NAGPRA, sec. 2[2]), the Bishop took a much broader view: "An alternative perspective, however, is to read 'shared group identity' broadly. The Museum may conclude that any organization meeting the NHO requirements of purpose, function and expertise in respect to Native Hawaiians has a relationship of shared group identity to the Native Hawaiian people of old (i.e. the 'identifiable earlier group'). The evidence for 'tracing' this relationship, in this alternative, is evidence of present day engagement in work perpetuating the Native Hawaiian culture generally, rather than tracing to tribe-like entities" (par. 16). The Bishop suggested that adherence to a narrow construction of NAGPRA's definition of cultural affiliation is extremely difficult within the Hawaiian context and would likely not be met by most NHOs. The breaking of the *kapu* system in 1819, the loss of many traditional practices during this period, and the rapid transformation of traditional forms of Hawaiian government and religion into Westernized variants complicate the tracing of items back to any specific "identifiable earlier group." But because of its direct descent from the national repository of the Hawaiian Kingdom and the Kamehameha line, the Bishop Museum serves as a legitimate steward of the Hawaiian past and therefore exhibits cultural affiliation. And although the Bishop recognizes the priority of proven lineal descendants in respect to human remains and associated funerary objects, the museum concluded that "as a Native Hawaiian organization, [the] Bishop Museum is culturally affiliated with all Native Hawaiian cultural items" (par. 17).

The third conclusion reached in the Bishop's proposed guidance document is that the museum holds in its collections no items of cultural patrimony or sacred objects as defined by NAGPRA. An item of cultural patrimony is defined in NAGPRA as "an object having ongoing historical, traditional, or cultural importance central to the Native American group or culture itself, rather than property owned by an individual Native American, and which, therefore, cannot be alienated, appropriated, or conveyed by any individual regardless of whether or not the individual is a member of the Indian tribe or Native Hawaiian organization and such object shall have been considered inalienable by such Native American group at the time the object was separated from such group" (NAGPRA, sec. 2[3][d]). The key component of this definition is that items of cultural patrimony must in some way be communally owned rather than privately held—only the community holds the right to transfer these objects outside of the group. The Bishop, seizing on this distinction, noted that "no objects in the Museum's collections from old Hawai'i appear to meet this definition, if for no other reason than all objects could in appropriate time and circumstances be conveyed, appropriated or transferred by a ruling chief" (par. 27). Therefore, the items in the Bishop's collection were privately owned by the chief, rather than communally owned by Native Hawaiians, and do not fall under the definition of objects of cultural patrimony.

Sacred objects as defined by NAGPRA are those objects "which are needed by traditional Native American religious leaders for the practice of traditional Native American religions by their present day adherents" (NAGPRA, sec. 2[3][c]). The Bishop holds in its collections numerous items of religious significance and noted that perhaps all cultural objects of old Hawai'i could be considered religiously important. However, the Bishop also suggested "that the objects of Hawaiian antiquity used in ritual were made new with regularity, and the power which the Hawaiians found in objects old and new was imbued through the complex and demanding rituals of the *kapu* system. The objects of antiquity are rare and priceless but other objects may be used in any present day religious practices" (par. 30).[7] Therefore, religious significance resides more in the proper following of ritual than it does in the object itself.

The final conclusion of the proposed guidance centered on the museum's claim of legitimate ownership of the artifacts in its collections. The museum noted that "NAGPRA does not require the repatriation of unassociated funerary objects, objects of cultural patrimony, or sacred objects if a museum has 'right of possession'" (par. 31). Under the definitions of NAGPRA, a museum has "right of possession" to an artifact if the artifact is "obtained with the voluntary consent of an individual or group that had authority of alienation" (NAGPRA, sec. 2[13]). Right of possession is also determined by applicable property law, including state laws. In its proposed guidance document, the museum claimed that the requirements for right of possession have been met and that under Hawai'i state property law the museum is the legitimate owner of the items in its collections. Furthermore, any NHO that claims that it—rather than the Bishop Museum—is the actual owner of an unassociated funerary object bears the burden of proof in demonstrating that the Bishop Museum does not have right of possession. Finally, repatriation to an NHO without the necessary demonstration of ownership amounts to violation of Hawai'i state property law and an unconstitutional "taking" (based on Fifth Amendment protections) of the museum's private property.

Responses to the Bishop Museum's Proposed Guidance Document

The conclusions of the Bishop's proposed guidance document were fairly sweeping and unprecedented, prompting a critical response from some members of the Hawaiian community, Native American organizations, and museum professionals. The most vociferous and visible criticisms came from Edward Halealoha Ayau, who served at that time as the head of the Hui Malama I Na Kupuna O Hawai'i Nei (hereafter referred to as "Hui Malama"), an organization founded in 1989 to assist in repatriation and reburial of Hawaiian human remains and artifacts and specifically listed as an NHO within the text of NAGPRA. In editorials printed in Honolulu newspapers, Ayau (2004a, 2004b) outlined Hui Malama's position on the Bishop's proposed guidance. Ayau stated that the proposed guidance document, if let stand, would

- Defeat the intent of Congress in enacting NAGPRA, which sought to redress harms to Native people caused when their human remains and other cultural objects were taken from them and put into museums.
- Represent a conflict of interest, in that the Bishop Museum would be able to claim cultural items from its own collections while at the same time hold responsibility for repatriation of such items under NAGPRA.
- Ignore the intent of NAGPRA by unlawfully obstructing the repatriation of unassociated funerary objects and sacred objects needed for cultural renewal.
- Allow the Bishop as an NHO to claim Hawaiian cultural items both in its own collections, and in the collections of other federal agencies and museums, which has the effect of countering the repatriation claims of legitimate Native Hawaiian organizations.
- Undermine the ability of Native Hawaiians to assert their *kuleana* (responsibility) to properly care for cultural items.

Ayau noted that "rather than being a mechanism for healing old wounds as NAGPRA was designed, this policy opens new ones" (Ayau 2004b). To begin healing and to end the continued paternalism of colonialism that the guidance represents, Ayau called for the rejection of the policy and the resignation of William Brown, the president of the Bishop Museum (Ayau 2004a, 2004b).

Hui Malama also disputed the legitimacy of the Bishop's ownership of these collections and suggested that the museum purchased many items in its collection from individuals who were nothing more than grave robbers. Ayau noted that immigrants to the state of Hawai'i—such as Joseph Swift Emerson (Apgar 2004a), David Forbes (Apgar 2004f), and Emma Turnbull (Apgar 2004c)—wrongfully removed from caves burial items (and sometimes human remains as well) that were intended to remain with the interred individuals. This wrongful removal demonstrates that these individuals had no legal title to transfer these items to the Bishop: "[President of the Bishop Museum] Brown ignores the fact that Hawaiian families placed these objects with their loved ones and that approval was not given to remove them. By assuming ownership, Brown is revoking our ancestors' decisions and usurping our *kuleana* (responsibility) to our *kupuna* (ancestors)" (Ayau 2004b). Ayau also argued that while the Bishop Museum does not hold the right of possession to important cultural objects such as bones and burial objects, neither does Hui Malama: "Hui Malama does not have 'sole possession' or any possession for that matter of the objects, as the *iwi kupuna* (ancestral bones) and *moepu* (burial objects) are back where they belong" (Apgar 2004g).[8] Ayau has further added that Hui Malama does not own anything but has only accepted the difficult kuleana of acting in accordance with what is right (NAGPRA Review Committee 2005: 25).

Senator Daniel Inouye (D-Hawaii), who serves as a member of the Senate Committee on Indian Affairs and was an instrumental player in the passage of NAGPRA, also voiced his concern about the Bishop's proposal. Inouye expressed his displeasure over the policy to the Bishop's board of directors, a move that likely caught the board's attention given Inouye's role in controlling the flow of millions of dollars into the museum (Apgar 2004b). Additionally, on behalf of Ayau (who had served on Inouye's staff during creation and passage of NAGPRA), Inouye sent an inquiry to the U.S. Department of the Interior, asking for a clarification on the "propriety of the Bishop Museum's self-designation as a Native Hawaiian organiza-tion and the legal effect on its obligation to comply with NAGPRA" (Ayau 2004a).

Despite the concerns of Hui Malama and Senator Inouye, the U.S. Department of the Interior ruled that the Bishop's self-declared status as a Native Hawaiian or-ganization was legal under federal laws governing repatriation (Apgar 2004b). But although the Department of Interior gave the Bishop Museum its blessing as an NHO, the Bishop Museum's board of directors voted unanimously against desig-nation as a Native Hawaiian organization (Apgar 2004d; see also Bishop Museum 2004b). This vote, however, was a hollow victory for critics of the museum. The board's vote against NHO status was an acknowledgment of "concerns over poten-tial conflict in (being a claimant and) judging claims on objects in its collection" (Apgar 2004d), rather than a resolution on whether the museum had the right to claim NHO status in the first place. Furthermore, the board did not reject the other provisions of the proposed guidance. In fact, Isabella Abbott, one of the seven Native Hawaiians on the museum's nine-member board, stated that when it comes to items in the Bishop's collection not covered by NAGPRA definitions, the Bishop "will defend those to the death" (Apgar 2004d). Abbott's strongly worded statement of support for the Bishop's policies regarding objects of Hawaiian antiquity stands in clear contrast to the views of Edward Ayau and Hui Malama. What lies behind these differing views will be addressed in the following sections.

The vote to reject NHO status did not result in an end to controversies surround-ing the Bishop Museum, stewardship of Hawaiian culture, and the value of artifacts. The actions of the museum and the response to those actions by organizations such as Hui Malama serve to highlight the complexity of NAGPRA implementation in

Hawai'i today. The questions concerning ownership of cultural objects and the appropriate goals of stewardship—as well as who is qualified to be the rightful steward of Hawaiian culture—persist and remain highly charged. And although NAGPRA is federal law, we must place the controversy surrounding the Bishop Museum's proposed policy on NAGPRA solidly within the context of Hawaiian tradition—especially those traditions that speak to stewardship and responsibility—as well as within the legacies of a colonial history.

Questions of Stewardship: Responsibilities and Families

Hui Malama has taken a leadership role in repatriation efforts and NAGPRA implementation in Hawai'i. Presumably this is attributable to the leadership of Edward Ayau, his close connection to Inouye's office and the crafting of the legislation, and the fact that Hui Malama is explicitly listed as a Native Hawaiian organization in the text of NAGPRA. Hui Malama, however, is not guaranteed the right to be the sole or even primary organization directing repatriation efforts on the islands. In fact, Hui Malama's designation within the text of NAGPRA does not automatically grant Hui Malama standing to bring repatriation cases. In the case of *Na Iwi O Na Kupuna O Mokapu v. Dalton* (894 F. Supp. 1397 [D. Hawaii]) the court noted that

> Hui Malama asserts that its inclusion in the definitional section of the statute effectively grants the organization standing. . . . While NAGPRA recognizes Hui Malama as a party with an interest in Native Hawaiian matters generally, the court does not construe this recognition as conferring standing. . . . The court construes Congress' mention of Hui Malama in the definitional section as providing an intended source of information that parties working under the provisions of NAGPRA may consult in order to better facilitate the statute's goal, namely proper repatriation of Native Hawaiian cultural items. The words of the statute convey nothing more. (Hutt, Blanco, and Varmer 1999: 330)

While the court did grant standing to the Hui Malama, the stated opinion makes it explicit that standing must be reestablished on a case-by-case basis.

Hui Malama's leadership role in repatriation has been strongly contested, as many other organizations and individuals have come forward to both criticize Hui Malama and assert their own rights in the process. This has resulted in a contentious struggle over who owns the right to care for Hawaii's heritage. Some have suggested that this struggle is the result of a definition of Native Hawaiian organization that is too broadly worded. They note that while NAGPRA may work for "American Indians who have recognized tribes with governing bodies that are authorized to make decisions on behalf of the entire tribe . . . native Hawaiians have no such governing body, nor do they have a native Hawaiian museum" (Apgar 2004i). The lack of a central governing body or Native Hawaiian museum has allowed some groups to "push their protocols and burial practices with total disregard for family opinions or decision capabilities" (Apgar 2004i).[9]

This concern over the role of families in repatriation is a recurring theme among those who criticize the power of Hui Malama. The fear is that Hui Malama has usurped responsibilities that in the past rightfully belonged to the family and that the organization incorrectly claims to be the only group knowledgeable about burial rights, when such protocols historically varied throughout the islands (Apgar 2004c). Isabella Abbott, a member of the Bishop Museum board of directors, expresses this point of view: "None of the members of Hui Malama who I have met are related to me, nor do I believe that they have any right to the bones of my ancestors. In fact, I would strongly protest any interference with the *iwi* of my Hawaiian family. In my Hawaiian family, handling the bones of others would have been strictly *kapu* (forbidden). . . How can it be *pono* to take the role that relatives should have, to fail in that role, and then to deny any responsibility?" (Abbott 2004).

Abigail Kawananakoa, a Campbell Estate[10] heiress who traces her lineage back to King Kalakaua, forcefully entered the repatriation struggle on December 7, 2004. She vowed to throw her support—and, more important, her wealth—behind La'akea Suganuma, the leader of the Royal Hawaiian Academy of Traditional Arts, an organization currently pitted in a legal battle with Hui Malama over control of reburied artifacts. Like Abigail Abbott, Kawananakoa stresses the role of family and states that her support of La'akea Suganuma "is my duty. I will do it with my money and it's a certainty I will do it with my lineage and my *koko,* or blood, and blood never lies" (Apgar 2004h). Kawananakoa's opinions are shaped by a strongly hierarchical worldview and her ali'i genealogy. She has referred to Hui Malama members as *maka'āinana* (commoners) and argued that at no time in Hawaiian history were commoners allowed to participate in ali'i burial rituals or handle their bones (Apgar 2005a). Furthermore, she believes that the refusal to return the property of the ali'i to the rightful custodians (in her view, the Bishop Museum fulfills this role) demonstrates profound disrespect for the central beliefs of Hawaiian people for thousands of years (NAGPRA Review Committee 2005: 26).

Others are less vociferous in their views but still bristle at what they view as the hubris of members of Hui Malama in asserting that they know best how to care for cultural artifacts. Many also criticize Hui Malama for ineptitude in properly handling repatriation responsibilities. At issue is the sale on the black market of many artifacts that had been repatriated by the Bishop Museum to Hui Malama (see Apgar 2004a; Gordon and Viotti 2004). Over a period of seven years, the museum repatriated items that were part of the J. S. Emerson Collection. Emerson had started "collecting" the items from a burial cave, known as Kanupa, as early as 1858. He eventually sold his collections to the Bishop Museum in the late 1880s (Apgar 2004a); upon repatriation to members of Hui Malama, the objects were reburied in Kanupa cave. Shortly thereafter, however, the cave was broken into and the objects were stolen, and some were secretly offered for sale to private collectors and antique dealers. Opponents of Hui Malama were quick to voice their concerns (see Abbott 2004), and many worried that reburying items in caves placed those objects at great risk. DeSoto Brown, the collection manager for the Bishop's archives, stated, "It's unrealistic to say that it's in the cave where the ancient Hawaiians wanted and that therefore we've done all right and it's all finished. . . . The items in a cave are subject to natural deterioration, which I know is what Hui Malama said should be their fate. But people can get into those caves and take things and they are not safe. This case brings this point into the open; the caves are not safe" (Apgar 2004a). Brown also noted that "this is why we have museums: to preserve, safeguard, and keep valuable artifacts" (Apgar 2004a). In March 2006, a man was arrested in connection with the theft of the Kanupa Cave items (Kobayashi and Pang 2006), but this did little to quiet concerns about the safety of reburied objects.

A second contentious case concerns the permanent reburial of items that were "loaned" to the Hui Malama by the Bishop Museum for a period of one year (Apgar 2004c, 2004f, 2004g). The loaned items consisted of eighty-three artifacts from the Kawaihae Cave Complex that had been taken from the cave in 1905 by Jack Forbes and eventually sold to the Bishop Museum (Apgar 2004f). On February 26, 2000, the Bishop Museum loaned the items to Hui Malama for a year, but when the museum requested their return, Hui Malama refused and stated that the objects had been reburied at a location that Hui Malama would not disclose. Hui Malama took the position that the "loan" had been merely the vehicle that the Bishop Museum used to release the items to Hui Malama for repatriation and that the Bishop's former director, Donald Duckworth, never expected to have the items returned (see NAGPRA Review Committee 2003, 2005 for details of the case; see also National Park Service 2003).

In response, two Hawaiian groups—the Hawaiian Academy of Traditional Arts and Na Lei Ali'i Kawananakoa—brought suit against Hui Malama and the Bishop Museum and demanded that the objects be returned and taken out of the control of Hui Malama (Apgar 2004g; Pang 2006a). Eventually, fourteen groups were involved in the lawsuit and requested some say in determining the fate of the objects. On September 7, 2005, U.S. District Judge David Ezra ordered that the eighty-three artifacts be returned by Hui Malama and stored at the Bishop Museum until all fourteen parties to the suit could determine their final disposition (Apgar 2005a). This decision was appealed, but the Ninth Circuit Court of Appeals in San Francisco upheld Judge Ezra's ruling (Apgar 2005b), and Hui Malama was ordered to provide the exact location of the items reburied in the chambers of the Kawaihae Cave Complex. Ayau, however, refused to reveal the location, stating that to do so would violate the kupuna (ancestors) and amount to an abrogation of his kuleana (responsibility). Ezra pronounced him in contempt of court and on December 27, 2005, ordered Ayau to prison (Mendoza 2005). In January 2006, the opposing parties in the dispute agreed to enter mediation, and Judge Ayers ordered Ayau released from prison and placed under supervised house arrest so that he could participate in the talks (Barayuga 2006; Pang 2006b). After four months of mediation, however, the differences between the parties remained unresolved; Judge Ezra ordered engineers to begin a plan for safely entering the caves and removing the items from within (Apgar 2006). In September 2006, representatives of the Bishop Museum entered the Kawaihae Cave Complex and recovered the disputed objects. Furthermore, Judge Ezra signed off on a settlement that released Ayau from house arrest but also ordered that the cost for recovery of the objects (approximately $330,000) be shared by both the Bishop Museum and Hui Malama (Johnson 2007: 150).

Responsibility to the Ancestors, Responsibility to the Descendants

Questions concerning ownership of cultural items and the role played by organizations, families, and individuals in directing repatriation work to shape the debate over control of the Hawaiian past. Two fundamentally different views of the value of artifacts and how best to care for objects of antiquity appear to lie at the heart of this debate. Sherry Hutt (2006: 12) suggests that when thinking about issues of ownership of artifacts, one should look at the perspectives of those asserting ownership rather than focusing on the artifacts. The chapter epigraphs (one from the Bishop Museum's proposed guidance on NAGPRA and the other from an article coauthored by Edward Ayau) exemplify this approach, embodying two very different perspectives on the value of artifacts and the role NAGPRA plays in connection to those artifacts.

The first epigraph represents the view of those, such as the Bishop Museum and many of the critics of Hui Malama, who stress that the value of artifacts lies in their ability to inspire and instruct the living and those to come. Renewal of cultural pride is accomplished through the return of historical objects, their celebration, and their availability to all of the people; NAGPRA serves as a mechanism for regaining and preserving those objects. The Bishop states that the role of the museum is to keep "the old for those who live now and who will live later" (Bishop Museum 2004a: par. 3). Many Native Hawaiians share this view and believe that the preservation and display of historical objects is important because "we don't need the original in our practice, but we do need access to the original to study and make our own. . . . the original is one of a kind. I want my grandson and future generations to be able to come back and see it. It should not be owned by just one" (Apgar 2004d). Revival of culture requires the survival and accessibility of artifacts. La'akea Suganuma, president of the Royal Hawaiian Academy of Traditional Arts, believes that the ancestors have made these culturally important objects available to the living for just this purpose: "I know what the ancestors want. From a Hawaiian point of view, if you think like the older folks, nothing is revealed unless there is a purpose for it. . . . They want the future generations to understand what they did, the things they created and how they were used. They want [the items] to be seen; otherwise nobody would have found them" (Sweetingham 2005). For Suganuma, these artifacts represent a tangible link to the past, and to ensure that this link continues to the descendants as well, their preservation and care is an obligation.

The second epigraph represents the views of the supporters of Hui Malama and Edward Ayau, who believe that their primary responsibility is to the ancestors, not to those living today. Their position is that these objects of antiquity cannot be owned by anyone living today but are purely the possessions of those with whom they were buried. The artifacts have little intrinsic value but are meaningful only in relationship to the ancestors whom they were meant to serve. Therefore, these items must be reunited with the iwi (bones), even if this means the deterioration or loss of historic artifacts, a fact that is lost on those who wish only to preserve these objects: "Opposition to the reburial of the Forbes Cave collection sought to shift the focus from the needs of the dead to those of the living, even though implementation of this contemporary view would have required a second looting of the *moepū* (funerary items). . . . The contemporary view reflects the Western practice of objectifying *moepū* as artifacts with inherent educational value, rather than as items intended to serve the needs of the deceased" (Ayau 2005: 195–96). Adherence to this contemporary Western view—in which preservation and display of artifacts occurs at the expense of doing what is right for the past—is symptomatic of a people who have lost their way because of colonization: "The emotionally and politically charged nature of the debate speaks to the various struggles we face as a colonized people seeking to reclaim our cultural identity. What were once fundamental values and beliefs to our ancestors regarding burial practices are now foreign to many in our current generation. Many Native Hawaiians now look to books and artefacts to learn about their past and forge an identity today" (Ayau and Tengan 2002: 184). The value of NAGPRA, therefore, is that it can serve as a tool for redress, a way of correcting the injuries that were done to the ancestors by a colonial power. In the process of correcting these injuries to the ancestors, present-day Native Hawaiians can learn the proper rituals, renew their culture, and move toward decolonization.

Decolonization is achieved not by studying figurines or preserving and displaying feathered cloaks in a museum. Rather, it is achieved by living your culture, practicing it every day, learning the teachings of the *kupuna* (elders) and passing it on to your *mo'opuna* (grandchildren) (see the testimony of Mr. William Aila, NAGPRA Review Committee 2005: 12).

Cynics might view this disagreement over caring for the past as a case of petty politics and indicative of a power struggle between Native Hawaiian factions. Edward Ayau, however, has stated that "this isn't about power or authority; it's about *kuleana* (responsibility)" (Apgar 2004i). I think that he is right. The complexities and struggles surrounding the repatriation, ownership, and ultimate fate of Hawaiian cultural objects reflect parties wrestling with how best to fulfill their responsibilities to the past, present, and future. Furthermore, we must remember that the stakes are very high. Forces of colonization attempted to separate Hawaiian people from their culture by destroying their customs and religions. Healing the wounds left by the legacy of colonialism and renewing Hawaiian culture is the goal of all the parties involved in the present case. The contentious nature of this case, then, is not a reflection of two parties struggling for power. Rather, it is a reflection of two parties who recognize how important the past is to people in the present but who have very different—and sincerely held—views about their responsibility to that past.

Notes

1. Section 106 requires that federal agencies must consider the impact of their activities on archaeological resources that are included in or eligible for inclusion in the National Register of Historic Places. The primary criteria for determining whether archaeological sites meet this criteria is evaluation criteria "(d) that have yielded, or may be likely to yield, information important in prehistory or history" (36 CFR 60.4). ARPA defines archaeological resources as objects that are "capable of providing scientific or humanistic understandings of past human behavior, cultural adaptation, and related topics" (43 CFR 7.3[b]).

2. The context for this chapter is the legal and political framework of the United States. My discussion—while certainly touching on issues regarding ownership and stewardship of antiquities that are repeated throughout the globe—is specific to the United States. Although comparing this case with similar cases internationally might prove informative, it is not within the scope of the current work.

3. The interim guidance document was consulted online at http://www.bishopmuseum. org/NAGPRAGuidelines.html (accessed on August 18, 2004). Because the document was consulted in Web-page format, paragraph number, rather than page number, is given for direct quotations.

4. The text of NAGPRA is reprinted in Mihesuah 2000: 307–19. Text citations, however, use the appropriate section and subsection designations.

5. An earlier version of the bill contained a provision requiring NHOs to have a majority Native Hawaiian membership. The removal of this provision from the final statute must be in-

terpreted to mean that Congress considered the provision but decided to reject it (McKeown and Hutt 2003: 161–62).

6. Ruta Ke'elikolani—the half sister of Kamehameha IV and Kamehameha V—died on May 24, 1883. Her extensive land holdings and collections were bequeathed to Bernice Pauahi Bishop, her second cousin and closest living relative. Bernice, who died less than a year and a half later, bequeathed her collections—which included a large Hawaiian ethnographic collection—to her husband, Charles Reed Bishop. Finally, Queen Emma, who died in 1885, also bequeathed her extensive collections to Charles Reed Bishop, with the understanding that a museum would be created to house and display these important items of Hawaiian history and culture (Rose 1980: 7–10). The Bishop Museum (named in honor of Bernice Pauahi Bishop) opened in 1890, and the core of its initial collection was formed by donations from these ali'i on the Kamehameha line.

7. Greg Johnson (2003; see also Johnson 2007) provides a discussion of the complex and contentious links between objects of antiquity, sacredness, religion, tradition, and political invention in the Hawaiian context. Johnson analyzes a NAGPRA case in which the Native Hawaiian organizations Hui Malama I Na Kupuna O Hawai'i Nei and the Office of Hawaiian Affairs requested repatriation of a Hawaiian ki'i (figurine) from the Roger Williams Museum in Providence, Rhode Island. Discussion of the relationship between Hawaiian objects and religion is also provided by Malo (1980) and Valeri (1985) in their descriptions of the Luakini Temple and Makahiki Festival rituals.

8. There is considerable disagreement over whether any of these items actually represent burial objects. Hawaiian historian Herb Kawainui Kane disputes Ayau's claims that these items were placed in graves as possessions of the deceased (Kane 2004). He also suggests that too many Hawaiians today have succumbed to the idea that the ancient ali'i were placed in tombs and "laid out in royal splendor surrounded by all the wealth of their time similar to the pharaohs of Egypt[;] . . . just the opposite is the case" (Pang 2006c). Some argue that many items of cultural importance were secreted away to burial caves to protect them from the burning and destruction of the "idols" that followed the abolishment of the kapu system in 1819. The physical proximity of cultural items to burials is therefore merely coincidental and not indicative of items purposely placed with the dead. This view, however, has been strongly criticized by anthropologists and archaeologists who state that there is ample ethnographic, historic, and archaeological evidence to suggest that the ali'i were buried with personal possessions (see the testimony of Ty Kawika Tengan and Kehaunani Abad, NAGPRA Review Committee 2005: 20).

9. The most recent version of the Akaka Bill (officially known as the Native Hawaiian Government Reorganization Act of 2007 [H.R. 505]) was passed by the U.S. House of Representatives in October 2007. The bill, if successfully passed by the U.S. Senate, would establish for Native Hawaiians the same level of federal recognition and right to self-government that is held by federally recognized Native American tribes and would perhaps lead to a centralized governing body for Native Hawaiians. While many Native Hawaiians support the bill, some non-natives are opposed, arguing that the bill would establish two separate race-based governmental and legal systems and therefore would promote discrimination. Those Native Hawaiians who support Hawaiian independence also tend to oppose the bill. They argue that federal recognition does not always work to the benefit of Indian tribes and that "domestic dependent" status prevents Native Americans from exercising full sovereignty.

They also feel that passage of the bill would only legitimize the long-term illegal occupation of Hawai'i by non-Hawaiians and diminish any hope of self-determination and independence.

    10. The Campbell Estate is a private trust created in 1900 to manage the assets of James Campbell and his wife, Abigail Kuaihelani Maipinepine. Campbell first arrived in Hawai'i in 1850 as a crew member on a whaling ship. He established a mill on the island of Maui and in 1877 used profits from the sale of that business to invest in 41,000 acres of land on Oahu. The discovery of a large reserve of fresh water on this land allowed Campbell to establish a large and financially successful sugar plantation. James and Abigail had four surviving children. The oldest of their four children married Prince David Kawananakoa of the House of Kalakaua. As of 2001, the Campbell Estate owned over 62,000 acres of land throughout the islands of Hawai'i and held assets valued at nearly $2 billion.

References Cited

Abbott, Isabella. "Hui Malama Failed in Its Self-Appointed Role." *Honolulu Star Bulletin,* September 5, 2004, Letters to the Editor.

Apgar, Sally. "Artifacts' Sale Investigated: Federal Agents Say that Several Items Returned to a Hawaiian Group Were Offered to Collectors." *Honolulu Star Bulletin,* August 11, 2004, News Section. [2004a]

———. "Museum Rethinks Artifact Proposal: Bishop Museum Can Declare Itself a Native Group, But Might Not Do It, After All." *Honolulu Star Bulletin,* October 3, 2004, News Section. [2004b]

———. "Group Contests Bishop Museum's Right to Artifacts: Hui Malama Cites a National Act to Protect Native Burial Grounds." *Honolulu Star Bulletin,* October 4, 2004, News Section. [2004c]

———. "Museum Votes against 'Native' Status: The Bishop Board Bows to Concerns over Potential Conflicts." *Honolulu Star Bulletin,* October 8, 2004, News Section. [2004d]

———. "Groups Inspect Sacred Burial Cave: Investigators Do Not Say What Was Found on the Big Island." *Honolulu Star Bulletin,* October 24, 2004, News Section. [2004e]

———. "Federal Panel to Revisit Artifacts Dispute." *Honolulu Star Bulletin,* November 3, 2004, News Section. [2004f]

———. "Bishop Museum Faces Allegations of Deception." *Honolulu Star Bulletin,* December 1, 2004. [2004g]

———. "Kawananakoa Support Preservation of Artifacts: The Campbell Heiress and Alii Descendant Promises a Fight over Reburied Objects." *Honolulu Star Bulletin,* December 5, 2004, News Section. [2004h]

———. "Hawaiians Call Law Too Broad." *Honolulu Star Bulletin,* December 9, 2004, News Section. [2004i]

———. "Showdown over Artifacts Unearths Spiritual Divide." *Honolulu Star Bulletin,* September 19, 2005, News Section. [2005a]

———. "Appeals Court Upholds Ruling against Hui Malama." *Honolulu Star Bulletin,* December 13, 2005, News Section. [2005b]

———. "Judge Orders Disputed Cave Artifacts Retrieved." *Honolulu Star Bulletin,* April 29, 2006, News Section.

Arakawa, Lynda. "Groups Blast Hui Malama." *Honolulu Advertiser,* December 27, 2005, Ethnic Affairs Section.

Arnold, Bettina. "The Past as Propaganda: Totalitarian Archaeology in Nazi Germany." *Antiquity* 64 (1990): 464–78.

Ayau, Edward Halealoha. "Museum Policy Further Threatens Artifacts." *Honolulu Advertiser,* August 8, 2004, Editorial Section. [2004a]

———. "Bishop Museum Doesn't Qualify as a Claimant to Artifacts." *Honolulu Star Bulletin,* August 29, 2004, Editorial Section. [2004b]

———. "Honour Thy Ancestor's Possessions." *Public Archaeology* 4 (2005): 193–97.

Ayau, Edward Halealoha, and Ty Kāwika Tengan. "Ka Huaka'i O Nā 'Ōiwi: The Journey Home." In *The Dead and Their Possessions: Repatriation in Principle, Policy and Practice,* edited by C. Fforde, J. Hubert, and P. Turnbull, 171–89. London: Routledge, 2002.

Barayuga, Debra. "Ayau out of Prison as Groups Agree to Start Mediation." *Honolulu Star Bulletin,* January 18, 2006, News Section.

Bishop Museum. "Interim and Proposed Final Guidance: Native American Graves Protection and Repatriation Act." http://www.bishopmuseum.org/NAGPRAGuidelines.html (accessed August 18, 2004). [2004a]

———. "Final Guidance: Native American Graves Protection and Repatriation Act, October 7, 2004." http://www.bishopmuseum.org/special/Final_NAGPRA_Guidelines.html (accessed May 26, 2006). [2004b]

Clavir, Miriam. *Preserving What Is Valued: Museums, Conservation, and First Nations.* Vancouver: UBC Press, 2002.

Gordon, Mike, and Vicki Viotti. "U.S. Investigates Sale of Hawaiian Artifacts." *Honolulu Advertiser,* August 11, 2004, News Section.

Groarke, Leo, and Gary Warrick. "Stewardship Gone Astray? Ethics and the SAA." In *The Ethics of Archaeology: Philosophical Perspectives on Archaeological Practice,* edited by C. Scarre and G. Scarre, 163–77. Cambridge: Cambridge University Press, 2006.

Habu, Junko, and Clare Fawcett. "Jomon Archaeology and the Representation of Japanese Origins." *Antiquity* 73 (1999): 587–93.

Hutt, Sherry. "The Year 2005: A Time of Examining the Meaning of Ownership of Cultural Property." In *Yearbook of Cultural Property Law: 2006,* edited by S. Hutt, 11–21. Walnut Creek, Calif.: Left Coast Press, 2006.

Hutt, Sherry, Caroline M. Blanco, and Ole Varmer. *Heritage Resources Law: Protecting the Archeological and Cultural Environment.* New York: National Trust for Historic Preservation, John Wiley and Sons, 1999.

Johnson, Greg. "Ancestors before Us: Manifestations of Tradition in a Hawaiian Dispute." *Journal of the American Academy of Religion* 71, no. 2 (2003): 327–46.

———. *Sacred Claims: Repatriation and Living Tradition.* Charlottesville: University of Virginia Press, 2007.

Kane, Herb Kawainui. "Gathering Place: Cave Artifacts Wrongly Deemed Sacred." *Honolulu Star Bulletin,* December 9, 2004, Editorial Commentary Section.

Kobayashi, Ken, and Gordon Y. K. Pang. "Arrest Made in Hawaiian Artifacts Trafficking Case." *Honolulu Advertiser,* March 17, 2006, News Section.

Kohl, Philip L., and Clare Fawcett, eds. *Nationalism, Politics and the Practice of Archaeology.* Cambridge: Cambridge University Press, 1995.

Lipe, William D. "A Conservation Model for American Archaeology." *Kiva* 39 (1974): 213–45.

———. "In Defense of Digging: Archaeological Preservation as a Means, Not an End." *CRM Magazine* 19, no. 7 (1996): 23–27.

Lynott, Mark J., and Alison Wylie. "Stewardship: The Central Principle of Archaeological Ethics." In *Ethics in American Archaeology*, 2nd rev. ed., edited by M. J. Lynott and A. Wylie, 35–39. Washington, D.C.: Society for American Archaeology, 2000.

Malo, David. *Hawaiian Antiquities*. Translated by Nathaniel Emerson. Honolulu: Bishop Museum Press, 1980. (Orig. pub. 1898.)

McGuire, Randall H. "Foreword." In *Ethical Issues in Archaeology*, edited by L. J. Zimmerman, K. D. Vitelli, and J. Hollowell-Zimmer, vii–ix. Walnut Creek, Calif.: AltaMira Press, 2003.

McKeown, C. Timothy, and Sherry Hutt. "In the Smaller Scope of Conscience: The Native American Graves Protection and Repatriation Act Twelve Years After." *UCLA Journal of Environmental Law and Policy* 21, no. 2 (2003): 153–212.

McManamon, Francis P., and Larry V. Nordby. "Implementing the Native American Graves Protection and Repatriation Act." *Arizona State Law Journal* 24 (1992): 217–52.

Mendoza, Jim. "Hui Malama Leader Jailed for Contempt." KGMB 9, December 27, 2005. Accessed online at http://www.kgmb.com.

Mihesuah, Devon A., ed. *Repatriation Reader: Who Owns American Indian Remains?* Lincoln: University of Nebraska Press, 2000.

NAGPRA. *The Native American Graves Protection and Repatriation Act of 1999*. Reprinted in *Repatriation Reader: Who Owns American Indian Remains?* edited by D. A. Mihesuah, 307–19. Lincoln: University of Nebraska Press, 2000.

NAGPRA Review Committee. Minutes, Native American Graves Protection and Repatriation Review Committee, Twenty-Fifth Meeting: May 9 and 10, 2003, St. Paul, Minnesota. http://www.cr.nps.gov/nagpra/meetings. [2003]

———. Minutes, Native American Graves Protection and Repatriation Review Committee, Twenty-Ninth Meeting: May 13 and 15, 2005, Honolulu, Hawaii. http://www.cr.nps.gov/nagpra/meetings. [2005]

National Park Service. "Native American Graves Protection and Repatriation Review Committee Findings and Recommendations and Minority Opinion Regarding a Dispute between the Royal Hawaiian Academy of Traditional Arts and the Bernice Pauahi Bishop Museum." *Federal Register* 68: 161 (2003): 50179–50180. [2003]

Pang, Gordon. "Dispute Delivers Praise and Scorn to Hui Malama." *Honolulu Advertiser*, January 13, 2006, News Section. [2006a]

———. "Judge Sets Ayau Free to Participate in Talks." *Honolulu Advertiser*, January 18, 2006, News Section. [2006b]

———. "For Museum or the Cave?" *Honolulu Advertiser*, May 21, 2006, News Section. [2006c]

Rose, Roger. *A Museum to Instruct and Delight: William T. Brigham and the Founding of the Bernice Pauahi Bishop Museum*. Honolulu: Bishop Museum Press, 1980.

Schmidt, Martin. "Reconstruction as Ideology: The Open Air Museum at Oerlinghausen, Germany." In *The Constructed Past: Experimental Archaeology, Education and the Public*, edited by P. G. Stone and P. G. Planel, 146–56. New York: Routledge, 1999.

Singleton, Theresa A., and Charles E. Orser, Jr. "Descendant Communities: Linking People in the Present to the Past." In *Ethical Issues in Archaeology,* edited by L. J. Zimmerman, K. D. Vitelli, and J. Hollowell-Zimmer, 143–52. Walnut Creek, Calif.: AltaMira Press, 2003.

Sommer, Ulrike. "Slavonic Archaeology: Groß Raden, an Open Air Museum in a Unified Germany." In *The Constructed Past: Experimental Archaeology, Education and the Public,* edited by P. G. Stone and P. G. Planel, 157–70. New York: Routledge, 1999.

Sweetingham, Lisa. "Native Hawaiians Refuse to Dig Up Artifacts Reburied for Their Ancestors." *Court TV,* December 23, 2005. http://www.courttv.com. [2005]

Thomas, Nicholas. *Entangled Objects: Exchange, Material Culture, and Colonialism in the Pacific.* Cambridge, Mass.: Harvard University Press, 1991.

———. *In Oceania: Visions, Artifacts, Histories.* Durham, N.C.: Duke University Press, 1997.

Trope, Jack F., and Walter R. Echo-Hawk. "The Native American Graves Protection and Repatriation Act: Background and Legislative History." *Arizona State Law Journal* 24, no. 1 (1992): 35–77.

Valeri, Valerio. *Kingship and Sacrifice: Ritual and Society in Ancient Hawaii.* Chicago: University of Chicago Press, 1985.

Watkins, Joe. "Artefacts, Archaeologists and American Indians." *Public Archaeology* 4 (2005): 187–91.

Wylie, Alison. "The Promise and Perils of an Ethic of Stewardship." In *Embedding Ethics,* edited by L. Meskell and P. Pels, 47–68. Oxford, U.K.: Berg, 2005.

10

Standpoints on Stewardship
in a Global Market for the Material Past

JULIE HOLLOWELL

I first headed to the Bering Strait for fieldwork to learn more about what was really happening on St. Lawrence Island, where I had heard that local residents were mining archaeological sites for artifacts to sell (Scott 1984; Staley 1993). To archaeologists, this represented a worst-case scenario: a community (a Native community, no less) that had decided to "loot" the record of its past to support livelihoods in the present. Reporters and archaeologists had called St. Lawrence Islanders "cultural cannibals" who were "plundering the past" and "selling their heritage."[1] As long as the Native corporations who owned the land did not object, this was completely legal. I wanted to know how diggers on the island saw their activities, who was digging, and why. Did people feel they were selling their heritage? If so, how did they rationalize what they were doing or conceive of their relationship to old sites and the artifacts within them?

People on the island did not particularly see the value in this topic, which focused on one aspect of their ongoing struggles to make ends meet, especially because this aspect was negatively portrayed in the media. Jobs are scarce, and selling what residents referred to as "old things" contributes toward many household incomes. Some families had been digging for generations, at the encouragement of traders and early archaeologists, who purchased as many so-called specimens as people could find. What community members wanted to know was "what happens to the things that leave our island?" This led me to a multisited study of the flows of people, materials, and information in the market for excavated materials.[2]

I soon realized that to really understand what I had come to know as "site destruction" and "looting," I had to de-center the archaeological standpoint and take into account the many different ways that people valued these old things. Archaeologists may have identified themselves professionally as stewards of sites and artifacts, but people living in places where subsistence digging is an accepted practice have their own notions of stewardship and ways of caring for archaeological sites and objects, as do collectors, dealers, and others.

Taking a more multivocal perspective on stewardship—one that treats archaeology as "one practice among others" (Foucault 1972: 186)—does not necessarily mean slipping into a relativism that accepts all standpoints as equally justifiable; instead, all accounts are subject to critique and evaluation (see Hollowell and Nicholas 2008: 78), and different standpoints can be evaluated using the same standards of clarity, coherence, and consistency that we apply to other analyses and to daily life (Wylie 2004). Trying to see a situation from other standpoints can cast one's position and interpretations in a new and critical light, revealing alternative ways of acting or consequences that may have previously gone unrecognized (Moody-Adams 1997).

Stewardship

Stewardship is a relationship between people and things that implies a responsibility for taking good care of something in the interest of someone else. Legal, cultural, economic, moral, or political interests typically underlie a stewardship relationship, raising fundamental questions about what or whose interests a steward serves and how the relationship is legitimated. At its heart, then, stewardship is a form of stake-holding—a term that more openly speaks to the role of interested parties (Sykes 2004). Just as there are multiple stakeholders in the past, so too are there many differing conceptions of what constitutes good or responsible stewardship. From one perspective, good stewardship might mean reburying grave goods without study; from another, it means keeping objects in well-labeled boxes on humidity-controlled shelves. What some archaeologists have called cultural cannibalism is, for others, a way to pay the bills. The ethical dilemmas surrounding the marketing of pieces of the past call for exploring how different entities involved in these practices see themselves as stewards.

Standpoints

One way to contextualize different perspectives on stewardship is by paying attention to *standpoints*. The concept of "standpoint" developed out of feminist critiques of the production of knowledge, which recognized the partial, contingent, and situated nature of all interpretations and accounts (Marcus 1998: 198; Wylie 1995). It has much in common with Giddens's (1979) notion of "situated practices," which interprets all actions as situated within a particular cultural and political context, but standpoint theory also explores how this situatedness both "shapes and constrains what we know" (Harding 1990). The term originally came from Marxism's demand for accounts of history and social movement from the standpoint of the proletariat. In the 1980s and early '90s, those conducting subaltern studies and feminist theorists applied the concept of standpoint as a way to correct for the lack of subaltern or female voices in research by purposefully privileging these voices. Recent readings reject the idea that any particular standpoint should automatically be privileged—say, just because one is an Alaskan Native or a trained archaeologist—while at the same time recognizing that certain life experiences and social positions give a person more (or less) authority to speak from a particular standpoint. Standpoint theory also must be wary of the tendency to essentialize a perspective as characteristic of a neatly delineated or bounded group—a problem built into the concept of "stakeholders" or of cultural groups in general (Handler 2003: 357). One way to address these critiques is to start from the stories and experiences of real people and to be explicit about one's own standpoint, experiences, and sources of data (or lack thereof).

Ethnographers in the field use standpoint theory all the time, when we give more or less voice or credence to certain perspectives on the basis of what we determine to be legitimate knowledge claims. Individuals' experiences or positions can lend them credibility to speak from a certain standpoint: a veteran artifact digger; an art dealer who has spent twenty-five years buying and selling Bering Strait artifacts; an archaeologist who has worked on St. Lawrence Island. Here I hope to further elucidate standpoints on stewardship held by some of the major stakeholders in the market for archaeological materials from the Bering Strait.[3] While the focus is on those who have the most at stake, the diggers, I also look at some of the ways that collectors, dealers, and the state of Alaska see themselves as stewards.

The Market

Along the coasts of the Bering Strait, people have long been digging for old ivory, bone, and artifacts to recycle, barter, or sell. In 1971, the settlement of indigenous land claims in Alaska created Native corporations and gave them land (and money) in return for extinguishing all future claims of aboriginal title (Arnold 1978). Faced with high rates of unemployment (up to 75 percent in many villages) and limited economic opportunities, several Native corporations in the ivory-rich Bering Strait region have exercised their rights under U.S. property law to allow shareholders to dig in old sites on corporation lands and sell materials that they find there. On St. Lawrence Island, home to a rich two-thousand-year-old tradition of ivory carving, digging for old things continues to be one of the only ways, besides producing arts and crafts for the tourist market, to generate cash from local resources. Today the islanders refer to what they do as "subsistence digging,"[4] which clearly aligns it with issues of cultural and economic survival and indigenous resource rights. Other Alaskan Native corporations and indigenous groups who do not allow digging or selling archaeological goods on their lands nevertheless support the decisions of St. Lawrence Islanders based on principles of sovereignty and self-determination.

Long-buried old ivory, or "fossil walrus," has constituted the main cash crop on the island since the crash of global markets for whale baleen and fox fur in the early 1900s. Today the bulk of the market consists of raw materials—whalebone beams from old houses, walrus bone from former butchering sites, and chunks of colorful mineralized ivory cached long ago for toolmaking. Dealers purchase old ivory and bone by the pound and sell it to a remarkable range of buyers—from workshops (some located in Indonesia) that mass-produce carvings for the Alaskan tourist market to artisans who create fine arts and crafts. International bans on other ivories have made St. Lawrence Island fossil walrus one of the only legal alternatives available to scrimshaw artists and instrument makers. In the early 1990s, dealers started buying whole pallets of old whale and walrus bone and flying it to Anchorage and Juneau to sell as a carving medium. Villagers saw this as a way to clean up the digging sites and were happy to find a market for all the bone that lay strewn around. A decade ago, somewhere around five tons of old walrus ivory and ten tons of sea mammal bone were leaving St. Lawrence Island each year.[5]

Worked artifacts on the market include everything from old ivory tools that sell as souvenirs and collectibles in Alaskan gift shops and on the Internet, to skillfully fashioned two-thousand-year-old animal and human figurines that end up in galleries, auction houses, and private collections of tribal art. Of the hundreds of unbroken artifacts unearthed each year, only a handful head for the art market. Prices for an extraordinary object have risen as high as six figures; five figures can mean a new boat and four-wheeler for a subsistence hunter. Fragments of worked artifacts, specialty bones, walrus teeth, and even chips of old ivory make up the rest of the market, along with locally created arts and crafts that incorporate ancient materials. In 1999, this amounted to an estimated one to two million dollars coming in from sales of archaeological materials each year, arguably making St. Lawrence Islanders the best-paid subsistence diggers in the world.

How pervasive is the digging? Many people told me that they "didn't have the patience" to dig. For others, it was a recreational activity for weekends or a long summer evening. Once in Savoonga, I asked classes at the high school how many had ever gone digging, and every hand went up. Yet perhaps only one in twenty people would really call themselves diggers, and fewer still would claim the status of professional digger, as one elder did on his answering machine.

On the Island

My first encounter with a digger took place a few hours after I arrived in Gambell. I was staying in the blue lodge, where the Native corporation rented cots to visitors and temporary workers. Arthur[6] was the last of half a dozen people who had lined up at the door that evening to find out whether I was buying ivory carvings, skin hats, or other crafts (I later learned that lining-up was the protocol for negotiating with artifact dealers and visitors alike). He produced a plastic bag holding two large chunks of old ivory, freshly dug, still wet and smelling like the floor of the 700-year-old Bering Strait dwelling I once excavated. One was the broken end of a pick, and the other was some kind of digging tool. He had found them that very day, extricating them from the permafrost with a pickax at a site near the village. "There must be lots more out there," he said, nodding toward the window, as if the artifacts were just waiting for someone to dig them up. Arthur's grandfather had worked closely in the 1920s and '30s with Otto Geist and Henry Collins, the first archaeologists to excavate on the island. His mother has kept some of the old things her family has found over the years, but others have disappeared.

A few days later, I was talking with a young woman who worked for the Native corporation. A digger had come into her office the day before with a beautifully carved artifact that would no doubt end up sold to an art dealer. "I hate to see people selling artifacts," she said, shaking her head. "But they need the money," I countered. "Yes, but they don't realize the consequences. We have already lost so much. Our past is all in oral history. The people are gone who remember. I just hope that in the future people will keep things of our culture *on* the island."

That summer, the village council was in the midst of negotiations under the Native American Graves Protection and Repatriation Act (NAGPRA)[7] for the return of human remains from the Smithsonian and the University of Alaska, the two institutions with the largest collections of excavated materials from St. Lawrence Island. Most council members wanted to see a museum on the island to house repatriated artifacts, but there were no funds for such a project, few tourists to make it sustainable, and other (more pressing) priorities in the village. A few months later, the ancestral remains were reburied on the island, but the artifacts would be kept, for now, at the university museum. Because of their value on the market, no one felt they would be safe on the island.

Digging as Resource Management

The Native corporations in Alaska are stewards in the literal sense of the word. They have a legal responsibility to manage their lands and resources in the interests of their shareholders; as private landowners, they also have the ability to make policies regulating access and use of their lands. On St. Lawrence Island, no formal regulations exist telling residents where or when they can or cannot dig, but many informal rules exist, such as about how to quicken a claim to a digging spot or what to do when a burial is found. However, the corporations strictly exclude anyone except their own shareholders from digging. Even spouses who have "married in" from another village do not automatically gain this privilege. The community-wide vigilance toward outsiders is even more palpable. Ships have anchored off the island's coast and let members of the crew off to dig, but I was told that they never get away with it for long. One day in Gambell, I was visiting a family when everyone broke out laughing at an announcement (in Yupik) on the ever-present CB radio. "A white man, probably a construction worker, is carrying some old bone across the village," they explained to me. "He thinks he can get away with it!" An archaeologist who had done contract work in Gambell admitted that when he walked around the village, he tried to never bend over or look at the ground, lest people think he was looking for artifacts.

Such protectionist attitudes toward sites and artifacts are part of a broader ethic of stewardship related to the land, sea, and their resources for which St. Lawrence Islanders are well known across the circumpolar region.[8] Like all other outsiders, if I wanted to venture beyond the outskirts of the village I was required to pay a $150 "land-crossing fee" and sign a statement that I would not collect fauna or flora of any kind. Whenever I went out walking, the corporation office would receive several calls from people asking whether I had paid my fee.

On St. Lawrence Island, good stewardship of archaeological resources has also meant trying to keep more of the end value of these goods in the community and ensuring that shareholders receive fair prices. Over the years, the island's two corporations have tried numerous ways to regulate dealers and other buyers—taxes, licensing fees, and setting fair prices, to name a few—without much success.[9] In 1999, a full-page article in the *Nome Nugget* announced the launch of Okvik, Inc.,[10] a business that would purchase old ivory and bone from diggers and gradually cut middlemen out of the trade. The long-term vision included selling artifacts, sponsoring scientific excavations, and building a world-class museum. The article's headline—"St. Lawrence Island 'Digs' Resource Management"—captured the distinctive local approach to stewardship (Silook 1999). I heard people argue, half jokingly, that as shareholders they each had the right to a percentage of the value of all materials sold from the island.

Outsiders often wonder whether diggers have a sense of conservation or whether they will continue to dig until the resource is gone—a "tragedy of the commons" scenario (Hardin 1968). Everyone I spoke with on the island had concerns about the supply of old ivory, in terms of both cultural loss and future economic loss. "Nowadays they have to dig down 10 or 12 feet to find it," one carver told me. "It's getting scarce," the manager of the ivory-carving cooperative admitted. "It's hard to find whole pieces; it's just the scraps, chunks. These are non-renewable resources so they don't grow like crops or other things that replaces year after year. They are there just one time. And once you find it, there's no more left." Both dealers and archaeologists have questioned why diggers do not use heavy equipment to mine sites faster or more efficiently, but people see benefits in digging conservatively. Not only will their inheritance last longer but also, if past decades are any indicator, values are likely to increase. Everyone seems to recognize that the digging will continue until an economic replacement exists.

Ancestors and Agency

On St. Lawrence Island, memories and histories are encoded in the land. Sites and rock formations are named for people or events that happened, and people are named after sites and places. Places on the land have agency; so do ancestors from long ago and artifacts in the ground. The act of digging actually strengthens connections with the past. People spoke of artifacts they found as gifts the ancestors had left for people to use in these days when cash is hard to come by. In this sense, archaeological sites are like a bank and their contents an inheritance.

One day in Wales, a digger came to show us a handsome ivory figurine, kept moist in a bag of wet sand. "I wish the ancestors would show me where to find some more!" he said with a gleam in his eye. When a digger unearthed a valuable artifact, there was a sense that it had allowed itself to be found. People told stories of smoke showing someone where to dig or voices warning that an object did not want to be found. This is similar to the stewardship ethic of subsistence hunters, based on a relationship of reciprocity, in which animals appear to the hunter who has a respectful attitude.[11] Good stewardship obligates the hunter (or digger) to take all that appears, as a gift that should not be refused. Human remains are treated differently. As in most places, the finest, most valuable objects are found in graves. Diggers would extract these gifts and carefully rebury any human remains as close as possible to the spot where they were found, often with offerings or prayers.

Other objects that people recognize as "dense with meaning" (Weiner in Myers 2001b: 307), such as family heirlooms or repatriated objects, resist commodification to a certain degree. Everyone had advised me to visit Arthur's mother, an elder known for her interest in cultural preservation (and her willingness to talk to outsiders). On one of my visits, she took two blackened wooden bowls from the back of her cupboard, handling them like treasures, and told me proudly that her family had dug two complete old *iglus* near their summer camp. She described the big pieces of flat rock pieced like tile on the floor, covered by thick walrus skins. Like others, she seemed to view digging not as a contradiction between heritage preservation and site destruction but as a connection with those who came before.[12]

Culture Loss

Diggers often felt emotionally torn between selling a unique object and wanting it to stay on the island. Some of the most ardent diggers were the same people seeking grants to fund a museum so that artifacts might stay in the community. "It's gone too far," one of the most inveterate diggers told a reporter in 1989. "Maybe as soon as the people get some employment, some kind of job" (Perala 1989: G3). Indeed, during the early 1990s, when running water and sewers were finally being installed in Savoonga, most diggers had a steady job, and dealers complained that there was hardly anything to buy.

Attitudes toward digging did not fall neatly along lines of age, status, or gender. Many saw the diaspora of archaeological artifacts in terms of regrettable cultural loss, caused by the lure of the market. Once in Savoonga, the head of the Native corporation called me into his office. On his computer were several digital images of an engraved harpoon foreshaft, black with age, held by the elder who had recently excavated it. "I may never get to see this piece again," he said, clicking through the images.

Some villagers believed that the digging truly caused harm. In Wales, they say that a digger who finds a "doll" (human figurine) will soon die. One day in Gambell, a respected elder paid me a visit. While we were talking, she became uncharacteristically quiet, then gestured ardently toward the window. "You see all those diggings out there? That's what made all the problems in our village, when people started doing that for money. All that digging never used to be there." Villagers generally placed the blame on early archaeologists who paid for whatever artifacts people brought to them and on the dealers who fly to the island with pockets full of money. People wondered whether future generations would hold them responsible. Still, they hesitated to restrict the activities of those who depended on digging to make ends meet.

In spite of their alienability, artifacts remained important cultural symbols for St. Lawrence Islanders, as when Merle Apassingok held up a two-thousand-year-old harpoon head at the Alaska Federation of Natives convention as documented proof of subsistence hunting rights (Apassingok 1998). The situation seems more an example of "keeping while giving" (Weiner 1992), a choice to keep the land, which people perceive as inalienable, and its intangible assets while giving up the old things embedded in it to meet economic needs.[13]

The Native corporation of Wales—whose old sites do not contain the same quantities of bone, ivory, or high-end artifacts as those on St. Lawrence Island—also allows its shareholders to dig but since the 1970s has prohibited them from digging on one mound inhabited in earlier centuries. The decision to protect the mound was based less on conserving the archaeological value of the site than on the risk to several burials of nearborn children. In recent years, the Wales Native Corporation has allowed an archaeological team (myself among them) to excavate on the mound, provided that sensitive areas were carefully avoided. The digging spots of local residents on the other side of town were in places a stone's throw from our trenches—proof that with mutual respect, negotiated consent, and compromise, two opposing (and seemingly incommensurable) standpoints on stewardship can coexist.

Dealers

I met with several wholesale dealers in Anchorage and Juneau who made trips to the island each year to purchase bulk quantities of old ivory and whale and walrus bone. These entrepreneurs can wield a great deal of power and influence over the market by stockpiling tons of these raw materials in warehouses to supply their clients. Some of these materials go to workshops where Asian or Russian immigrants produce "Native-style" carvings for the Alaskan tourist market. One wholesaler I interviewed felt that people on the island were making a big mistake by selling off all of their valuable old ivory as a raw material, but he called the supply of bone "inexhaustible." Most wholesalers seem to envision old ivory, bone, and even artifacts as resources much like gold or silver that Native diggers should be managing for their own benefit and profit. "If they can serve a purpose, why not mine them. The more they can get for them, the better," one of the biggest ivory traders told me. This argument, based on a capitalist notion of stewardship as "wise use," contends that if a resource exists, it should be used and its profits maximized.

The few dealers who purchase objects for the art market directly from diggers typically would spend several weeks in Nome in the late summer at the end of the digging season. Eager to tell me their stories, they had no trouble imagining themselves as stewards whose role is to shepherd ancient ivories from relative obscurity into the cosmopolitan art world. From their standpoint, good stewardship (and good business) means promoting the circulation and appreciation of art on the global market. They carefully position themselves as gatekeepers to mediate and control, as much as possible, flows of objects and information between the island and the art world, as well as within the art world,[14] so that a Bering Strait ivory rarely surfaces in the art world without their knowledge. One dealer explained to me that without a constant trickle of new ivories entering the market through his efforts, and someone like himself constantly pushing for their appreciation, collectors would soon lose their interest in this particular genre and turn their acquisitive appetites elsewhere.

Art dealers feel a special attachment to objects that have gone through their hands. "All the pieces I sell have to go to a good home," one emphatically told me. "If I don't think the person appreciates them, I might even raise the price." Dealers also take great care in conserving and restoring objects, giving newly excavated pieces special treatment while they dry, and teaching conservation techniques to diggers and collectors. Their reputation is based on an experienced eye that can recognize fine art or spot a fake. Many have an extensive library to help them research and authenticate objects and current market values.

All dealers, whether of high-end art, artifacts, or raw materials, justified what they did as stewardship in another important way. They perceived their entrepreneurship as providing economic benefits to local people that far exceeded anything archaeology had to offer. One ivory trader estimated that he spent around $250,000 a year on St. Lawrence Island. "I couldn't just quit. . . . There are lots of people, whole families, that depend on me out there," he said, standing next to his truck, which was loaded with goods for people on the island. None of the dealers had an accurate understanding of the role that in situ provenience plays in archaeology, however. One dealer repeatedly told me that he could easily "get [diggers] to take a picture and measure how far down an object was found." He had offered to send this information to the Smithsonian and was irritated when they did not seem interested.

Art Collectors and Artifact Collectors

In tracking down old Bering Strait ivories, I met with more than twenty private collectors, often in their homes. No two were alike—indeed, collecting is a good way to express idiosyncrasy (Belk 1995)—but they were all primarily interested in the aesthetic qualities and universalist appeal of an object. They divided roughly along the lines of whether they saw themselves as collectors of art or as collectors of artifacts.[15] Most of the art collectors had acquired "ancient Eskimo ivories" owing to their interest in tribal art (sometimes still referred to as primitive art), a genre that typically includes objects from Africa, Oceania, or the Americas. One collector had become enamored with the so-called ancient Eskimo ivories during a visit to an art dealer's office after having been struck by their likeness to Cycladic and pre-Columbian forms. He limited his acquisitions to human or masklike forms (not surprisingly, the most valuable objects on the market); everything else was "too ethnographic" for his taste. Some collectors "lived with their pieces," while others brought them out of deep storage especially for my visit. Only two or three individuals I met specialized in ancient Eskimo ivories as their primary collection. They tended to be self-trained scholars, interested in a broad range of forms and styles, from functional objects to fine art. Very few of the art collectors I met had any desire to visit St. Lawrence Island.

Connoisseurship and wealth allow these collectors to remove old ivories from the promiscuous realm of commodity and envision themselves as worthy stewards of immortal works of art (Appadurai 1986a; Belk 1995; Myers 2001a). More often than not, the diggers who produce the very objects that art collectors so revere are erased from the art-world frame, as if they have no relationship to the objects at all. In fact, many collectors (and art museums) seem to feel that information about the economic or social contexts of artifacts or diggers amounts to little more than inappropriate political correctness, perhaps because these ruptures dilute the transcendental aura of objects and raise questions about the legitimacy of collectors or museums as stewards.

The artifact or relic collectors I encountered were just as interested in the technical and functional aspects of "Eskimo" artifacts as in the aesthetics. They were always eager to show me their collections of old tools; some had them stashed away in bags and boxes, but others were carefully mounted in cases. Some had purchased their ivory artifacts from traders, shops, and flea markets; others had found pieces on the Internet. Artifact collectors generally relished Bering Strait prehistory and often collected archaeological reports from the Bering Strait region. A few had made a pilgrimage to St. Lawrence Island, and others hoped or had dreams to visit the island someday.

Clearly, collecting these "old things" denotes a very individualistic and personal relationship with objects, frequently as markers of quest, distinction, or identity (Baudrillard 1988: 45; Belk 1995). At the same time, the collectors I met had several things in common. They saw themselves as temporary stewards of objects whose qualities transcended time, place, and their own mortality. They all felt that the care and appreciation they gave objects was equal to, if not better than, that of most museums. Many told me they would rather sell their collections than donate to a museum where things would be "locked up in dark basements." They complained about the difficulties of gaining access to museum collections that were supposedly held in the public trust (some museums do, in fact, have double standards for researchers and members of the public in access to collections). The threat of repatriation had also made some reluctant to donate to museums, out of fear that objects might be returned to communities where they would not receive the proper care.[16] They saw their collecting as philanthropic, done in the interest of safeguarding worthy objects that otherwise could end up unappreciated or uncared for or might be subjected to an even worse fate (such as being sawed up for use as a raw material).

Collectors often alluded to the animosity between themselves and archaeologists.

But like dealers, few understood the actual role that in situ evidence plays in archaeology. Frequent comments from collectors such as "archaeologists can't dig it all" or "don't they have enough of these already" suggest that archaeologists have failed to communicate how they produce knowledge from the material past or why it might be important to others.

The Tourist Market and the State

In one of the biggest tourist shops in Anchorage, I interviewed a young clerk, who took me into the back room to show me boxes of still-wet bits and pieces of ivory artifacts, received in the mail from diggers who expected to be paid for them by the pound. I asked him whether the stream of artifacts from St. Lawrence Island seemed to be slowing at all. "They're still coming in like crazy," was his reply. Artifacts that could not be sold as curios were destined to be used as raw materials and reincarnated into jewelry, belt buckles, scrimshaw, or myriad other goods for the tourist market. "I still hate to see anyone take a nice artifact and chop it up to make other things, like some people do," the young man added. Ironically, many people seemed to draw the line at cutting up unbroken worked artifacts, as if this were immoral or bad stewardship. On Juneau's main tourist drag, I spoke with an artist who uses old artifacts to create wall hangings that sell in her shop for thousands of dollars each. "I don't use any really good artifacts in my work," she told me, "but in fact, I consider using artifacts in art the ultimate in recycling. And in the villages, they need the cash."

One man who owned a small shop on the outskirts of Haines, Alaska, where he fashioned ivory artifacts into necklaces and knife handles, was quick to justify his use of ivory artifacts to me with the following arguments, numbering them as he spoke.

1. What more is there to learn that we don't know already?
2. There is so much of this stuff, and most of it is very similar and already out of context, so why not use it?
3. Since people need the cash, why not charge archaeologists to dig and make them employ diggers?
4. These things are just sitting around in the ground until someone digs them up, and the Natives need the cash.

While he thought it was fine for Eskimos (as he called them) to dig and sell ivory from their own lands to make money, when I asked whether he would feel the same way if an important archaeological site were destroyed in the process, he had to think for a minute. From his standpoint, it came down to the legal right of landowners to use their land as they saw fit. "Grave robbing is another story," he added. "That's a personal issue. I wouldn't want someone digging in the graves of my ancestors."

Alaska's Division of Commerce and Economic Development has supported the marketing of archaeological materials, first, because it is legal, and second, because of its importance to the retail tourist industry. The state justifies this as good stewardship on its part by arguing that sales of locally available resources provide much-needed economic support for Native livelihoods.

In 1993, the State of Alaska came head-to-head with archaeologists from the National Park Service (NPS), the agency charged with enforcing the protection of archaeological resources on federal lands. The Alaska office of the NPS had designed a brochure, "Saving Alaska's Heritage," that mildly discouraged tourists from buying artifacts or old ivory because of the potential damage to archaeological sites. At the same time, the NPS issued a ban on selling arts and crafts made from archaeological ivory to retailers who leased shops located on federal government property. State officials, ivory dealers, carvers, retailers, and Native groups joined forces in a groundswell of opposition to the ban and the brochure. Though the loss of profits was certainly a major concern to retailers, most of the arguments against the NPS policy were about the moral, economic, and legal injustice of preventing Native villagers from using a legal source of income. An editorial in the Juneau paper accused federal bureaucrats of "robbing present-day villagers in order to preserve relics from the past" ("Feds Must Redo Ivory Plan," *Juneau Empire,* June 3, 1993). "The Park Service should get their nose out of it," one shop owner insisted. "They can't tell the Natives what to do with their own stuff! I've had archaeologists come in here very upset about the fact [that] we sell these things, but they need to put their efforts where their mouth is and go out there and show people how to dig." Under pressure, the NPS retracted the ban and revised the brochure's wording.

Archaeologists

Until recently, from an archaeological standpoint, the scientific value that archaeologists could extract from objects in the ground outweighed all nonscholarly interests (Champe et al. 1961). Claims of archaeological privilege were supported and legitimated by federal legislation throughout the 1960s and '70s (in other countries as well as the United States), which authorized archaeologists as managers and protectors of archaeological resources for the state (Smith 2004; Watkins 2000). By the 1980s, as stewards for the state, archaeologists had been compelled to recognize the interests of other stakeholders in the past (Prott and O'Keefe 1984) and the multiplicity of values that sites and objects held for different people (Lipe 1984). The state (more so in some countries than others) has continued to underwrite archaeological stewardship and use the expert knowledge, skills, and scientific authority of archaeology to legitimate its claims over sites, objects, and "heritage" (Smith 2000, 2004; see also Appadurai 2001: 44). Terms such as *stewardship, heritage management, archaeological resources,* and *preservation* have come to describe very specific practices performed under state mandates and regulations.

Stewardship "For All People"

In 1996, the Society for American Archaeology (SAA) adopted "stewardship" as its primary principle of ethical responsibility for the profession (SAA 1996). The principle encourages archaeologists to work to conserve and protect the archaeological record for the benefit "of all people," presumably as part of a world heritage belonging to "all of humanity" but owned and ownable by no one. Groarke and Warrick (2006: 164–65) have called the SAA's interpretation of stewardship "inconsistent in light of the multiple and often contradictory interests that diverse groups have in various manifestations of the archaeological record." Indeed, serving in the interests of *all* is rarely, if ever, possible, and all stakeholders have certainly not shared equally in the production of knowledge or other benefits of archaeology. Appeals to stewardship in the name of the "public trust" or "all of humanity" tend to obscure competing voices or less well-positioned interests (Salmon 1997: 59) and as such have been used to conceal nationalist agendas and in some instances to justify confiscation of land, material goods, or resource rights. As Alison Wylie (2005) suggests, such universalist notions beg further scrutiny. What interests do they serve, and what actions do they justify?

On the Ground

I spoke with several archaeologists working in Alaska who offered their personal perspectives about the situation on St. Lawrence Island.[17] Their opinions fractured more or less along the lines of those who had firsthand experience working in Native communities (who tended to be more empathetic) and those who did not. Only one, a hard-line NPS enforcement officer, unconditionally condemned the digging.

One archaeologist who worked for the state felt that selling and digging artifacts had become such an integral part of the economy on St. Lawrence Island that changing the situation would be difficult, if not impossible. He blamed early archaeologists who had purchased artifacts from anyone who offered them for sale. One commonality he had found among Native communities in Alaska was that they all felt that archaeologists had come and taken their old things, leaving little or nothing in return. Over the years, he had come to see that most Native communities perceived cultural preservation from a very different standpoint than did archaeologists; instead of thinking in terms of preserving sites, old structures, or material objects, they wanted support for language camps, storytelling with elders, and ways to document and teach cultural practices.

The state archaeologist (at the time) prefaced his remarks by warning me of his unorthodox views. He readily acknowledged that St. Lawrence Islanders had a legal right and an economic need to dig for artifacts, but he considered the Native corporation policy unjust and racist because it allowed only shareholders to dig. Thinking about this later, I had to disagree. If the corporation allowed only Yupik people to dig and banned all non-Yupiks, the policy would be racialist, but country clubs restrict their property and activities to members, so why should a Native corporation not be allowed to do the same?

I had spent four summers working for an archaeologist who directed the excavations mentioned above in Wales, where villagers also dug for the market. It had been very difficult for him to look out the window and watch people digging on summer evenings. Each year, he approached village authorities for permission to return, and each year he received their full approval. Everything we excavated (including the piles of seal bones) was to be returned to the Wales Native Corporation after analysis, and they could do with it as they chose. He had approached the corporation with a plan to curate the artifacts, but at the time, he was not certain what their answer would be.

Later when I spoke with the head of the NPS Alaska Division, he began and ended our conversation with the disclaimer that he was not speaking from an official standpoint. He granted that Natives had the right to sell artifacts from their lands, but he added a cautionary tale: "In twenty or forty years they will probably be angry with us for allowing them to sell these things off and once again use the rationalization that white men ripped them off, even though it's their own decision. . . . But for those prices, I would probably be selling, too."

A Failure of Archaeological Stewardship

Archaeological stewardship has long been synonymous with posing science as an interest that trumps others because of its rational, authoritative knowledge that sets archaeologists up as *the* representatives of all publics, the ones who should be entrusted with the material remnants of the past (Wylie 2005). However, in this case, the interests of diggers, dealers, collectors, and the state (justified by legal and economic arguments) have overruled those of archaeology; archaeological values, except as they enhance these other claims, have carried the *least* weight in the politics of stewardship. Additionally, the geographic and social distance between various standpoints have added to the opacity and lack of understanding among them.

Why did some archaeologists go so far as to call St. Lawrence Islanders cultural cannibals in the press? Could it be because this is a situation over which they have little control, one in which the economic lure of the market and legal property rights combine to trump archaeological privilege and expertise—a failure of stewardship from an archaeological standpoint? Without a legal leg to stand on or backing from the state, opponents to the market for archaeological materials resorted to a strong moralist argument to justify their standpoint. But from another standpoint, who are the real cultural cannibals here? Archaeologists have a legacy of digging up graves and taking the contents far away, turning them into intellectual and economic capital that benefits careers, theories, and lifestyles and, until recently, giving little in return.

The stewardship practices of St. Lawrence Islanders clearly transgress romanticized notions of native people as primordial stewards or "original ecologists" (Nuttall 1998: 53; see also Roseberry 1989: 223). But how can we fault indigenous entrepreneurs for following in the footsteps of the economic practices and desires of the First World? Do archaeologists hold subsistence diggers, who have few other economic options, to a higher standard than developers and others who mine resources for economic gain? How can we expect diggers to choose conservation until other stable and more reliable forms of income exist for them? Once this happens, people may find themselves in a position where they can say no to dealers and the global market and begin to reevaluate their decisions about how to use the unique archaeological materials on their island.

Multiple Standpoints on Stewardship

What constitutes good stewardship obviously depends on whose interests are being served. Archaeologists consider themselves experts when it comes to archaeological resources and their management, but diggers also regard archaeological sites as a resource they are managing.[18] Yet underlying these divergent viewpoints on stewardship among and within groups of stakeholders are some common threads. One is a notion that stewardship is based on a special relationship characterized by a transcendent interest that claims to be the best way to manage or care for sites and objects, whether that interest is scientific knowledge, appreciation of great art (and the ability to buy it), wise resource use, or cultural affiliation.

Second, deeds euphemized as stewardship almost always involve "enclaving," an act that signals a person's claim to an object (or idea) by making it inaccessible to others or diverting it from the commodity realm (Strathern 1996). The politics of enclaving are attempts to control the movements and value of things: whether by collectors building up economic or social capital, by dealers trying to control supply and demand, or in nationalist claims of cultural property. Archaeologists engage keenly in enclaving when they insist on curating archaeological goods for the research value of those objects. St. Lawrence Islanders are able to enclave old things while these remain on the island, but they have little power to do so once things leave, other than through repatriation.

Third, Leo Groarke and Gary Warrick (2006: 168–69) have recently criticized the idea that archaeologists could serve as stewards in the interest of the archaeological record as if this "anthropomorphic fiction" had interests or desired to be studied or preserved. However, I found that all stakeholders did indeed envision themselves as serving the needs and interests of the objects, whether as immortal art that deserved to be seen, old tools that needed a good home, or gifts from the ancestors imbued with "money power." A similar notion characterizes the relationship of aboriginal peoples who see themselves as custodians *for* the land or the ancestors, both of which continue to have agency in contemporary life. The one exception to this might be the wholesalers who deal in bulk quantities of old bone and ivory, but carvers who use these raw materials often say that they are "releasing the spirit of the bone."

In any case, as Groarke and Warrick (2006: 165) point out, stewardship defines a political stance more than an ethical one, a stance that blatantly privileges certain interests and contradicts others. We can, as Arjun Appadurai (2001) suggests, ask which standpoints on stewardship are less exclusive or less predatory, which bring about a more equitable distribution of resources, or who is silenced or confined to the margins. We can look to see where double standards exist and why certain interests trump others in a particular context. We can also consider the potential for harm and the unintentional consequences that arise from exercising a certain standpoint (Bannister and Barrett 2004). The needs of living people, for example, ought to outweigh the interests of objects (Hollowell 2006), and greater weight might be given to the standpoints of subsistence diggers because of their marginal political and economic position and legacy of dispossession. That said, stewardship has never been necessarily egalitarian or altruistic and can often be exclusive and elitist. In fact, the stewardship practices on St. Lawrence Island are exclusive, unsustainable, and, from the standpoint of some, predatory. But what other choices do people feel they have?

A Role for Ethnography

Philosopher Michelle Moody-Adams (1997) discusses how too often our judgments of others lack information about moral practices or standpoints that might help us see how other people rationalize their situations and conceive of what they do. Ethnography has a role to play in casting light on different iterations of how people claim the past and the dilemmas this can create for others. Epistemologically, attending to diverse and divergent standpoints is a way for ethnography to produce less partial accounts. Moreover, the reflection that comes from examining one's position in relation to others can "lead one to see oneself, one's relations to others, and one's place in the world [standpoint] in a different way" (Moody-Adams 1997: 139), opening up the possibility of doing things differently. Ultimately, understanding the nature of contested standpoints on heritage stewardship or finding real common ground among them requires an understanding of what impels people to make the choices they do.

Notes

1. See Perala 1989: G7; Eppenbach 1991: D6; Yesner 1989. For a counter interpretation, see Crowell 1985: 26.

2. See Marcus 1995 and Marcus 1998 for a discussion of multisited ethnography.

3. Each of these standpoints also has its own history, which I do not revisit here; see Hollowell 2004.

4. The term *subsistence digging* was first used by David Staley (1993: 348), an archaeologist who worked on St. Lawrence Island. He defined it as artifact digging when the proceeds are used to support a subsistence lifestyle.

5. These estimates come from 1997, when I helped a consultant hired by the Native corporations of St. Lawrence Island conduct a study of bone and ivory leaving the island, and from a 1999 business report, for which I supplied information.

6. I have changed the names of individuals who participated in field research, unless they have previously been publicly cited.

7. NAGPRA is a U.S. law passed in 1990 that requires federally funded institutions (including museums and federal agencies) to return human remains, grave-related materials, and sacred or communally owned objects, upon request, to any federally recognized tribal entity that can prove substantive affiliation, as defined by the law itself.

8. Both Native corporations had thus far rejected all offers by outsiders that would compromise control over their resources (for example, licenses for mining or communication towers), and in the 1980s the Village of Gambell had taken its case to the Supreme Court when exploratory oil drilling on the outer continental shelf threatened subsistence rights. More recently, St. Lawrence Islanders put pressure on government agencies to clean up toxic waste at abandoned military posts on the island—all indications of a deep sense of stewardship and its close connection with sovereignty.

9. In 1995, the Village Council passed an ordinance dealing with VTRs (valuable tribal resources)—defined as live animals, local plants, archaeological materials, and old ivory—which required anyone intending to take these from the island to register and pay a severance tax, but there was no way at the time to enforce these measures.

10. *Okvik* means "place where walrus haul out" and is the name that archaeologists have given to the style and period associated with the supposedly oldest artifacts from the region, now extremely valuable.

11. For interpretations of indigenous concepts of hunter-animal relationships and appropriate uses of abundance, see Brightman 1993; Fienup-Riordan 1986, 1990; and Nadasdy 2003.

12. Aron Crowell (1985: 27) observed a similar attitude among diggers during his survey of archaeological sites on the island in 1984.

13. Fred Myers (2001a: 25) suggests a similar interpretation when he describes how Australian Aboriginal artists willingly alienate ritual objects called *tjurunga* while keeping both the land and the power of the material object.

14. By controlling the flows of information and materials through the market, dealers manipulate supply and in this way manage uncertainty, prevent collusion among buyers, create scarcity and exclusivity, whet demand, and enhance values overall (see Alsop 1982; Becker 1982; Moulin 1987). In his study of the African art market, Christopher Steiner noted that the success of the middleman depended on keeping buyers and sellers separate (Steiner 1994: 151).

15. There is a history to this art/artifact divide (see Hollowell 2004). Edmund Carpenter pointed out how the Surrealists changed Eskimo masks from ethnographic artifacts into "art" in the 1930s simply by moving them across town from a dusty museum to an art gallery (Carpenter 1975: 11; Clifford 1988: 237–39). In many art museums, the privileging of aesthetics at the expense of cultural context still pervades the entry of tribal, or "primitive," materials into the art world and distinguishes them from artifacts.

16. There are, of course, exceptions to this. Members of the American Indian Ritual Object Repatriation Foundation have purchased objects from auction for the sole purpose of returning them to source communities (www.repatriationfoundation.org). John Putnam was another exception. Until his death in 2002, he volunteered tirelessly at the Burke Museum (Seattle) and donated a large collection of fine archaeological ivories, purchased from diggers while he was a teacher on St. Lawrence Island in the early 1970s, just before the art market boom. Unfortunately, when I visited the collection, the condition of the objects had deteriorated considerably because of the museum's lack of climate controls.

17. All who worked in government positions began their conversations with me with a disclaimer that their opinion was not the official standpoint.

18. Ethnographers have found that subsistence diggers elsewhere also view antiquities as a resource to be exploited, much like other natural resources (Heath 1973: 263; Matsuda 1998; Paredes Maury 1998).

References Cited

Alsop, Joseph. *The Rare Art Traditions: The History of Art Collecting and Its Linked Phenomena Wherever These Have Appeared.* New York: Harper and Row, 1982.

Apassingok, Merle. "Subsistence Statement from Gambell, AK, October 21, 1997." *Cultural Survival Quarterly* 22, no. 3 (1998): 81.

Appadurai, Arjun. "Introduction: Commodities and the Politics of Value." In *The Social Life of Things: Commodities in Cultural Perspective,* edited by A. Appadurai, 3–63. Cambridge: Cambridge University Press, 1986. [1986a]

———, ed. *The Social Life of Things: Commodities in Cultural Perspective.* Cambridge: Cambridge University Press, 1986. [1986b]

———. "The Globalization of Archaeology and Heritage." *Journal of Social Archaeology* 1, no. 1 (2001): 35–49.

Arnold, Robert D. *Alaska Native Land Claims.* Anchorage: Alaska Native Foundation, 1978.

Bannister, Kelly, and Katherine Barrett. "Weighing the Proverbial 'Ounce of Prevention' versus the 'Pound of Cure' in a Biocultural Context: A Role for the Precautionary Principle in Ethnobiological Research." In *Advances in Economic Botany,* vol. 15, *Ethnobotany and Conservation of Biocultural Diversity,* edited by T. J. Carlson and L. Maffi, 307–39. Bronx: New York Botanical Garden Press, 2004.

Baudrillard, Jean. "Consumer Society." In *Jean Baudrillard: Selected Writings,* edited by M. Poster, 32–59. Cambridge, U.K.: Polity Press, 1988. (Orig. pub. 1970.)

Becker, Howard S. *Art Worlds.* Berkeley: University of California Press, 1982.

Belk, Russell W. *Collecting in a Consumer Society.* London: Routledge, 1995.

Brightman, Robert A. *Grateful Prey: Rock Cree Human-Animal Relationships.* Berkeley: University of California Press, 1993.

Carpenter, Edmund. "Collecting Northwest Coast Art." In *Indian Art of the Northwest Coast,* edited by B. Holm and B. Reid, 9–49. Seattle: University of Washington Press, 1975.

Champe, J. L., D. S. Byers, C. Evans, A. K. Guthe, H. W. Hamilton, E. B. Jelks, C. W. Meighan, S. Olafson, G. S. Quimby, W. Smith, and F. Wendorf. "Four Statements for Archaeology." *American Antiquity* 27 (1961): 137–39.

Clifford, James. *The Predicament of Culture: Twentieth-Century Ethnography, Literature, and Art.* Cambridge, Mass.: Harvard University Press, 1988.

Collins, Henry B., Frederica De Laguna, Edmund Carpenter, and Peter Stone. *The Far North: 2000 Years of American Eskimo and Indian Art.* Washington, D.C.: National Gallery of Art, 1973. (Reprint, Bloomington: Indiana University Press, 1977.)

Crowell, Aron. *Archaeological Survey and Site Condition Assessment of St. Lawrence Island, Alaska, 1984.* Washington, D.C.: Smithsonian Institution; Gambell, Alaska: Sivuqaq Native Corporation, 1985.

Eppenbach, Sarah. "Thieves of Time: Looting of Archaeological Sites Is Threatening Alaska's Native Heritage." *Anchorage Daily News,* September 8, 1991, D6–7.

Fienup-Riordan, Ann. *When Our Bad Season Comes: A Cultural Account of Subsistence Harvesting and Harvest Disruption on the Yukon Delta.* Anchorage: Aurora Press, 1986.

———. *Eskimo Essays: Yup'ik Lives and How We See Them.* New Brunswick, N.J.: Rutgers University Press, 1990.

Foucault, Michel. *The Archaeology of Knowledge and the Discourse on Language.* Translated by A. M. Sheridan. New York: Pantheon, 1972.

Giddens, Anthony. *Central Problems in Social Theory: Action, Structure and Contradiction in Social Analysis.* London: Macmillan, 1979.

Groarke, Leo, and Gary Warrick. "Stewardship Gone Astray? Ethics and the SAA." In *The Ethics of Archaeology: Philosophical Perspectives on Archaeological Practice,* edited by C. Scarre and G. Scarre, 163–77. Cambridge: Cambridge University Press, 2006.

Handler, Richard. "Cultural Property and Cultural Theory." *Journal of Social Archaeology* 3, no. 3 (2003): 353–65.

Hardin, Garrett. "The Tragedy of the Commons." *Science* 162 (1968): 1243–48.

Harding, Sandra. "Starting Thought from Women's Lives: Eight Resources for Maximizing Objectivity." *Journal of Social Philosophy* 21, no. 2–3 (1990): 140–49.

Heath, Dwight B. "Economic Aspects of Commercial Archeology in Costa Rica." *American Antiquity* 38, no. 3 (1973): 259–65.

Hollowell, Julia J. "'Old Things' on the Loose: The Legal Market for Archaeological Materials from Alaska's Bering Strait." Ph.D. diss., Indiana University, 2004.

———. "St. Lawrence Island's Legal Market in Archaeological Goods." In *Archaeology, Cultural Heritage, and the Antiquities Trade,* edited by N. Brodie, M. Kersel, C. Luke, and K. W. Tubb, 98–132. Gainesville: University Press of Florida, 2006.

Hollowell, Julie, and George Nicholas. "A Critical Assessment of Ethnography in Archaeology." In *Ethnographic Archaeologies: Reflections on Stakeholders and Archaeological Practices,* edited by Q. E. Castañeda and C. N. Matthews, 63–94. Lanham, Md.: AltaMira Press, 2008.

Lipe, William. "Value and Meaning in Cultural Resources." In *Approaches to the Archaeological Heritage: A Comparative Study of World Cultural Resource Management,* edited by H. Cleere, 1–11. London: Unwin Hyman, 1984.

Marcus, George E. "Ethnography in/of the World System: The Emergence of Multi-Sited Ethnography." *Annual Review of Anthropology* 24 (1995): 95–117.

———. *Ethnography through Thick and Thin.* Princeton, N.J.: Princeton University Press, 1998.

Matsuda, David J. "The Ethics of Archaeology, Subsistence Digging, and Artifact 'Looting' in Latin America: Point, Muted Counterpoint." *International Journal of Cultural Property* 7, no. 1 (1998): 87–97.

Moody-Adams, Michele. *Fieldwork in Familiar Places: Morality, Culture, and Philosophy.* Cambridge, Mass.: Harvard University Press, 1997.

Moulin, Raymonde. *The French Art Market: A Sociological View.* Translated by A. Goldhammer. New Brunswick, N.J.: Rutgers University Press, 1987.

Murray, Tim. "Aboriginal (Pre)History and Australian Archaeology: The Discourse of Australian Prehistoric Archaeology." In *Power, Knowledge, and Aborigines,* edited by B. Atwood and J. Arnold, 1–19. Bundoora, Victoria: LaTrobe University Press in association with National Centre for Australian Studies, 1992.

Myers, Fred R. "Introduction: The Empire of Things." In *The Empire of Things: Regimes of Value and Material Culture,* edited by F. R. Myers, 3–61. Santa Fe, N.Mex.: School of American Research, 2001. [2001a]

———. "Interview with Annette Weiner." In *The Empire of Things: Regimes of Value and Material Culture,* edited by F. R. Myers, 269–313. Santa Fe, N.Mex.: School of American Research, 2001. [2001b]

Nadasdy, Paul. *Hunters and Bureaucrats: Power, Knowledge and Aboriginal-State Relations in the Southwest Yukon.* Vancouver: University of British Columbia Press, 2003.

Nuttall, Mark. *Protecting the Arctic: Indigenous Peoples and Cultural Survival.* London: Routledge, 1998.

Paredes Maury, Sofia. *Surviving in the Rainforest: The Realities of Looting in the Rural Villages of El Petén, Guatemala.* Foundation for the Advancement of Mesoamerican Studies, August 1998. http://www.famsi.org/reports/95096/index (accessed March 29, 2009).

Perala, Andrew. "Pillaging the Past." *Anchorage Daily News,* June 25, 1989, G1, Arts Section.

Prott, Lyndel V., and Patrick J. O'Keefe. *Law and the Cultural Heritage.* 3 vols. Abingdon, Oxon: Professional Books, 1984.

Roseberry, William. *Anthropologies and Histories: Essays in Culture, History, and Political Economy.* New Brunswick, N.J.: Rutgers University Press, 1989.

Sahlins, Marshall. "What Is Anthropological Enlightenment? Some Lessons of the Twentieth Century." *Annual Review of Anthropology* 28 (1999): i–xxiii.

Salmon, Merilee H. "Ethical Considerations in Anthropology and Archaeology, or Relativism and Justice for All." *Journal of Anthropological Research* 53, no. 1 (1997): 47–63.

Scott, Stuart. "St. Lawrence Island: Archaeology of a Bering Sea Island." *Archaeology* 37, no. 1 (1984): 46–52.

Silook, Susie. "St. Lawrence Island 'Digs' Resource Management." *Nome Nugget,* July 22, 1999: 15.

Smith, Laurajane. "'Doing Archaeology': Cultural Heritage Management and Its Role in Identifying the Link between Archaeological Practice and Theory." *International Journal of Heritage Studies* 6, no. 4 (2000): 309–16.

———. *Archaeological Theory and the Politics of Cultural Heritage.* London: Routledge, 2004.

Society for American Archaeology. "Principles of Archaeological Ethics." *SAA Bulletin* 14, no. 3 (1996): 5, 17.

Staley, David P. "St. Lawrence Island's Subsistence Diggers: A New Perspective on Human Effects on Archaeological Sites." *Journal of Field Archaeology* 20 (1993): 347–55.

Steiner, Christopher B. *African Art in Transit.* Cambridge: Cambridge University Press, 1994.

Strathern, Marilyn. "Cutting the Network." *Journal of the Royal Anthropological Institute* 2, no. 3 (1996): 517–36.

Sykes, Karen. "Negotiating Interests in Culture." In *Transactions and Creations: Property Debates and the Stimulus of Melanesia,* edited by E. Hirsch and M. Strathern, 132–50. New York: Berghahn, 2004.

Watkins, Joe. *Indigenous Archaeology: American Indian Values and Scientific Practice.* Walnut Creek, Calif.: AltaMira Press, 2000.

Weiner, Annette B. *Inalienable Possessions: The Paradox of Keeping-While-Giving.* Berkeley: University of California Press, 1992.

Wylie, Alison. "Alternative Histories: Epistemic Disunity and Political Integrity." In *Making Alternative Histories: The Practice of Archaeology and History in Non-Western Settings,* edited by T. C. Patterson, 255–72. Santa Fe, N.Mex.: School of American Research, 1995.

———. "Why Standpoint Matters." In *The Feminist Standpoint Theory Reader,* edited by S. Harding, 339–51. New York: Routledge, 2004.

———. "The Promise and Perils of an Ethic of Stewardship." In *Embedding Ethics,* edited by L. Meskell and P. Pels, 47–68. Oxford, U.K.: Berg, 2005.

Yesner, David R. "Looting Gravesites Is 'Cultural Cannibalism.'" *Anchorage Daily News,* December 21, 1989, C11, Forum.

11

Archaeology on the Periphery

Locating a "Last Great Place"

CHIP COLWELL-CHANTHAPHONH

The extant literature makes clear that most archaeologists deem their work and the objects of their inquiry to be of great significance in the human experience. We are told that monumental sites are the symbols on which nations are founded and destroyed (Atkinson, Banks, and O'Sullivan 1996; Kohl, Kozelsky, and Nachman 2007); that museums have been and often continue to be the instruments of colonialism and imperialism (Barringer and Flynn 1998; Smith 2006); that archaeological objects are central to native identities and increasingly their assertions of intellectual and cultural property rights (Brown 2003; Nicholas and Bannister 2004); that some of the Third World's poor sustain themselves by selling their material heritages through global markets to First World elites (Brodie et al. 2006; Messenger 1999); and that archaeological sites and their contested interpretations are the source of ethnic violence (Härke 2000; Meskell 2005a). Even as archaeology has undeniably been enmeshed with nationalism, global economics, colonialism, identity formation, and war, the material past and its study are not always the focus of a community's gaze and not always at the heart of regional, national, or global politics. Despite archaeologists' understandable focus on the importance of archaeology, in fact, in many times and places, the material past is more at the periphery of the human experience than at its core.

The San Pedro Valley, in Arizona's southeastern corner, is what we might call a "persistent place" because the lush waterway has been occupied nearly continuously for 13,000 years. Its history is primarily a history of Native America: of the appearance of the big-game hunters, the emergence of agriculture, the movements of Indian communities, and the rise of Euro-American colonialism. Through the generations, Native American communities have maintained their connections to the San Pedro Valley in myriad ways—for example, today Apaches have more than sixty place-names in the valley, while Hopis still regularly offer prayer feathers for their ancestral villages to the south (Ferguson and Colwell-Chanthaphonh 2006). When the first Europeans arrived in the region, they took note of its many ruins. From the observations of Francisco Vázquez de Coronado in 1540 (Hartmann and Lee 2003) to those of Eusebio Kino in the 1690s (Bolton 1936) and the first American, James O. Pattie, in 1826 (Battman 1998), ancient sites have found a place in the colonial imagination. Around 1869, the first excavation—consisting of the haphazard diggings of a curious U.S. Army captain—took place in the San Pedro Valley (Bourke 1971: 1). Formal surveys and excavations by some of the Southwest's preeminent scholars, including Adolph Bandelier, Jesse Walter Fewkes, and Byron Cummings, soon followed. Charles Di Peso conducted the first major archaeological expeditions in the region in the 1950s, excavating pueblos, as well as the Spanish fort of Terrenate (Di Peso 1951, 1953, 1958). Into the 1960s, the region drew further attention with the discovery of several mammoth kill sites (Haury, Sayles, and Wasley 1959; Lance 1953), including the Murray Springs site, among the most celebrated Paleo-Indian sites in North America (Haynes and Huckell 2007).

What the San Pedro Valley lacks in monumentality—it has nothing akin to Cahokia or Mesa Verde—it makes up for in antiquity and quantity, as hundreds of sites have been recorded attesting to millennia of Native American history (Clark, forthcoming). And yet, despite the valley's continuing meanings for Native Americans, its long focus of archaeological research, its immense antiquity, and its tangible material past, archaeology is not a major concern or interest for people in the region today. Like those of Mexico's Yucatán, the ruins of the valley would have little intrinsic archaeological merit without the presence of professional archaeologists but would be seen as "both mysteriously and imprecisely 'ancient' . . . a 'natural' as opposed to built feature of the terrain" (Breglia, this volume). Why and when archaeology has been pushed to the periphery and why and when it shifts to the center of people's lives is the concern of this chapter.

In the contemporary context of tourism, development, and environmentalism in the San Pedro Valley, archaeology has largely been marginalized. These three primary issues converge on the question of the San Pedro River's very survival. In 2000, the Nature Conservancy—a multimillion-dollar organization, self-described as "a leading international, nonprofit organization dedicated to preserving the diversity of life on Earth"—listed the San Pedro River valley as one of its two hundred "last great places," supposedly making it among the "most unique and endangered nature preserves and sanctuaries on earth."[1] Locating—socially, politically, and topographically—the San Pedro Valley as a "last great place" is the conceptual beginning point for this chapter because the phrase so intriguingly captures the values of place: Who decides what makes a place "great," and by what criteria can it be said to be among the "last"? How are the boundaries that define a place constructed and configured? Who, after all, gets to decide what a place means for its inhabitants and visitors?

As the politics of place in the San Pedro Valley have shifted in recent years to questions of biodiversity and the continued existence of the valley's ebbing river, archaeology has not been (if it ever was) the center of public debate. As emergent interest groups engage in the politics of the valley's place-making, we are led to further questions about why archaeology has been relegated to the back seat, when elsewhere it plays such a vital element in identity formation. How do these interest groups think about and interact with the valley's history? What do tourists value about the landscape and the valley's ruins, and how do tourism interests figure into the politics of culture, nature, and development? How do proponents of development think about the valley's Native American past? Why do environmentalists in the region refrain from drawing more heavily on the trope of Indians living in symbiosis with the natural world?

Because we know that the valley is important to both archaeologists and contemporary Native Americans (Doelle and Clark 2003; Ferguson, Colwell-Chanthaphonh, and Anyon 2004), here I focus on interest groups in the valley that have heretofore been given far less attention—tourists, development proponents, and local environmentalists. Drawing on recent work at the intersection of ethnography and archaeology (Abu el-Haj 2001; Castañeda 1996; Handler and Gable 1997), my research methodology—conducted between 2001 and 2004—ranges from participating in an archaeology tour to a close reading of brochures, visitor books, and Web sites to semistructured interviews with local environmentalists and political leaders. My work is perhaps an "archaeological ethnography" with its focus on material and social positionalities (Meskell 2005b), but at the same time I see this research as a kind of behavioral archaeology, defined as the study of the relationship between humans and their material world in all times and places (Schiffer 1995). I want to understand the intersection and exchange between people and things—how people fashion their world from ancient objects and places, and how ancient objects and places fashion people.

In tourism, for example, a deep Native American past has been silenced in exchange for an emphasis on the "outdoors" and the "Old West." This helps direct what tourists experience when visiting a ruin in the San Pedro Valley. Based on an observation of a tour and a textual analysis of visitor books, I argue that archaeology is largely on the periphery of the tourist experience in the valley—even when tourists are visiting an actual archaeological site. Local environmentalists do occasionally use archaeology, first to provide an added value of place (as when a bird-watching festival includes some archaeological tours), and second as a morality tale (in which the ruins are a symbolic reminder of the fragile nature of human society). Development proponents do not depend on the deep history of the region as a marketing tool to attract tourists and new residents; the subtle—that is, nonmonumental—archaeology of the region is a harder sell than is the "Old West." Some development proponents also suggest that the Indian past offers a lesson, but in contrast to environmentalists, they see the region's deep history as positive proof that the valley has a long future—that human use of the valley is inevitable and right.

What these perspectives share is also what distinguishes them: how very differently concepts of place are employed. My basic assumption is that places are never given but instead must be conceptually made and corporeally marked from the vast spaces of our lived experiences (Feld and Basso 1996; Low and Lawrence-Zúñiga 2003); even "natural places" are not self-evident (Bradley 2000). As Lynn Meskell eloquently observes elsewhere in this volume, "Over vast expanses of time, the texture of memory cannot cohere in its original form; it is constantly reworked, fabricated, and cast as politically desirable. Selectively, the past is remembered and forgotten in the present, and thus, certain pasts are sanctioned as heritage." In other words, the "San Pedro Valley" is neither timeless nor fixed but must be located and made as a distinct place through cultural and sociopolitical imaginings. Building from this postulation, I argue that tourists, local environmentalists, and development proponents distinctly perceive notions of "interior" and "exterior" landscapes—that is, people perceive objects to exist inside and outside of a given place (Tuan 1977: 25). Exterior landscapes are those exotic and unfamiliar spaces perceived to lie beyond a border, whereas the interior is the internal portion of an area deemed to be comfortable and familiar. The use of these expressions—*interior* and *exterior*—is in some measure artificial, because few people in the valley speak explicitly in these terms. But these words are useful because they draw attention to the ways in which places are fundamentally defined through the creation and maintenance of *boundaries*—the conceptual and material expressions of "here" and "there," the means by which places are distinguished within the infinity of space (Muir 1999: 75–84). Ultimately, I am trying to demonstrate that archaeology is linked to these constructions of place but that this process of place-making is inherently selective. Archaeology is not a given, but rather, as Julie Hollowell and Lena Mortensen posit in the introduction to this volume, is merely one *iteration* of a past that has multiple meanings and lived experiences. In this way, archaeology is not always or necessarily vital to communities but may often be defined by its absence.

A Last Great Place

Cochise County, in the southeastern corner of Arizona, is a region of great scenic beauty and carefully preserved cultural heritage. Connect with nature and explore the gorgeous scenery, breathe the fresh mountain air and view the abundance of birds and other wildlife. Step back into time and encounter some of the nation's most colorful history ever written.

Advertisement distributed by the Cochise County Tourism Council

This statement on a flyer aims to entice visitors to Cochise County, which embraces much of the San Pedro Valley—to learn about its history, to enjoy its wildlife, and ultimately to spend tourist dollars. As with most advertisements of the San Pedro Valley's southern reaches that are geared toward tourists, this one highlights the twin themes of nature and culture. "Nature" and "culture" are not universal or unitary categories, however; in this case, these motifs are constructed from limited notions of the "outdoors" and the "Old West." Another brochure neatly unites these concepts with the tag line, "Cochise County: Where the Old West Meets the Great Outdoors."

History in Cochise County is largely confined to the theme of the Old West, presented repeatedly throughout the commercial literature—an array of brochures, advertisements, and maps. The Old West, popularly imagined as a time of romance and excitement, was largely born from the "desert aesthetic" that emerged in the early 1900s, as America's western frontier was closed (Teague 1997). The image of the Old West remains the predominant trope of history in the San Pedro Valley. For example, in one brochure the chair of the Cochise County Tourism Council writes, "Few places on earth display the rich tapestry of history and natural beauty that is woven throughout Cochise County. . . . This land embodies the romance of the Old West—and visitors can relive the raucous days of cowboys, miners, and saloon girls at storied sites throughout the county."[2] Nothing in the guide mentions the oldest known sites of Native American ancestry in the San Pedro Valley such as Murray Springs, even though an interpretive trail has been built there, but it repeatedly reiterates the Old West through images and stories of places including Cochise's Stronghold, Tombstone, and Fort Huachuca. These recent histories are certainly entwined with deeper American Indian histories, but they selectively capture only the very end of native history in the valley and tend to downplay its significance.

Even with the rich Native American presence in the valley over the millennia, there are few visible reminders of American Indians in towns such as Sierra Vista. The handful of Indian place-names that exist in southern Arizona appeared when Indian peoples lost control over traditional lands, as a way for new residents to project "a sense of somehow being indigenous to the area, a sense of inherent right and belonging" (Colwell-Chanthaphonh and Hill 2004: 192). In the late 1800s, as the Apaches were being subdued in southern Arizona, the county embracing much of their former lands was named after their famed though fallen leader—Cochise. Anglos recognized the power of place-names when, in 1955, local leaders changed the town name of Fry (with the implication of frying in the Arizona heat) to Sierra Vista (with the authentic Hispanic allusion to beautiful mountains). As the town grew (table 11.1), new streets were occasionally named in a miscellany of Indian tribes: Choctaw Drive, Papago Trail, Hopi Avenue, Apache Avenue, Cree Avenue, Cherokee Avenue, Shawnee Drive, Nez Perce Avenue, Sioux Avenue. Yet the sal-magundi of names signifies not an honoring of local Indians but merely a generic, nonspecific reference to Indian-ness. People relocating to a new home are often in-secure in their belonging to a place yet feel a desire to be part of the community (Chavez 1994: 53–56). Indians, as the first inhabitants, denote a sense of legitimacy by first occupancy and depth of time, which are essential aspects of belonging. At the same time, the reference to Indians must not too specifically reference the local native peoples, because then these symbols would serve to remind new residents of the dispossession that preceded them (Lowenthal 1985: 67).

One way in which Indians appear throughout Cochise County is via a string of convenience stores, each with a giant cowboy and Plains Indian carved out of wood (figure 11.1). Tourist brochures reinforce such generic (and stereotypical) character-izations. On the back of one brochure is one of the few references to American Indians I could find: an advertisement for a local art gallery showing a sensual,

Table 11.1. U.S. Census data for Cochise County

Year	Population	Change
2000	117,755	20%
1990	97,624	14%
1980	85,686	38%
1970	61,910	12%
1960	55,039	75%
1950	31,488	-10%
1940	34,627	-18%
1930	40,998	-12%
1920	46,465	34%
1910	34,591	274%
1900	9,251	—

Figure 11.1. One of the few visible representations of Indians in the San Pedro Valley. (Photograph by Chip Colwell-Chanthaphonh.)

Noble Savage type of Indian, a gaudy bronze sculpture of a nude woman barely covered by a buffalo hide.[3] The appropriation and distortion of the image of American Indians goes back centuries (Bataille 2001; Berkhofer 1978), but its effect in the San Pedro Valley is to foster a conspicuous presence of native peoples, which depends in part on the absence of references to local, more deeply rooted Indian communities and histories.

The portrayal of "nature" in the San Pedro Valley is similarly selective. Although many of the brochures discuss the "wild mountains" and "verdant valley," few opportunities are missed to emphasize the range of birds drawn to the valley, which is occasionally referred to as the "Hummingbird Capital of the United States."[4] A recent survey conducted by the Sierra Vista Chamber of Commerce determined that most visitors come for an outdoor experience, mainly birding.[5] The representation of the valley as a birding haven simultaneously draws from and highlights the Nature Conservancy's title: a "Last Great Place."[6] But unlike the Nature Conservancy's representation of the San Pedro Valley, which characterizes the place as unique in itself, tourist brochures emphasize these natural locales as an outdoor playground, a place that exists for human consumption. "This is one of the country's premier bird watching areas—especially for hummingbird viewing," another brochure notes.[7] From the tourist promoters' viewpoint, the value of the valley's birds comes from their ability to provide entertainment, not their contribution to the region's biodiversity.

As is true of many tourism constructions worldwide, the San Pedro Valley brochures simultaneously accent the valley's modernity. Though subtle, this characterization is important because it draws attention to how the "outdoors" (embodied in the natural landscape of the San Pedro Valley) is constructed in contrast to the indoors (embodied in hotels and restaurants)—that is, an interior/exterior dichotomy as a culture/nature divide. These texts underscore that even though visitors can spend their days in the wild, exploring the natural wilderness and the untamed settings of cowboy history, at night they can retreat into "civilized" comfort. As stated in one guidebook that is representative of many others, "Habitats ranging from mesquite shrub land, desert grassland and lowland riparian (streamside), to high mountains with Douglas Fir and Quaking Aspen are all within a two hour drive of Sierra Vista's 1100-plus hotel, motel and bed & breakfast rooms and over 85 restaurants."[8] In one sentence, the guidebook effectively links the range of possible wilderness experiences with the luxury of modern hotels and eateries.

Tourists in the Valley

In the San Pedro Valley, visitors have easy access to only a few archaeological sites. One of these is the Presidio de Santa Cruz de Terrenate, a Spanish fort occupied in the late eighteenth century. In the autumn of 2002, I took part in a formal tour of the site given by a local nonprofit group, Friends of the San Pedro River, which gave me a glimpse into how the Spanish presidio and other sites on the tour were experienced as places "outside," exterior to the comfortable modernity of Sierra Vista and its counterparts. Of the eleven people on the tour, none expressed a clear interest in history or archaeology, but almost all indicated that they had come to hike in good company.[9] Although this tour was billed as a "walk through history," many people paid more attention to the natural scenery and to bird-watching, as evidenced by their frequent exclamations about the valley's beauty and the use of binoculars they wore around their necks. A mountain lion's pawprint in the sand encountered during the tour garnered as much attention as, if not more than, the artifacts they later saw at Terrenate.

The physical geography of the walk and the signs posted along the way further demarcated each tourist's transition from an interior landscape of modernity to an exterior landscape of nature. The trail provided a means to bridge these worlds, and fences clearly delineated types of landscapes: places interior and exterior. As we left the parking lot to begin the tour, walking along the trail, we passed through a barbed wire fence that separated the ancient/wild land from the present/civilized one. On the one side were our cars, the town of Fairbank, picnic tables, well-trimmed mesquites, and outhouses. Passing through a gate, we confronted a sign that read, "The San Pedro Trail will take you to the Fairbank Cemetery (.4 mi.) and to the Grand Central Mill Ruins (1.7 mi.) . . . Please Take Plenty of Water and Watch for Venomous Creatures," making clear that ruins and wilderness lay ahead, and civilization behind. The tour expressed not merely that these places were outside spatially but also that the past was something exterior to our modern lives. The tour guide made such distinctions clear in his talk about Terrenate, frequently telling us how difficult it was for the Spanish to live back then, even to accomplish such simple tasks as getting water from the river (figure 11.2). The Apaches were fierce and violent, as they had pushed at earlier O'odham communities and then battled Spanish imperialists; they

Figure 11.2. Tourists gather around tour guide at Terrenate. (Photograph by Chip Colwell-Chanthaphonh.)

even ate horsemeat, the guide said. "This must have been a living hell here," he kept repeating, conjuring an image that patently contradicted the serene and beautiful terrain in which we stood, some 222 years after the denizens of the presidio had left Terrenate. One woman was trembling in delight to find a rusty nail at an abandoned mining area; for her, this rather common and somewhat ordinary object was incredibly exotic.

The constructions of pastness/modernity and wilderness/civilization on this tour are mirrored in statements made by visitors in guest books left at Terrenate, which offer a glimpse of the experiences of hundreds of visitors over the years.[10] Of those who recorded their visit in the guest books between 1999 and 2002, 250 had left a comment of some kind, indicating their thoughts or feelings about the site and its presentation to the public.[11] I coded comments according to whether they specifically referred to history, the natural environment, or both.[12] Of these respondents, 48 percent wrote only about the natural environment, 35 percent wrote only about history, and 17 percent wrote about both. These provisional divisions, and their weights, generally match those derived from a single guest book placed at Terrenate between February 1999 and November 2000, which (unlike the other guest books) specifically asked visitors to indicate (by checking a box of preselected choices) why they had visited the site.[13] Of the total number of responses in this source, 59 percent indicated that the visitor had come for the hiking; 24 percent of the respondents indicated that they had come for touring; 9 percent indicated that they had come for birding; and still smaller percentages obtained for hunting, horseback riding, backpacking, picnicking, and bicycling. These numbers indicate that visitors were coming to experience Terrenate, a site noted for its historical values, in large part for its location in a "natural" landscape, as a place to hike and to be out of doors. For most of this audience, the past mattered little, if at all.

Environmentalists in the Valley

The boundary between interior and exterior is further complicated by the perspectives of self-proclaimed environmentalists in the region who tend to distinguish the San Pedro Valley's value as a place independent of human needs. These environmentalists are acutely involved in the debates over the San Pedro Valley's current use and uncertain future, largely because the valley is valued for both human development and natural conservation. As one of the last free-flowing rivers in North America and a key stopping point for migrating birds, environmentalists see the San Pedro Valley as a "last great place" of biodiversity in the world. At the same time, developers envision the San Pedro Valley as a place of incredible growth potential—in no small part because it is a "Last Great Place." That is, the valley's socio-ecological value as nature becomes its socioeconomic value as a space of development. As a result, over the past decade, a battle has raged over the San Pedro Valley's future, a conflict that has revolved around how, paradoxically, expanding communities such as Sierra Vista are threatening the very landscape that makes the region attractive for visitors and residents alike. Many of the region's most vocal environmentalists live in the valley and are thus consuming the very resources they seek to save.

Tom Wood, a naturalist who has been on the front lines of these clashes since the late 1980s, observed in an interview with me that people's attitudes in the area have changed over the past ten years. When he first began working on water issues as an employee of the Nature Conservancy in the area, he met people "who felt that the San Pedro was not special, and then there was a segment that felt that the water use in the area was not connected to the San Pedro [River]." However, in recent years, Wood has noticed that there is still plenty of "disagreement and lots of polarization" but at least now "nearly everyone thinks that there *is* an issue. Even this wasn't the case years ago." But interviews, newspapers, and reports make clear that there remains much controversy over the precise terms of the debate. Is the problem simply too little water, or is it how water is used? Is the problem growth itself or merely unbridled growth? Is the problem one of tourists consuming too many natural resources, or contributing too few monetary resources to offset their impacts? The answers to these questions are now the rhetorical ammunition used in the battles over the valley's future.

These dilemmas are not simply economic or political. A spatial aspect, as Carl Steinitz and colleagues (Steinitz et al. 2003) suggest, is also present because multiple groups desire one topography that cannot be had by all. By focusing on the constructions of place, we can see how contemporary environmentalists in the San Pedro Valley distinguish interior (human) from exterior (natural) landscapes by constructing "nature" as a place devoid of humans.[14] Some of the most vocal development proponents, in turn, are concerned with extending inside spaces to the outside; often, no distinct boundary is drawn between these kinds of landscapes, as all spaces are seen to be open to fulfill human needs. Although in practice organizations such as the Nature Conservancy rely heavily on invasive management techniques, local environmentalist discourse concentrates on establishing vast areas of wilderness sheltered from human activity. Lands outside of urban areas are defined as "nature," pristine and untouched. These landscapes are seen to demand preservation in perpetuity.

Of course, environmentalists in southern Arizona recognize that human beings depend on nature, water, and oxygen, but their solution to sustaining human life often involves divorcing people from these unsullied spaces. The Nature Conservancy, for instance, has purchased several large ranches in the San Pedro Valley for millions of dollars, shut down all agricultural activities, and created conservation easements to prevent further development.[15] These land tracts are often resold, but to new owners who cannot do much to the land (because of the legal conservation easements) except maintain it as natural landscape. This separation of human needs and the land that provisions those needs is also conveyed in much of the Nature Conservancy's printed literature. The organization's 2002 annual report, for instance, featured dozens of photographs of natural places, stunning vistas of glacier-capped mountains, vast grasslands, and placid wetlands. However, only one picture included people actually *in* these scenes of nature's grandeur (several people on a boat in a lake). The report included many other pictures of people, but these were taken in a studio and then laid over the photographs of natural places—a clean division between nature pristine and beautiful, and humans contained and discrete.

The environmentalists I interviewed often spoke about having to learn to value the San Pedro Valley as a natural place. When Tom Wood was hired in 1988 by the Nature Conservancy to manage the Ramsey Canyon Preserve in the Huachuca Mountains just west of Sierra Vista, it was the first time he had ever been in southeastern Arizona. "I was kind of surprised when I got here because I knew it was a hotspot of [bio]diversity," he recalled. "And so when I came for an interview to Sierra Vista it was just mesquite and brush flats. It wasn't much." However, with time, Wood came to see the river as "a real jewel." Similarly, Patricia Gerrodette, an environmental activist, moved to Sierra Vista from California in 1995, but upon her arrival, she felt disoriented. She knew that Sierra Vista was not a major city, yet when she drove through the valley for the first time at night, she recalled that "there was a solid string of lights across the valley." The next day, she drove down one of Sierra Vista's main streets, Fry Boulevard, but "wasn't terribly impressed." She was struck by the valley, which was "clearly pretty," but grew distressed as she drove outside of town. "I have a vivid recollection of driving down Hereford Road and I was shocked by the *rural sprawl,*" she said (her emphasis); "one-acre ranchettes just horribly chopping up the landscape." She subsequently grew to love the valley and became involved in the local Sierra Club and Audubon Society, eventually becoming president of the Southwest Wings Birding Festival. The experiences of Gerrodette and Wood underscore that the San Pedro Valley is not intrinsically or patently a "natural" place. Rather, individuals come to see the landscape in a particular way given time, new information, and novel encounters.

Some local environmentalists do emphasize the temporal dimension of the San Pedro Valley, drawing attention to the ancient places in the valley. The Southwest Wings Birding Festival—"Arizona's longest running nature festival . . . an educational celebration of the diversity of birds, mammals, reptiles, and insects, in their unique habitat"—for example, in some years offers a tour to Terrenate or Murray Springs in addition to various birding activities.[16] More broadly, local environmentalist discourse focuses less on the valley's pastness than on what the valley's history says about a shared future. As naturalist Roseann Beggy Hanson (2001: 5) has written, "The San Pedro is truly a 'last great place,' as named by the Nature Conservancy, where we can see our past—the stories of our ancestors—where we can read the story of all life in the Southwest, and our future as well, in the health of the trees and water." A similar view was expressed by the celebrated novelist and essayist Barbara Kingsolver in "San Pedro River: The Patience of a Saint," published in *National Geographic* (2000). This article highlights the San Pedro's dizzying diversity of plants and animals without disregarding its long human history. As with Hanson's book, Kingsolver's article warns of the human thirst for land and water. The future is written in the past. But Kingsolver is buoyant and finds solace among the ruins she stumbles upon alongside the brook: "It's tempting to see these remnants as reassurance," she writes, "to believe our own century's claims on the river will someday disappear just as gracefully into the San Pedro's patient embrace" (Kingsolver 2000: 93).

Development in the Valley

Economics directly links tourism and environmentalism to development. Environmentalists and development proponents alike told me that they believe tourism brings millions of dollars a year to southeastern Arizona. An interview with Kay Daggett, then executive director of the Sierra Vista Convention and Visitors Bureau, confirmed the importance of tourism to the local economy. Data from her office suggest that most tourists in the area can be categorized as "nature-based tourists" (specifically, bird-watchers). Those tourists who do not come for birds likely come for the romance of the Old West, she said. When I asked why so little attention was given to the many archaeological sites in the area, Daggett explained that although nearly anyone can watch birds, not everyone can understand the significance of archaeological finds (see Shakley 2001: 8). In reference to sites such as Murray Springs, she said, "It's hard to say that under the dirt this happened. There are no reenactments and no current digging. So from a marketing standpoint, that's a real challenge." This "marketing challenge" explains why tourism brochures printed by Daggett's office rarely mention the ancient archaeology in the area. However, there are interpretive trails at Terrenate and Murray Springs. Several archaeologists told me that their efforts to develop more-substantial archaeological interpretive centers had not received support from local government offices. Hence, development proponents seem, in some measure, to be *choosing* not to focus on the valley's ancient history.

Places of the ancient past play a minor part in the language of local development. After scanning literature put out by developers in the area, as well as local policy documents and newspaper articles, I was struck by how little reference is made to archaeology. In the development discourse, the ancient past is defined by its absence. Arthur M. Jones is a leading development proponent in the area and held a seat on the Sierra Vista City Council when I interviewed him. Like many of the environmentalists, he had not been especially impressed by the region when he first arrived. But unlike the environmentalists who recoiled from the chain of city lights, Jones suggested that folks should visit for the first time at night, when they would see "lights strung across the valley from horizon to horizon when it looks like there is a lot there." Jones, when pressed, said that he occasionally visits archaeological sites in the San Pedro Valley, such as Terrenate and Murray Springs. He recently went to Kartchner Caverns—a popular cave tour with no archaeological remains that the State of Arizona opened in 1999—and found it "magnificent." The lesson of that place, for Jones, was human vanity. "Sure, we could destroy something like Kartchner in a moment, but for all of mother-nature, she wouldn't feel it. It's *vain* to think that we can have a lasting effect on nature, at least on her time scale. That is vanity of the highest order" (his emphasis). Archaeological sites teach us the same lesson, according to Jones: "Murray Springs is twelve thousand years ago. That's nothing. That's not even a hiccup."

Whereas the discourse of environmentalism often invokes a separation of interior and exterior landscapes, the rhetoric of development endorses a figurative and literal leveling of the earth, so that all spaces are indistinct and therefore open to human consumption. The events I witnessed in southern Arizona echo Gastón Gordillo's (this volume) phrasing of Henri Lefebvre's statement that the logic of capitalism creates "abstract spaces" free of cultural meanings in order to open geographies to new economic opportunities. The disparity between environmentalism and development is not limited to Arizona, as many communities face decisions about how to satisfy human needs without devastating the biosphere on which we, and other life-forms, depend. Mary Curran (2003), for instance, has written about how the people of Montana have struggled to mediate between its two contradictory aphorisms, "The Treasure State" and "The Last Best Place." The latter motto reflects the New West, the hope of building a future from natural landscapes, which was superimposed on the former saying, which exhibits the values of the Old West, the desire to extract and exploit. Similarly, Deborah McLaren (1999: 28) argues, "Tourism, like other western-style industries, encourages the use of open land by seeking out and developing the 'last unspoiled places on earth.'"

In the San Pedro Valley, archaeology becomes implicated in these debates but only obliquely, on the periphery, as environmentalists and advocates of development each use it to bolster their point of view. For those who support development, archaeology may serve as cultural capital, a means of enticing tourists and new residents. Sites presenting Arizona's cultural heritage are something to "do," like birding or golfing. "When you live in a state with more than a thousand years of Native American culture—first visited by the Europeans in the 16th century and later the stomping ground of cowboys, outlaws, and sheriffs—you're bound to find some wonderful historic places," a brochure about retiring in Arizona says between articles titled "The Golf State" and "Opportunities for Hobbies." The findings of archaeologists are also used to justify the expansion of cityscapes into nature, because the long Native American history makes the presence of humans in the San Pedro Valley seem timeless and inevitable. "People have been here forever" was a common refrain I heard from those sympathetic to development. Despite this long history of human occupation, the river still runs and the birds still come year after year; therefore, the thinking goes, there is nothing we can do to nature today that has not been done before.

Conclusions

One might suggest that archaeology is on the periphery in many if not most locales and that a scholarly predisposition is what has created the illusion of archaeology's vital importance. Perhaps because in recent years researchers have typically begun their investigations with a monumental site, monument, battlefield, memorial, park, or museum and then moved outward to the nested social relations invariably formed around such sites, they have in some measure presupposed that archaeology is of distinctive significance. The predominant effect of the present literature covering the social context of archaeology nonetheless suggests that archaeology is of preeminent concern—that archaeology's body of knowledge and material objects are quintessential sites of sociopolitical contestations and identity formations. This is not to deny that archaeology is critical in some times to some communities—from Israeli nation-building (Zerubavel 1995) to Celtic ethnic identity (Dietler 1994)—but such a statement invites the question of why, when just about every place on earth has been touched by the depths of human history, are some places imbued with the special status of antiquity while other places of equal age and record are ignored, dismissed, or marginalized?

If we trace the San Pedro Valley's past, an immense story of human life and survival could be told, a narrative that begins with ice age Paleo-Indians following the roaming mammoths and goes virtually uninterrupted to the modern-day "snow birds" looking for a peaceful place to retire. Archaeologists have examined this story in detail, recording hundreds of sites, and they have helped establish a handful of sites that the public can visit and learn from. Yet the power relations among stakeholders in the valley undermine, or at least profoundly delimit the development of, an expansive archaeological "industry" (see Mortensen, chapter 8, this volume). In other words, the groundwork for a deep and meaningful public engagement with archaeology is countered in several fundamental ways. To begin with, Native Americans are predominantly represented in the valley today generically and stereotypically—this generic image is embodied in the convenience store statues and vividly depicted in the art and advertisements of tourist brochures and in streets named after distant tribes. Additionally, those in positions with power to encourage visitors and residents to visit ancient sites (namely, the bosses of the Sierra Vista Visitors Bureau) explicitly deem the San Pedro Valley's ancient though non-monumental sites as unmarketable. And so the valley's ancient past is not marketed. Furthermore, even as the valley's ancient remains are de-emphasized, its qualities of nature are overwhelmingly accentuated. But this portrait of "nature" is largely devoid of humans, instead consisting of a place "outdoors," a wilderness of birds and flowing water, distinct from the modern landscape of Sierra Vista with its hotels and restaurants. Archaeology is not completely disregarded in the valley, but its significance is mostly drawn into the constructions of place; archaeology then becomes only one part of the formation of place, which is in essence born from the formations of boundaries for interior and exterior places.

The case study of the San Pedro Valley demonstrates that while archaeology can and does play an important function in place-making, its character as a tangible marker of histories and identities is not prescribed. Place-making is fundamentally a process of discrimination, akin to memory, as Marc Augé (2004: 17) has recently written: essentially "gardener's work" of selecting and pruning. Thus, researchers need to focus on the way in which archaeology is not simply or obviously present in a community or a landscape but instead must first be *seen*—recognized, crafted, and then sustained in the collective imagination of different publics. Archaeology's role in places, then, may be defined as much by its absence as by its presence.

Notes

1. http://www.lastgreatplaces.org/index.htm (accessed November 2002).
2. *2001–2002 Official Guide to Cochise County.* No additional publication information is available for these guidebooks.
3. *2001–2002 Official Guide to Cochise County.*
4. *2002–2003 Greater Sierra Vista Area (Chamber of Commerce).*
5. Kay Daggett, personal communication 2002, based on a quantitative survey conducted by the Sierra Vista Convention and Visitors Bureau.
6. http://www.lastgreatplaces.org/index.htm (accessed November 2002).
7. *Arizona Living, 2001–2002.*
8. *Sierra Vista Official Visitors Guide.*

9. Three in the group were women; everyone except me appeared to be more than forty years old; most were decked out in standard hiking clothes (jeans and flannel shirts, wide-brimmed cloth hats, sturdy boots); several people were passing through the area, while all the others were recent transplants to the valley. I went on this tour as a participant: the tour guide knew of my research, but because it was a public tour, the others did not explicitly know about my research although everyone could see me taking notes and photographs.

10. Jane Pike Childress of the U.S. Bureau of Land Management generously provided me access to the guest books gathered over the years from Terrenate, Murray Springs, and Fairbank. For this analysis, I used the books from Terrenate covering a forty-four-month period from February 1999 to November 2002 (except for July to September 2000, when no books were available for tourists). The basic statistics from these books constitute minimum counts.

11. A score of one was given to those statements that were entirely negative ("Disappointed to see black and yellow plastic in walls. How much more is fake?"), two for statements that indicated some negative part of the tourist experience ("BLM: Do more to mark and in-terpret"), three for neutral statements ("Bike touring across America!"), four for generally positive remarks ("Great glimpse of the past"), and five for extremely positive statements ("Gorgeous! Cool! Cool!"). On the basis of these statements, the comments were ranked as negative or positive on a scale of one to five (five being highest) as a proxy measure of whether people enjoyed their visit. The average score was 3.8, indicating that people, on average, felt neutral or were basically happy with their experience. Breaking down these scores based on where people came from did not produce any discernable differences: people from Arizona had an average response of 3.9; people from outside of Arizona, 3.9; and people from places unknown, 3.7.

12. Comments on history include statements such as "Best BLM interpretation I've seen"; comments about the natural environment include "I love the river"; and comments on both include "Gorgeous views. Neat adobe walls."

13. Respondents could write more than one response; not all visitors responded. Numbers are minimum counts.

14. Environmentalism here is defined as the advocacy for or work toward protecting the natural environment from unchecked development, destruction, or pollution. Development here is defined as the promotion for or work toward making the land progressively useful and profitable for human consumption.

15. *Arizona Daily Star,* September 6, 2002.

16. http://www.swwings.org/who.html (accessed May 2005).

References Cited

Abu el-Haj, Nadia. *Facts on the Ground: Archaeological Practice and Territorial Self-Fashioning in Israeli Society.* Chicago: University of Chicago Press, 2001.

Atkinson, John A., Iain Banks, and Jerry O'Sullivan, eds. *Nationalism and Archaeology.* Glasgow: Cruithne Press, 1996.

Augé, Marc. *Oblivion.* Minneapolis: University of Minnesota Press, 2004.

Barringer, Tim, and Tom Flynn, eds. *Colonialism and the Object: Empire, Material Culture and the Museum.* London: Routledge, 1998.

Bataille, Gretchen M., ed. *Native American Representations: First Encounters, Distorted Images, and Literary Appropriations.* Lincoln: University of Nebraska Press, 2001.

Batman, Richard, ed. *Personal Narrative of James O. Pattie.* Missoula, Mont.: Mountain Press, 1988.

Berkhofer, Robert F. *The White Man's Indian: Images of the American Indian from Columbus to the Present.* New York: Vintage Books, 1978.

Bolton, Herbert Eugene. *Rim of Christendom: A Biography of Eusebio Francisco Kino, Pacific Coast Pioneer.* New York: MacMillan, 1936.

Bourke, John G. *On the Border with Crook.* Lincoln: University of Nebraska Press, 1971.

Bradley, Richard. *An Archaeology of Natural Places.* London: Routledge, 2000.

Brodie, Neil, Morag M. Kersel, Christina Luke, and Kathryn Walker Tubb, eds. *Archaeology, Cultural Heritage, and the Antiquities Trade.* Gainesville: University Press of Florida, 2006.

Brown, Michael F. *Who Owns Native Culture?* Cambridge, Mass.: Harvard University Press, 2003.

Castañeda, Quetzil E. *In the Museum of Maya Culture: Touring Chichén Itzá.* Minneapolis: University of Minnesota Press, 1996.

Chavez, Leo R. "The Power of the Imagined Community: The Settlement of Undocumented Mexicans and Central Americans in the United States." *American Anthropologist* 96, no. 1 (1994): 52–73.

Clark, Jeffery J., ed. *Migrants and Mounds: Classic Period Archaeology along the Lower San Pedro River.* Tucson: Center for Desert Archaeology, forthcoming.

Colwell-Chanthaphonh, Chip, and J. Brett Hill. "Mapping History: Cartography and the Construction of the San Pedro Valley." *History and Anthropology* 15, no. 2 (2004): 175–200.

Curran, Mary. "Dialogues of Difference: Contested Mappings of Tourism and Environmental Protection in Butte, Montana." In *Mapping Tourism,* edited by S. P. Hanna and V. Del Casino Jr., 132–60. Minneapolis: University of Minnesota Press, 2003.

Dietler, Michael. "'Our Ancestors the Gauls': Archaeology, Ethnic Nationalism, and the Manipulation of Celtic Identity in Modern Europe." *American Anthropologist* 96, no. 3 (1994): 584–605.

Di Peso, Charles C. *The Babocomari Village Site on the Babocomari River, Southeastern Arizona.* Dragoon, Ariz.: Amerind Foundation, 1951.

———. *The Sobaipuri Indians of the Upper San Pedro River Valley, Southeastern Arizona.* Dragoon, Ariz.: Amerind Foundation, 1953.

———. *The Reeve Ruin of Southeastern Arizona: A Study of a Prehistoric Western Pueblo Migration into the Middle San Pedro Valley.* Dragoon, Ariz.: Amerind Foundation, 1958.

Doelle, William H., and Jeffery J. Clark. "Preservation Archaeology in the San Pedro Valley." *Archaeology Southwest* 17, no. 3 (2003): 1.

Feld, Steven, and Keith H. Basso, eds. *Senses of Place.* Santa Fe, N.Mex.: School of American Research, 1996.

Ferguson, T. J., and Chip Colwell-Chanthaphonh. *History Is in the Land: Multivocal Tribal Traditions in Arizona's San Pedro Valley.* Tucson: University of Arizona Press, 2006.

Ferguson, T. J., Chip Colwell-Chanthaphonh, and Roger Anyon. "One Valley, Many Histories: Tohono O'odham, Hopi, Zuni, and Western Apache History in the San Pedro Valley." *Archaeology Southwest* 18, no. 1 (2004): 1–15.

Handler, Richard, and Eric Gable. *The New History of an Old Museum: Creating the Past at Colonial Williamsburg.* Durham, N.C.: Duke University Press, 1997.

Hanson, Roseann Beggy. *The San Pedro River: A Discovery Guide.* Tucson: University of Arizona Press, 2001.

Härke, Heinrich, ed. *Archaeology, Ideology and Society: The German Experience.* Gesellschaften und Staaten in Epochenwandel 7. Frankfurt: Peter Lang, 2000.

Hartmann, William K., and Betty Graham Lee. "Chichilticale: A Survey of Candidate Ruins in Southeastern Arizona." In *The Coronado Expedition: From the Distance of 460 Years,* edited by R. Flint and S. C. Flint, 81–108. Albuquerque: University of New Mexico Press, 2003.

Haury, Emil W., E. B. Sayles, and William W. Wasley. "The Lehner Mammoth Site, Southeastern Arizona." *American Antiquity* 25, no. 1 (1959): 2–30.

Haynes, C. Vance, Jr., and Bruce B. Huckell, eds. *Murray Springs: A Clovis Site with Multiple Activity Areas in the San Pedro Valley, Arizona.* Anthropological Papers of the University of Arizona 71. Tucson: University of Arizona Press, 2007.

Kingsolver, Barbara. "San Pedro River: The Patience of a Saint." *National Geographic* 197, no. 4 (2000): 80–97.

Kohl, Philip L., Mara Kozelsky, and Ben-Yehuda Nachman, eds. *Selective Remembrances: Archaeology in the Construction, Commemoration, and Consecration of National Pasts.* Chicago: University of Chicago Press, 2007.

Lance, John F. "Artifacts with Mammoth Remains, Naco, Arizona: Description of the Naco Mammoth." *American Antiquity* 19, no. 1 (1953): 19–24.

Low, Setha M., and Denise Lawrence-Zúñiga, eds. *The Anthropology of Space and Place: Locating Culture.* Oxford, U.K.: Blackwell, 2003.

Lowenthal, David. *The Past Is a Foreign Country.* Cambridge: Cambridge University Press, 1985.

McLaren, Deborah Ramer. "The History of Indigenous Peoples and Tourism." *Cultural Survival Quarterly* 23, no. 2 (1999): 27–30.

Meskell, Lynn. "Sites of Violence: Terrorism, Tourism, and Heritage in the Archaeological Present." In *Embedding Ethics,* edited by L. Meskell and P. Pels, 123–46. Oxford, U.K.: Berg, 2005. [2005a]

———. "Archaeological Ethnography: Conversations around Kruger National Park." *Archaeologies* 1, no. 1 (2005): 81–100. [2005b]

Messenger, Phyllis M., ed. *The Ethics of Collecting Cultural Property: Whose Culture? Whose Property?* Albuquerque: University of New Mexico Press, 1999.

Muir, Richard. *Approaches to Landscape.* Lanham, Md.: Barnes and Noble, 1999.

Nicholas, George P., and Kelly P. Bannister. "Copyrighting the Past? Emerging Intellectual Property Rights Issues in Archaeology." *Current Anthropology* 45, no. 3 (2004): 327–50.

Schiffer, Michael B. *Behavioral Archaeology: First Principles.* Salt Lake City: University of Utah Press, 1995.

Shakley, Myra. *Managing Sacred Sites: Service Provision and Visitor Experience.* London: Continuum, 2001.

Smith, Laurajane. *Uses of Heritage.* London: Routledge, 2006.

Steinitz, Carl, Hector Manuel Arias Rojo, Scott Bassett, Michael Flaxman, Thomas Maddock III, David Mouat, Richard Peiser, and Allan Shearer. *Alternative Futures for Changing*

Landscapes: The Upper San Pedro River Basin in Arizona and Sonora. Washington, D.C.: Island Press, 2003.

Teague, David W. *The Southwest in American Literature and Art: The Rise of a Desert Aesthetic.* Tucson: University of Arizona Press, 1997.

Tuan, Yi-Fu. *Space and Place: The Perspective on Experience.* Minneapolis: University of Minnesota Press, 1977.

Zerubavel, Yael. *Recovered Roots: Collective Memory and the Making of Israeli National Tradition.* Chicago: University of Chicago Press, 1995.

Contributors

O. Hugo Benavides is associate professor of anthropology, Latin American and Latino studies, and international political economy and development at Fordham University, where he also directs the M.A. program in humanities and sciences.

Lisa Breglia is a cultural anthropologist who teaches global affairs at George Mason University. Her research explores the politics of patrimony in Mexico, looking at the oil industry on Yucatan's Gulf Coast. She is the author of *Monumental Ambivalence: The Politics of Heritage* (2006).

Quetzil E. Castañeda is founding director of OSEA—the Open School of Ethnography and Anthropology—and teaches in the Department of History and in the Latin American and Caribbean Studies Program at Indiana University. He is the author of *In the Museum of Maya Culture* (1996), co-filmmaker of *Incidents of Travel in Chichén Itzá* (1997), and co-editor of *Ethnographic Archaeologies* (2008). Castañeda directs the OSEA Heritage Ethnography Field School in Yucatán, Mexico.

Chip Colwell-Chanthaphonh is curator of anthropology at the Denver Museum of Nature & Science. He is the author of *Massacre at Camp Grant: Forgetting and Remembering Apache History* (2007) and coauthor (with T. J. Ferguson) of *History Is in the Land: Multivocal Tribal Traditions in Arizona's San Pedro Valley* (2006).

Jon Daehnke is a postdoctoral fellow at Stanford University and a graduate of the University of California, Berkeley. Jon's research interests focus on the relationship between archaeologists and descendant communities, archaeology and the law, and human interaction with landscapes and place.

Gastón Gordillo is associate professor in the Department of Anthropology at the University of British Columbia. He is the author of *Landscapes of Devils: Tensions of*

Place and Memories in the Argentinean Chaco (2004, winner of the 2005 AES Sharon Stephens Book Prize), *Nosotros vamos a estar acá para siempre: Historias tobas* (2005), and *En el Gran Chaco: Antropologías e historias* (2006).

Richard Handler is professor of anthropology and associate dean for Academic Programs in the College of Arts and Sciences at the University of Virginia. His books include *Critics against Culture: Anthropological Observers of Mass Society* (2005), *The New History in an Old Museum: Creating the Past at Colonial Williamsburg* (with Eric Gable, 1997), and *Nationalism and the Politics of Culture in Quebec* (1988).

Julie Hollowell is a research associate with Indiana University's Center for Archaeology in the Public Interest and Department of Anthropology and co-editor of the World Archaeological Congress Research Handbooks in Archaeology series (published by Left Coast Press). She is currently at DePauw University as the Nancy Schaenen Visiting Scholar with the Prindle Institute for Ethics and as a visiting professor of anthropology.

Jennifer Jacobs is a linguistic anthropologist whose research focuses on vocalizing and sentiment. She teaches at the University of California, Berkeley, where she is writing a book on the acoustic form and circulation of Middle Eastern ululation.

Christopher N. Matthews is associate professor of anthropology at Hofstra University. He is the author of *An Archaeology of History and Tradition* (2002) and co-editor (with Quetzil E. Castañeda) of *Ethnographic Archaeologies* (2008). He specializes in American historical archaeology and methods of community engagement.

Lynn Meskell is professor of anthropology at Stanford University. Her most recent books include *Object Worlds in Ancient Egypt: Material Biographies Past and Present* (2004), *Embedding Ethics* (co-edited with Peter Pels, 2005), *Archaeologies of Materiality* (ed., 2005), and *Cosmopolitan Archaeologies* (ed., 2009). She is founding editor of the *Journal of Social Archaeology* (Sage) and of the Material Worlds Series (Duke).

Lena Mortensen is assistant professor of anthropology at the University of Toronto, Scarborough. Her research interests include the politics of heritage and identity, archaeological tourism, and discourses of the past.

Matthew Palus is a doctoral candidate in the Department of Anthropology at Columbia University and author of *They Worked Regular: Craft, Labor, and Family in the Industrial Community of Virginius Island* (with Paul Shackel, 2006). He is currently living in Takoma Park, Maryland, and completing his dissertation on the role of public utilities in the annexation of Eastport into the City of Annapolis during the twentieth century.

Benjamin Porter is an archaeologist who co-directs the Dhiban Excavation and Development Project in Jordan. He teaches at the University of California, Berkeley, and is writing a book on Near Eastern marginal communities.

Helaine Silverman is professor of anthropology at the University of Illinois, Urbana-Champaign, where she also co-directs the Collaborative for Cultural Heritage and Museum Practices. She is editor of the journal *Latin American Antiquity* (2008–11). Her current research focuses on intersections of archaeological tourism, production of identity and nationalism, and economic development.

Laurajane Smith is a reader in heritage studies and archaeology at the University of York (U.K.). She previously taught Indigenous studies at the University of New South Wales, Sydney, Australia. Her recent books include *Uses of Heritage* (2006), *Archaeological Theory and the Politics of Cultural Heritage* (2004), and (coauthored with E. Waterton) *Heritage, Communities and Archaeology* (2008).

Index